A History of Gnosticism

Date Due

BRODART, CO.   Cat. No. 23-233-003   Printed in U.S.A.

A HISTORY OF GNOSTICISM

Giovanni Filoramo

Translated by Anthony Alcock

Basil Blackwell

English translation copyright © Basil Blackwell 1990
First published in Italian as *L'attesa della fine, Storia della gnosi* © *Gius.
Laterza & Figli*

First published 1990
Reprinted 1991
√
Basil Blackwell Ltd
108 Cowley Road, Oxford OX4 1JF, UK

Basil Blackwell Inc.
3 Cambridge Center
Cambridge, Massachusetts 02142, USA

British Library Cataloguing in Publication Data

A CIP catalogue record for this book is available from the British Library.

Library of Congress Cataloging in Publication Data

Filoramo, Giovanni.
    [Attesa della fine. English]
    A History of Gnosticism / Giovanni Filoramo; translated by Anthony
Alcock.
        p.   cm.
    Translation of: L'attesa della fine.
    Includes bibliographical references.
    ISBN 0631-15756-5
    1. Gnosticism. I. Title.
BT1390.F5513 1990   89-27513
299'.932—dc20   CIP

Typeset in 10 on 12 pt Sabon
by Photo-graphics, Honiton, Devon
Printed in Great Britain by TJ Press Ltd., Padstow

Contents

VI.3	*AuthLog*	*Authoritative Teaching*
VI.4	*Noēma*	*The Concept of Our Great Power*
VI.5	Plat. *Rep.*	Plato, *Republic* 588 b–589 b
VI.6	*OgdEnn*	*Discourse on the Eighth and Ninth*
VI.7	*Or*	*Prayer of Thanksgiving* (+ scribal note)
VI.8	*Ascl*	*Asclepius 21–9*
VII.1	*ParSem*	*Paraphrase of Shem*
VII.2	2 *LogSeth*	*Second Treatise of the Great Seth*
VII.3	*ApcPt*	*Apocalypse of Peter*
VII.4	*Silv*	*Teaching of Silvanus* (+ colophon)
VII.5	*StelSeth*	*Three Steles of Seth*
VIII.1	*Zostr*	*Zostrianos*
VIII.2	*ApPt*	*Letter of Peter to Philip*
IX.1	*Melch*	*Melchizedek*
IX.2	*Nor*	*Thought of Norea*
IX.3	*TestVer*	*Testimony of Truth*
X	*Mars*	*Marsanes*
XI.1	*Inter*	*Interpretation of Knowledge*
XI.2	*ExpVal*	*Valentinian Exposition*
XI.3	*Allog*	*Allogenes*
XI.4	*Hyps*	*Hypsiphrone*
XII.1	*SSex*	*Sentences of Sextus*
XII.2	*EvVer*	*Gospel of Truth*
XII.3	*Frgm*	*Fragments*
XIII.1	*Prot*	*Trimorphic Protennoia*
XIII.2	*OrigMund*	*On the Origin of the World*

BG · Berlin Gnostic Codex 8502

Individual treatises in BG

SJCH	*The Sophia of Jesus Christ*
1 LJ	*First Book of Jeu*
2 LJ	*Second Book of Jeu*
EvMar	*Gospel of Mark*

General

| *ARW* | *Archiv für Religionswissenschaft* |
| *Aug* | *Augustinianum* |

BCNH	*Bibliothèque copte de Nag Hammadi*, ed. J.É Ménard (Quebec, 1977–)
Bibl	Biblica
CG	(Papyrus) Cairensis Gnosticus
CH	*Corpus Hermeticum*
DBSup	*Dictionnaire de la Bible*: Supplements, L. Pirok et al. (eds) (Paris, 1928–)
ERJ	*Eranos Jahrbuch*
GCS	*Die griechischen christlichen Schriftsteller der ersten drei Jahrhunderte* (Leipzig–Berlin, 1897–)
Greg	*Gregorianum*
HR	*History of Religions*
HThR	*Harvard Theological Review*
JAC	*Jahrburch für Antike und Christentum*
Mus	Museum
NHS	Nag Hammadi Studies (Leiden, 1971–)
NT	*Novum Testamentum*
NTS	*New Testament Studies*
Num	Numen
OLZ	*Orientalische Literaturzeitung*
PCol	*Papyrus Coloniensis*
POxy	*Papyri Oxyrhynchi*
PW	A. Pauly and G. Wissowa, *Real-Encyclopädie der klassischen Altertumswissenschaft* (1893–)
QS	Qumran Scrolls
RAC	*Reallexikon für Antike und Christentum* (Stuttgart, 1941–)
RevHR	*Revue d'histoire des religions*
RevSR	*Revue des sciences religieuses*
RevThPh	*Revue de théologie et de philosophie*
RGG	*Religion in Geschichte und Gegenwart*[3], ed. J. C. B. Mohr (Tübingen, 1958)
RHE	*Revue d'histoire ecclésiastique*
RSLR	*Rivista di storia e letteratura religiosa*
RSPhTh	*Revue de sciences philosophiques et théologiques*
RSR	*Recherches de sciences religieuses*
SMSR	*Studi e materiali di storia delle religione*
ThRu	*Theologische Rundschau*
TLZ	*Theologische Literaturzeitung* (Leipzig, 1876–)
TW	*Theologisches Wörterbuch zum Neuen Testament* (Stuttgart, 1933–)
TZ	*Theologische Zeitschrift*

VetChr	*Vetera Christianorum*
VigChr	*Vigiliae Christianae*
ZNW	*Zeitschrift für die neutestamentliche Wissenschaft*
ZRGG	*Zeitschrift für Religions- und Geistesgeschichte*
ZKG	*Zeitschrift für Kirchengeschichte* (Gotha, 1877–1930, Stuttgart, 1931–)
ZThk	*Zeitschrift für Theologie und Kirche*

Introduction

GNOSIS AND MODERN CULTURE

Are we witnessing a rediscovery of Gnosis? To judge from the many indications that may be found collectively or singly in contemporary culture, the answer would seem to be 'yes'. However, in contrast with specialist usage, different interpretations and the inevitable ideological manipulation, there is a common need to collate and to verify hypotheses and influences, echoes and intuitions with the historical object that has been disfigured, but not entirely obliterated, by a complex of concealment and repression.

The discovery in 1945 of a library containing original Gnostic writings in Coptic (see chapter 1) has certainly stimulated a renewed interest in a religious world that for too long has remained the exclusive preserve of academic research. In fact, before this, the most that the vanguard of specialists had been able to do was to hesitate (or to hope) to confront the persistent esoteric tendencies of Christianity. There has, however, been the danger that, by some strange irony of fate, they would render themselves liable to the accusation of transmitting that same religious traditionalism also recognizable in a certain conception of Gnosis.[1] If there was an alternative to this (to say the least) embarrassing situation, it was to maintain close, though misleading, encounters with that group of theologians, the heirs of the ancient Christian heretical tradition, which as the new *malleus gnosticorum*, or 'hammer of the Gnostics', wages its missionary struggle against the menacing Gnostic hydra, at times without distinguishing in its attacks the scholar of Gnosis from the object of his research.[2]

It took almost a 'secret production', therefore, as in the case of other romantic archaeological and manuscript discoveries of recent decades, for the very means of the discovery to bring it to the attention of a wider public, investing it with the exotic and provocative aura of a

Middle Eastern setting, in addition to the suspense created by a series of carefully orchestrated situations.

So, if this discovery indicated a decisive shift in the field of specialist studies in respect of the new primary sources available for research, the repercussions were bound to be varied once the new material was brought to the attention of a wider section of the public: the more so since certain areas of the cultural panorama showed a disposition, a particular sensitivity to the lively and interested reception of these texts, recovered in such an extraordinary manner, which dealt with a phenomenon that they themselves had in some way helped to keep alive.

Jung's reflections had long been immersed in the thought of ancient Gnostics to such an extent that he considered them the virtual discoverers of 'depth psychology'.[3] It was Jung himself who promoted the famous meetings at Ascona, annual conferences attended by some of the greatest specialists in Gnostic thought,[4] including Gilles Quispel, a Dutch scholar deeply attached to Jungian psychology. In his works Quispel helped to construct a bridge between ancient and modern Gnosis: inasmuch as it involves research into the ontological self, a cognitive technique that anticipates the modern process of individuation, ancient Gnosis, albeit in its form of universal religion, in a certain sense prefigured, and at the same time helped to clarify, the nature of Jungian spiritual therapy.[5]

This vital link, this hermeneutic circle between ancient Gnosis and its modern metamorphosis also affected the studies of Hans Jonas.[6] A pupil of Heidegger at the beginning of the thirties, Jonas recognized in *Sein und Zeit* an interpretative premiss necessary for the penetration of the dualist, anti-cosmic and nihilist vision of ancient Gnosis. Thus to the attentive reader the implication was that there must be a sort of subterranean umbilical cord between ancient Gnosis and modern existentialism, strengthened by more than external historical continuity: profound similarities, secret relationships, elective affinity which were alive and rooted in analogous forms of sensitivity, if not in identical critical positions *vis-à-vis* the world and existence. In this way Heidegger's pessimism, while it helped towards a better understanding of Gnostic nihilism, drawing it into the orbit of the dramatic questions posed by modern existentialism, was at the same time elevated by its recognition of a worthy, if somewhat unfortunate, predecessor in the ancient religion.[7]

In modern culture, therefore, the Gnostic *Weltanschauung* predated the postwar discoveries in terms of the channels of diffusion. At first sight these appear to be traceable to a particularly important point from which they radiated: classical German idealism. In this revived form Gnosticism was in this very sphere to undergo a profound, decisive transformation that would render it more suitable to the requirements of the modern world. Thinkers such as Hegel and Schelling incorporated into their systems the ideal principles of Gnosticism in such a way as to make them unrecognizable.[8] From the Gnostic myths of the second century AD, first via Manichaean dualism and then via the Bogomil and Cathar myths, what had appeared as a radically pessimistic view of the world for more than a thousand years now emerged, in the most typical representatives of speculative idealism, in the seductive guise of an optimism and an idealistic, progressive, unquenchable rationalism, a monistic pantheism which seems to have little or nothing in common with the ancient matrix. Nevertheless, the spirit of Gnosticism reverberates throughout these systems. Beneath the more abstract trappings of a gnoseological principle it presents itself as acute longing, nostalgia for authentic origins and at the same time as a possibility of total knowledge, without any vestige of what is divine in man, indeed, of his substantial divinity. In its aspiration towards the 'encounter with the self', which is fundamental to the Hegelian system, ancient Gnosis appears subdued, stripped of its mythological apparatus and sacred values, sunk into a horizon of optimism and immanence which deprive it of its most violent aspects of protest and rebellion against the rulers of this world. Wearing this mask, it was better equipped to penetrate into many unsuspected and hidden places, where it would be discreetly preserved.[9]

The metamorphoses of ancient Gnosis in modern European culture have yet to be investigated. It will be a delicate task, thankless and full of pitfalls. It will in fact involve research into areas historically diverse and remote, following divergent paths, in some cases penetrating ideological minefields destined to provoke unavoidably hard feelings and controversies.[10]

The faith of more or less restricted groups who, in the name of their own divine origin and nature and of a more or less radical rejection of the world, its creatures and institutions, struggled against religious and political power supported by an armory of ideas in a battle destined to be lost,[11] was up to a point substantially unitary in socio-historical circumstances that were diverse, but not too dissimilar. With the advent first of Humanism, then of the Renaissance, the complex tradition of Gnostic thought, in conjunction with Cabbalistic modes of thought and imbued with the new fevers of Hermeticism, abandoned its ancient nihilism and threw aside its dualistic attire, refashioning its constituent nucleus: self-knowledge as consciousness of the encounter with the Self, in keeping with the new requirements of the age. Thus it has inspired the thought of Cabbalistic Christians,[12] it is at the centre of Rosicrucian movements,[13] it blooms in the many ventures into the occult,[14] it pervades the reflections of the great mystics, the spiritual thinkers and alchemists, particularly the Germans of the sixteenth century.[15]

We see a veritable efflorescence of Gnostic mythology in Jacob Böhme,[16] the new Valentinus. Known to his contemporaries as the 'Philosophus Teutonicus', he stands, with the depth and daring of his visions and his theosophical speculations, at the origin of the modernization of Gnostic esoteric traditions,[17] destined, especially among the Germans, to leave an often profound influence on thinkers such as Goethe[18] or, specifically, Hegel.[19] Friedrich Oetinger, the greatest German esoteric specialist of the eighteenth century, openly refers to him,[20] as does Franz von Baader (A. W. Schlegel's 'Boehmius redivivus') one of the most acute minds of the first German Romanticism.[21] And in his letters Schelling acknowledged his debt to this 'theogonic nature'.[22]

Even in the early writings of Marx we find a positive reference to Böhme.[23] This is no accident. Some years ago Ernst Topitsch, in an important, if sometimes debatable, essay on the history of ideas, had detected the influence of a tradition of Gnostic thought in the shaping of the founder of Marxism.[24] And there are a number of political scientists who have wanted to see in Leninism and its conception of the single party as a group of elect already saved because they possess the keys of knowledge (the party being a political substitute for the self) yet another metamorphosis of ancient Gnosis.[25] The political scientist Eric Vögelin, who has tried to isolate in a certain conception of Gnosticism a fundamental category for discovering the roots of modern nihilism, has maintained in many of his works that 'Gnostic thinkers, ancient and modern, are the great psychologists of alienation, the bearers of the Promethean revolution.'[26]

While not going so far as to hold, with Jean Guitton, that 'the Gnostic spirit is always present and continues to inspire philosophy and politics even today', this brief survey may help to conjure up a picture, however partial and arbitrary, of the many streams into which ancient Gnosis appears to be divided today. If we omit the important evidence afforded throughout the history of European art, from the Manichaean visions of Hieronymus Bosch to those of William Blake, which have been nourished by a mythology in which 'the tempestuous wind of ancient Gnosis gently blows',[27] there still remain the large number of its appearances in literature. If it is true that only with Romanticism did the literary act begin to be conceived as a sort of attempt to make direct contact with the Absolute, and its result as a revelation, the foundation of this literary creativity might easily be discovered in the magical idealism of Friedrich von Hardenberg, otherwise known as Novalis.[28] In his brief life, which appears to have been spent with Werther's genius as its model, a thirst for knowledge and a poetic flair merge in a literary output transcending the boundaries of the traditional compartments of knowledge. In his poetry it is not difficult to discern the guiding lines of ancient Gnostic myth, with its accounts of the Fall from the Pleroma and the reconstruction of primordial unity. It is the language of the poet that will finally re-establish Paradise Lost, the language of a visionary poet able to discover the hidden relationship between the visible and the invisible worlds. The poet is therefore endowed with an extraordinary, magical power: he arouses – as it were creates – what he evokes. This is Promethean power, which Novalis, like so many other writers attracted by the esoteric, believes to derive from occult and Cabbalistic traditions of a Gnostic variety as well as from the mysticism of numbers or from the visions of a Swedenborg.

With his 'mysticism of knowledge', Novalis provides a typical example of the aspect of German literature that makes it incomprehensible 'without the mystical doctrine that the essence of self is at one with the essence of essences – God, Universe, Being – and that the quest for the true or inward self holds out the promise of proximity or even union with the divine in the realization of selfhood.'[29] On the other hand, with his visionary intuitions, he is in many ways a forerunner of French symbolist poetry, so very open to esoteric suggestions and permeated with mythical Orphic and Cabbalistic memories.[30] Gérard de Nerval was a fervent student of books on the esoteric, magic and theosophy.[31] As a good Mason, he wanted to be initiated into the mysteries of theogony and destiny. *Amélia* and *Les Chimères* prefigure the Baudelairian ideas of the later *Correspondances*. And, of course, there is also Victor Hugo. His religious ideas 'are the most grandiose of all Romanticism: we find there an extremely complicated metaphysics, myths of a Gnostic tendency, a doctrine of reincarnation.'[32] There is no point in multiplying the examples: 'Beginning with pre-Romanticism, the theme of desolate nature, considered as the remains, or the marred image of a more glorious state destroyed by the Fall, runs through Western literature.'[33] How many poets in their writings do indeed express a longing for a pure, harmonious world, to be recovered by a revelation of the type used by the initiate culminating in experiences that reach the roots of existence, at the same time maintaining continuous rapport with the spirits that fill nature, on the wave of a cult of night and death, which have by now become the metaphysical principles of inspiration?

Even movements such as Surrealism seen to reappear in the lost paradises of ancient Gnosis, with their Promethean aspect and their search for an absolute power – a search often pursued by means of esoteric and Cabbalistic techniques.[34] Nor does modern crisis literature suffer from any shortage of spontaneous outbursts, with its recurrent variations on the themes of the absurdity of the world, the omnipresence of an unavoidable Evil Principle, mutable and adopting many forms, the resulting feeling of estrangement, the acute desire to escape from it by means of impossible flights into the past world of one's own memories. On the Gnostic nature of these themes 'the work of Kafka, Faulkner and many other great writers would provide material for very constructive observations.'[35] This brief list of writers could not, of course, be complete without the name of Hermann Hesse, 'the clearest example of Romantic Gnosticism in the twentieth century'.[36] One has only to think of *Demian* (a youthful work), a typical expression of the Gnostic sentiment that is at the same time 'the Romantic sentiment *par excellence*: the sentiment of the limits imposed by destiny and the desire to break through these limits, to destroy the human condition, to break out of everything.'[37]

Finally, what is one to say of those attempts of some groups of scholars who, in their reconstruction of a modern Gnosis as global knowledge, with no traces of the mystery of the universe and of man, have tried to see a possible solution to the anxiety and despair that beset modern man?[38]

But it is time to abandon this journey through the metamorphoses of Gnosis, as fascinating as it is fraught with pitfalls. Indeed, there is a danger of losing all contact with the historical reality of the object of one's research. The term 'Gnosis', in many of these cases, instead of evoking a concrete historical world with its fears and anxieties, hopes and promises of salvation, conjures up rather the lifeless phantasm of Gnosis as a universal category of the human spirit, an 'eternal' form of knowledge, a universal label, an empty box refilled with different contents hurriedly pushed onto the intellectual market by cultural fashions.[39] Might it not be more appropriate to speak of oblivion than of rediscovery? The terminological uses and abuses of the reappearance of the term 'Gnosis' in the different scientific languages may have been made possible precisely because the veil of historical oblivion conceals the concrete reality of ancient Gnosticism.

THE REDISCOVERY OF GNOSTICISM

If one is to speak of rediscovery[40] or to speculate on its probable causes or possible results, one must look in another direction. The question must be asked whether, behind the renewed interest in Gnosis, there is not something other than merely a taste for the exotic or the volatile search for the esoteric, whether there is not hidden the intuition of a secret affinity between our age of crisis, riddled with anxiety and at the same time avid for change and thirsting for novelty, and the historical period between the second and third centuries AD when ancient Gnosticism established itself as a religious response to the acute problems of an 'age of anxiety', an original and sometimes victorious response. A more careful analysis would reveal analogies of situations and responses that deserve to be treated in greater depth. At a superficial glance, however, this might appear surprising; but one has only to think for a moment about the peculiar nature of the modern world, viz. the secularization imposed by various revolutions as much in the area of science as in that of industry, as much in politics as in religion.

However, certain religious events in recent years compel one to reconsider the problems of the divorce of modern cultural values from religion in other terms. Today some historians are indeed beginning to ask themselves if it is not more appropriate for European societies with a Christian heritage to speak of dechristianization.[41] The hasty identification of Christianity with religion has in fact caused serious errors of evaluation. And the new religious movements that have emerged in the last decade have helped to shed more light on this ideological myopia.[42]

We are confronted with a situation analogous in some respects to that characterizing the official religious life of the Roman Empire, in which polytheism was restored as a result of Augustan reform. For centuries religion had fulfilled the function of the unification of society. But, once having transcended national boundaries, it found itself facing an impossible task. Official paganism was, in fact, throughout the imperial period the religious ideology of restricted groups of intellectuals, blockaded in their cultural citadels in defence of values that were no longer generally acceptable to society. Compared with the present situation, the striking aspect, apart from the obvious differences due to the diversity of the social and cultural worlds or to the heterogeneous nature of the two religious worlds, is the analogous dysfunction which then, as now, characterized the official religious structures of paganism and Christianity respectively over a long period. The end of a certain monopoly of religious goods is at the same time cause and effect of a radical change in the market for the exchange of holy ideas. Today, as then, there is clearly a religious pluralism unparalleled in the history of the West. New faiths come from the East, others are offshoots of official religion, sometimes breaking the umbilical cord. The trade in faiths is quite brisk, thanks to a competition in products that promise the same success, the same health, the same salvation, physical and spiritual, as the oriental prophets declared at the time of the Empire. A radical restructuring of the religious scene[43] is taking place. The protagonists of this change are the children of those silent revolutions, collective and anonymous, that have been developing over the last two millennia in periodic waves against the grandiose backdrop of city life. On each occasion different patterns appear to be sketched against the same background. As places where goods and ideas are exchanged, urban centres exude wellbeing and wealth, while at the same time harbouring acute tensions and contradictions. The old professions are queried, new trades and new social groups burst upon the scene. Mobility becomes a distinctive trait in the social microcosm – upward mobility, made easier by the circulation of wealth, but also sideways, because the change is due to the abandoning of ancient links and the construction of new ones. Traditional religion, continuously changing in this universe, loses its principal function of consolidating origins and traditions. The emergence of a new sociocultural identity poses problems to which the replies of traditional religion appear dated and untenable. New religions, able to respond to the new religious needs, arise and assert themselves.

In the world of late antiquity, which is already beginning to take shape in the second century, the new religious order appears in the forms of Christianity, the oriental cults and Gnosticism. These reveal a scene of contrast in the religious field. At the centre is the individual with his need for personal salvation, his search for internal experiences, authentic and guaranteed by an unimpeachable seal of approval: recourse to techniques of ecstasy, visions, dreams, revelations, the discovery of sacred writings which, it is hoped, will provide a new basis for one's own identity, both individual and social, the invention of new symbols or the recovery of old, forgotten myths, whose enchantments will help to commit the vicissitudes of history to oblivion; the attainment of divinely guaranteed knowledge, complete and definitive, based on a reality other than that of this world, which will once and for all dispel the doubts and uncertainties of a reason prey to its own syllogisms and incapable of renewing itself when confronted by the fantastic world, rich in emotions, from which the dormant illusions of an immemorial past flow.

At this point it is not surprising that those who study the new religious phenomena of the last decade can look with increasing interest and sympathy at the ancient world of Gnosticism as a historically important parallel to help them towards a better understanding of the present.

> We are in for an interlude during which an increasing number of people in urban-industrial society will take their bearings in life from the I Ching and the signs of the zodiac, from yoga and strange contemporary versions

of shamanic tradition. The quest for a communal reality assumes the shape of a massive salvage operation, reaching out in many unlikely directions. I think it is the greatest adventure of our age and far more humanly valuable than the 'race for space'. It is the reclamation and renewal of the old Gnosis.[44]

This opinion may sound odd, coming as it does from a prophet of the American counter-culture. And yet, beyond historical distortions and facile generalizations, it sheds light on an actual fact, which constitutes the *raison d'être* of this book. Every phase of modern research into Gnosticism, beginning with the pioneering work of Gottfried Arnold,[45] has seen the problems of its own age reflected in the ancient Gnostics.[46] Indeed this is quite natural, since all historical research has its origin in an impassioned, lucid participation in the problems of the present. Today we are invited to consider the religious world of the ancient Gnostics as a pertinent guide to those processes of social restructuring, of ideological transformation, of change in religious sentiment, that characterize our age also.

But reflection on the changing course in the history of Gnosticism will enable us to avoid the pitfalls of an archaeological re-examination (both academic and pointless) only at a price: facing up to the siren song of Gnostic mythology, allowing it to let loose all its fascination, but not to force its seductive ways upon us so that we forget the difference.

Acknowledgement

The publishers wish to thank Sonia Argyle, for her help and expertise in the editorial preparation of this book.

1

Fragments of a Lost Faith

DISCOVERY

In the month of December[1] farmers in the area of Nag Hammadi, in ancient Egypt, situated at the bend of the Nile as it flows north between Luxor and Assiut, usually fill their camels' saddlebags with *sebakh*, a particular type of soft soil rich in nitrates, with which they fertilize their fields. At the end of 1945 two brothers, who lived in a hut in the village of al-Qasr (ancient Chenoboskion, a fourth-century centre of Pachomian monasticism), like others, saddled their camels to go off in search of the precious fertilizer. They made for the area near Nag Hammadi, to Gebel el-Tarif, a hillside with over 150 natural caves, some of which proved in subsequent archaeological investigations to have been painted and used as tombs from the time of the Sixth Dynasty (about 4,300 years ago). The two brothers, Muhammad and Khalifah Ali of the al-Samman tribe, made a strange discovery as they were digging: a jar about 1 metre high, which seemed to promise all manner of treasures. Many years later Muhammad again described to his interviewers the terror that seized him as he broke open the seal of the jar, for fear that it might have contained a jinnee or local spirit of some sort. But spurred on by the thought that it might even contain gold, he broke it open with a pick-axe. Instead of the dreaded spirits or the gold they sought, from the fragments that poured out, they found books. He and his brother quickly gathered them together, mounted their camels and returned to their village.

And so began the travels of the Nag Hammadi library. Thirty years were to elapse before its final publication. All sorts of circumstances helped to delay this, from Nasser's *coup d'état* to the Suez crisis, the Arab–Israeli War of 1967, as well as the more banal and petty exchanges of rivalry and jealousy between scholars engaged in the battle for the right to publish the precious corpus.

Publication was to have a profound effect on the state of the knowledge of Gnosticism. In fact, apart from a few authentic documents of uneven quality, which were difficult to interpret, scholars of previous generations had to rely on a sufficiently large and systematic heresiological literary output, the outcome of the struggle of the defenders of Christianity from the mid-second century, in order to repel what seemed to them a mortal threat to the life of the Church. The picture that emerges from it is unavoidably scrappy and distorted. If we want to assess the full importance of the Nag Hammadi corpus, we must therefore begin with a preliminary investigation, momentarily leaving the two brothers as they return to their village with the precious manuscripts. How did the Gnostic landscape appear to the scholar before this discovery? What were its principal features, who were its principal inhabitants, its situation and background? In what colours was it depicted? These are some of the questions to which we must now turn our attention.

THE GNOSTICS AND THEIR MASK: THE PROBLEM OF THE HERESIOLOGICAL SOURCES

It is a strange fate to be able to speak only through the mouth of one's opponents. And yet it is a widespread fate common to minorities, dissidents and fringe groups, whether religious or political, whose writings have been scattered or destroyed by their conquerors and whose image is thus filtered through, or distorted by, the eye of the opposition. How is one to overcome this obstacle – the voice of the heresiologist, the prosecutor in a witch hunt, the conquistador describing the colonized tribes – which stands between the historian and the actual reality of the protagonists? How far is it possible to eliminate the errors of perspective made by these necessary, but distorting and biased, witnesses?

It is a delicate and difficult task. Not least because, as contemporary research on Gnosticism shows, the same scholars sitting in judgement on history have not always been slow to display calmness and objectivity. Gnosticism, the first and most dangerous heresy among the early Christians, has by no means been a neutral subject. It has provoked burning theological debates, in which the present has cast its shadow over the past.

This clearly produces a vicious circle. Critical study of the heresiological sources[2] has attempted to break the circle by setting itself essentially two objectives: to study the mutual interdependence of the anti-Gnostic writings and to isolate the criteria used by Christian polemicists in their attacks. The results, however limited, have not been without value and will be considered here, albeit briefly.

In the first place one could not expect the ancient heresiologist to offer what he could not offer: scientific objectivity and exactness. Justin, Irenaeus and Hippolytus were complying with essentially theological requirements when they wrote their refutations: a defence of the doctrine of the Church against an attack that threatened to destroy its foundations. To achieve their goal, they were permitted to use the most diverse means, provided that they did not violate the accepted norms of professional ethics. The interpretative views of Gnosticism used by the heresiologists were prompted, unconsciously and consciously, by the sole logic of presenting the adversary in the most sinister and unfavourable light. Thus it was that Gnosticism was presented as an evil within the Christian body, to be singled out and expelled. Or on the other hand, it was an epidemic imported from outside, the virus of the incurable disease of pagan philosophy. There was even an attempt to attribute the thousand streams of Gnosticism to a single source: the Devil. This was followed, almost as a natural corollary, by accusations of magic, witchcraft, incest and libertinism.

It is now time to enter the gallery containing the family album of this anti-heretical tradition, which occupies over a millennium. However, we are in for a surprise. The founding father, who must have been the model for a fortunate series of successors, is represented only by an empty frame. In fact, the first work of this kind known to us, the *Syntagma* or *Compendium against All Heresies*, compiled in the mid-second century by the apologist Justin, who was martyred in Rome *c*.165, is no longer extant, and attempts to reconstruct it (now almost entirely abandoned) have proved unsuccessful.[3] The position of honour, therefore, goes to the *Adversus haereses* of Irenaeus, Bishop of Lyons (140/50–200), a work in five books, originally written in Greek, but surviving in complete form only in a Latin translation.[4] As he states in the preface, Irenaeus was persuaded to compose this work of refutation by a friend who wanted to know more about the teachings of the followers of Valentinus, a particularly important Gnostic school,[5] and by his own experience as a bishop, seeing the Church's dangerous opponents making relatively good progress in the populous, rich valley of the Rhône. So he had firsthand knowledge of the Valentinian school whose theological writings he had read and studied. To attack it at its roots he tried to trace it – by following a path probably derived from Justin[6] – to the heresiarch *par excellence*, Simon Magus of the Acts of the Apostles. From this diabolical character, through a succession of Gnostic teachers and schools, were descended those who had initiated the various contemporary Gnostics, the most important heirs being the Valentinians.

Irenaeus is a precious source: 'Nag Hammadi has done much to confirm the conclusions already drawn by Förster and Sagnard in relation to the substantial reliability of Irenaeus.'[7] He appears to be well informed about the Valentinians, Ptolemy and Marcus; but the genealogical tree that he claims to pass on appears today to be in many ways an arbitrary ideological reconstruction, which tells us something about the Bishop of Lyons's intentions, but is far from a trustworthy guide through the tangled forest of the groups of Gnostics.[8]

We are indebted to Hippolytus of Rome, a personality who, at the beginning the third century AD (d. *c*.235), played an important part in the Roman community, where doctrinal and ecclesiastical controversy was rampant and rife. He has left us a heresiological work that is second in order of time and importance.[9] This is the *Refutation of All Heresies*, also known as the *Philosophoumena* (Philosophical discussions), written in Greek. There were ten books, and thanks to a manuscript discovered in 1842, we have Books 4–10 (the first book has been known since 1701). The work, probably written after 222 – and its Hippolytan authorship has been questioned both recently and on several other occasions[10] – revolves around a basic theme: all heresies are merely travesties and adaptations of pagan philosophy. The first four books are therefore devoted to an exposition of pagan errors, from philosophy to magic, from the mysteries to astrology, errors later to be absorbed by Gnostic sects (thirty-three, to be precise), whose systems Hippolytus describes in the extant books. For this purpose he uses primary sources, still valuable today, even though his geography of the Gnostic sects (like that of Irenaeus) seems artificial.

With the author of the *Philosophoumena* heresiology can be established as a genre, on a literary as well as on a doctrinal level. It clearly presupposes the existence of 'heresy'.[11] And it is no accident that the Christian writer who has contributed most to the legal definition of the concept, the great African polemicist Tertullian (*c*.150–*c*.225), had made lengthy, direct attacks against the Gnostics, especially the Valentinians.[12]

Like Irenaeus before him, Tertullian testifies in his work to a historical problem of great importance. The history of the early Church was profoundly influenced, between the second and third centuries, by the struggle against the Gnostics. Irenaeus, for example, is impelled precisely by this confrontation to work out and establish fundamental theological and doctrinal issues: the doctrine of the visible, public Apostolic Succession, which he uses to refute the esoteric, unverifiable oral traditions of the Gnostics: the doctrine of *creatio ex nihilo* (creation out of nothing) which he refines and argues, together with the vigorous defence of the uniqueness of the Creator and the goodness of the cosmos, in clear contrast to the dualistic theories of his opponents;[13] the doctrine of the resurrection of the body, linked with the elaboration of an anthropological perspective undoubtedly stimulated by the typically Gnostic attitude of rejecting carnal reality.[14] Even Tertullian, who grasps the essential features of Gnosticism, is prompted by them to confirm his extremist defence of the primacy of a *pistis*, or faith, separate from, and opposed to, *ratio*, or reason.

A new theme emerges with the Alexandrian school: the intermingling of 'odi et amo', or love and hate, which joins two spiritual worlds, divergent, but united by certain elective affinities. If Tertullian had rejected and attacked the influence of pagan culture, asking the rhetorical question, 'What has Athens to do with Jerusalem or the Academy with the Church?', Clement of Alexandria (140/50–211/15) takes the opposite position, and in the *Protrepticus* and the *Paedagogus* attempts to recover the positive aspects scattered throughout the pagan world. So different a perspective entails a new solution to Tertullian's problem of the relationship between faith and reason, and this is most evident in his principal extant work, the *Stromateis* (Miscellanies). Clement opposes false Gnosis with the true Gnosis of the Christian.[15] By means of good, healthy living, knowledge of the principles of faith and growth in the spiritual dimension, the Christian is able to achieve the status of a true Gnostic, of one who aspires to know God through the Son. So Clement shows that in many sensitive areas, such as those of ethics and theology, he is quite familiar with the writings of his opponents. Indeed, it might be argued that his formulation of a balanced, moderate position owes something to the criticism of Gnostic ethics with its extremes of radical asceticism and unbridled libertinism, as is shown in his discussion of the problems of matrimony in *Strom.* 3.[16]

Origen (who died *c*.253–4), the greatest thinker and most important Greek writer of the Church, also had a complex relationship with the world of Gnosis, with which he established a dialectical relationship, not without its dangers and misunderstandings.[17] He had perceived an important historical truth. Thinkers like the Valentinians in their theological works had laid the foundations for rational reflection on the Christian God. On the other hand, in his *Commentary on the Gospel of John* this same Origen has left us forty-eight passages of a commentary on the same Gospel by the Valentinian Heracleon (second half of the second century), the first such commentary on an Evangelist that is known to us; and in his polemic against the Gnostic teacher, he ends up adopting the same allegorical principles as his opponent and shares with him, in addition to interpretative accuracy and virtuosity, a taste for getting to the bottom of the mystery of the Scriptures, in which he reads those events concerning the pre-existence of the soul and its fall, those 'principles' of the divine world that are to be found in the same atmosphere as the reflections of those under his attack.[18]

After the Alexandrian School there are one or two gaps in our portrait gallery. They are not accidental. As we shall see in chapter 10, from the middle of the third century the Gnostic system as a whole underwent a gradual process of erosion both for internal reasons and as a result of attacks from the True Church. Moreover, Christian thinkers began to turn their attention to more pressing doctrinal problems, such as those raised by the Trinitarian controversy; while on the horizon was the ever-increasing threat posed by the institutional crisis of the Empire, which would help to put in motion the wheels of persecution. Apart from a few hints that can be found in the *Ecclesiastical History* of Eusebius of Caesarea (d. 339), we have to wait until the second half of the fourth century to find another important writer engaged in the hunt for heretics, especially Gnostic heretics. This is Epiphanius,[19] born *c.* 315 at Eleutheropolis, not far from Gaza in Palestine. As a young man he visited the most celebrated monks in Egypt; he returned to Gaza and founded a monastery, over which he presided for about thirty years. This helped to provide him with an aura of sanctity, an advantage when the bishops elected him as Metropolitan in 367. He thus became Bishop of Constantia (ancient Salamis). And from there he fought his battles, both theological (he was an implacable opponent of Origen and his followers) and heresiological.

With his *Panarion* (Medicine Chest) (374–7) he intended to offer a reliable antidote to those who had been bitten by the poison of heresy, as well as protection and encouragement to those who had remained true to the faith. That heresy flourished at that time there can be no doubt: one has only to think of the endless theological controversies begun by Arius. That Gnostic groups continued to flourish is a matter of less uncertainty. Nevertheless it is significant that Epiphanius in some cases has had firsthand experience of his opponents (see chapter 11 below). That the heresies from Simon Magus to those of his contemporaries, the Messalians, reappear and are rounded up to the prophetic number eighty, to which Epiphanius limits them, is a further example of the ancients' love of arithmetical speculation (cf. the parallel of the eighty concubines in Song of Songs 6:8) and certainly not an actual historical fact. The heresiological material is subdivided or multiplied according to this numerical scheme, with results and problems for the modern scholar that may easily be imagined. Moreover, Epiphanius, with his Tertullian-like hatred of over-audacious philosophical or theological speculation (to which may be added his failure to understand it, unlike the African writer), appears as the exact antithesis of modern scientific method. The heretics are finally consigned to an increasingly fantastic genealogical pedigree, painted in the gloomiest colours, charged with the worst sins and condemned to the harshest penalties.[20]

The Bishop of Salamis may be considered virtually the last in the gallery of heresiological masks. Comparable later works, from the Augustinian *De haeresibus* (428), to Theodoret of Cyrus (395–466) and finally the *Book of Scholia* by Theodore bar Konai (791/2), are essentially no more than lists or catalogues of heresies, usually repeating what has been said before. If they occasionally contain valuable information on heretical movements that are closer and more familiar to the writer, they have almost nothing more to say about ancient Gnosticism.

Another mask was put on the face of Gnosticism by those pagan thinkers and polemicists who fought them just as vigorously as the Christians whom they hated, for example by Celsus, author of a *True Discourse* (*c.* 178), known to us partly from the attack on it by Origen in his *Contra Celsum* (AD 246).[21] But the main critic was Plotinus. The great philosopher had some Gnostic pupils, he had read their texts and rejected their dualistic doctrines, in which he saw a systematic attack on the very principles of the classical vision of the world.[22] Plotinus' evidence is very important, despite the difficulties involved in interpreting it, because the philosopher spreads his attacks on the Gnostics more or less by allusion and aims them not so much at individual schools, but rather more at what we would today call the structure of Gnostic thought.[23] It is precisely through his particular viewpoint and his contemptuous reaction that we can appreciate how the 'barbarous' wisdom of these new intellectuals must have appeared to an educated Greek of the third century.

This picture partly matches the description of certain 'new men' made towards the end of the third century by Arnobius, an African convert to Christianity who wrote an attack on paganism, *Adversus nationes*.[24] Arnobius' 'new men' too, like Plotinus' Gnostics, claim to be the bearers of a new religious message, which appears formidable and is rejected on the grounds that it is a new container for the old wine of the religious world of the second century, a world that appears to the modern scholar to be tinged with Hermetism.[25]

IN SEARCH OF A THEME: GNOSTICISM AND ITS INTERPRETATIONS

Apart from the few original fragments scattered through the heresiological texts, before the discovery at Nag Hammadi, the likelihood of hearing the actual words of the Gnostics lay in the discovery of a few original documents in Coptic at the end of the eighteenth century. It is also true that contemporary religious literature offers some traces of Gnostic beliefs. Certain themes typical of second-century Gnostic systems (the preaching of rigorous asceticism and the consequent rejection of the body and its passions, aspiration to perfect knowledge, i.e. the desire for direct attainment of the divine source) were in fact part of the more general religious atmosphere of the period and are detectable in various contemporary documents. At first sight there is often a danger of attributing the label of Gnosticism to material that is not Gnostic simply because they share a common cultural background and an identical atmosphere. An example is the *Odes of Solomon*, a collection of poetry probably from the second century (whether they were originally written in Greek or Syriac is disputed), richly evocative in images, which often echo, but are not identical with, parallel themes in Gnosticism.[26] Other examples are found in the Apocryphal Acts of the Apostles.[27] In particular, the *Acts of Thomas*[28] contains a good example of this type: the *Hymn of the Pearl* tells the story of a prince sent by his father to Egypt (the symbol of evil) to recover a hidden treasure, the Pearl. He falls prey to worldly pleasures, forgets where he has come from and his mission and has to be reminded of his task by a messenger. He recovers the Pearl and is able to put on the royal cloak again, and return once and for all to his country. Symbolic of the wanderings of the soul lost in worldly pleasures and forgetful of its divine origin, the story has often been interpreted as a poetic model of that process of Gnosis fundamental to Gnostic myths, based on the word of a divine messenger, whose task is to reawaken in the Gnostic the memory of his origin and thus to communicate the true Gnosis to him.[29]

This is quite different from two particular types of original sources: Hermetism and Mandaeism.

The *Corpus Hermeticum*[30] is a collection of texts attributed to Hermes Trismegistus ('thrice greatest'), compiled in Greek between the sixth and ninth centuries, but originating in the third, or perhaps the second, century AD. In the form of gentle, scholarly dialogues in which Hermes teaches a closed group of disciples, the *Corpus* contains many themes typical of contemporary philosophical syncretism, presented in a discursive and unsystematic fashion: the nature of the Supreme God who is invisible and good; the nature of the cosmos, a beautiful and visible god; the structure of the cosmos and the relationship between its elements; the nature of disorderly, irrational matter; the relationship between the macrocosm and that particular microcosm that is the human being. They are by no means original themes, and moreover their presentation is confused and sometimes contradictory, but – as is typical of contemporary speculation about God – they are imbued with genuine religious sentiment, a characteristic *pietas* and an irrepressible desire for knowledge of God. The ideological structure of the *Corpus* is *eusebeia meta gnōseōs* (piety with knowledge), an attitude of genuine, deep devotion as the way to knowledge of oneself and of God.[31]

Many of the documents reflect the traditional conception of the cosmos as a beautiful ordered world (as the Greek *kosmos* implies), a mirror of the invisible God, itself a living God whom one must contemplate and love. Essentially optimistic, they incline towards a pantheism that wants God to be present in everything and everything to be present in God.[32] Hermetism is not, however, a coherent philosophical system; beside these positive expressions of the world and God, there are in the same collection documents pervaded with a pessimistic view of life and characterized by a dualistic conception of the world and of humankind.[33] The world seems to be 'the epitome of evil'. Because it is alien to their true nature, human beings must renounce it and flee from it in order to be able to return to their heavenly home. To achieve this aim they must possess Gnosis, be reborn in their true nature, and be baptized in the cup of knowledge into which the divine intellect has been poured.[34] The documents containing these themes represent a typical example of Gnosis, free from Christian influence, which preaches new, difficult paths towards a rebirth of the Gnostic type, using Platonic themes.[35]

Unlike the Hermetists, of whose social identity we know nothing, the Mandaeans were an actual, living community. Essentially a Baptist sect, they produced an enormous literature in a Semitic dialect (eastern Aramaic) and managed to survive the vagaries of history,[36] so that even now they number about 1,500 initiates, still living as they did on the banks of the Tigris and the Euphrates. The writings of the Mandaeans reveal a mythological world and thought structure that is typically Gnostic. Their publication, which took place largely between the two wars and is still continuing today,[37] has caused some debate and controversy. Even their assignment to the first century AD[38] is now shown to be hypothetical (in fact the definitive compilation was made many centuries later). Accordingly, to use them as the basis for reconstructing the historical framework in which Gnosticism arose and established itself is, to say the least, problematic. Dated too precipitately to the beginning of our era, these writings were also used in the historical explanation of some fundamental conceptions of the Gospel of John.[39]

Two further documents must be mentioned, both discovered towards the end of the eighteenth century and containing original material in the Coptic language. The Codex Askewianus (named after the English Doctor Askew), which is in the British Library, was brought to the attention of the academic public in 1778 by C. G. Woide, though it was not made more generally accessible until 1851 in a Latin translation from the original Coptic. Compiled between the fourth and fifth centuries, it contains the *Pistis Sophia* or 'Faith Wisdom', which goes back to the third century.[40] The contents are an interminable, rambling series of revelations made by the risen Jesus to his disciples. While they might have gladdened the hearts of theosophists and spiritualists,[41] they left the specialist perplexed, irritated or frankly disappointed. With its tendency to multiply pleromatic entities and intermediate worlds, the treatise seems to afford evidence typical of a regressive phase and of the irreversible decadence of a Gnosticism no longer capable of speculative originality. As for the other document, the Codex Brucianus (named after its Scottish owner, J. B. Bruce), now in the Bodleian Library in Oxford, it contained the *Two Books of Jeu*, similar in form to the *Pistis Sophia*, but even more inclined to regard magical formulae and mystical cryptograms as the way of gaining access to the divine mysteries, and an untitled theological treatise, difficult to interpret.[42]

Confronted by this situation, scholars of the interwar years found themselves driven into the clutches of the heresiologists in an attempt to recover the authentic face of Gnosticism. The critical question that was bound to be asked had to be formulated in either of the following ways: is Gnosticism a Christian heresy, risen within the doctrinal controversies and theological debates of the first two centuries, a Christian heresy whose content might originate in the most diverse religious traditions, given its syncretistic makeup, but whose spirit is rooted and grounded in the gospels? Or must one finally reject this mask, which some heresiologists have already imposed on a religion which by its nature had nothing to do with Christianity and whose origins were independent of, and perhaps earlier than, the gospel message itself and, indeed – as the Gospel of John seems to show – may even have influenced it?

The problem of origins is thus clearly interwoven with that of determining the essence of Gnosticism. In the course of the nineteenth century a typical interpretative pendulum began to be constructed. It was F. C. Baur (1792–1860), a Hegelian, founder of the important exegetic theological school at Tübingen, who initiated modern critical research on Gnosticism with his publication of *Christliche Gnosis* in 1835.[43] He regarded the Gnostics as the first philosophers of the Christian religion, the vanguard of a type of reflection that was to manifest itself many centuries later in the Gnosis of the Hegelian system (his work is still a valuable account of the fortunes of Gnosticism). This interpretation was based on a distinction, destined to become canonical, between popular Gnosticism as represented in the mythological systems and a philosophical Gnosticism typical of original, speculative thinkers like Basilides and Valentinus, who had begun, under the inspiration of Greek philosophy, to reflect on the mysteries of the Christian message.

This thesis was given a classic formulation at the end of the century in the *History of Dogmas* by the great Protestant church historian and theologian, Adolf von Harnack (1851–1930). He regarded Gnostics as the first Christian theologians and Gnosticism as the extreme Helleniz-ation of Christianity,[44] an anticipation of religious modernism which had introduced into the citadel of the original message of Jesus the enemy destined to distort it: Greek rationalism.

This view was not radically overturned until the beginning of this century (though there had been sporadic indications of a change during the nineteenth century) by some of the more important members of the History of Religion School at Göttingen.[45] Stimulated by a renewal of interest in the phenomenon of folklore and popular culture, they turned their attention to mythological systems. Their style had nothing in common with the western speculative tradition; they were products of the East. And if one wished to discover the origins of Gnosticism, one had to look towards the East. In the reconstructions of a Bousset[46] or a Reitzenstein,[47] Gnosticism consequently appeared to be a non-Christian religion of eastern origin. But at the same time it is a system of thought that has nullified the vital spark of this remote influence. The oriental mythological themes that make up its framework, from the celestial journey of the soul to belief in the great Mother Goddess, so full of life and colour in the original Babylonian religion, had, in the religious syncretism of the imperial period, become lifeless survivals, spectres flitting about in vain in a world of shades deprived for ever of their life blood.

Disengaged from the heresiological matrix and no longer viewed from the perspective of ecclesiastical history, Gnosis could now move in the less restricted areas of the history of religions, though this was extremely far-reaching and dangerously unlimited territory. It now assumed a quite different perspective. Related, if not prior, to Christianity, it had arisen independently, based on oriental texts and ideas, a genuine religion, in which the *logos* (word/reason) was the son of the *mythos* (myth) and Christianity one of several elements that came together to make a difficult puzzle.

At this point tension inevitably developed. According to tastes and specialities, the Gnostic 'Orient' fragmented into various directions,

which the individual scholar pursued retrogressively according to his or
her own inclinations, looking now at Babylon, now at Persia and Egypt
as possible sources of mythological Gnostic material. But how could
these fragments of mythical worlds, light years away from the second
century AD, continue to be the subject of beliefs and practices? What
gave life to these survivors? The theory of 'survival' revealed its limits
in this case too.

A certain section of German youth in the thirties, influenced by
Spengler to regard the crisis of the Weimar Republic as the crisis of the
West and its values, and responding to the promptings of both Nietzsche
and Heidegger to search desperately for an answer to the historico-
political tragedy that was happening before their eyes, began to look to
the East, so precious to an entire German philosophical and literary
tradition;[48] in its Gnostic guise, the Orient was able to become a
valuable symbol, an antecedent and at the same time a possible answer
to the existential dramas of their own time. A new life blood flowed
from the East. New conceptions and new ways of existence arrived, and
communication with imaginative forms that an arid, cold Greek
rationalism had suppressed or marginalized.[49]

The voice of this *Stimmung*, or mood, in the field of Gnostic studies
was that of a brilliant young German philosopher, a pupil of Heidegger
trained in the rigorous philological and exegetical school of Rudolf
Bultmann: Hans Jonas. Using the traditional sources, Jonas succeeded,
perhaps better than anyone else, in grasping the originality and specific
nature of the Gnostic world.[50] There are several reasons for this. Jonas's
philosophical training was particularly important. German philologists,
even when, like Dieterich and Reitzenstein, they rejected the exasperated
classicism of Wilamowitz who dominated the scene at that time,
continued to impose rationalist prejudices on the Gnostic Orient. How
is one to assess certain theological constructs? Bousset opposed Harnack
and his interpretation, typical of *fin de siècle* liberal theology. Bousset
was concerned with similar theological preoccupations, even if they did
reflect a contrary viewpoint: the non-Christian origins of Gnosis and
its possible influence on Christianity were bound to elicit yet another
attempt to study Christian origins from a religious-historical angle,
based on an elaborate theory formulated by Ernst Troeltsch.[51]

Jonas approaches the Gnostic world without the aid of these deceptive
screens. A philosopher seduced by the subtle fascination that Heidegger's
lectures exerted on an entire generation of young German scholars,[52]
he aims at penetrating the heart of the Gnostic systems. Abandoning all
misleading theories about the survivors, he seeks to take the inner pulse,
to rediscover the forms of a phenomenon that he regarded as a living

organism and not an archaeological fossil. The secret life blood of the various Gnostic worlds is a radically dualistic concept, which pits the body against the spirit, this world of shadows against the world of light; a vision nurtured by, and rooted in, *Dasein*, or existence, in a way of being in which problems and solutions of modern existentialism are anticipated. The Gnostic is the Stranger *par excellence*, the 'alien' propelled to exist in a cosmos that is strange to him, to live a life that does not belong to him, because it is rooted in illusion. His is an anxious search for *gnōsis*, for a knowledge that will save him; this will be revealed to him as a call from above, a cry that will arouse him from his existence of sleep and shadows to remind him of his true origins, which know nothing of becoming and of death, and to show him the road to salvation.

With Jonas's work on Gnosis and the spirit of late antiquity, the classical period of Gnostic research comes to an end. And not by chance. Never before, as there is in the *juvenilia* of this scholar, had there been any impression that the subject of Gnosticism, freed of so many shadows accumulated around it by history, was now finally in a position to speak with its own voice.

A VOICE FROM THE DESERT: THE NAG HAMMADI LIBRARY

Research into Gnosticism had reached this point when the two Ali brothers made their startling find. What they took back to their village was a library of Coptic texts. Many of these were Gnostic works, previously known often only by title and thought to be irretrievably lost. But a variety of obstacles was still to be erected against the voice of these records of the past.

Back in the village of the two brothers, the library found itself in the midst of a blood feud. The father, a night watchman of the irrigation system for the neighbouring fields, had some months previously surprised a thief during one of his tours of inspection and killed him. The following morning, in accordance with a widely held tradition of vendetta, he too was murdered. About a month after the discovery of the library, Ahmad, a molasses dealer who was passing through, fell asleep in the midday heat near the house of Muhammad Ali. A neighbour informed Muhammad Ali that the unfortunate man was his father's murderer. Muhammad Ali thereupon rushed home to tell his brothers and his mother the good news. The whole family set upon the victim, and literally tore him limb from limb. The climax of the blood feud was to cut up his heart and divide it among themselves.

This bloody turn of events had quite an unexpected effect on the subsequent fortunes of the library. The police issued a warrant for Muhammad's arrest and frequently visited his home. Believing these writings to be Christian because they were written in Coptic script, and also in order to remove what was beginning to look like the source of his misfortune, Muhammad thought that they would be safer in the house of the village Coptic priest until matters improved. Coptic priests can marry, and the wife of this priest had a brother who gained a living as a peripatetic teacher of English and history in the neighbouring schools of the Coptic Church. When he arrived back at al-Qasr, his sister decided to show him one of the codices, and he immediately recognized its potential value. He persuaded his brother-in-law to let him have one of them, Codex III. In Cairo he showed it to an academic interested in the Coptic language, Georges Sobhi, who in turn took it to the Department of Antiquities. After lengthy negotiations the codex was bought by the Coptic Museum in Cairo on 4 October 1946.

Meanwhile Muhammad Ali's mother, thinking that the books were worthless, had burned some of them (perhaps Codex XII, of which only fragments remain). Illiterate Muslims from near by bought the others at a derisory price. A certain Nashid Bisadah, who had acquired one of them, gave it to a gold merchant from Nag Hammadi, who sold it in Cairo and divided the proceeds with his business partner. Most of the codices were acquired by Bahy Ali, a one-eyed criminal from al-Qasr, who took them to Cairo with the help of a local antiquities dealer, Dhaki Basta, to make sure that the maximum amount could be got for what looked like a promising investment. After an unsuccessful attempt at selling them to an antiquarian, they finally managed to dispose of the whole lot to Phocio J. Tano, from whose hands the precious goods eventually passed to the Department of Egyptian Antiquities. After Nasser seized power, even the Coptic texts were nationalized. Deposited at the Coptic Museum in Cairo, they entered upon a new phase of life. The struggle for their acquisition and preservation was replaced by the struggle for their publication.

Codex I, the so-called Jung Codex, underwent a separate fate.[53] It fell into the hands of a Belgian art dealer, Albert Eid. Afraid that the Egyptian government would confiscate it, he had it taken out of Egypt. Once abroad, it was offered, unsuccessfully, first to the Bollingen Foundation in New York and then to the Bibliothèque Nationale in Paris. With the owner's death, there were then complicated problems of inheritance. The credit lies with Gilles Quispel for having rescued the precious document. Thanks to his interest, it was in fact acquired by the Jung Institute in Zurich on 10 May 1952 and offered to its celebrated founder as a gift. The text was published and eventually returned to Egypt after negotiations between the Institute and the Coptic Museum in Cairo. Today the entire library is one of the major attractions of this extraordinary Museum.

Many years, however, were to elapse before the completed publication of the entire library in a photographic edition in 1977, under the auspices of Unesco.[54] A whole generation of specialists had been denied access to these extraordinary sources. This deplorable situation was caused partly by the rivalry between schools and scholars. The less said about this the better.

By making the texts more generally available, the photographic edition put an end to the various monopolies which had been jealously guarded. Thus, recent years have seen a whole series of editions. There is now a complete English translation,[55] and many translations of individual texts. Different projects for a critical edition have reached an advanced stage.[56]

What are the contents of this collection that lay hidden for more than a thousand years until it was uncovered by Muhammad Ali's pickaxe? To whom did it belong? Why had it been so carefully concealed? These are questions that must be attended to, a necessary stage to pass through before the impatient reader is allowed to enter the world of Gnostic mysteries and myths.

The Nag Hammadi library primarily represents a considerable corpus to the scholar previously accustomed to work upon a few scattered documents: thirteen books containing fifty-three texts, a total of 1,153 pages (almost 90 per cent of the original).[57] Of these texts forty-one were previously quite unknown; of the remainder six are either duplicates of writings already extant, and six were previously known. Many of those texts (about thirty) have come to us in good condition, and only ten are particularly fragmentary.

The contents of the library are not specifically Gnostic.[58] Apart from a passage of Plato's *Republic* (588 b–589 b in NHC VI.5) and a Coptic translation of the *Sentences of Sextus* (NHC XII.1), a second-century Christian text of ascetic origin known to specialists for some time, there are also the *Teachings of Silvanus* (NHC VII.4), another example of Christian wisdom literature, which most probably has a monastic provenance and which, despite many exegetical attempts to the contrary, has no specific Gnostic content.[59] On the other hand, the ascetic nature of the teachings might also have attracted the attention of the Gnostic reader; indeed, one might regard the text as a Trojan Horse designed to introduce its own religious message into a Christian stronghold susceptible to ascetic teaching. Similarly, the *Acts of Peter and the*

Twelve Apostles (NHC VI.1) belongs to the romance genre typical of the other apocryphal acts, shot through with the elements of the Greek romance, with travels, disappearances and rediscoveries, though of course the erotic element of the pagan model was sublimated in the censored, Christian version, which provided noble examples of virginity and ascetic practice. In these *Acts of Peter* there is nothing specifically Gnostic; but motifs like the journey, the stranger, the hidden pearl, typical of this work, might well have lent themselves to Gnostic exegesis, which could easily identify[60] them as metaphors and symbols of its own mythical world.

There are also three Hermetic texts: a partial version of the *Asclepius*, previously known from a Latin version (NHC VI.8); a typically Hermetic prayer (NHC VI.7), previously known from a Greek version (*Papyrus Mimaut*) and a Latin translation (*Asclepius* 41); and *On the Ogdoad and the Ennead* (NHC VI.6) on spiritual regeneration.[61]

The specifically Gnostic writings contain a significant variety of literary genres. Besides the apocryphal texts (e.g. the *Apocryphon of John*), which were meant to remain hidden and secret (*apokryphon*), and the pseudepigrapha, a common genre favoured in antiquity by a certain kind of mentality (and a far cry from modern problems of copyright), which came to be attributed to the revelations of a famous person of the past, we find epistles, treatises and prayers. Generally speaking, they are literary fictions,[62] which, like modern advertising slogans, always ultimately conceal the same message – a literary framework typical of that period in literature. This is the case, for example, with the apocalypses[63] scattered throughout the codices, which reproduce a literary genre of ancient, noble Iranian origin and not very successful in the Graeco-Roman world (not naturally given to eschatological revelation), but well known in the Judaeo-Christian tradition. It is indeed not surprising that it found new life in Gnosticism, for by its nature it is revealed soteriological knowledge. On the other hand, some Gnostic writers even went so far as to invent a new literary fiction (as if the available ones were not enough): the Gnostic revelation discourse,[64] e.g. the *Pistis Sophia*, essentially based on a New Testament *topos*, or passage. The Gospels record that Jesus spent forty days[65] with his disciples after the Resurrection, though the Evangelists say little or nothing of the particular revelations he is supposed to have made to them.[66] It was the Gnostics' intention to fill this gap. This period became a privileged source of possible esoteric traditions. In those days (whose number could be multiplied at will, up to the twelve years of the *Pistis Sophia*), Jesus no longer spoke in parables, in veiled terms that concealed the truth and were intended for the masses, but openly, communicating the true Gnosis to the elect.

Finally there are the so-called Gnostic 'gospels'. As in the case of the well-known *Gospel of Thomas* (NHC II.2),[67] they are collections of sayings of Jesus, originally not Gnostic, which nevertheless owe their present form to the subtle, but clearly recognizable, work of a Gnostic author. Or, as in the case of the *Gospel of Truth* (NHC I.3), we are dealing with a homiletic exposition of the good news, Gnostic in character.[68]

Is this variety of literary forms attributable in its doctrinal content to definite schools and trends of thought? This is a most difficult and controversial aspect of the entire Gnostic dossier and, at the present state of research, it is not yet possible to arrive at a satisfactory reply.

The heresiological sources had provided a fairly broad, well-formed picture of the Valentinian school. This fixed point of reference has allowed various writings to be attributed to the Valentinians, the most important being the *Gospel of Truth*, the *Epistle to Rheginus* (NHC I.4), a short, but important, treatise on the Gnostic concept of resurrection and the nature of the spiritual body; the long *Tripartite Tractate* (NHC I.5), so called[69] because in allusive, cryptic language, which conveys its esoteric nature, the anonymous author systematically reflects on the three phases of the Gnostic myth (upper or pleromatic world: fall of the pneumatic or spiritual principle and formation of the world and man; and creation of three classes of men and their destiny); the so-called *Gospel of Philip* (NHC II.3), a collection of Jesus' thoughts and sayings, of which the most important, as we shall see, concern the sacrament of spiritual marriage; finally, a treatise from Codex XI on baptism and the eucharist. The school's influence can therefore be traced in different stages and steps in other writings in the corpus, which are further confirmation of the theological relevance, and also of the success enjoyed by the Valentinians.

Sometimes the writings provide texts whose titles were already known from the heresiological tradition. For example, the *Paraphrase of Shem* (NHC VII.1) may be related to the *Paraphrase of Seth* mentioned by Hippolytus;[70] in abstruse and often impenetrable language, the origins of the elements, the fall of the spiritual principle and the history of the salvation of the elect are outlined. The apocalyptic texts *Zostrianus* (NHC VIII.1), *Marsanes* (NHC X.1) and *Allogenes* (NHC XI.3) appear to be related to certain apocalyptic treatises mentioned by Plotinus[71] in which the mysteries of the upper world are communicated to the protagonist in the course of a celestial voyage in the customary fashion of apocalyptic literature.

However, it has not always been possible to find any correspondence between external evidence and the Nag Hammadi documents. The scholar is thus compelled to resort to internal comparison, a necessarily more hypothetical terrain. This in-depth analysis has revealed that many of these writings share a common background.[72] The Gnostics in question seem to agree on a common spiritual ancestor in Seth, the patriarch, Biblical son of Adam; and in identifying the most characteristic elements of the divine world and in defining the way in which the story of salvation is unfolded. Thus it has been conjectured that these writings belong to a common ideological world of a more or less unitary nature commonly called 'Sethian', rather than to clearly identifiable sectarian groups.

The heterogeneous nature of the library reflects a movement that by its nature avoided dogmatic systems and rigid divisions. The very presence of more than one version of the same text, e.g. the *Apocryphon of John*,[73] which contain significant variant readings, is confirmation not only that the same text could circulate in different editions, but that, unlike sacred books subjected to the rigid standardization of the text, these treatises could easily be enlarged or corrected; and this shows both the essentially fluctuating nature of the myths and the divergent theological interests.

The texts that have come down to us are fourth-century translations in various dialects of Coptic, the language of Christian Egypt, based on Greek originals of the second or third century.[74] Various elements that can be deduced from the binding of the codices indicate that the translations were made in a monastic environment in the late fourth century, a period when Pachomian monasticism was flourishing. An attempt has therefore been made to see the corpus as the private library of one of these monasteries.[75] It is an enticing hypothesis, but has yet to be proved. However, these and other texts, perhaps no longer extant, may have been assembled with the aim of refuting a movement that was still thriving in the middle of the fourth century; or rather it may have been a private collection of monks who, zealous predecessors of modern esoteric specialists, were thus preserving the memory of a religion that now, two centuries after its heyday, looked like a relic of the past.[76]

The reader who has been patient enough to follow this survey of the various problems posed by a study of this library, after looking through so many side doors, with a fleeting glance at the introductory rooms, and arriving at the last door, may legitimately ask: Do these writings reveal the true face of Gnosticism? In cases of this sort one must proceed with extreme caution. Today it is possible to outline the Gnostic planet with more precision and accuracy. We can now distinguish the two great continents already partially discovered by the History of Religions School. In addition to a Gnosis that arises and has established itself upon the very framework of Christianity and draws sustenance from it, there is clearly another, non-Christian Gnosis.[77] The boundary between the two is still disputed territory. It will certainly be one of the most difficult tasks of future researchers to explore this no man's land. It is also possible to depict more clearly the relationship between this area and other areas of the ancient religious and cultural world, e.g. the Graeco-Hellenistic world,[78] especially in its Platonic aspects, the Jewish world[79] and oriental traditions, especially those of Iranian origin.[80] The relationship with the True Church in the second and third centuries may also be examined in greater detail, and some scholars have already tried to reopen the thorny dossier of the conflicts between orthodoxy and heresy[81] or the still more delicate question of the relationship between Gnosis and the New Testament.[82]

However, it is above all the internal life of this world that becomes better known. The first explorers of the Nag Hammadi texts found themselves confronted by a veritable mythological jungle. But the achievement of the first attempts to penetrate it are beginning to show results. The mythological Gnostic world in its rich complexity is one of the most significant aspects of the history of second-century thought. Some aspects of the cult life of particular groups are even better known, even if the present state of our knowledge makes it difficult to attain a sociologically acceptable understanding of Gnosticism. To some extent, after all, one can sketch out more solid hypotheses on the actual history of this movement, on its eventual origins and the principal phases of its development.

But the true face of Gnosticism must remain for the time being a mystery. However, we are quite happy to leave this for others to discover. What we propose here is a more limited task: to lead the reader to discover the complex problems of the mythical world of Gnosticism. We shall enter it after a brief reconnaissance of contemporary religious beliefs, which may help us to sketch the essential framework of the social and religious universe in which Gnosticism and its mythology arose and became established.

2

Between Demons and Gods:
an Age of Revelation

A TWO-HEADED JANUS: THE CENTURY OF THE ANTONINES

The Gnostic drama has its own unity, if not of place, at least of time. History decided to lift the curtain on the drama between the first and second centuries AD at the beginning of the Antonine era.

What Gibbon considered an age of indolence, what to many subsequent historians continued to present itself as an age in decline, concealing behind the veil of economic development and public munificence the symptoms of a spiritual canker, an irreversible crisis of classical enlightenment and rationalism, appears today, in the new perspective on the late antique world, in a new form and a different light.[1]

This crucial century was a watershed between the two decisive periods of imperial history: the Augustan Restoration and the 'crisis' of the third century. Its Janus-like quality becomes clearer when one considers its religious life.

One of its faces continues to gaze imperturbably at the past. The traditional forms of civic religion, albeit with the necessary changes and adaptations entailed by alterations in the power structure, continued to fulfil an important function within the vast social body of the Empire. The routine of official cults was now the instrument to ensure social cohesion of local elites.[2] Generally speaking, and contrary to a widely held opinion (even of such authoritative witnesses as Plutarch[3]), the traditional channels of religious consensus, at least in certain social classes, still enjoyed widespread respect. Oracles, though consulted less than previously, still exercised considerable influence, if not on the more general political events that escaped the control of local gods, certainly on the everyday life of the many petitioners who thronged to the doors of prophets and prophetesses in the hope that the 'god of the day' might deliver through them answers to the perennial questions and problems: the outcome of a birth, the fortunes of a marriage, the prospects for business.[4] The desire to know one's destiny and to be able to control, to evade or to use it is a dimension of the human spirit that appears to be limitless. The documents provide us with evidence of the fortunes of astrologers, magicians, fortune-tellers, practitioners of the occult in a traditional society that was afraid of threatened changes and in need of both outlet and constraint.[5] In his workshop the magician continued to provide ready-made recipes designed to deceive or to furnish hope to the disappointed lover, to quench the betrayed lover's thirst for revenge, to cure aches and pains that had defeated the remedies provided by conventional medicine.[6]

The fashion for the occult that appears to invade Hellenistic cities in the first centuries of our era (occasionally, as we know from astrology, in the garb of a pseudo-science) is none other than the urban version of popular religion typical of the countryside. On the other hand, it is hardly surprising in a world, physical and cultural, in which the very cities, even in the period of their greatest expansion and pride, continue to be islands in a sea of countryside (or desert), that rural religious life, through yet another change, acquired certain features of its urban counterpart. It is a face, therefore, that at that time was turned towards the past, lost in escapist traditions and daydreams, and, when compared with the other currents of the religious panorama, tranquil and indolent. Then ripples begin to appear on the peaceful surface, betraying at times unsuspected tensions and anxieties. One begins to see a landscape populated by major characters with a new kind of religious temperament. Lucian,[7] an acute and sceptical observer of his time, depicts the changing spiritual climate vividly and with subtle irony. From behind a screen of disparaging accusations, his 'group photography' depicts the typical representatives of a religious world in ferment. His writings are full of itinerant preachers, prophets bearing divine messages, Christians thirsting for martyrdom, 'theomaniacs' and 'holy sinners'. These people have a new rapport with the divine: they represent a sort of barometer of the profound changes taking place in religious mentality.

The other face of the century reveals, if not an age of anxiety,[8] then certainly the emergence of new problems, questions and shared religious responses from the rejection of traditional solutions, a newly formed geography of the realm of the sacred, a different conception of the biorhythms of religious life and a paradoxical way of imagining, and giving shape to, the relationship between the human and divine.

NEW RELIGIOUS HORIZONS

The ancient representation of the world, that of the pre-Socratics as a flat disc floating in space, was replaced from the beginning of the Hellenistic period by a new geocentric configuration that was to remain fundamental to astronomical (and astrological) thought until the modern revolution of Kepler and Galileo. The earth, centre of the universe, is surrounded by seven planetary spheres, concentric circles on the ideal surface of which another seven planets rotate: three (the Moon, Mercury, Venus) under the Sun and three (Mars, Jupiter, Saturn) above it.[9] The eighth sphere, situated beyond the planetary spheres (according to an opinion also shared by Aristotle), finally supports the heaven of the fixed stars, so called because, unlike the varied movements of the planets, it was characterized by a single unitary movement.

This revolution in astronomy had enormous consequences for the religious geography of the Beyond. Alongside belief in the subterranean Underworld, the concept of a sublunar Underworld began to emerge, located between the Earth and the Moon.[10] On the other hand, Elysium itself had also been shifted, moving upwards from distant areas of the Earth to ever higher regions in the celestial world.[11]

This rearrangement of the mythological landscape is never an end in itself. The geography of the other world acquires a rich complexity, as in the famous descent of Virgil's Aeneas,[12] a forerunner of the many increasingly detailed and complex descriptions of the afterlife in Jewish and Christian apocalyptic texts. On the other hand, whereas Aeneas, following the paths of tradition, had to find the entrance to the Underworld in a cave, the Gnostic Saviour of the second century AD, making his soteriological descent across the heavens, saw that the Underworld had changed and become one with the cosmos itself.

This demonization of the cosmos,[13] which extends the place of the Underworld to the planets and the heavens of the fixed stars, is in fact the barometer of a more general revolution in religious concepts.

Traditional paganism had for centuries been expressed by impersonal forms, such as the universe itself, mobilizing and conveying emotions towards objects and sacred rites. Even where Greek *pietas* seems to reach its most sublime expression,[14] there remains nevertheless the residuum, irreducible in the classical forms of religion, of a rapport with a god who continues to confine man within rigid ethical rules of socially acceptable behaviour. This same impersonal concept of divine power as expanding energy that penetrates the different parts of the universe, sometimes in the traditional, familiar forms of the classical pantheon, sometimes spilling over into the esoteric spheres of magic and astrology to the point where it reaches the dimensions of cosmic energy pervading and animating everything,[15] continues to represent the basso continuo of many religious concepts, even during the imperial period.

Jewish apologetics, though with little success, had helped to question the classical concept of the divine.[16] Between the first and second centuries both the spread of the Christian message and the introduction of new religious cults based on a more intimately personal relationship were travelling much of the way in parallel in pursuit of the traditional relationship between God and human beings.

The drive towards these different traditional religious forms was fuelled by an actual change in the self-awareness of the individual. Many experienced the sensation of having something infinitely precious in themselves, an extraordinary gift that raised them above the anonymous mass of believers, but also estranged them, sometimes painfully, from the surrounding world. 'In interiore homine habitat veritas' (truth lives in the inner person): an ancient tradition of thought, going back to Plato himself, but overlaid with diverse religious and philosophical elements from the vast sea of Hellenism, had had the effect of emphasizing, in the same human microcosm, the spiritual and invisible at the expense of the material and tangible.

Contact with this delicate, penetrating sensitivity revealed that the material, empirical human being was an outer covering that with its suffocating, deceptive coils envelops the chrysalis of a new reality: the inner person, the true, essential person.[17] Endowed with the ability to taste spiritual reality, to hear celestial harmony, to understand and to penetrate within the recesses of the divine world, this new anthropological reality imposed itself at the same time as the promised goal of competing revelations and the outcome of the ascetic processes of strict self-discipline and rigid observance.

With regard to the models of the Socratic-Platonic tradition, learning to know oneself now involved a double shift in emphasis.[18] Superimposed on the ethical dimension of the self was a concrete spiritual reality, an *anthrōpos* (man, human being) who, given a moment's attention, saw that he or she was invested with a vitality of his or her own, ready to emerge into a new life in whoever was prepared to undergo the spiritual birth-pangs. For this purpose the verbal instruments of Socratic midwifery proved to be increasingly inadequate. The 'truth' that one carried inside oneself was not an abstract reality, which could be produced aseptically in scholastic disquisitions or in self-serving meandering reflection. Those who turned, out of boredom or disgust with the eternal world, to their own interior microcosm, did so with a new keen sensitivity of the

imagination, that enabled them to respond to the signs of the formation
of a new life, which to many now appeared to be the true one: indeed,
it now partook of the same life as the Godhead, perhaps even coinciding
with it.[19]

What had once been the destiny of heroes and demigods now became
the privilege of anyone who succumbed to the blandishments of some
god's itinerant minstrel or who heeded the persuasive voice of the 'inner'
person. Classical Greece had established solid barriers between humans
and the gods; to violate them, even in thought, was to commit the
infamous sin of hubris. Now the new spiritual climate positively insisted
that one transcend these barriers and become a *hyperanthrōpos* (a super
human).[20] This now became the goal in a spiritual contest destined to
attract increasingly numerous and enthusiastic competitors.

This was inevitable. From aristocratic privilege maintained in terms
of *philotimia* – decorum, honour and respect for the ground rules in a
hierarchical society where the social boundaries were clearly defined –
the assimilation to the divine *kata to dynaton* (as far as possible) was
tending to become a possibility on offer, at least theoretically, to
everyone, indeed to anyone able to undergo the experiences of spiritual
conversion and rebirth that constituted the principal commodities of
this religious market.

But how was this to be attained? The major obstacle in the new
structure of religious reality was the new place assigned to divine power.

The spiritual principle, which aspired to return to its divine home at
the end of its sojourn on earth, was obliged to make long, tedious
planetary journeys.[21] Only after crossing the gate of the Hebdomad, the
traditional seat of the Cosmic God, was it able to enter the limitless
space of the divine kingdom. For this was now inhabited by a God
who, according to the most consistent theory, appeared to be *atopos*,
without a place that could in any way confine him.[22]

In reality, an absolute transcendence, like that of the contemporary
Theos agnōstos (unknown God), ignores or despises *analogia entis*
(comparison of being).[23] A common language, that of negative theology,
links the God of the Christians, the Gnostics and the Platonists. God
cannot be predicated; or rather, what one can say about him is what
he is not; he is not this or that quality or aspect of being. But while
one surrounds him with negative predicates, the mystique of the
ineffable[24] builds around him the soft protective barrier of a language
that fends off the attacks of anthropomorphism and removes him to
the recesses of a sovereign solitude.

And yet God was active in history and, moreover, in a world replete
with dark – indeed demoniacal – forces. The problem of theodicy

deepened, to bristle with unusual difficulties. Philo, a Hebrew philosopher from Alexandria in Egypt, educated as a Greek at the beginning of our era, was acutely aware of this. If God was the *summum bonum*, or highest good, and if, on the other hand, matter, which he had created, was essentially something negative, because it was by nature subject to change and corruption, how could God have anything to do with this world of death – the perceptible cosmos? In view of the origin of humankind, it was a problem destined to have serious repercussions. The human's dual nature, a spiritual principle set within a corruptible body, and a soul continually deflected from its course towards the heavenly home by all sorts of longings and desires, compelled one to reconsider the mystery of original creation. How was it possible for evil to arise from creation, an intrinsically good divine act?[25] Was there, then, some possibility of mediation between absolute divine transcendence and the corrupt nature of the world and humankind?

The problem of mediation, which so acutely characterizes the thought of the time, receives different responses, according to the various situations. What these responses have in common is the general multiplication of intermediate principles, powers that mediate between the ineffable God, unknown and transcendent, and the transitory, corruptible world of matter. In Philo the monotheistic God of the Hebrew tradition is obliged to rely on the assistance of hypostases,[26] self-supporting forms of the one divine reality. Their function is to collaborate in the work of creation, assuming the most delicate and problematic aspects, e.g. that of the angels who fashion the matter for the human body.[27]

The tendency to multiply the intermediate figures between God and the cosmos, to populate the *intermundia* (the worlds in between) with countless divinities, was typical of the period. It was not a matter simply of finding a provisional and sometimes uncomfortable arrangement for the company of gods and divinities in the traditional pantheon unceremoniously evicted from their positions of primacy. As we are told by Plutarch, and reminded by the Neoplatonic tradition,[28] the ancient gods were now called upon to fulfil a new function. Interposing themselves between human beings and a God who, as in paganism, was beginning to assume the traits, if not monotheistic, certainly henotheistic, of a unique principle of the universe, they acted as an image of a complex divine reality, a mirror which refracted and allowed one to see the multiplicity of functions and activities that were at work in the divine world, while presenting a boundary that might not be crossed in order to preserve the absolute independence and transcendence of God.

Like the *deus otiosus*, or inactive god, of archaic mythology, the unknown and unknowable God, who is at the top of the divine pyramid gives the extra push that sets in motion the great machine of the cosmos and seems to have retired to his palace, inaccessible to humankind. The entities generated by him now have the task of realizing concretely the plan conceived from the beginning of time. From among these entities there emerges a distinct *deuteros theos*, a second god, son and perfect image of the Father: he is the *Logos* (Word) of the Christians, the *Nous* (Mind) of the Middle Platonists and of the Gnostics. He has the dual function of manifesting and setting up the plan conceived by the Father within the divine world and of realizing it in the external world.

In the theological systems of the period the *Logos* becomes the mediator by antanomosia.[29] His fate is bound to the multifaceted ideological heritage that the concept itself involved. Creation could not have taken place without the intervention of the word (*logos*), which is word-discourse, the principle of order, rationality and programming of the divine plan, at once destined to find their natural theological incarnation in the *Logos*.

In certain cases, the *deuteros theos* might directly assume the demiurgical tasks of creation;[30] but generally this was a task delegated to obedient servants. This band of assistants was thus faced with a thankless job: to fashion matter that was recalcitrant, if not directly rebellious.[31]

In the cosmologies of the period the nature of matter[32] constitutes one of the most obscure and controversial issues. In terms of philosophical syncretism, though its eternity was not discussed, its essence caused quite a few problems. The spread of positions was fairly diverse, even if many subscribed to the belief that its negativity was bound up with its own nature of an element deprived of *logos*, and consequently irrational and chaotic, subject to disordered tensions and movements.

How could particles of the divine *logos* be inserted in matter without deforming it? Basically, everything depended on the limits imposed on the presence of this negativity. According to the Hermetic *Asclepius*,[33] it would have been possible to confine the irrationality of *hylē* (matter) to the lowest strata of the cosmos, which was forming in ever more harmonious, close structures, approaching the very source of harmony, the vault of heaven, the cosmic God. Evil appeared as a *minus habens*, a deficiency of the being and the fullness that were able to subsist in their ontological purity only at the highest levels of the divine hierarchy. This solution, destined to find its more solid and rigorous foundation in the works of Plotinus,[34] thus had the advantage of solving the actual problem of evil by denying its ontological consistency.

Among Christians the problem of mediation assumed a position of decisive importance. It is true that the world was good and could not be otherwise, as God's creation. Evil was no longer a natural, but rather a moral, fact, a consequence of the abuse of free will. However, evil went to the very root of the history of the world and humans' own nature, to such an extent that only intervention from above might have been able to save humankind from its sinful condition. Hence, the decisive function of the Saviour, the Mediator *par excellence.*

Compared with the Hellenistic saviours,[35] the Christian Saviour was able to boast at least two radically new attributes. His act of salvation aimed at rescuing and preserving the higher spiritual principle of humankind, of all humanity. He therefore had to be a personal, historical Saviour, embodying the essence of mediation in his nature of God and man.

WAYS OF SALVATION

The road to liberation, however, was fraught with all manner of difficulties. In order to understand the nature of these difficulties better, a short digression is now necessary.

For those of olden times religion was like an item of clothing, received at birth and worn on certain ritual occasions, but able to be discarded in everyday life without any special traumas.[36] At the same time it was an atmosphere, a particular aura, which one learned to breathe early in life, an ambience in which one was taught to move and behave correctly by means of an approved series of social and religious initiation ceremonies.

The first centuries of Hellenism had not known genuine religious revolutions. Indeed, in the cities of the Diadochoi (the successors of Alexander the Great), there are signs of a certain attitude of scepticism, if not of indifference, towards the typical religious problems associated with death and ways of survival.[37] Epicureanism elevated this attitude to theoretical dignity and a code of behaviour. The traditional world of belief is characterized rather by the emergence of those typical Hellenistic divinities, such as Tyche, Fortune, Destiny, Fate, Necessity. Even the religion of the Stoics is a religion of the intellect or, at most, of strict will power, but not of the heart.

Religious life continued along traditional lines. Those surviving ecstatic movements and cults of possession that, like the cult of Dionysus, shook the routine of Greek religious life in the fifth century BC, had assumed the easily controllable forms of 'mysteries', socially acceptable and legally recognized religious clubs that required membership and functioned in accordance with the laws governing spiritual meetings.[38]

Even when oriental cults began to achieve wider recognition (from the second or first century BC) and to attract the interest and attention of a growing number of followers,[39] the mechanism of religious individualism did not undergo radical change. It was possible to belong to one of these cults without prejudice to one's daily life, family affections or social relationships.[40] In certain cases the new gods were openly petitioned in the hope of improving one's fortune or of accelerating one's *cursus honorum*, or career. For the rest, these gods were to some extent the same.[41] It was possible to move from one cult to another as easily (relatively) as it is for today's soccer fans to adopt a new idol.

But prophetic religions, such as Mazdaism or Judaism, had imposed different models of religious self-identification. The very nature of Ahura Mazda or of Jahweh did not tolerate rivals. The decision to belong to these faiths had therefore a different kind of importance in the life of the individual. It is also true that such decisions were bound up with the family, the clan, the group, indeed the *ethnos* (race), of which these prophetic religions were a fundamental manifestation. This trait, more prominent in Mazdaism, which represented to Iranians a means of ethnic and social identification, is also typical of Judaism. On the other hand, even if, especially in the Hellenistic period, there is evidence of proselytism in the Judaism of the Diaspora,[42] it is still only a marginal phenomenon. Nor was the life of a proselyte an easy one. He not only incurred the contemptuous criticism and abusive looks of the outside world for the Hebrew race, but had also to put up with the innate suspicion, if not the downright hostility, felt by pious Jews towards any member who was a stranger or lived on the fringes of the community.

And yet, right in the heart of Judaism, between the second and first centuries BC, there is evidence of a radical transformation in religious consciousness. What we now know of the life and beliefs of the community at Qumran proves that the model of religious identity had, in this restricted group, undergone a change fraught with consequences.

Though beset by difficulties, the way of a pagan who had wanted to convert to Judaism was still characterized by clear symbols: circumcision, profession of faith, and a certain life-style. But even these signs of recognition were considered for an interim period too transient and superficial for the person who expressed the wish to live the revelation of Jahweh right to the full. So-called 'inter-testamental' Judaism is now regarded by historians as a period of profound religious transformation, the consequence of the dramatic events that marked the life of the Chosen People from the second century BC; a world in movement, in which traditional divisions between factions, groups, sects or parties were being revised. The very plurality of religious opinion, on the other hand, helped to reconstruct on a new basis the problem of the authentic nucleus of the faith. In this multiplicity of messages, who was the real interpreter of the divine message? To what signs could one appeal as evidence for the authenticity of inspiration? But this problem, though long-lasting, received a new solution at Qumran. What the community offered was the seal of election, the guarantee of predestination. To acquire this mark of salvation, to enter the community of the 'Children of Light', one now required a conversion, a radical change, interior rather than external, in one's own life.[43]

The idea of election, in itself free from any notion of compromise, must sooner or later, as we know from its long and troubled history (from Paul to Augustine, from Luther to Calvin), come to sensible compromises with actual reality. In an age replete with revelations of all kinds, what were the signs that permitted the elect to be absolutely sure of their vocation? Later on we shall see the Gnostics' reply. At Qumran, the first sign was the very fact of the decision to enter into the life of the community with its rules and observances. This common life was thus the first fundamental guarantee against external enemies, the Sons of Darkness.[44] Moreover, divine revelation continued to make its voice heard through the privileged medium of scriptural exegesis, which by means of certain exegetic techniques (*pešer*) allowed one to reinterpret sacred history as the needs of the community required.[45] But above all it was necessary to scrutinize one's inner self: according to a model we find operating in the Master of Justice himself, God was able to enlighten the heart of his elect directly, granting them access to the most hidden mysteries.[46]

Charis, or divine grace, thus became a decisive factor in conversion, the chemical change in the spiritual substance of the individual. Only thanks to its help and intercession could the obstacles cutting off the road to rebirth be overcome.[47]

These obstacles were of various types. In addition to the usual difficulties encountered by the pious in their craving for the divine, there were others, symptomatic of the changing spiritual climate. In the thoughts and struggles of humanity in search of God, the demons had finally established themselves as the most dangerous enemies.[48] In the religion of the Homeric poems the *daimōnes* do not figure prominently.[49] The Pythagorean *daimōn* is more like the Socratic demon, a sort of protective genius of the individual, than the malevolent spirits of later generations.[50] Only with Hellenism does the *daimōn* begin to assume exclusively those negative associations destined to characterize it in the history of western religion.[51] There are two possible reasons for this: the influence of religious trends such as Mazdaism, in which armies of malevolent demons are deployed in the world in the service of the Lord of Evil, or the internal transformations of a demonological heritage like that of Judaism.

Neither pagan nor Christian demons are immune from this contagion. Among pagan demons there appears a veritable bureaucracy of the invisible.[52] At the lower levels are the malevolent demons, associated with the most violent, brutal aspects of human nature. As the steps of the pyramid rise, one begins to breathe a purer air. The higher demons correspond to the traditional gods, who follow the course of human events from their celestial homes both actively and passively. It is to these demons, to their power, that the theurgist turns, he who, in his capacity as the benevolent instrument of that positive divine power that descends from the higher demons, wishes to do good; he is the forerunner of the Renaissance magician who would like to put his natural magic at the service of mankind.[53] On the other hand, the *goëtes* (wizards) are the precursors of diabolical magic. Malevolent, terrestrial demons, who find themselves in contact with irrational matter, are the ultimate source of their power. They turn to them and to their terrible *dynamis* (power), confident of obtaining the necessary malign force to work evil deeds and to practise sorcery.

For their part, the Jewish, and later the Christian, traditions had also made provision for the imposition of order in this agitated world, characterized in the interim centuries of the Christian era by an impressive rate of demographic development. Against the ranks of malevolent demons are now ranged the equally numerous crowds and battalions of angels.[54] The world becomes a battleground of invisible, but none the less terrifying, armies. Not only individuals, but groups, people and nations now have their guardian angels.[55] Interpretative angels appear as celestial messengers in apocalyptic texts to explain divine revelations about the end of time;[56] they intervene in human history;[57] they accompany the destiny of individuals.[58] They are a counterforce grown up in the shadow of the increasing power of the demons; the career of certain archangels reveal that they are destined for speedy, positive promotion in the inner workings of the celestial bureaucracy.[59]

Christian beliefs also played their part in this work of progressive demonization in the world. The apologists of the second century, even on the basis of certain statements in the New Testament, testify to us often of the expansion in the power of malign spirits, which extend and multiply their functions to the point where they seize control not only of the physical world, but also of the very heart of humankind.[60]

Indeed, this gradual interiorization of the spiritual struggle is perhaps the most significant characteristic of the transformation of ideas and beliefs that we have been outlining. The really decisive battle begins to take place in the wanderings of the individual psyche. Cosmic conflict between the Archons, lords of this world, and the angelic Christian forces or the divine Gnostic entities are in fact only an echo or a reflection, however vivid and dramatic, of a much more terrifying internal conflict. Having now become the passive scene of a conflict in which they stand helplessly by, human beings appear incapable of overcoming the new limitations imposed on religious knowledge. In order to save themselves they now require divine intervention from on high: a revelation.

ECSTASY AND REVELATION

The gods were accustomed to communicating with men, to transmitting their plans and informing them of their intentions. All ancient religions were familiar, in one form or another, with that special communication between the divine and human worlds that we call revelation (not always an appropriate term).[61] The technique of these communications, however rudimentary, was not without effect. In the various forms of divination, dreams, oracles and visions, there was a speedy, multiform line of communication (by now well tested), which maintained a continuous link between the two worlds.

However, access to this line of communication was not vouchsafed to the ordinary mortal. Rather, one was obliged to rely upon the aid of appropriate technicians: from intermediaries of the official cults and priests to prophets, astrologers, magicians and interpreters of dreams. Even if the god did condescend to speak to the ordinary person in dreams, it was in such an allusive and cryptic way that the person required the services of a professional interpreter of dreams.[62] Those who, tired of seeing their attempts at a career impeded, or anxious for promotion, went in search of a powerful god able to provide a kind of recommendation in keeping with the times (a particular recipe or formula), had only to knock at the door of those who were practised in sacred matters, who often lived in the shadow of famous old temples, in order to enjoy the privilege of direct communication with the god.[63]

This search for a vision that would produce direct contact with the highest point of the hierarchical scale, for an experience that would guarantee a one-to-one (*monos pros monon*) meeting with the divine, even in matters of commercial transactions or problems in one's career, is at the same time valuable evidence of a significant change; communication with the divine was now being sought, a profound experience to be accomplished in the first person, without assistance from intermediaries or interpreters. It is on this theme that Hellenistic mysticism will construct its virtuoso variations.[64]

In a famous dialogue Plato had theorized the two fundamental types of mania or possession.[65] In its literal sense 'ecstasy' means 'being put outside oneself'. This could happen in two ways: either by alienating the actual spiritual principle from the prison of the body to allow it to unite with the god; or else by allowing the god himself, as in the oracular tradition, to penetrate the body of the seer, momentarily to subdue him and to speak through him. In both cases, however, the distance and the distinctions between human and divine were preserved.

Between the first and second centuries AD in contrast, we witness a new type of possession. Many of the itinerant prophets and divine men wandering about the Empire[66] claim to incarnate those two aspects of ecstasy that Philo had previously kept rigidly separate. They were not simply an instrument of the divinity, because in some sense they were the divinity. Divine power no longer limited itself to penetrating their body, using it as an instrument, for the simple reason that the body had become a permanent residence of the god. The first requirement of these new professional candidates thus became the capacity, not so much of having divine power to hand, but more of being the incarnation of divine power. The proof of this transformation consisted in the acquisition of special thaumaturgical qualities. Miracles were thus important, not only for their therapeutic effects (and these were certainly considerable), but rather because they confirmed that one was dealing with a divine reality.

At the same time these individuals proposed a new form of mediation, a type of revelation previously unknown. The 'true' revelation had to be unique and definitive. Instead of the thousands of privileged communications, many of these people had an experience, unique and definitive, that radically changed their life. On the other hand, this revelation had to correspond with a change in the religious landscape.

God had withdrawn from the world, often having no interest in it. The world had thus become easily susceptible to hostile forces, which oppressed humankind to such an extent that humans were obliged to think, as the Gnostics taught, that they were diabolical creatures. The thirst for the divine could no longer be quenched, in these cases, by drinking at the traditional fountain of accidental revelations, connected with the innumerable events of everyday life. They needed something else for their salvation. The sheet-anchor was intended to save them once and for all from the catastrophes of the present life.

Thus form and content of the revelations change. Jewish apocalyptic had already indicated the way to be travelled. For the visionaries of these apocalypses, almost all of which were composed between the second century BC and the second century AD, it was now possible to contemplate the terrible scenes of the end of the world and to see the destiny that awaits the just and the wicked.[67] In their celestial journeys they have the opportunity of a careful study of the topography of punishment and reward.[68] Some visionaries, like Enoch, might even be granted the singular privilege of access, not only to the mysteries of the end, but even to those of the beginnings of human history.[69] This is not surprising, for the destiny that awaits the just is written in a celestial book in which the history of the world is established.[70]

In this way the revelations about the end occasionally reveal a need destined to appear in Gnostic apocalypses. The content of the revelation expands to the point where it encompasses beginning and end of cosmic and individual history. Both are in fact closely connected and interdependent. The reader of apocalyptic texts knows that 'mea res agitur' ('this is my concern'): if he or she can make the right decision, no less than eternal victory is at stake. Human destiny runs parallel to that of a world that is hurrying to its destruction: to seize the opportunity has now become an existential problem, in which it is a matter of spiritual life or death.[71]

But not all the many visions and revelations of the period are equivalent. Contrary to the visionary experiences of Aelius Aristides, who was accustomed to turn to Asclepius as one might nowadays turn to a psychoanalyst[72] (financial circumstances permitting), what unifies the visions of Lucius in the *Metamorphoses* of Apuleius, the Montanist prophetesses and the Gnostics Valentinus and Marcus is their formative character.[73] A barrier, invisible, but for that reason the more insurmountable, was now placed between life before and after, separated by this new spiritual ridge. Isis, appearing in a dream to Lucius while he is still in the form of an ass, promises to release him forthwith, with the warning, 'Remember, and bear in mind for ever, that the rest of your life must be dedicated to me up to your last breath.'[74] In exchange, he will have access to the ineffable mysteries that will provide a new basis for his existence. And this is precisely the point: to lay the foundation of a new religious and social identity.

The visionary experience thus becomes the ideal meeting-place for a variety of experiences that may appear at first sight remote, if not contradictory. Montanus, the second-century instigator of the Montanist heresy, like Lucius, arrogates to himself the protective hand of a sublime divinity, of a divinity that guarantees the possession of a sacred reality, ineffable and infinitely precious.[75] This communion with the divine is not a privilege of birth, wealth or education, but rather the heritage of 'those of goodwill'. The sense of a mysterious call or divine choice may find in this experience of the numinous an effective confirmation and its seal of approval. It sets in motion the mechanism of rebirth.[76] Enlightened by the spirit and touched by a particular vision, this divine humanity can now, according to some Hermetic treatises, drive out the negative forces so as to allow the new human to enter into them.

IN SEARCH OF A NEW IDENTITY

The new spiritual identity is based on, and helps to nurture, a new social identity. The protagonists of this decisive internal revolution, carried out silently in the depths of an intimacy cultivated, loved and known with vivid recognition, were in fact none other than 'the rootless and the weary who had been cut adrift and were searching for a new life',[77] children of a society that was expanding and continually changing, a world that was cosmopolitan and open to the most diverse experiences. It was a world that encouraged travel and trade, but undermined family ties, bonds of friendship and social relationships to the point of destruction.

Merchants and businessmen, constantly on the move, now disem-barked in crowded harbours and made for the great commercial centres, certain of being able to surmount linguistic differences and ethnic and cultural barriers in their search for deeper spiritual bonds, visiting temples and practising cults that went beyond the confines of the old ethnic religions.[78] The initiates of the various oriental cults, soldiers who felt at home in the military atmosphere surrounding the myths and ceremonies of Mithraism, or emigrants, former slaves and freedmen mindful of their eastern origin, who met and knew each other in the orgiastic celebrations of the followers of Cybele and Attis or in the rites of Dea Syria (described by Lucian): all moved in the same religious climate. What they now have is a new identity-card, which enables them to recognize each other and meet together, a passport that allows them to surmount ethnic barriers and social differences. The vertical axis of the divine progeny intersects with the horizontal axis of brotherhood with fellow believers, spiritual co-ordinates not without effect even at the social level.

The feminism of the time provides important confirmation of this. The satirical writers of the early centuries of the Empire frequently satirize women who want to discuss everything and to occupy themselves with poetry, dancing and music. It is a pertinent indication of the general change in the position of women, at least in the leisured classes, which had affected the life of increasing numbers of women in the Hellenistic cities.[79] They 'were everywhere involved in business, social life, such as theatres, sports events, concerts, parties, travelling – with or without their husbands. They took part in a whole range of athletics, even bore arms and went to battle.'[80] And, we might add, they lived a new intense religious life, free of parental ties or matrimonial duties.

The new techniques of salvation were presented as a privileged way of confirming and ratifying what society was in its turn bringing about. In the secret meetings of the oriental cults many women devoted themselves to Isis or Cybele.[81] Christian groups often had to come to terms with the problem of female inspiration and to try to bring into line the charisma of prophecy which, according to Paul, apparently ought to remain a male privilege.[82] It is no accident that in Montanism, the *terra sacra*, or sacred territory, of prophetic inspiration *par excellence*, the prophets preferred by Montanus were women.[83] The spirit blows where it will; and the chosen women of the spirit were the various Mary Magdalenes of the Gnostic cliques.

The extensive reshuffling of the social cards in the second century was bound to affect religion, which then, more than today, was the area in which the corresponding ideological attitudes were reshaped, measured and tested. This becomes clearer when one considers the fate of certain intellectuals.

Some of the heirs of Dio Chrysostom continued to use up their rhetorical skill and dialectical inheritance celebrating the Establishment, together with its educational system, of which they were the most solid support. Others, more restless, curious and mobile, looked out onto the changing reality that surrounded them. The curiosity of an Apuleius, typical representative of an intelligentsia on the move, is one example.[84]

He seems to be the one called upon to perform the function of cultural mediation whose religious equivalent we have already discussed. His birth and education placed him at the boundary between two worlds which he bridges, but also makes distinct. They are the world of the provincial African periphery where he was born, between Numidia and Gaetulia, and the world of the great urban centres, such as Athens, Alexandria and Rome, which provided him with his education; the world of Middle Platonist philosophy[85] and the mysteries and cults, of which he became an initiate,[86] the world of the calm light of practical theurgy and the sinister flashes of black magic, which here and there leave traces on his face.[87] This systematic ambivalence, this wavering between cultural universes and remote social situations, is not really surprising. Apuleius is a child of his time. Continual travel brought him into contact with different worlds; his thirst for experience enabled him to embrace the diverse social worlds; his curiosity pushed him to the limits of the impossible.

The *Metamorphoses* themselves reveal the need for mediation. The form of the Greek novel, which normally performed the function of diverting and entertaining a largely popular audience, is transformed in the able hands of the African writer into a form able to respond to the needs of a new public made up of the well-to-do populace with a modicum of learning, that constituted a fourth class in contemporary cities: respectable artisans, prosperous freedmen, citizens who lived in the shadow of the exclusive aristocracy and wished to emulate them even at a cultural level, businessmen eager to embellish their social climb with evidence of cultural know-how. Using a popular narrative form, Apuleius sets out to reach this kind of public in order to bring to it 'the interpretative categories (and the ideological potential) of the doctrinal system of the elite, because they act as a fixed point in the disorders of human history and the chaos of the perceptible world.'[88] Because this is the message of the Apuleian parable: what he presents, against the background of contemporary social and cultural change, is a redefinition and a restructuring of the external boundaries and the internal structure of the concept of the individual. Old cultural models, concepts such as cosmos and virtue, seem to be experiencing a crisis from which there is no turning back. As Lucius' symbolic experiences, which to some extent illustrate those of Apuleius, reveal, a possible solution lies in the response that searches for a new identity, which is obtained by rapport with a new divinity (from a changed perspective) able to provide new certainties.

Even with his obvious individuality and originality, Apuleius seems to be a typical representative of an important social group, the 'new men' (*viri novi*): orators, lecturers, teachers who constitute a sort of turbulent, lively intellectual proletariat. He is characterized by a *cupiditas viarum*, an insatiable desire for travel through different cultures in different countries, intellectual journeys that develop amid philosophical experiences and religious initiations. In the same way, the philosopher Justin, later a Christian apologist and martyr, experimented with various fashionable philosophies before settling on the Christian revelation.[89] A thirst for experiences also characterizes the Gnostic teacher Valentinus, who was educated in the cosmopolitan worlds of Alexandria and Rome, open to the influence of mythology and, at the same time, like Apuleius, ready to use this popular medium to transmit his more subtle tenets of doctrine.

These new intellectuals, men of the frontier, astute and active representatives of a century in transition, while reflecting the ambiguities and contradictions of their age, also indicate some possible solutions. It is now time to consider one of these solutions: Gnosticism. Its radical originality will be understood better if it is considered against the background, both social and ideological, that we have outlined, a background common to pagan and Christian thinkers and an integral element in any such consideration. Gnosticism, like the intellectuals who produced it, is a child of its time: its background is a religious world in ferment, a cultural universe in which syncretism had become an ideological garment, in which oriental blood had now been flowing for centuries in the somewhat anaemic body of the West.

The novelty of the Gnostic message is to be sought neither in the origins of the mythological material that it borrowed and used from various sources, nor in any so-called vital force of eastern origin, but in the solution that it attempted to bring to the problems of its own time. It is now time for us, like Theseus, to put our trust in Ariadne's thread and prepare to enter the mythical maze of the Gnostic labyrinth.

3

The Gnostic Imagination

THE NATURE OF GNOSTIC KNOWLEDGE

Anyone who embarks on a description of the Gnostic *fabula* or story, inevitably does so with a growing sense of unease. And this is understandable. To one familiar with the plastic figures of classical mythology or to an inquisitive reader of the mythical stories of preliterate peoples, the mythological Gnostic structure is surrounded by quite a different atmosphere with its galleries of divine ancestors with pallid, metaphysical faces; its rooms thronged with lifeless, monotonous shapes of aeons, entities and hypostases; its Underworld peopled with monstrous archons and demons.

But, like every labyrinth, the Gnostic one too has a centre from which flow the vast streams of mythical narrations, thence to mingle and intertwine. This heart of the mythological body is a reality less remote and strange than may appear at first sight. What the myths all record is: the fate of the divine spark present in humanity and its fall into a hostile world of shadows, where it forgets its true home, while unconsciously longing to return there; its wanderings and hopes, and the eventual arrival of a Saviour who will reveal its true origin and thus enable it to regain consciousness of its essential alienation from this world of shadows. In other words, do they not perhaps conceal the secret of acquiring knowledge of the self, the principle of individuation that has fallen into the fatal embrace of Lethe?

But all foreknowledge, however necessary, inevitably entails some risks. To avoid, from the outset, the impression of wanting to see the Gnostics as simple precursors of modern depth psychology, it will be necessary to consider further several points in order to remove any ambiguity and to restore the historical difference between the two. In this sense, the use of the very term 'Gnosis' offers us a privileged way.[1]

In classical Greek the terms *gnōsis* and *gignōskō* indicate true knowledge of 'what is' (*ta onta*) in contrast to mere sense perception (*aisthēsis*) or opinion whose truth is not guaranteed (*doxa*). Unlike *epistēmē* (understanding), the term is hardly ever used in an absolute sense, but requires an object in the genitive case: it emphasizes the act of knowing rather than knowledge itself.

But what sort of cognitive process is meant? In keeping with the Greek predilection for the organ of vision,[2] *gnōsis* is presented as knowledge obtained by discourse and dialectic, beginning with visual, direct observation. Of course, in the case of invisible realities, knowledge will come through the eyes of the mind, which are able to grasp the realities of the ideal world (as, e.g., Plato's reflections on mathematics suggest[3]). To achieve this knowledge one does not require a particular organ or special method, but simply the coherent, systematic application of the natural ability to see, to verify and to check the data received along the way.

In Gnostic vocabulary the term has undergone a profound transformation. *Gnōsis* is now also used in an absolute way to indicate a form of meta-rational knowledge, which is the gift of the divinity and has in it the power to save the one who achieves it. It enables one to take possession of the keys to the cosmic mystery, to solve the enigma of the universe by absorbing the *axis mundi*, or world axis, of archaic cosmogonies into the very essence of one's being. The sacred strength of *gnōsis* reveals 'who we are, what we have become, where we have been cast out of, where we are bound for, what we have been purified of, what generation and regeneration are.'[4]

If it is true that the doctrinal content of Gnosticism is also cosmological and aims at revealing 'what is upon earth, in heaven, and anything that is perhaps above heaven',[5] it is also true that the acquisition of this teaching is not an end in itself, but a function of the knowledge of the mystery of human beings and therefore of their salvation. Gnosis is the 'redemption of the interior man',[6] that is, the purification of the spiritual being and at the same time knowledge of the Whole. The *Gospel of Truth* puts it as follows:

> Therefore if one has knowledge, he is from above. If he is called, he hears, he answers, and he turns to him who is calling and ascends to him. And he knows in what manner he is called ... He who is to have knowledge in this manner knows where he comes from and where he is going. He knows as one who having become drunk has turned away from his drunkenness, and having returned to himself has set right what are his own.[7]

In Gnostic texts the term has become synonymous with *epignōsis*, recognition of one's own true reality: that is, the ontological self that constitutes and is its basis. It would seem to be no more than a revival of the Delphic 'Know thyself' and Plato's interpretation of it, put into the mouth of Socrates.[8] But on the contrary, the change could not be more radical. The 'self' of which the Gnostics speak does not refer to the ethical, practical sphere within the individual consciousness, but is a concrete reality, which rather runs counter to this consciousness.

The Gnostic self,[9] the ontological ego, the reality that makes one divine, must neither be regarded as an impersonal force that, as in ancient Dionysiac ecstasy and Apolline prophecy, penetrates the individual and expels the individual ego, suspending the individuality and the consciousness of the possessed during a period of ecstasy, nor must it be interpreted, in terms of modern depth psychology or the blandishments of currently dominant subjectivism, as a reality for the Gnostic within one's own consciousness and therefore attainable by a simple act of inner reflection, a withdrawal into oneself. The 'return to the self', the leitmotif of Gnostic knowledge, is not only a bare movement of the mind, by means of which the empirical ego, the 'me' of everyday consciousness, the subject immersed in the world of becoming, is able to intuit and thence to grasp his or her ontological base, but also (and principally) an objective process, which develops outside the 'me', which fulfils itself upon meeting the self, the divine and celestial counterpart of the Gnostic (variously named in the Gnostic texts[10]), which is the intermediary of revelation and at the same time its ultimate object and purpose. The character of subjectivity takes nothing away from the metaphysical claim to absolute objectivity, which the Gnostic tends to attribute to this fundamental experience. The visionary moments of ecstasy in which it takes place are always meetings with reality 'other than me', the empirical 'me', the transient 'me', with which the Gnostic is led to identify his consciousness.

It follows that this divine reality cannot be known through the ordinary faculties of the mind. Illumination, revelation, the intervention of a celestial mediator is required. He descends from above to call the Gnostic, to rouse him from earthly sleep and drunkenness, to take him back to his divine homeland. It is the particular nature of the Revealer that gives Gnostic knowledge one of its most characteristic traits. The channel for the communication of Gnosis, the person of the Revealer is consubstantial with the element present in the Gnostic destined to receive it. In other words, one could say from the Gnostic point of view that revelation is possible only because within the Gnostic there somehow pre-exists a disposition, a capacity, a potential fitted for testing and getting to know that particular reality. Only like can in fact know like. Only spiritual beings can perceive, receive and understand the spiritual.

This affirmation, of Platonic origin,[11] the basis of ancient and modern hermeneutics alike,[12] is grafted by Gnostic reinterpretation onto a typically mythical landscape. Indeed, it presupposes the pre-existence of the ontological basis, the separation and the fall of a part of the self into the world of darkness, with the resulting 'finitization' of this infinite principle in a finite individual, in whom it now constitutes the precious, but forgotten, reality.

This process of recognition, which sometimes appears to be confused with the ancient art of memory (Platonic *anamnēsis*), is quite different from it in both its subject–object relation and its purpose. If 'to know' in Gnosis means 'to recognize' one's true nature and divine origin, this is possibly only because one is reborn to the true life. Rather than a cognitive procedure of the intellect alone, Gnostic knowledge is experience, a lived experience of spiritual regeneration. It is a transforming knowledge, whose immediate effect is salvation. To know, in fact, is to know one's own origin, who one truly was at the beginning. And to know one's own *archē* (beginning) is also to know one's own *telos*, or end; the destiny that awaits will be reunion with the celestial counterpart of one's ego, the definitive return to the divine world, one's real homeland.

This analysis of terms has allowed us to glimpse a profound change of attitude, which, with regard to the relationship between knowing subject and known object, conflicts radically with the picture of classical gnoseology. 'To know' now means 'to become that same reality that is known', to be transformed through enlightenment into the actual object of knowledge, overcoming and removing the dichotomy between subject and object.

If we measure this particular gnoseology against classical rationalism, we cannot help but feel that the gap that separates them cannot be filled. But this is not quite right. Not only because the Gnostic way of knowing has some of its roots in particular currents of the same Greek thought, but especially because it is a species of the type of knowledge (certainly more complete and perhaps more radical) found in the thinkers of the first centuries of the Empire.

The 'divine' Plato had already assigned a particular place to intuition as the suprarational organ of knowledge. Beyond the *logos*, or reason, there was *nous*, or intellect, the faculty capable of perceiving the divine, the instrument *par excellence* of contemplation.[13] His attempt to introduce traditional methods of achieving mystic knowledge (from prophetic madness and ecstatic possession up to their secularized version, poetic ecstasy) into a more complex vision of the cognitive capacity of human beings did not drive him so far as to confuse intuition with rational knowledge or to value it more highly. Unlike intuition, rational knowledge was able to test its basis.[14] In this fashion, however, the way was open for a full appreciation of *nous* as an intuitive capacity, to the detriment of the inductive and discursive faculty *par excellence*, the *logos*. Aristotle, on the other hand, invites us to abandon the old norm of life that confined the human being within the barriers erected by the divinity.[15] In fact, the human is 'quasi mortalis deus' (almost a mortal god),[16] by virtue of possessing a divine reality, the intellect, capable of approaching God and enabling him or her to know God. And Zeno, the founder of the Stoic school, within a rigidly pantheistic framework, pushes this concept to its extreme: the human intellect not only has an affinity with God, but is part of the same divine substance in the pure, active state.[17]

Substantially homogeneous in spite of their diversity, these various solutions, put forward to solve the problem of knowledge of the divine, lost consistency and validity when the divinity, in the classical sense, was replaced by a God transcendent and unknowable, at least by the normal methods of reason. With this change in one of the two terms of the rapport (the actual object of knowledge), the quest for new forms and cognitive techniques came to prominence, especially if this new problematic within the tradition of Greek thought was grafted onto a theological concept, such as the Jewish one, which thinks of the divinity in terms of an entity not only transcendant, but also personal. In this sense Philo's speculations on the intellect assume particular importance.

The dualism between the immutable and incorruptible spiritual world and the mutable and corruptible terrestrial world actually induces Philo to postulate the existence of two intellects. The first, created together with terrestrial beings and bound up with the body and the process of becoming, is the part of the soul that performs the functions of perception, memory and reaction to impulses.[18] Even where, linking up with Stoic theory, he makes the intellect a hot, fiery breath,[19] a particle detached from the divine being,[20] one has the impression that it is at most a faculty that, inasmuch as it draws its origin from the World Soul,[21] can intuit the latter by natural affinity. However, in some passages Philo appears to go beyond these boundaries.[22] If it is true that we can contemplate light by means of light, that we can perceive God by means of God,[23] he sometimes affirms that human intellect, as an *apospasma theion* or a divine fragment, is of the same pneumatic substance as the Higher God.[24] It is this substantial identity between divine *pneuma*–intellect and human *pneuma*–intellect that is fundamental to affinity with God and makes suprarational intuition possible. In this way, in intuition 'the spirit is "transformed" into the object to be understood, "sends out its rays" and in this manner eliminates the tension between the cognitive subject and the object of cognition.'[25]

From this privileged observation point the Gnostic solution to the problem of knowledge of the divine no longer appears so remote. Beyond the decisive differences, what links Philo's theory of spiritual knowledge to the Gnostic one is the pressure towards overcoming the subject–object dichotomy by means of a particular doctrine of the *pneuma* that establishes and makes possible the identity between subject, object and the means of knowledge. (Philo's theory is also based on a certain dualism and applies to a divine world, which revolves around the personal God of the Bible.)

Philo's gnoseology belongs to the intellectualist tradition typical of Greek thought. And this is quite different from the roots of another theory of knowledge, which for our purposes is equally important: that revealed in the Qumran texts.

The centuries that straddle the early Christian period in the Jewish world are characterized by a very deep need for knowledge, as is evident from canonical and apocryphal texts. 'The Book of Wisdom (7:18–20) provides us with a picture of the subjects the wise man must know: zoology, astronomy, the study of the angels, psychology, botany and pharmacology. The Book of Enoch (2–5 and 72–82) speaks of botany and astronomy: the ultimate goal of knowledge has become knowledge of "everything": that is, not only the knowledge of things, but also of their meaning and history.'[26] The Qumran manuscripts help us to understand the mechanisms and purpose of this knowledge. Above all, the change of object, which is no longer confined to the Law, or content with prophetic warnings or promises, but lays claim to the totality, raises the question of the primacy of the Mosaic revelation, which is replaced by the possibility of personal illumination. With the aid of these, there is the possibility of access to the mysteries of the history of salvation, established from the beginning in the project of the divine mind. This particular form of knowledge is the privilege of a pre-destined few who belong to a select group of 'the friends of God'. In this way knowledge tends to be contrasted with faith, where the spirit, the organ of knowledge, is seen not only as a divine gift, but rather as a human quality that permits intuition of the Whole.[27] As the *Rule of the Community* says, 'From the source of his righteousness comes the light of judgement in my heart; from his marvellous mysteries in the eternal present my eye gazes upon a wisdom hidden from men.'[28] This knowledge of the divine mysteries is possible because God himself 'has made the light that illumines me spring up from the fount of his knowledge so that my eye has been able to behold his marvellous deeds, and the light of my heart the mystery to come.'[29]

Though not explicit in theoretical terms, it seems possible to grasp an interpretative principle that Philo holds dear: only the light can know the light; only because it is illuminated by the divine light can the eye of the intellect now grasp, instantaneously and wholly, the object in its totality.

But at Qumran intuitive knowledge remains subordinate to moral action; and in Philo the gap between creature and God is never abolished. Some Middle Platonist philosophers of the second century appear to have overcome this gap.[30] For Numenius, as for the author of the *Chaldaean Oracles*, God is knowable only by recourse to a special method.[31] He hides in marvellous solitude, ready to appear occasionally like the little boat lost at sea.[32] How can one attain to him, except by way of intuition? The method of achieving this aim seems to re-echo certain Buddhist teachings. One must empty the mind of all positive content and make the intellect void;[33] only thus can one be absorbed into God to the point where one can identify with the same Divinity and 'deal with the Good on a one-to-one basis'.[34]

Numenius' thinking is (even chronologically) so close to that of the Gnostics that one might be tempted to equate them.[35] But this would be wrong. The novelty of Gnostic knowledge consists in its need to fuse together not only subject and object, but also the means of knowledge with them both. This is because the cognitive process is grafted onto a special experience. The intuition of one's true nature and of the essence of the divine world is not pure, disinterested contemplation, but immersion in the vital, throbbing reality of origins, the ability to tune into the divine energy, to allow oneself to be penetrated by it to the point where one is possessed and transformed by it. This reaching out for spiritual rebirth, so widespread and typical of the period, thus receives its specific characteristics in Gnosticism by means of the umbilical cord that binds it to the desire for total knowledge, giving rise to a specific gnoseological constellation: enlightment.[36]

The presupposition of the Gnostic theory of enlightenment is a metaphysics of the light that arises and is established throughout the Christian era.[37] Instead of simply being a means of knowledge, a 'how' of existence, as is typical of the classical tradition, the light becomes its privileged object. It is transformed in fact into a force, a power that is life, incorruptible, divine life.[38] Between the divine world, luminous and resplendent, and this world, dark and shadowy, an ever deeper division is being opened up. A desire is born, an acute longing to open itself to that light world of the divine life, to return once again to rest in the calm, tranquil bosom of primordial light. In its more radical formulations, this nostalgia for its origins means only the drive to become and to be light, to participate in that particular life to the point of identifying with the divine light that constitutes the substance of the world of the pleroma – that is, of the fullness of divine reality.

To form an idea of this process, let us consider the opening treatise in the *Corpus Hermeticum*, the *Poimandres*. To begin with, Hermes has a vision: Poimandres, the shepherd of men, the archetypal Nous, appears to him. Having addressed him, this Intellect suddenly changes its appearance; and at this point, Hermes says, 'everything suddenly opened up before me. And lo, I saw an indescribable vision. Everything became a calm, joyous light. And when I saw it, I fell in love with it.'[39]

Hermes' cognitive process takes root and ultimately becomes a lived experience, grounded in the vast depths of the subject. Hermes is involved in a cognitive act whose protagonists are bound together by secret affinity. Hermes, or rather his *nous*, the most sublime and divine part of his being, is the individual counterpart of the Nous of Poimandres, the general, universal intellect.[40] In this way a hermeneutic circle is established, based on the identity of subject, object and means of knowledge. Hermes is able to know his own true nature because he has the means, his own *nous*, a particular moment of the general Nous, which guarantees him substantial identity with the object at which his thirst for knowledge is directed: the world of the divine intellectual powers. The light that he contemplates, then, is no longer simply a means of cognition, but the same substance as the divine world, primordial, archetypal light. He can now know it and its content. Indeed, in his intellect Hermes sees 'the light becoming an incalculable number of powers and a world without boundaries'.[41] What he now contemplates is the very nature of God in its dynamic dimension. But since his intellect is in fact part of the divine Nous, which he intuits, what can all this mean except that he is now seeing his own nature?

Two other Hermetic treatises, ideally related to the *Poimandres*, reveal what the vital, emotional stages of this process of spiritual regeneration are: treatise XIII on regeneration and the Coptic text *De Ogdoade et Enneade*. They describe in a wealth of detail (which cannot be included here)[42] the movement of Gnostic knowledge in its profound dimension of vital experience. The background is typical of this kind of process: the setting is on a mountain[43] and includes the theme of the expulsion of the 'old man', represented as an agglomeration of *dynameis*, or negative forces, and their replacement by a new spiritual reality.[44] Hermes insists in his warnings to his disciple Tat on the fact that one reaches Gnosis by reflection. But this is only a preparatory phase, however indispensable; discussion with one's teacher, meditation and reflection train the will and exercise the intellect.[45] But these alone cannot achieve the goal. Therefore the external intervention of a luminous power is required to initiate a profound emotional experience. It is in this phase, crystallized by the mystical silence,[46] that regeneration takes place. Tat now feels a new quickening lifeblood circulating within him.[47] 'Incipit vita nova' (new life begins), a life modelled and condensed into the image of an essential man, endowed with that consubstantiality with the divine world that has generated him. Grafted onto this new life, knowledge can now take shape Gnostically as the recognition of one's true essence and hence of the very essence of the divine.[48]

To the reader of these texts, the fact that it is not simply a matter of a psychological process is confirmed by a decisive element: the mythological framework in which the events are placed, as the *Poimandres* indicates. This raises a new problem: the relationship between knowledge and myth in the structure of Gnostic thought.

MYTH, THOUGHT AND SOCIETY

The privileged object of Gnostic mythology is constituted, as was said above, by the events of the self, of the most profound ontological reality of the Gnostic. It is a theme that may, in its simple, elementary details, be repeated *ad nauseam*. But at the same time it was the starting-point for the various Gnostic schools to construct imposing intricate variations that eventually obscure the elemental nature of the initial accounts. Indeed, they are typical variations of mythical narrative, which is always open to the invention of ever new motifs, contrasts, ramblings, linking events and confusing characters. But one may ask: why on earth did Gnostics ever have recourse to myth in the construction of their systems? And it is worth while asking first: what does 'myth' mean in this context?

It is no idle question. It actually touches upon one of the fundamental aspects of the Gnostic system. Gnostic mythology appears, at first sight, to be a singular phenomenon in the religious panorama of the second century. According to the accusations of Christian apologists, the pagan world was able to go on living on myths, but from time immemorial these had been repeated to no avail. The struggle between *mythos* and *logos* appeared to have been settled in the enlightened Athens of the fifth century.[49] Had not Plato himself expelled myths from his Republic?[50] And had not Aristotle, in his *Poetics*, perhaps completed an even more radical, corrosive process of internal clearance, interpreting *mythos* as a purely narrative framework?[51] Seen in this light, the successive revivals of mythology can only appear as survivals of a past long dead, but yet as external excrescences, microbes and infectious germs (here, as in other parallel cases, of oriental origin), ready to attack the essentially healthy body of Greek rationalism. In fact, this view is too partial and one-sided not to provoke radical criticism. Various scholars today incline to a contrary viewpoint. The structure of mythology did not disappear in Greece with enlightened criticism of religious traditions. On the contrary, it pervades the whole of the ancient world, for the simple reason that it concerns an explanatory mode fit for the human mind and other than that of logic and discourse.[52] This argument, if accepted, is just as dangerous as the preceding one (perhaps more so[53]), but it does have the undoubted merit, especially in its early and most balanced formulations, of stating the problem of ancient mythology in new terms.

If we try for a moment to look at the religious world of the Mediterranean with the eyes of a contemporary, it appears to us, in the phrase of Plutarch 'a goblet seething with myths'.[54] The oriental cults, whether applied to Isis and Osiris, Mithras or Dea Syria, were a source of fascination, in the exotic character of their mythical tales, in the interest provoked by bloody and dramatic events (e.g. those involving Attis and Cybele). The encounter with traditional classical mythology was a foregone conclusion: the lifeless world of Homeric gods and the Roman pantheon was confronted by a living universe, quickened by powers and divinities whose activities acquired exemplary value in the eyes of the believer. On the other hand, even in a rigidly monotheistic world such as that of Judaism, mythological representation was able to make itself known by means of appropriate, seductive changes: apocalyptic scenery is filled with material and concepts that reflect a traditional mythological heritage.[55]

Events within the history of classical culture itself had contributed to the persistence of mythological successes in the early Empire. The struggle between *mythos* and *logos* had an important background: urban life, literate society, systems of communication and control dealt a mortal blow to the *mythos* of oral tradition.[56] In this sense the process is irreversible: in the veins of the *polis* (city) there runs, however weak it may be, a blood characterized by the march of progress.[57] In contrast to those forms of reiteration and assurance of existence that distinguished the mythological beliefs and ritual practices of ancient societies, a world of continuous change is now being introduced, which must find new parameters to measure its own growth. The urban origin of the *logos* shifts the terms of encounter to a different territory from which there is no escape, even though the power shift will not be painless and the new will continue to merge with the old in unforeseeable and surprising ways, albeit obliquely and elusively.

To cite just a few examples, one need think only of the ideological function of legitimation that myth, stripped of its most refined, manifestly sacred values, began to perform once again between the fifth and fourth centuries BC in thinkers nostalgic for the past, like Plato, Isocrates and Demosthenes; it indicated the birthplace of the foundation and perpetuation of a political ideal in crisis and overwhelmed by events themselves.[58] It seems almost that, through a sort of trick of reason, the very *logos* of history will reawaken, by means of an unrealizable, utopian nostalgia, the ghosts of an irrecoverable past, to the point where 'the reality of myth remains and works within the very core of those narratives that are presented as explicitly historical.'[59] It is a process, paradoxical only at first sight, of emptying, by means of the *logos*, a mythical shell whose substance is at the same time continually taken up, reread and reconstructed, as one sees in the fifth-century tragedians, who project upon them the preoccupations and problems of contemporary society.[60] This process of metamorphosis experienced a revival under the Diadochoi, a period in which mythology was enlisted for the purposes of apotheosis and the legitimation of dynastic power.[61] On the other hand, even the Roman world, though providing few myths, had its *hieroi logoi* (scriptures) and sacred events. What else, from this particular point of view, are Titus Livius' genealogical reconstructions if not an attempt (more or less conscious) to provide a mythical and religious foundation charter for a state that is beginning to extend its imperial rule throughout the world?[62]

This secret capacity of *mythos*, which, taking root in urban soil, shows its capacity to resist by existing parasitically at the expense of the *logos* itself, is also true of the ancient allegory.[63] Originally a means of defending the traditional religious heritage from attacks launched by rationalists, allegory continued to enjoy an equivocal status. It fragmented the narrative backcloth of ancient *fabulae*, or stories, to rediscover, in the guise of narrative, contents and problems that were the concern of the interpreter. These might be historical, as in the case of the Euhemerists (rationalizing interpreters of myth); physical, the struggles between the gods being no more than the contrast between elements of nature; or finally moral and symbolic, as in the entire Neoplatonic tradition of allegory.[64] At the same time, however, the allegorist often unconsciously reversed, in the empty cases that had contained the old mythological figures, a complete network of symbolic relationships endowed with new mythical values.

In this connection Philo is an important example, all the more if we remember that he was a pious intellectual Jew, an enemy of all idolatry and an ardent defender of the monotheistic faith of his fathers, growing up in the Diaspora, open to every cultural change, in an intellectually active ambience like that of Egyptian Alexandria. Inevitably he fought strenuously against pagan mythological beliefs. Yet 'there is consistent evidence in his works of the fact that he was influenced by pagan myth at a deeper level than that of literary allusion.'[65]

Philo's polemic against pagan mythology, under Platonic influence, turns principally on its patent immorality: the second commandment forbids not only the construction of idols, images and statues, but also the acceptance of mythical invention about the births and marriages of gods, their innumerable scandals and the inexhaustible lasciviousness associated with them.[66] Criticism is consequently directed against some aspects of the content, not the mythological process as such. And this, in fact, becomes quite clear when, as we have seen, Philo's discussion of the complicated relationship between God and the world starts to flag. Philo's hypostases, such as the Logos or Sophia, do not seem to be mere abstractions or, even less, interpretative hypotheses; nor can they be reduced to the type of medieval allegory, but they take shape more as particular mythological characters now called upon to perform a new drama: the action of God towards the world.

It is no accident that Philo betrays his Platonic influences in this particular mythopœic process, in which the reflective *logos* of the thinker has to guide the movement of invention and organization of the relationships between these particular entities. Of the various factors that have helped to keep alive a mythological potential in the tradition of classical and hellenistic thought, the example of Platonic mythopœic fabrication is among the most significant.

However one evaluates the position of myth in Platonic thought,[67] it is certain that, through the ancient tradition associated with it, the mythopœic momentum continued to provide an example of decisive importance. The mythical stories were a possible means of entry into being. Apart from their pedagogic, instrumental function, some narratives, from that of the chariot to the eschatological myth of Er and the theme of Eros and the androgyne, acquire the function of propaedeutic metaphysics. To these in some way the *logos* seems bound to concede a certain value of 'reality'. Against the background of individual imagination the stories make up the scenario intended to stimulate *anamnēsis*, or recollection, the bridge to the world of ideas. Myth, far from being simply an ornament or an instrument, acquires in Plato's thought a privileged gnoseological status, to the point where 'mythical thought is extended in the same measure as it is transformed.'[68]

The Platonic conception of myth was bound to find disciples. Plutarch is an authoritative witness to this.[69] Reviewing the mystic and symbolic tradition of exegesis of the mythological heritage that had established itself in his beloved Pythagorean circles, and at the same time foreshadowing later positions of the Neoplatonic school, he approaches the repertoire of ancient images to inject new life blood into them. One idea dominates the mythopœic thought of this pious believer and zealous Platonist: the myths are no more than a projection of the 'epic of the soul on its journey to salvation'.[70] But he does not confine himself to rereading and interpreting the old mythologies; following the master's model, he himself will compose three typical eschatological stories on the destiny of the soul after death.[71]

That Plutarch makes use of mythical creation is due not merely to the categorical imperative of following in Plato's footsteps. There are other reasons, mostly connected with contemporary problems. He was quite conscious that in his self-imposed task of conserving and purifying the heritage of religious traditions, the mythical story could become a privileged instrument of secret persuasion to reach the greater mass of *apaideutoi*, the illiterate, the social strata that adhered to the persisting mythical and religious traditions, but were also eager for new myths.[72]

In addition there was a particular rereading of the Platonic heritage, consistent with a philosophical tradition of many centuries. Had not perhaps Plato himself taught that myth intervenes and occurs at the junction between being and becoming?[73] While it takes on a gnoseological function, this is also a basis for truth. On this point Plutarch is a faithful witness of an age in which philosophy is open to mysticism and questions the primacy of the *logos*.[74] In short, 'for a true, proper inversion of the mental process, reason establishes itself to some extent in myth.'[75] Even where he confines himself to using and reinterpreting pre-existent mythological material, his exegesis is not an end in itself, but exercises its *logos* as if letting itself be guided by a principle of free symbolic associations, which aim at illuminating, in the mass of traditional material, vast, harmonious principles on which the universe is supposed to exist. So for the modern interpreter it is difficult, if not illegitimate, to separate in this form of thought what for the author is mythical and symbolic and what in contrast is presented in the forms of an ordered, rational vision of the cosmos, since the two planes are continually intersecting, superimposed on each other to the point where they merge. Thus, to choose only one example, the relation between the sun and the moon, which in some essays Plutarch treats according to the scientific canons of the age,[76] in other writings appears to be marked by the most genuine mythological imagination, the same that underlies the widespread astrological beliefs of the period. The moon is a divinity and a seat of the gods. It is a female reality and, as such, receives the seminal power of the sun, the generator of intellects.[77] These images are inserted within a typical symbolism, whose mythological roots are ancient. Everything in heaven is arranged as in a human body. Indeed, heaven is a *macroanthrōpos* (large-scale human being), an image and at the same time a living model of the human microcosm.[78] The sun is the heart of this world. The moon, placed between the earth and the sun, as between the belly and the heart, is their messenger. Hence its role of intermediary, attested also by its androgynous nature: 'it transmits heat here below from above, while it filters the lower exhalations, purifying them by a species of cookery, making them rise around it.'[79] The great law of universal sympathy, which binds all the elements of the animate and inanimate world, establishes between them pseudo-scientific relations governed by occult laws, which require armies of demons for their concrete realization.[80]

The ambiguity of the status of myth in Plutarch's thought is, in conclusion, bound up with its actual function of mediator, of intellectual placed on a changing boundary line. He looks at the mythical and religious traditions with a nostalgic, vigilant and conscious eye; he seizes upon the new ferments of the religious society of his time, exposing himself to the influence of barbarous myths and beliefs.[81] Myth constitutes the bridge for the defenders of tradition, but also for a public open to, and thirsting for, novelty and with a hunger and desire for exoticism. A mediator of these forms of popular religion,[82] he does not confine himself to recording the latest kind of change, but to making a subterranean transformation of it. Myth, a myth profoundly imbued with reflection and *logos*, now narrates the activities of the god–human and the divine principle exiled and longing for return to the heavenly home.

THE NATURE OF GNOSTIC MYTH

The mythological revival of the Gnostics is not an isolated phenomenon and cannot be explained simply by means of oriental influences. If it is true that the mythological material on which Gnostic thinkers' work derives from the available religious traditions of diverse provenance, it is equally true that they generally transform them, endowing them with new meanings. And if it is true that Gnostic myths are myths in their own right because they are the basis of the realities of this world, because of their particular narrative form, the structure of their underlying thought and their characteristic richness and varied symbolic values, it is equally true that their content is not unrelated to history. In other words, as structural analysis has shown, myth as the manifestation of primitive thought possesses an independent form of expression, which prevents it from being reduced to the level of a mere mirror of reality or an aetiological explanation. At the same time, above all in literate societies, it cannot be attributed solely to a combinatory mechanism endowed with a particular logic removed from the influence of historical changes. Gnostic myth thus no longer relates the activities of gods separate from humankind, but only those of that original *Anthrōpos* (human being), from whom individual *anthrōpoi*, or humans, are descended through fragmentation and dispersal. The change of emphasis is decisive and betrays the centrality that reflection on humankind has acquired.

In this respect Gnostic myth has only one predecessor: ancient Orphism.[83] This was a religion of the book, inspired by holy scriptures from which it derived its doctrines and purificatory practices. These scriptures contain and transmit a mythical story of Dionysus' assassination by the Titans[84] – in a form that reverses the view of traditional mythology of the type recorded by Hesiod. If the mythical account in the *Theogony* develops, as it does, from the indistinct to the distinct, from the void to the full, from chaos to cosmos, from atemporality to the affirmation of a *chronos*, or time, the Orphic myth is inspired by a contrasting aim to explain, to justify itself and at the same time to establish the passage from an initial ontological plenitude to the existential void of the present.[85] In this way the Orphics seem to condemn the traditional mythical structures that are used to affirm the primacy of existence and to guarantee hierarchies and equilibrium between humankind and gods, and consequently within humankind itself.[86]

This transformation acquires greater significance when seen against its historical background: the changes and contradictions experienced by the Athenian *polis* between the sixth and fifth centuries BC. Since the Orphics rejected sacrifice (and this is typical of ascetics who make up a community of 'saints'), what are they if not a significant indication of this profound social upheaval, a response that, even though destined to be marginalized and forgotten, is nevertheless creative and original in the face of historical change?

Gnostic mythology also adopts this reverse perspective as the result of its own radical dualism. It is now a matter of understanding, intuiting and reliving the original drama, the initial situation that provoked the rise, the establishment and the triumph of evil, an evil that has now acquired an ontological toughness and substance. This cosmos is incurable and must be rejected. Myth thus acquires the functions of salvation. It describes the way of salvation, reminding the Gnostic of his true origins and showing him how to escape from the cosmos. But above all, like all myth, that of the Gnostics is essentially a story of origins: there lies the key of all that one thinks one possesses. But the 'origins' of the cosmos coincide with the pouring forth of Being, a Being that is the *Anthrōpos*, for the human has now become the predicate of the divine. The manifestation of God to himself: this is the heart of Gnostic myth, that seeks access, like all theosophy, to the mystery of that first throb of Being, that initial moment, that original conflagration from which the pleromatic universe would emerge.

And this manifestation can only take place through the medium of the imperfect narrative that pertains to the era of myth. As *Geschichte*, or history, a succession of archetypal events that proceed from plenitude to deficiency in order to establish and thereby explain it, this divine self-manifestation cannot be described in logical and discursive terms. In the heart of the individual Gnostic it takes shape as an individual process, which is, however, at the same time a moment in a more general process and thus in that same manifestation of God to himself. The mythological narrative form is thus the only channel, the necessary bridge between Being and its becoming.

On the screen of imaginary myth the Gnostic thus projects divine events and exiles that to the modern interpreter can appear only as stages in the search for a new identity, the attempt to refashion a different basis for a conception of the individual in crisis, to which the underlying *logos* of the Gnostic *mythos* is striving to restore its original and archetypal unity.

Gnostic mythological accounts reveal a profound cultural transformation. The Gnostics' is a conscious and reflected mythology. Using pre-existing material, the Gnostic shuffles them round and gives them a new task and a purpose both profound and original: by penetrating the divine mystery to circumscribe and to clarify the same mystery of humankind.

4

In the World of the Pleroma

GNOSTIC DUALISM

'The world came about through a mistake. For he who created it wanted to create it imperishable and immortal. He fell short of attaining his desire.'[1] That the world in which one lived might not be the best of all possible worlds was an opinion, if not widespread, by no means alien to certain schools of thought in the early centuries of our era.[2] While Plato had already offered in the *Timaeus* the spectacle of a Creator-Demiurge of a harmonious, beautiful cosmos,[3] in other dialogues he had helped to introduce serious doubts as to the possibility of human existence not at odds with the laws of the cosmos, with his doctrine of a radical opposition between the essential world of ideas and the transient, corruptible world of appearance. These doubts were translated, then, into a concept of the human body as, if not a prison, certainly an obstacle to the free development of the life of the spirit.[4]

Moreover, we know from some sources, e.g. from Plutarch,[5] that the concepts of Mazdaean dualism also were so widespread in this period that Zarathustra had become one of the most acclaimed 'prophets of the Orient'.[6] According to his teachings, the evil present in the world is attributable to the existence *ab aeterno* of two opposing principles: good and evil; and the world is merely the stage upon which the struggle between Ahura Mazda, the Lord of Good, and Angra Manyu, the Lord of Evil, is played out in periods that are varied and complex.[7] But still the world itself is not evil; indeed, it is intrinsically positive. Likewise, the dualistic element is ethically oriented, and its goal is to restore the positive nature of the renewed, regenerated cosmos by the definitive defeat of evil.[8]

Hellenism had once again taken up the ancient concept of the World Soul which presides over cosmic events[9] and to which it seems natural to attribute the evils that beset the earth.[10] With the growth of astrological beliefs, this concept was reinforced and grafted onto a vision of the earth subdivided into zones which, with their climates, influence for good or evil the events of a world whose positive nature is not questioned.[11]

We have already alluded[12] to an important parallel to this theme in the thought of late Judaism. According to Deut. 32:8, the Supreme God had established boundaries for the nations in accordance with the number of his angels. The disorderly nature and squabbles of these angels, whom Philo significantly identifies with the stars,[13] are made responsible for wars, rebellions and pestilence, with all their accompanying evils.

But the angels are only subordinate elements; they are not opposed to the One God of Judaic monotheism, and the world, even in the most radical forms of apocalyptic pessimism, is not the product of a mistaken calculation or the failed hope of an ignorant Demiurge.

That Gnostic dualism, with its anti-cosmic stance and uncompromising rejection of the beauty and positive aspects of the cosmos, is to be placed at the opposite end of the spectrum of ancient thought, is confirmed most clearly by the anti-Gnostic polemic of Plotinus: 'No one should reproach this world as if it were not beautiful or the most perfect of corporeal beings.'[14] It is true that the cosmos, disturbed by the presence of matter, can only share in the beauty and the life of the Supreme Being: indeed, as the product of Divine Providence, it is so beautiful, according to Plotinus, that there is none more so.[15] Hence the great philosopher's attack upon the denigrators *par excellence* of the cosmos, the Gnostics.[16] They censure and denigrate its authorities; they identify their ignorant Demiurge with the Platonic World Soul, to which they attribute the same passions as those of individual souls.[17] In reality, even this cosmos comes from God and reaches out to him. Thus, those who condemn the nature of the world do not know what they are saying or where their audacity may lead them. How can a devout person deny that Providence penetrates into this world and into all its creatures? Who among such unreasonable and proud people is as well ordered and provident as the All?[18]

And yet Plotinus knows perfectly well the origin of that audacity and arrogance that he so passionately rejects: 'Denying honour to this creation and this earth, they claim that a new earth has been made for them, a land to which they will turn when they have departed from here.'[19] A new land that is at once their original home, the pleromatic world of light, which represents for them the one true reality.

Compared with that world, the cosmos appears at best a pale, gloomy reflection, which is frequently painted in sinister colours: the product of an ignorant, arrogant Creator, it is for the Gnostic the very incarnation of evil. But in this way the Gnostic, in Plotinus' view, falls victim to a hopeless contradiction. If the Gnostics think that the cosmos is not the outcome of a process of continuous, eternal illumination, which instantaneously and totally originates from the One and is mediated through the Nous and the World Soul and whose purpose is to maintain it in its constant, uniform beauty and positive aspect,[20] what is the origin of the evil that is believed by the Gnostics to pervade it?

> It is indeed necessary [says Plotinus] that this illumination be according to nature or contrary to it. But if it is according to nature, it will remain for ever. If, however, it is contrary to nature, then the unnatural element will be one of the Intelligibles themselves and evil will predate this world. Thus, the Intelligibles, and not the cosmos, will be the cause of evil; and it is not the cosmos, but they (i.e. the Intelligibles) that will be the cause of evil; and the Soul will not acquire evil from the world, but will itself be the instrument of bringing evil and the argument will derive the imperfection of the world from the first principles.[21]

'Unde malum?' Where does evil come from? The reply given by Plotinus' Gnostic opponents, a reply that he understood perfectly well, could not be more radical. It originates in the very bosom of the divinity, in the universe, in the Pleroma, the world of plenitude and divine perfection,[22] which is the special subject of the speculatively most audacious of the Gnostic myths. It is to these accounts, their peculiarly original dualism[23] and the way in which their narration explains the origin of evil that we should now turn our attention.

PROLOGUE IN HEAVEN

The Gnostic universe is three-dimensional. Hippolytus gives us the following account of the teachings of one group, the Peratae:

> The universe is one, having three parts. One part of their threefold partition is as it were a single principle like a great source, which can be divided by the word into an infinite number of divisions. The first and most important division in their view is a trinity, and is called 'perfect goodness', a paternal power; but the second part of their trinity is like an infinite number of powers which have originated from themselves; the third is the particular. And the first is unoriginate and is good, the second good [and] self-originate, the third is originate. Hence they explicitly speak of three gods, three words, three minds, three men.[24]

The first consequence of this tripartite division is spatial. The contemporary opposition between visible and invisible cosmos is reinterpreted and corrected: there is now an intermediate place, destined to perform the function of cushion and mediator between two conflicting and apparently irreconcilable spheres of reality. It is the 'place in the middle' between the world of divine plenitude and the place of deficiency and non-being. The pleromatic world, ungenerated in the sense that it derives generation only from itself, is opposed by the world of generation: between the two is an intermediate world bound to Sophia, the last of the aeons, whose sin, not by chance, consisted in an attempt to generate itself. An analogous tripartite structure reappears, as we shall see below, in the divine hierarchy itself, in its first, most complete manifestation: the Triad.

The tripartite division also affects the concept of time. The mythical, basic time of the Beginning is followed by an intermediate time, which affects the life of the Gnostic, a prelude (however interminable it may appear) to that final time that precedes the definitive dissolution of time itself. There is also a triple division of humankind: between the hylic, or material, part and the pneumatic, or spiritual, part there is in fact the psychic dimension. It is an anthropological division that reflects a three-class sociological stratification: the Gnostics, the perfect, destined for salvation; the hylic, material beings condemned to perdition and identified with Jews and Gentiles; finally, the psychic, identified by many Gnostic groups (who were both influenced by, and in dispute with, the True Church) with Christians themselves.

A single law, however, regulates this universe, which may appear, at first sight, to be fragmented or stratified into contradictory levels. Beneath the dualism that (externally and on a vertical axis) separates this world from the divine Pleroma and (internally and on a horizontal plane) contrasts pneumatic reality with hylic reality (both present in humanity) is an underlying tendency of thought that obscures its monistic inclinations, using and exalting in particular a conceptual figure (and its mythological correlates) already familiar to us: mediation or, in Gnostic terms, image. 'The truth did not come naked into the world, but in types and images.'[25]

This cosmos of ours is a pale, eroded, if not deformed (and upside-down) image of the true world. The upper world, by means of a series of agents, imposes its seal upon inert, passive matter, in such a way that 'what is manifest has been conceived out of what is hidden.'[26]

This is the origin of the particular interest that certain systems of Gnostic thought, e.g. Valentinian and Sethian, have in the celestial world. In their depths are concealed the archetypal models according to which the Demiurge created human beings and shaped the world. So, to recover the truth in its fullness, one must return to these models, contemplate these ideal forms and penetrate this divine world.

The process of Gnosis is, in the final analysis, a movement of penetration into the recesses of the Pleroma, which coincides with an *anachōrēsis*, a return to one's own origins, and an *epignōsis*, a remembering of one's own celestial home, which lead to the recovery of the family tree. Allogenes (foreigner, stranger to this world, belonging to another race), in the treatise of the same name, relates to his son Messus the revelations received from a celestial character, Youel. This character (45. 1 – 57. 23) first describes the supreme entities of the Sethian pantheon, dwelling particularly on Barbelo.[27] Thus the same Allogenes (57. 24–64. 19), in accordance with a model typical of Gnostic apocalypses,[28] visits the celestial world, ascending the various steps up to the Supreme Triad. This mystical adventure, destined to transform Allogenes' nature by regenerating it, culminates in ecstatic silence: 'There was a stillness of silence within me, and I heard the blessedness whereby I knew myself as [I am].'[29] The vision of the Gnostic pantheon thus has a decisive effect: how Hermes, Allogenes, knowing his true ego, becomes the reality that he sees, because he actually is that reality.

The richness and complexity of the pleromatic worlds may bring surprise and confusion as a result of the special hypostatic nature of persons that are in it and as a result of the variety of their names, attributes and functions. If this latter aspect is to be explained by taking account of the fluid nature of Gnostic theological reflections that put down their roots in a sociological situation of meetings and small groups not subject to dogmatic principles, but sometimes expressly in open dispute with each other,[30] it is more difficult to justify the special nature of the protagonists in Gnostic theogonies.

In one sense, it could be said that Gnostic theology radicalizes tendencies present in contemporary theological reflection to the point where they become unrecognizable. Divine unity is affirmed by the demonstration of the complex, omnipotent nature of God. Those divinities that in the polytheistic pantheons of classical religions represented distinct spheres of activity in the world of an impersonal divinity have been transformed in Gnostic theology into subordinate modes of the complex manifestation of a unique, substantially unitary, personal God.

God is, in fact, Anthropos,[31] Man/Human, or rather the archetypal Androgyne, in whose breast take place cognitive, volitional processes that are a model and at the same time a reflection of structures of thought and modalities of action typical of the Gnostic. These processes are actualized mythologically in a series of hypostases and entities, which

Gnostics call 'aeons',[32] and which represent self-subsisting moments in the dynamic expansion of divine reality. From a situation of initial stasis and immobility, which reveals a plenitude in some way unresolved, there is a sort of explosion, as a result of which the great machine of Gnostic theogony moves into action.

It has already been pointed out that Gnostic theogony, unlike other ancient theogonies, begins with an initial plenitude that ends in that 'crisis' (the sin of Sophia) that will attack the periphery of the Pleroma. In this downward movement, which takes place within the Pleroma, a single protagonist is actually concealed behind a multiplicity of *personae*, the masks assumed in the Gnostic drama:[33] the *pneuma*, or divine spirit,[34] a formal active dynamic element and at the same time a luminous, pure, uncontaminated substance. It is from this starting-point that various pairs of aeons emanate from the divine bosom in accordance with the divine plan to form that perfect number of entities into which the Pleroma is divided and whereby it is completed. This process of emanation,[35] of the progressive issue of the divine substance, by means of which God manifests to himself the totality of his infinite potentialities, is a process of enrichment, but also of impoverishment. Indeed, only by the concrete manifestation of the complex articulation of his potential nature can God truly know himself. But, equally and contradictorily, this movement entails a flowing of divine substance, which disperses itself in the pleromatic space and, moving progressively away from its ideal centre, loses in stability, solidity, strength and vigour. And it is no accident that the Pleroma experiences, just at its outer periphery, in its final aeon (generally identified with Sophia), a crisis which threatens its unity and stability and which will be solved only by the elimination of the cause of this disturbance, i.e. with the expulsion of an actual part of spiritual matter as a sort of scapegoat. This will be placed in a region outside the Pleroma, where it will give rise to a successive phase in the process: the creation of the world and of human beings. Naturally, in turn, these successive processes will bring a further degradation of the spiritual element, now become a prisoner of the world of darkness and the human body. To recover and to save it, it will be necessary to send a Revealer, a Saviour, to gather the particles of light dispersed in the cosmos and to restore them, purified, to their home.[36]

THE MYSTERY OF THE ARCHETYPAL ANDROGYNE

Before taking his rest in the calm of divine grace and revelation, the Gnostic is a being in search of truth,[37] as the Gospel says. This person is therefore subjected to doubts about the true nature of the world and its Creator. The author of the *Tripartite Tractate*[38] says that people are incapable of knowing the course of things. Some appeal to Providence, basing their reasoning on the stability and conformity of cosmic movement.[39] Others, dissatisfied, consider that there is a principle outside the cosmos, but they reject the Stoic concept of Providence and are once again faced with the difficulty of the problem of evil. Others again are simply fatalists; they maintain that 'the things that happen are destiny.' The author criticizes other existing opinions. They all have a common element, however: in their search for causes the philosophers who hold these opinions draw the line at the visible, the existent. The wisest of the Greeks and barbarians (among whom the Jews are also included) never managed to get beyond faith in the Demiurge. And with good reason: 'The powers themselves seem to hinder them, (appearing) as if they were the Totality.'[40] This illusion falsifies every perspective: 'neither philosophy nor types of medicine nor types of rhetoric nor types of music nor types of logic' correspond to the true principles; 'they are opinions and theories.'[41] Therefore the truth must be re-established. This is possible only by gaining access to the mystery and the very basis of reality, the unknown God.

Gnostics like to emphasize his nature of absolute transcendence, employing doxologies typical of contemporary negative theology. In the *Apocryphon of John* Jesus reveals to his disciples:

Nobody dominates the Spirit, for it is a monarchy (that is, it rules alone). The True God, Father of All, the Holy Spirit, the Invisible, Who is above all, Who exists in His incorruptibility, He is in the pure light, which the light of the eye cannot look at. It is impossible to think of the Spirit as a god or that He exists in a certain mode. For He is above the gods. He is an *arche* (principle) and nobody dominates Him. Nobody exists before Him and He needs nobody. He has no need of life, for He is eternal. He has no need of anything, for He cannot be perfected, for He has no need of anything to be perfect. At every moment He is utter perfection. He is light, He is without boundaries, for there is no pre-existent being to set boundaries. He cannot be judged, for there is no pre-existent being to judge Him. He has no measure, for no one else has measured Him. He is invisible, for no one else has seen Him. He is the eternal, which is forever. He is indescribable, for no one has apprehended Him to describe Him. He is the one whose name cannot be pronounced, for there is no pre-existent being to name Him. He is the immeasurable light, the holy and pure purity, the unspeakable, the perfect, the indestructible. He is neither perfection nor happiness nor divinity, but above these things. He is neither boundless nor bounded, but above these things. Neither incorporeal nor corporeal. Neither great nor small. He has no measurable

size. No creature or person can comprehend Him. Above all, He is nothing
of that which exists, but is above that.[42]

But meanwhile the negations open the way, as is proper in the rhetoric
of the indescribable, to a series of positive attributes that define the
special mode of being of the Gnostic God and prefigure his specific
form of action.

For the author of the *Tripartite Tractate*, God the Father is a unity,
the first, but also the only one.[43] On the other hand, he is not a solitary
individual, but rather reminds one of a root from which the tree with
its branches and fruit grow – that is to say, the Son and the company
of aeons. In strict terms, he is also a pre-Father, for, unlike ordinary
fathers, He knows no father. He is therefore *agennētos*, ungenerated.
He is thus without beginning and without end, because he is stable and
immutable. More traditionally, he is also the good *par excellence*,
without any evil. No name can be given to him, even though it is
possible to use all names for his honour and glory. But none of them
can reach his true essence and form.

The idea emerges clearly from other texts that androgyny is the
distinctive trait of this God: 'I am androgynous. [I am Mother and]
Father since [I copulate] with myself,'[44] proclaims the Protennoia, the
First Thought of the Father, the protagonist in the treatise, the
Protennoia.

The symbolism of the androgyne, so widespread in the history of
religions and found alive in ancient mythological thought also by virtue
of the particular good fortune enjoyed by the Platonic androgyne,[45]
tends to express as its most general content the concept of *coniunctio
oppositorum*, or joining of opposites,[46] to embody the conquest of all
duality in an image that for the most part is constructed on a sexual
paradox, by denying sex itself or affirming the wealth and fruitfulness
of a full sexual life.[47] The androgynous God of the Gnostics is thus
open, in the mystery of his dual nature, to more interpretative possibilities.

A way of imagining the relations between male and female within the
archetypal Anthropos was offered by numerological speculation, which
Neopythagorean opinion had helped to popularize. If the male principle
is seen as monadic, the female counterpart will appear as dyadic.[48]
Consider the *Three Stelae of Seth* (NHC VII.5), a typical Sethian
apocalypse,[49] in which the instrument of revelation is represented,
according to a form that was widespread, by three stelae said to have
been composed and hidden by Seth, the Father of the Living Race, and
rediscovered by a certain Dositheus, who communicated them to the
elect. They are devoted to the Divine Triad, the head of the Sethian

pantheon. In increasing order of importance, they contain invocations to the Son, to the Mother Barbelo, and to the God who is non-being and pre-existent existence. The text affirms that Barbelo, while remaining one, has become numerable and therefore subject to division.[50] Thus, the female principle, the Dyad, presents itself as the very possibility of revealing all the numerical potentialities present in the initial Monad, which would otherwise remain unexpressed.

An analogous concept emerges in which, to represent the mystery of the androgyne, recourse is had to the image of logical reflection and verbal expression, with the help of certain Stoic speculations.[51] The Triad is presented as Thought, Voice and Word. Thought lives in itself, immersed in light and silence. Its female dimension is imagined as the Voice of silent Thought. 'I am a Voice . . . within the Silence',[52] exclaims the Protennoia. From Voice proceeds the Son, Logos or Word, who has in himself the Name and hence the possibility of naming the multiplicity of particular beings destined to be generated.

But the most natural and obvious way of representing this androgyny is, as has been said, by recourse to sexual imagery. According to Ptolemy, a Valentinian thinker, there is

> in the invisible and ineffable heights a pre-existent, perfect aeon, whom they also call Pre-beginning, Forefather, and Primal Cause (Bythos). He is incomprehensible and invisible, eternal and ungenerated, and he has existed in profound stillness and serenity for infinite aeons. Along with him there existed also Ennoia (Thought), whom they also name Grace and Silence (Sige). Once upon a time Bythos determined to produce from himself the beginning of all things and, like a seed, he deposited this production which he had resolved to bring forth, as in a womb, in that Sige who was with him.[53]

From this relationship between the Father and his female counterpart proceeds the Son or Nous.

The spiritual self-fertilization of the archetypal Androgyne is also represented, in a favourite theme of ancient thought, as contemplation of the male principle in the female 'mirror' that constitutes its vital and emotional dimension. 'He is the First Father Who has no beginning. He sees Himself in Himself, as in a mirror.'[54] That theme,[55] which, in certain mythological traditions, served to highlight the temptations of narcissism or to take up the Platonic motif of the lifeless nature of the copy as compared with the original, when it is applied to the pleromatic world, seeks, on the other hand, to express the perfect identity of the Father with himself. What reflect him are the pure, luminous, virginal waters of life that surround him, the spiritual substance from which the pleromatic world originates. He 'understands Himself in His own light that surrounds Him, that is, the source of the waters of life, the light of full purity.'[56] The different images transmit the same fundamental concept. The female counterpart of the androgyne, with which he copulates, is his vital dimension, his generative potential, a spiritual, luminous substance, which is at the same time virginal and 'male' and emphasizes the characteristics of purity and the absence of all corruption, which at this level of being are the mark of generative modalities.[57] As Ennoia or Protennoia, this female dimension will indicate the Father's ability to reflect upon himself in order to achieve, by means of the emanation of the Son (his Nous or Intellect by design) a form of self-awareness.[58]

How could the Father, who is by definition perfectly stable,[59] be at the same time the principle of that movement destined in some measure to disturb his own stability? At this point the answer ought to be obvious. Movement is the essential characteristic of his female dimension. When Allogenes, in his celestial journey towards the First Principle, reaches Vitality, its female dimension, he stops and stands upright. Though calm, he is not stable (stability being the nature of the male principle). And it is at this point that he sees around him eternal movement, intellectual and undivided: the movement, in fact, of Vitality.[60] It is in fact the movement that moves in every creature,[61] the vital breath that animates all aeons,[62] transmitting their life to them.

This basic sketch outlines the complex nature and decisive function that the female dimension of the Androgyne is called upon to perform. It is essentially a work of mediation: on the one hand, it questions the stability, the Father's situation of *estōs*, or standing, denying his nature of solitary and self-subsisting being; on the other hand, it also lays the foundations on which the process of emanation from the Pleroma is constructed.[63]

DIVINE HIERARCHIES: THE STRUCTURE OF THE PLEROMATIC FAMILY

Compared with that Infinite that is the Father and the infinite possibilities of realization that the Father contemplates by means of his Ennoia, the Son is presented as the first basic passage to the finite, the first determination of the will of the Father. In the *Three Stelae of Seth*[64] he is Father through a Father, a unity that comes from a unity through a unity, a word that proceeds from a command. Self-generated[65] and thrice male[66] to indicate the triple male potential present in the Triad, which is manifested in him, he is the First Man, or rather the complete, determined manifestation of the original Anthropos;[67] he is the name[68] and the Nous of the Father, i.e. his possibility of intellectual knowledge.

This last attribute is especially revealing. To a mode of thought dominated, as Gnosticism is, by the imperative of immediate, intuitive knowledge of God, the Son, as Nous, seems the obligatory way to achieve that goal.[69] He is at the same time a barrier interposed between the Father and other aeons, signifying from a cognitive point of view the impossibility of exhausting the Father's infinity.[70] Finally, the Son is the one who possesses knowledge of all the aeons. In the words of the *Tripartite Tractate*,

> without falsification, [he] is of all the names, and he is, in the proper sense, the sole first one, [the] man of the Father. He it is whom I call the form of the formless, the body of the bodiless, the face of the invisible, the word of [the] unutterable, the mind of the inconceivable, the fountain which flows from him, the root of those who are planted. . .[71]

But the Son, 'though co-eval with the light that is before him, is not equal to it in power.'[72] This is a delicate point in the formation mechanism of the pleromatic hierarchies. The divine world is a world made up of a special substance, the luminous *pneuma*. Applying an originally Stoic doctrine of the *pneuma*,[73] Gnostic thinkers have nevertheless tried to strip it of its initially material characteristics, providing it with qualities such as luminosity and purity. But this spiritualizing operation was only partially successful. If it is true that the fiery nature of the pleromatic spirit is not to be confused with that of the cosmic fire, only by acceptance of the relative materiality of this spirit is it possible to explain how certain authors have been able to imagine the emanation of the Son. Thus Jeu, in the *First Book of Jeu*, the equivalent of the Sethian Son and the Valentinian Nous, describes his birth: 'I shone in this small shape as one who proceeds from the Father. I bubbled up and flowed from that. The latter emanated, and in this I was the first emanation. I was his entire likeness and image.'[74] Why did the Son bubble up, unless he is the product of a bubbling up, of an increase and an explosion of the heat and fire that generate life and animate the movement of the 'small shape', the equivalent of the Ennoia?[75]

Moreover, this heat that animates the luminous spirit, that gradually recedes from its origin, is destined inevitably to lose strength, vigour and vitality, to cool until it changes first into a psychic, then into a hylic, element.[76] Some texts have rendered this movement by using the image of 'perfume'.[77] For the author of the *Gospel of Truth* the sons of the Father are his perfume, because they emanate from the beauty of his face. Therefore the Father loves his perfume and reveals it everywhere. But, when mixed with matter, it becomes cold and thus a psychic element. Only 'if a breath draws it' does it 'get hot. The fragrances . . . that are cold are from the division.'[78]

In this way, the emanation process entails almost of necessity, as in the case of the Son, an imperceptible, but slow, continuous drop in level which, as we shall see below, gradually brings about the final crisis represented by the sin of Sophia.

So far, we have examined, underlining their common features, the processes by which two Gnostic schools of thought, the Sethian and the Valentinian, dealt with the mystery of the Initial Triad. This choice was justified, despite the profound differences that exist between the two systems, by the similarity in their attempts to present the nub of theogonic generation. However, when one begins to examine the world of the hierarchy of the aeons, the differences become clear, despite certain constant features; and they require separate treatment. The theological texts that provide the treatises typical of a Sethian type have not in fact been Christianized, or they have been subjected to merely superficial Christian influence.[79] Although there are important differences of detail which we cannot go into here, the process of emanation proceeds in them according to the following instructions.

From the Son four luminaries are sent forth, four aeons called Harmozel, Oroiael, Daveithe and Eleleth.[80] Each one is endowed with other entities, to indicate the rich variety of their functions and the extent of their sphere of activity. This Tetrad (or Dodecad, since each luminary has three aeons) sums up and at the same time prefigures the stages of the future history of salvation. According to the *Apocryphon of John*, this Dodecad 'of the First Knowledge and the Perfect Intellect' is followed by 'the perfect true Man, the first manifestation, through God and with the agreement of the Great Invisible Spirit and of the Self-generated One. He called him Adam.'[81] Adam is placed in the first luminary, Harmozel. Adam is followed by Seth, who is placed in the second light. In the third is placed in turn the seed of Seth, the souls of the perfect and of the elect, and in the fourth the souls of those who knew their perfection, but did not repent immediately and persisted for a while in their sin, until they finally repented.[82] In this way the four luminaries are presented as the genetic code, mythically based, that contains the archetypal model of the protagonists, of the development and the outcome of the future history of Sethian salvation: the creation of Adam and Seth (see chapter 5 below) and the destiny of the Elect.

Not to mention the quadruple division of time: the age of Adam, the age of Seth, the age of the Sethian patriarchs and lastly the present age.[83]

The nature and dynamic of the Valentinian Pleroma immediately reveal the profound influence of Christianity.[84] The myth recounts the activities of a Saviour who is the celestial prototype of the earthly Jesus with a speculative richness, depth and boldness which we can only hint at here.

According to the system of Ptolemy, the generation of androgynous Nous, whose companion is Aletheia (Truth), together with Abyss and Silence, makes up the primordial Tetrad. Since he possesses Truth and knows why he has been generated, Intellect in his turn emanates the pleromatic couple or pair, Logos and Zoe (Word and Life), 'Father of all beings said to have come into existence after Him and Beginning and Formation of the entire Pleroma'.[85] In its turn this couple emanates Anthropos and Ecclesia. Thus is formed the Firstborn Ogdoad, the root and foundation of all things.

We now witness a double emanation process. In order to glorify the Father, Logos and Zoe emanate ten more aeons, to which are added twelve aeons proceeding from Anthropos and Ecclesia: this makes a grand total of thirty aeons (Ogdoad, Decad, Dodecad).

Strictly speaking, the pleromatic world should not comprehend the First Tetrad, but only those aeons (starting with the Logos) whose knowledge of the Father is not intellectual (proper to Nous), but rather, logical and rational, since it belongs to Logos. In a sense the aeons are nothing but the projection in hypostatic form within the bosom of the original Anthropos of a totality of human cognitive, volitional processes, which range from the emergence of a first thought to the overcoming of obstacles that it meets on the way to its final realization. The difference between the First Tetrad and the genuine Pleroma, in Valentinian terms, is that, while formation according to substance and formation according to Gnosis coincide in the First Tetrad, for the Pleroma, formed in respect of substance, Gnosis is the *telos*, or end, of a drama that takes place within itself and becomes evident with the appearance of a certain *pathos* (a sensation described as cognitive by the Valentinians and erotic in some Sethian texts). The cognitive tension, controlled and almost inhibited, is destined, however, sooner or later to explode in the sin of Sophia.

An interesting aspect of the Valentinian Pleroma is the way in which it reinterprets the motif of the androgyny of the aeons. Also in Sethian accounts, the various pleromatic entities, images of the archetypal

Androgyne, are androgynous. But this fruitful theme has been exhausted in all its rich variety only by Valentinian thinkers. In Ptolemy's system the male dimension of the various couples in the Ogdoad (Nous, Logos, Anthropos) responds to the need to provide a principle of individuation, a formal criterion that will circumscribe and delimit a female dimension by itself transient and amorphous. The Logos thus represents the divine economy projected outwards and the Anthropos represents the personal individuation of the Nous. In the whole, the Son is thus characterized in his intellectual, logical and anthropological functions. It should also be emphasized that there is a fundamental difference between Decad and Dodecad. The former, an emanation from Logos–Zoe, orchestrates the perfections of a world that knows neither increase nor decrease in its completion of rational life, refracting in the various aeons and synthesizing in their generative pair the perfection of a complete spiritual economy right from its beginnings. Like the decad of the *Apocryphon of John*, it reveals the fullness of the divine attributes in their logical articulations, in their capacity to think discursively and to articulate the divine project. The Dodecad, on the other hand, parallel to the Sethian Dodecad, revolves around the problem of Man (Anthropos/Adam). It thus appears directly finalized at the specifically human moment to which the God–Man is directed, epitomizing the spiritual economy of an Anthropos destined for that development with which every 'history' is necessarily familiar. The Pleroma thus contains within itself and, at the same time, is the basis of the successive history of the world and humankind.

THE SIN OF SOPHIA

The disharmony, the intimate contradiction that both underlies the life of the Pleroma and betrays an element of potential deficiency, reaches the point of no return with the emanation of the ultimate aeon: Sophia.

The paradoxical, yet original, character of the Gnostic Sophia is quite striking. Contemporary philosophical technique had reshaped Sophia, in her capacity as knowledge of the divine mysteries,[86] as projected upwards. Her forebears in Wisdom, however, had endowed her with a dynamism of the opposite sort. As companion of God in the work of creation, this hypostasis, the ideological twin of the contemporary *Anima mundi*, or World Soul, summed up in its functions the divine plan and action as regards the cosmos.[87] As we are about to see, Gnostic Sophia, Sethian or Valentinian, certainly performs the function of mediator between God and matter, between the divine economy and its fulfilment.

But her specifically Gnostic feature derives from her special function and place in the delicate balance of divine kinship structures. The paradox is just this: Biblical Wisdom has here become the most complete expression of divine deficiency. The long version of the *Apocryphon of John* relates that, when the emanation of the Dodecad is complete,

> ... the Sophia of the Epinoia, being an aeon, conceived a thought from herself with the reflection of the invisible Spirit and foreknowledge. She wanted to bring forth a likeness out of herself without the consent of the Spirit – he had not approved – and without her consort and without his consideration. And though the personage of her maleness had not approved and she had not found her agreement, and she had thought without the consent of the Spirit and the knowledge of her agreement, yet she brought forth. And because of the invincible power which is in her, her thought did not remain idle and a thing came out of her which was imperfect and different from her appearance, because she had created it without her consort.[88]

Sophia's fault consists in a particular sin of hubris: the audacity to generate without the contribution of the male principle. But what drives her to break the androgynous harmony? The text hints at an invisible *dynamis*. The nature of this force is revealed to us by the parallel passage of the shorter recension. She emanates from herself solely because she is unconquerably *prunikos*, or lewd.

This decisive detail leaves no room for doubt about the true nature of her sin. The term, which generally indicates a situation of prostitution or lewdness,[89] when applied to Sophia, reveals that the generative force is concentrated within her and that she is the repository of those aspects of seduction and courtship typical of a certain concept of the female, which accompany (secretly, but necessarily) and mark out the activity of various female hypostases during the formation of the Pleroma.

That this is the situation is confirmed by an interesting series of parallels. *Brontē* (*The Thunder* NHC VI.2)[90] is a short treatise, which in the form of a revelation discourse pronounced by a female entity, represents, with contradictory, paradoxical statements, a typically Gnostic way of affirming the presence in the cosmos of the spiritual principle, at the same time emphasizing its absolute transcendence. Using the stylized form of self-declaration,[91] the work begins with these words:

> The Thunder, Perfect Mind. I was sent forth from [the] power, and I have come to those who reflect upon me, and I have been found among those who seek after me. Look upon me, you who reflect upon me, and you hearers, hear me. You who are waiting for me, take me to yourselves.

And do not banish me from your sight. And do not make your voice hate me, nor your hearing. Do not be ignorant of me anywhere or at any time. Be on your guard. Do not be ignorant of me. For I am the first and the last. I am the honoured one and the scorned one. I am the whore and the holy one.[92]

The concept of the 'holy sinner' that characterizes Brontē serves to illustrate the paradoxical nature of Gnostic Sophia.[93] Irenaeus says of the so-called Barbelognostics that 'from the first angel (that stands beside the Only Begotten) derives the Holy Spirit, which they call Sophia or Prunikos.'[94] Sophia's spiritual, and therefore virginal and holy, nature is inextricably bound up with the tendency to sin conceived in terms of sexuality.

For this reason some Gnostics, Irenaeus' so-called Ophites, anticipate a typically Valentinian solution and postulate the existence of two Sophias. According to them in fact,

> . . . there is a first light in the power of the 'deep', blessed and incorruptible and boundless, which is the Father of All and is called the First Man. His Ennoia which proceeds [from him] they call the Son of the one who emits him, and he is the Son of Man, the Second Man. Below these is the Holy Spirit, and below the Spirit on high the elements are separated, water, darkness, Abyssus, Chaos, over which they say the Spirit hovers; and they call it the First Woman. Thereafter, they say, as the First Man rejoiced with his Son at the beauty of the Spirit, that is the Woman, and illuminated her, he begot from her an incorruptible light, a third male, whom they call Christ the Son of the First and Second Man and of the Holy Spirit the First Woman, since both the Father and the Son lay with the woman, whom they call the Mother of the Living. Since she was unable to carry or contain the greatness of the light, they say she was overfull and bubbling over on the left side; and thus only their son Christ, as being on the right and lifted up into higher parts, was at once transported with his mother to the Imperishable Aeon . . . The power which bubbled over from the Woman, having a trace of the light, fell downwards, they teach, from the Fathers, but by their will retained a trace of light: they call it, on the left, Prunikos Sophia and Androgyne.[95]

Here the task of the seduction of the primordial Anthropos by the beautiful lady (it should be borne in mind that 'spirit' in Hebrew is feminine) is quite unmistakable: it is necessary for the birth of Christ, but its negative effects are concentrated in Sophia Prunikos and thus expelled from the Pleroma.

But perhaps the most important example is provided by the Helen of Simon Magus' followers, a myth to which we shall return. Here it is enough to say that, in the Simon legend, the Ennoia of the Heavenly Father is none other than the celestial prototype of a certain Helen, a prostitute from Tyre whom the Father himself, incarnate in Simon, is said to have liberated. The Simonian Helen, also called Prunikos with good reason,[96] reflects the underlying theme of the myth of the Sethian Sophia: the spiritual principle can purify itself of any negative residue only by passing through the dark gates of evil (here seductively attired as female sexuality).

In the Valentinian reinterpretation, this motif continues to re-echo,[97] but against the background of an interpretation now influenced deeply by Christianity. Sophia is the thirtieth aeon and, as for Christ the arrival of the thirtieth year coincides with his maturing and with the beginning of the tragic epilogue, Sophia represents the ripening of *pathos*, or suffering, in the Pleroma as it arrives at its moment of crisis, the need to abandon anonymity in order to fulfil (in this case, beyond the Pleroma) the mission of salvation conceived and desired by the Father *ab aeterno*.

His consort here is Theletos, spontaneous, natural will.[98] Thus, at the lowest level of life in the Pleroma, an androgynous situation is reproduced, analogous to that of the archetypal Androgyne. Sophia, in fact, is the equivalent of the Father's Ennoia, even if (in keeping with her Biblical origins) she may be a thought of God who looks at the world. As for Theletos, it represents an essential element in the Gnostic Pleroma. Will is, in fact, a typical trait of the Valentinian God. In a passage in the *Tripartite Tractate* we learn that the will of the Father is the spirit that breathes in the aeons, inspiring them – that is, providing them with the thought, the idea of the Unknown God that reawakens latent possibilities and arouses the desire to know him.[99] According to some Valentinians, then, the Abyss, the Primordial Principle, has two consorts, Ennoia and Thelesis; for he first thought what he wanted to produce and willed it to happen.[100] Will, therefore, is a potentiality of the Father in this divine, sexually divided universe, imagined as male and thus able alone to set in motion the generative process. According to a theory that we might define as 'communicating vessels', will is also *pneuma*, a generative male power and therefore a function capable of impressing forms on the underlying amorphous female substance.

With respect to the Theletos–Sophia couple, Sophia's transgression in the Sethian texts consisted, as has been noted, in the fact of wanting to generate without the consent of her partner, breaking the androgynous harmony of the Pleroma. In the Valentinian tradition the cause of the transgression changes. The passion that now moves Sophia is in fact the search for the Father, for she wishes to understand his greatness.[101]

According to Ptolemy, the reason was that 'she was unable to undertake this impossible task and was suffering because of the immensity of the depth and the inscrutability of the Father and her love for him, constantly stretched forward because of his sweetness. In the end she would have been absorbed and dissolved in the universal substance',[102] had it not been for the intervention of a power, Horos (Limit), placed by the Father to guard his inscrutability.[103]

A vague hint of Oedipal conflict inevitably underlies the pathological family relations in which Sophia's act is submerged. The desire to imitate the Father in fact conceals a libido for sexual union, which is made clear by the motif of ascending to the Abyss and the corresponding brusque rejection by the Limit. At all events, what counts from the Gnostic point of view is that Sophia has broken the basic rule in the games of kinship: indeed in generated beings the female element produces the substance and the male element the form.[104] Thus the product of her sin cannot be other than an abortion.

For the moment let us leave the 'formless entity' produced by Sophia to its own fate. What happens now to the lost aeon? Thanks to the intervention of Horos, the male entity which, as we have seen, performs the double function of impassable boundary to protect the mystery of the Father and stabilizing element for Sophia, she puts aside her *enthymēsis*, or intention, destined in turn to become a new hypostasis, Sophia beyond the Pleroma. The abandoning of this guilty intention coincides with the conversion of pleromatic Sophia. Her plea to be pardoned and restored to her original position is also supported by the other aeons, especially by Nous. The Father agrees, and Sophia is restored to her partner.

With the cause of her passion expelled, formation according to Gnosis can now take place. According to the Father's plan, the Only Begotten produces another couple, Christ and Holy Spirit, quite deliberately. Indeed, the Gnosis of the Father, which coincides with the spiritual formation of the Logos, can only reach the genuine Pleroma from an entity outside it: as the Holy Spirit descended from above upon Jesus to anoint and sanctify him on his thirtieth birthday.

The function of Christ is to teach the aeons

the nature of their partnerships, that they, being begotten, could not understand the unbegotten one; and he proclaimed among them the knowledge of the Father. That he cannot be understood or comprehended, that he cannot be seen or heard, but is known only through the Only-begotten one; and that the reason for the eternal permanence of the others is the fact that the Father is incomprehensible, and that the reason for their origin and formation is that which is comprehensible in him, that is, the Son.[105]

In keeping with a teaching that, aiming at the vision of God and beatific union with him, puts hearing before seeing and the kerygmatic message and teaching before contemplation, Christ instructs the aeons, preparing the way for the intervention of the Holy Spirit. His task is to illuminate them, definitively shaping them in the Gnosis of the Father and introducing them to true repose. What he performs is not a process of substantial transformation (the aeons already have substantial form), but a qualitative one.[106] Within the Pleroma every difference disappears. Equal in form and will, the male elements have all become Intellects, Logoi, Anthropoi; the female elements have become Truths, Lives, Churches.[107]

The underlying idea is simple and profound. The life of the Pleroma is guided by a double movement: expansion and contraction (*diastolē* and *systolē*). In its centrifugal momentum the Firstborn Anthropos expands, revealing the internal richness of the divine plan and at the same time emphasizing its fundamental unity, for the same syzygial relationship is repeated at lower levels in the pleromatic world. The point of arrival of this movement, the expulsion from the Pleroma of the most amorphous spiritual substance, coincides with the projection of the life of the God, of his female dimension, into the void, the *kenōma*. Movement in the opposite direction, of the (so to speak) male nature, will then tend to return to unity. When distinctions and oppositions are overcome, the archetypal Androgyne will be able to lie in himself, in definitive repose, stable and calm for ever.

The pleromatic activities of the Valentinian Sophia are therefore the paradigm of the activity of the Gnostic: it is the mythical basis and dramatic representation of those internal processes of conversion that have made him susceptible to the message of revelation and the communication of Gnosis.

5

The Arrogance of the Demiurge and the Creation of the World

SOPHIA'S DISRUPTIVE BEHAVIOUR

Plotinus was right. For the Gnostics the origins of evil are to be found in the life of the Pleroma itself, in the process of emanation and of inevitable decay, which takes place within it. The gradual cooling of the spirit is paralleled, on the subjective level,[1] by the crisis the last aeon, Sophia, undergoes: *pathos*, the negative element in the pleromatic life, is given concrete expression and then expelled.

But, as the Valentinian myth of Sophia Achamoth[2] reveals, it is a matter of negativity *sui generis*; the Intention of pleromatic Sophia being none other than the spiritual seed, destined by the Father to be cast into this world so that she may return to the Pleroma after purification from her contact with matter.

Sophia's first task, after being thrown out of the Pleroma, is to supervise the formation of *hylē*, primordial matter, and the generation of the Demiurge, the divine craftsman charged with shaping it and forming the world in which the Church of the Spiritual beings will be established.

At this point in the myth, certain texts make use of a theme well known in antiquity, the cosmogonic veil.[3] In *On the Origin of the World* (NHC II.5), whose treatment of the origin of the world is clearly at odds with traditional cosmogonies, we learn that

> After the nature of the immortals was completed out of the boundless one, then a likeness called 'Sophia' flowed out of Pistis. ⟨She⟩ wished ⟨that⟩ a work ⟨should⟩ come into being which is like the light which first existed, and immediately her wish appeared as a heavenly likeness, which possessed an incomprehensible greatness, which is in the middle between the immortals and those who came into being after them, like what is

above, which is a veil which separates men and those belonging to the
[sphere] above.[4]

The Sophia in our text, who corresponds more or less to the
Valentinian Sophia Achamoth, is given the task of generating the cosmos.
The veil that she forms has a dual function: it is a place of separation
and a place of joining between the upper and lower worlds. It seeks in
fact to separate the luminous world of the Pleroma from external
darkness, a darkness that in this type of Gnostic thought tends to acquire
an ontological dimension. But it also joins the two worlds. As an image
of the upper world, the veil contains the types, the models, the archetypal
principles from which the lower cosmos can be formed. Sophia's task
is to transmit to unformed, dark matter those luminous seals, those
ideal traces of the Pleroma from which, by a sort of inverted law of
example,[5] by the play of distorting mirrors, our world will be generated,
an abortive cosmos, a pale image, a distorted reflection of the harmonious
beauty of the pleromatic world.

The protagonists in the cosmogonic drama have entered the stage.
Above, waiting for her celestial seat, Sophia–*Anima mundi*; below,
formless, chaotic darkness. What will Act I of this drama bring?

In this type of system the darkness performs (even when it changes
its nature) a typical 'female' function, analogous to that of the primordial
waters of life. It contains within it the substance of this world, but is
incapable of generating it itself, since it does not possess its form.
Therefore the first decisive step must be taken by the male principle
active at this level, that of Sophia.[6] She reveals herself to the darkness,
illuminating it.

This is no mere repetition of the creative theme of 'fiat lux', or 'let
there be light.' Cosmogonic (like pleromatic) illumination obeys the laws
of a particular generative concept of the period,[7] here adapted to the
proper needs of Gnostic myth. Sophia, revealing herself to the darkness,
spiritually fertilizes it, transmitting to it the *dynamis*, the spiritual
principle, the genetic code that contains the forms of the pleromatic
world.

The first effect of Sophia's illumination is the formation of primordial
matter from dark chaos. The second effect, the product of the second
illumination, will be the generation of the Demiurge.

But, it will be said, in illuminating the underlying darkness, is there
not a risk that the divine principle will be captured and swallowed up,
as it were, by Chaos? The answer to this question, in the structure of
Gnostic thought, is of a strategic importance. Let us return to Plotinus'
objections. The Sophia of his Gnostic opponents appears there in a

logically contradictory situation. After having thought the cosmos, elaborated the project and established the concept, she bends down to the lower world, illuminating its darkness. This bending down entails a 'local', i.e. a spatial, movement. To illuminate the darkness, Sophia is obliged to move towards it. Plotinus' Gnostics, however, maintain that she remains where she is and does nothing when confronted by darkness.[8]

This contradiction is not an invention of Plotinian polemic. Plotinus was criticizing mythical accounts. A characteristic of mythic symbolism is its variety, its capacity for using certain pregnant images in order to represent plastically what seems irreconcilable with logic. The representation, then, of relations between Sophia and darkness derives from an Aristotelian concept of the relations between a male and a female element.[9] The male principle in generation is the giver of movement, but, above all, the bringer of form. It finds itself confronted by a female principle conceived as the element providing the substance. Moreover, the male principle is a *dynamis*, a fertilizing power, which, in its meeting with the female substratum, is limited to activating it without loss or diminution of its own nature.

Equally, in the process of illuminating the darkness, Sophia (here represented in her male dimension of fertilizing power, as Philo had already taught) confines herself to emitting a *dynamis*, an effluvium,[10] a luminous seed, which penetrates the matrix of lower matter (this is the local movement); but this does not mean a union with darkness or, worse still, a change in her nature. Fertilized by this spiritual spark, the primordial waters of Chaos are now ready to generate the various elements.

This typically mythological way, characteristic of Sethian systems, of depicting the creation of matter appears to constitute the background upon which Valentinian cosmogonic reflection probably drew. In chapter 4 we left Sophia Achamoth outside the Pleroma at the moment when, alone and abandoned, she was reflecting on her destiny.

Separated as a result of her passion, she began to seethe,[11] hot spiritual matter waiting to be fertilized, but by herself without form or appearance, like an abortion. At this point, the intervention of Christ becomes necessary. He forms her first of all according to substance; he orders and arranges that basic material, leaving it with a suggestion of immortality, a hint of the divine world. Thence he returns immediately to the Pleroma. Achamoth, thus formed, becomes conscious. However, suddenly abandoned, she sets off in search of the light. But she is stopped by the Limit, because she is still too consumed by passion: 'abandoned alone outside, she fell into all sorts of suffering which has many forms and varieties: she experienced sorrow, because she had not comprehended; fear, lest he might abandon her, as light had done; and, in addition, perplexity. All these [she suffered] in ignorance.'[12] Purified of these passions, Sophia Achamoth now experiences a new fundamental disposition: that of conversion, of return to the Logos, to the Christ who had given her life.

From the passions of Achamoth, a manifestation beyond the Pleroma of the internal *pathos* pervading it, matter was formed; and from matter the world emerged. In contrast, in the conversion, as a positive act, originates the psychic element and its representative *par excellence*, the Demiurge. The other elements arise from fear and pain:

> Indeed, from her tears was born all wet substance, from her laughter all luminous, from her pain and consternation all the corporeal elements of the world. Indeed, at times she wept and was in pain, as they say, because she had been abandoned alone in the darkness and void; at times, however, she thought of the light which had abandoned her, took comfort and laughed, then again she felt pain and at other times she was seized by uneasiness and astonishment.[13]

Thus Achamoth's passions reproduce the higher Sophia's passions in a pattern now familiar, according to which the same event is repeated at gradually descending levels of reality, an indication of the substantial unity of the divine world; but equally of the gradual receding of the *pneuma*, or spirit, until real 'crises' break out, taking the form of substantial changes. In the case of Sophia Achamoth, the passions provoke more than a simple change inside the same pneumatic substance; they provoke a contrast, which is the symbol of the mixture (between hylic and spiritual, by means of the psychic), representative of the actual Gnostic situation.[14]

As for the effects of the passions, they are the outcome of the action of that particular spiritual Demiurge, the Christ–Logos. Indeed, by his intervention he brings form and distinctiveness to the potentialities and virtualities that reside in Achamoth, shapeless spiritual matter. Thus, the elements from which our cosmos will be formed are already present; a cosmos destined to become familiar with the activities of its lord, spiritual humanity.

As a result of her conversion, Sophia Achamoth is now ready to return to the Pleroma. It is the moment of formation according to Gnosis. She pleads with the light that has abandoned her, namely Christos. He then sends her the perfect fruit of the Pleroma, the Paraclete or Comforter promised by the Gospel, who comes down upon Achamoth, surrounded by his angels: 'Seized with reverence, Achamoth first covered her face with shame, but, having seen him with all his fructifying power, she ran to him and received strength from his appearing.'[15]

Achamoth, symbol of the soul of every Gnostic, after being converted to the spiritual principle is thus able to rejoin her consort and, purified of all *pathos*, to reconstitute the primordial union. This spiritual marriage generates 'a spiritual product born like the companions of the Saviour',[16] the seed that, cast into matter, will make up the church of the spiritual. As for the Saviour, he completes the work of consolidation of incorporeal matter, distinct at two levels: psychic substance capable of conversion, and hylic substance, destined to perdition.[17] Thus everything is ready for the appearance of the Lord of this world, the Demiurge.

'WOMAN BORN OF WOMAN': THE BIRTH OF THE DEMIURGE

The Demiurge is a central figure in Valentinian and Sethian mythology. While he may be completely absent[18] or of secondary importance in other systems,[19] in the myths under examination here he is presented as a complex figure, whose origins, through Sophia, are traceable to the very life of the Pleroma.

The antecedents of this figure, generally identified with the God of the Old Testament, are, like other figures in Gnostic mythology, multiple, and not traceable to a single cultural tradition.[20]

Greek thought had devised a theory of demiurgic activity, in which it is not difficult to detect reflections of quite precise social situations. The Demiurge is the artificer, the artisan who gives order to matter that is, by itself, without spirit; he injects into it a form that is superior to it. As Plato shows with the example of the divine artificer of the *Timaeus*,[21] and Aristotle emphasizes with his observations on technical work,[22] the creation itself is for ancient humankind more perfect than the Creator, and humans are smaller than their work. Contrary to what we might now be tempted to think, neither the spirit of initiative nor the capacity for reflection is required of artisans: their function and virtue, according to Aristotle, consist in obedience.[23] This is the point: the artisans are not the producers of the 'form' that they impose on matter; rather, the form, as beginning and end of the process, in a sense overcomes the artisans.

In every demiurgic production the artisan is the driving force: he acts on a material (a material cause) to give it form (a formal cause), which is that of the finished work. At the same time this form constitutes the end of the whole operation (final cause). It is this that directs the whole of demiurgic activity: the true causality of the operation process does not reside in the artisan, [but in the one who sends him].[24]

This concept, typical of the ancient division of labour, was boldly applied by the Gnostics to God the Creator, of the Old Testament. Jahweh, far from being the single Lord of creation, is its simple artificer, uncouth and ignorant. Moreover, boasting of being the only god and believing himself to be the true Creator, he does no more in his arrogance and stupidity than emphasize his blind folly. In reality, he is for the Gnostics the simple instrument of a complex divine plan, whose formal cause is represented by Sophia, who in her turn is moved by the final cause of the whole process, that is to say, the soteriological plan of the Father, understood and manifested by his Intellect, the Son.

The distinctive trait of the Sethian and Valentinian Demiurge is that of being the abortive outcome of the sin of Sophia. 'Woman born of woman'[25] was a widespread concept of the time, which regarded the abortion not as a failed man, but as *mulieris portio*,[26] a part of a woman; it was a concept that lent itself (by analogy), as we learn from parallels in Plutarch, to regarding cosmogony itself as a failure.[27] On the other hand, the outcome of Sophia's conception could not be other than formless and destined to failure; for she is a woman who dared to generate without the contribution of her consort. This is repeated over and over again by certain cosmogonic Sethian texts. The short recension of the *Apocryphon of John* relates that when, no longer able to contain the passion that was in her when she conceived, 'her thought could not remain inactive, and the product of her work came forth, incomplete and odious in its form, for she had generated it without her partner. He did not have the form of the mother; he had another form ... He had the form of a serpent and a lion. His eyes cast a light of fire.'[28]

Certainly, in the construction of this image, whose eyes shine like fire and whose body has the monstrous appearance of a serpent and a lion, there are elements drawn from more ancient traditions, e.g. the Orphic[29] (and this is typical of mythical bits and pieces). It is also probable that some Biblical reminiscences favoured the idea of a Demiurge transformed into an abortive product.[30] But what matters is the new significance that this material has assumed in the Gnostic construction. The Demiurge is part of the Mother. When she sees the product of her thought in that horrible form, she moves it away from herself because none of the immortals can perceive it, except the Holy Spirit, destined, as we shall see, even at the point of contact, to perform a soteric function towards it. The name he receives is Ialdabaoth.[31] He is the First Archon, who has in himself the power of the Mother.[32]

To put a further stage between the pleromatic world and the demiurgic product, some Sethian texts seem to want to attribute the formation of the Demiurge to an entity intermediate between Sophia and Ialdabaoth; they favour a multiplicity of plans typical of Gnostic thought. According to the *Hypostasis of the Archons* (NHC II.4), a short but important cosmological treatise, which recounts the origin of the lords of this world. Sophia, wanting to create something on her own, without her consort, forms a veil between what is above and the lower aeons, 'and Shadow came into being beneath the veil; and that Shadow became Matter; and that Shadow was projected apart. And what she had created became a product in the Matter, like an aborted fetus. And it assumed a plastic form molded out of Shadow, and became an arrogant beast resembling a lion.'[33] This androgynous being is the Demiurge, who appears not as the abortive product of Sophia, but that of her shadow. But who conceals this shadow?

In Gnostic thought the theme of the shadow is a substitute for the theme of the image.[34] Like the image, the shadow may have a positive value and constitute the perfect copy, in some way degraded in the identity of substance, of the *Urbild*, the archetypal model.[35] In some cases, however, the shadow, like the image, refers to a deformed reproduction, to a mirror that reveals and disfigures the features reflected in it.[36] In the case in question, there is little doubt about its potentially negative values. If in some respects it appears to recall Philo's Logos, 'the shadow of God . . . of which He has made use in order to create the world',[37] the shadow in the Gnostic text is presented as a degraded hypostasis of Sophia. This hypostasis must in all likelihood be identified with Samael, an angel on whose activities the text will subsequently dwell.[38] The whole of the extract seems to contain a Gnostic interpretation of a Jewish myth, that of the origin of the *Nefilim* or giants, frequently found in Old Testament apocryphal literature.[39] The fall of the angels and their sin with the daughters of men had become a favourite theme in some apocryphal texts, which discovered in them an answer to the basic question of the origin of evil. The Gnostics, with the sin of Sophia, provided a celestial predecessor to this drama. For the author of the *Hypostasis of the Archons* the creation of the celestial veil which Sophia performs (and in which, one might think, the positive angelic powers took up their residence) is paralleled by the second creation, the work of the Shadow. Having materialized, the shadow descends from the veil into the lower world. The product of this encounter with matter is the Demiurge in leonine shape.

In the parallel text, *On the Origin of the World*, on the other hand, the generation of the Demiurge is preceded by that of *hylē*, matter, in a more systematic and coherent way. It will be recalled that here too cosmogony begins with the formation by Pistis of a cosmogonic veil. That automatically brings into existence the lower shadow, which corresponds to the Chaos of traditional ancient cosmogonies, the Abyss, from whose midst matter will be formed in successive stages. In other words, the lower Triad of Shadow, Darkness and Chaos takes shape as the negative correlate of the celestial cosmogonic veil: a totality in the purely potential state, matter which waits like a woman (this reveals its ill-fated potentiality) to be activated and fertilized by a higher power. This is Pistis' task. One of her first manifestations causes the birth of those negative hypostases that constitute a recurrent theme in descriptions of the primordial world. This is the case with envy:[40] like a spiritless abortion, envy is born in the same watery substance from which *hylē* later emerges: 'Just as all the useless afterbirth of one who bears a little child falls, likewise the matter which came into being from the shadow was cast aside.'[41] The scene is now set for the psychic element to emerge from *hylē* in its representative *par excellence*, the Demiurge. In fact, one is witnessing a final manifestation of Pistis, this time to *hylē*, lying immersed in boundless darkness and water. The outcome is a lifeless abortion. Pistis follows it. When she decides that 'the one who had no spirit [should] receive the pattern of a likeness and rule over the matter and over all its powers, a ruler first appeared out of the waters, lion-like in appearance, androgynous, having great authority within himself, but not knowing whence he came into being.'[42]

The synthetic nature of our exposition prevents us from pursuing those variants that constitute the elusive object of all mythological analysis. One might ask: why is it Sophia who acts in one text, Pistis in another? What lies behind the various accounts of the genesis of the Demiurge? In fact, behind these variants there are different theological traditions, controversies within groups and factions, which were expressing themselves in a different, competing interpretation of this or that detail of a common mythical heritage. One must remember that in the particular texts under review we are dealing with true mythical accounts, which, as has already been confirmed, prefer the vivid richness of symbols and the fascination of a narrative rich in pathos to the rigorous logic of a theoretical treatment.

In contrast, these aspects tend to disappear in the Valentinian re-elaboration of the figure of the Demiurge. The depth of theological reflection, the search for a theoretically coherent and convincing answer, leave little room for mythical imagination. The multiplicity of symbols is replaced by a precise, penetrating exegesis of myth, but one that violates its intimate nature. Ptolemy merely affirms that Sophia Achamoth, after being formed according to Gnosis and after giving birth to the spiritual substance, 'from the psychic substance she formed the Father and king of all those things which are of the same nature as he is, that is, the psychics, which they call the Right.'[43] The author of the *Tripartite Tractate* notes that the Logos–Sophia established an Archon–Lord over all creatures, an emanation of the Logos as the representation of the Father of the aeons; and thus the Demiurge is equipped with every name and every glorious quality and property as a copy of the heavenly Father.[44]

The Valentinian authors thus make explicit in their reflections a theme that, in the mythological web of the Sethian accounts, was presented in allusive form and lent itself more easily to divergent interpretations. The Demiurge, as an abortion of Sophia, continues to possess it or (according to some variants in which he is formed after *hylē*) receives it later from the Mother (usually without his knowledge), a part of the Mother's spiritual substance. And it is precisely by virtue of this participation in the spiritual world that he can now tackle his appointed task: the formation of the cosmos.

SETHIAN AND VALENTINIAN COSMOGONIES

The lower world is created in the image of the pleromatic. Sethian cosmogony thus gives notice of a theme that will appear at its most relevant at the moment of the creation of human beings. The cosmos is created in the image of the pleromatic world and in the likeness of the substance of the Demiurge and his Archons.

According to the *Apocryphon of John*, Ialdabaoth withdraws, once he has been generated and powerfully equipped by his Mother. He builds for himself an aeon of fire in which he decides to live. He then unites with his companion, Aponoia (lack of sense), the negative counterpart of the archetypal Ennoia and symbol of the Demiurge's intellectual blindness.[45] The cosmos that he creates is superficially not unlike the one familiar to the ancients. The great difference is its nature: instead of being the living image of the living God, it is the deformed copy of an abortive God.

The stages in the cosmogony are to some extent inevitable. They are confined to a negative reinterpretation of the origin of the basic elements of contemporary Hellenistic cosmology, from astral bodies to the formation of Earth and Tartarus, the underlying lower world.[46] But now between Tartarus and the celestial spheres there is no longer a substantial difference: both are the outcome of the irrational creation of Ialdabaoth. First of all he generates twelve angels, each according to the model of the incorruptible aeons.[47] Of these, seven command the planetary spheres and five the chaos of the lower world. To each of these angels, who have barbarous names and a horrific appearance,[48] are given seven more angels. Moreover, each angel is assigned three powers and other beings, a total of 360, 'in agreement with the manifestation of the pre-existing model'.[49] Thus there is the formation of both space and time, with its basic units of division. When the work of creation is finished, the Demiurge can now exclaim, 'I am God and there is none other beside me.'[50]

This recurring exclamation of arrogance, a Gnostic reinterpretation of Isaiah 45:6, seeks to emphasize the essential characteristic nature of the Demiurge. He has created a world under the misapprehension that he is the only true artificer. This is the lie behind the statements of the Old Testament God. And it is the mystery that the Gnostic, in the light of his revelations, is now in a position to uncover. The God of the Jews, creator of a cosmos threatened at its roots by incurable disease, is nothing but an unconscious puppet manipulated by the invisible strings of higher powers.

The image of the Demiurge usually portrayed in the Sethian texts is negative. Apart from anti-Jewish and anti-Christian polemic, there are internal reasons for this, specifically the function of the psychic element represented by the Demiurge. This element is not, as for Valentinians and other Christians Gnostics, the seat of free will, but a moment (that of animation) in the hylic dimension and, like it, destined to perdition.[52] This is the radical difference from the Valentinian Demiurge, the latter being representative of a psychic element that is also called upon to participate in the work of salvation.

Devoid of scarifying characteristics, Ptolemy's Demiurge is simply the Creator of the Seven Heavens, who lives above them. What the Valentinian scholar wishes to emphasize is the deep meaning of the Demiurgic myth:

> They say that the Demiurge believed that he had created all this of himself, but in fact he had made them because Achamoth had prompted him. He made the heaven without knowing the heaven; he formed man without knowing him; he brought the earth to light without knowing it. And, in every case, they say, he was ignorant of the ideas of the things he made, and even of his own mother, and imagined that he alone was all things.[53]

If the Demiurge is the Lord of the Hebdomad, the Devil or Cosmocrator is the Lord of the terrestrial world. Like all the other elements, he derives from one of the passions of Sophia, the conversion.[54] As has been said already, the elements of this world are born from other passions:

> The corporeal elements of the universe sprang . . . from the terror and perplexity, as from a more permanent [the Greek reads 'more ignoble', but has to be emended] source: earth, as a result of the state of terror; water, as a result of the agitation of fear; air, as a result of the congealing of sorrow. Fire is inherent in all these elements as death and decay, just as they also teach that ignorance is hidden in the three passions.[55]

The scene is now set for the appearance of the Lord of the Cosmos; humankind. But we must first consider how other Gnostics, sometimes differing greatly from the systems of thought considered so far, portrayed the origin of the world.

GNOSTIC VARIATIONS ON COSMOGONIC THEMES

Gnostic thinkers did not always see the creation of the world as the negative result of the process of emanation within the Pleroma. In some cases (not frequent, but none the less important), they postulated the existence *ab aeterno* of two principles: Light and Darkness.[56] The clearest example is that of the so-called Sethians, described by Hippolytus,[57] whose type of dualism has been confirmed in a Nag Hammadi text, the *Paraphrase of Shem* (NHC VII.1). It contains the revelation that Derdekeas, the son and image of the Supreme Entity, the pleromatic Light, has been allowed by the Light to grant to Shem:

> My mind which was in my body snatched me away from my race. It took me up to the top of the world, which is close to the light which shone upon the whole area there. I saw no earthly likeness, but there was light. And my mind separated from the body of darkness, as though in sleep.
>   I heard a voice saying to me, 'Shem, since you are from an unmixed power and you are the first being upon earth, hear and understand what I shall say to you first concerning the great Powers who were in existence in the beginning, before I appeared. There was Light and Darkness and there was Spirit between them. Since your root fell into forgetfulness – he who was the unbegotten Spirit – I reveal to you the truth about the Powers. The Light was mind full of attentiveness and reason. They were united into one form. And the Darkness was wind in [. . .] waters. He possessed the mind wrapped in a chaotic fire. And the Spirit between them was a gentle, humble light. These are the three roots. They reigned

each in themselves, alone. And they covered each other, each one with its power.[58]

This concept is substantially the same as that attributed by Hippolytus to certain Sethians. The universe here consists of three separate principles, each one provided with an unlimited number of powers: Light, Darkness and, between them, Pure Spirit.[59] A characteristic feature of these two systems is that Darkness, depicted as a product of threatening waters, is not without an intelligence of its own. It does its best to retain this element, thus clashing with the task of Light, which aims to restore to their proper dignity the particles of Nous that belong to the Darkness. In the *Paraphrase of Shem* Light is replaced by the soteriological figure of Derdekeas.[60] As for the genuine cosmogony, it is the outcome, in the case of the Hippolytan Sethians, of the mutual impact that the powers of the three principles experience at a certain point. They leave their imprint and their form on lower matter. Thus, the first impact produces a great seal shape, that of the sky and the earth, formed like a matrix with the umbilical cord in the middle. From successive impacts further seals are formed, in accordance with which are shaped innumerable creatures, including humans, who populate our world.[61]

A distinctive feature of this cosmogony, therefore, is the opposition of two principles right from the beginning, in a scheme that foreshadows Manichaean dualism and, like Manicheism, tends to conceive the shades of Darkness as a mobile, active principle.[62]

But like other Gnostic cosmogonies, it insists upon the triple division of the universe: 'He who says that the universe proceeds from one principle is mistaken; he who says that it is from three, speaks the truth and will give the description of all.'[63] This is the belief of the Naassenes of Hippolytus. We have already mentioned the triple division of the Peratae. Their world consists of the Perfect Good, the Self-Generated and of what is generated and particular. The Self-Generated, or intermediate principle, moves between the Supreme God and Matter. He has the features of a serpent: assuming for himself the powers of the Father, this Ophite Logos, without form or quality, descends to impress the seals of the Father upon matter. He then recovers those formal principles to bring them back to the Father. Thus there seems to be a self-generating process of circularity, in which nothing is created and nothing destroyed,[64] a process that is well illustrated by the ancient image of the serpent biting its tail[65] or, as in the case of the Naassenes, symbolized by the movement of the Ocean descending from above to below, to bring its currents back to the original source.[66]

The image of the cosmos thus derived is far from negative. It is the passive receptacle of the divine forms, the place of their manifestation.

The theme recurs, with its triple division, in the *Apophasis Megalē*, a 'great revelation' attributed by Hippolytus to the followers of Simon Magus.[67] We have here a unique infinite power, which stands upright, immobile and facing only itself. It manifests itself in three aeons: 'those which stand upright are indeed there.'[68] The divine element 'who stands on high in the unoriginate power, who took his stand below in the chaos of waters when he was begotten in the image, who will stand on high with the blessed infinite power if he be fully formed.'[69]

The first manifestation of the infinite power, the second aeon, consists of six roots born in couples: Intellect and Thought, Voice and Name, Reason and Reflection. As is typical of Gnostic thought, these couples, which express the forms in which the world is realized by the operation of a unique principle (which meditates when forming a thought, speaks when giving a name, reasons when generating reflections), also contain the outcome of the creative process: 'Now of the six powers . . . he calls the first pair mind and thought, [or] heaven and earth . . . But "voice" and "name" mean sun and moon; "reflection" and "conception" mean air and water.'[70] In them the higher power is present and diffused. It operates until the spiritual elements mature in their earthly sojourn, changing into perfect images of the infinite power. As for the earth, it is far from being the seat of evil, 'while the earth below receives her kindred intelligible fruits brought down to earth from heaven.'[71]

This weakened form of dualism finds its most original expression in the system of Basilides (an acute Gnostic thinker who lived in the first half of the second century), as Hippolytus tells us. When the non-existent God[72] wanted to create the world, he hurled down the seed that contained all the semen for the world, i.e. he emitted the immaterial substratum from which three principles emerged: Basilides calls them 'sonships', and they were in every way consubstantial with God.[73] The first, the most subtle, returned straightway to the non-existent God (it represents the paternal Nous). The second, more opaque and unable to return above, provided itself with wings; Basilides calls it the Holy Spirit, thus Christianizing an originally Platonic motif. However, this Spirit, unlike the Spirit in the Sethian system, is not consubstantial with the Father. So when the second sonship, which corresponds to the *Anima mundi*, returns to the non-existent God, the Spirit cannot follow it, but stops near the blessed place of God, keeping within itself the virtue of sonship, the odour of its perfume. Like the cosmogonic veil in some Sethian systems, it constitutes an intermediate space separating the upper and lower worlds, the firmament placed between the supramundane and mundane regions. As for the third sonship, the most opaque, it represents the spiritual substance in need of purification, 'that has remained in the huge mass of seeds to make and receive benefits.'[74]

At this point the creation of the world can take place. Basilides duplicates this creation. According to the plan and the will of the non-existent God, two Demiurges are in fact created from the seed, the first charged with creating the Ogdoad, the heaven of the fixed stars and the planets, helped by a Son who is superior to him; the second creator of the Hebdomad, i.e. the sublunar world. The great Archon, the Head of the world is 'greatness, beauty, inexpressible power'.[75] Inasmuch as he is unaware of the existence of the non-existent God, his characteristics are certainly not those terrifying and despicable characteristics of the Sethian Ialdabaoth.

When creation is over, the work of salvation begins. The gospel descends in the form of a hypostasis from the upper world and first illuminates the Demiurge, then descends in turn upon Mary and becomes incarnate in Jesus, whose duty it will be to form spiritually the third sonship. In the eschatology of the text one receives a clearer idea of the more positive traits of Basilidian cosmology: 'When the whole Sonship thus arrives [above], he says, and is beyond the boundary, the Spirit, then the creation will receive pity ... God will bring on the whole world the great ignorance, so that everything may remain in accordance with [its] nature, and nothing desire anything contrary to its nature.'[76]

Bathed thus in eternal oblivion, the creatures of this world not destined for eternal salvation will not know the final destruction that characterizes the eschatology of other systems. It is possible to detect in this cosmology definite echoes of Greek concepts of the eternity of the cosmos. However much it may have been devalued, the cosmos, the seat of purification of the elect, seems worthy of divine compassion.

There are also traces, even in Sethian texts, confirming the possibility of a more positive evaluation of the cosmos. Marsanes, a typical Gnostic visionary, in the eponymous apocalyptic text, enters into possession of the divine mysteries during a celestial journey. Among other revelations he learns that 'in every respect the sense-perceptible world is [worthy] of being saved entirely.'[77] This is probably a late development of Gnostic dualistic cosmology which, influenced by Christianity or, as here, by Neoplatonic ideas,[78] brought out more clearly in the third century the monistic, optimistic themes already present in authors and systems of the second century.

The stage is now set for the central act of the demiurgic operation: the creation of humankind.

6

And God Said, 'Let Us Make Man in Our Image and Likeness'

INTRODUCTION

'In the final analysis Gnosis is anthropology: man stands at the centre of Gnostic interests.'[1] This statement, which since the time of Feuerbach can be applied to all religions, is certainly true of Gnosticism. Precisely because the Gnostics made central to their myths the creation of Adam, on whose story the way to salvation is mythically based and revealed, they have also been able to place a God Anthropos at the top of the divine hierarchy.

Seen in this perspective the cosmogonic stories appear as the framework in which the true drama takes place, the backdrop erected just in time for the entrance of the principal actor: the human being.

As is typical of Gnostic thought, there is an event at the basis of the creation of human beings which repeats, at the anthropogonic level, a process verified already both theogonically and cosmogonically. The Demiurge, Creator of humankind, the Creative God now surrounded by a cohort of faithful Archons, is a simple artificer. He shapes hylic and psychic matter, whose forms he does not possess, but which he derives, by way of illumination, from the upper world. In the creature thus shaped he will insert, at a favourable point, the strength inherited from the Mother, which will be the spiritual substance of Adam. For the possession of this substance there will henceforth be war between malevolent and luminous forces. The malevolent forces, made aware of the superiority of Adam, will be struggling to destroy the divine seed and its progeny. The luminous forces will be endeavouring to restore to the Pleroma the fallen luminous substance which, in the Gnostic history of salvation, is the leaven of the important events of this world.

Adam's actions, his spiritual seed, his wanderings and his salvation are grafted onto a structurally dichotomous anthropology in the Sethian accounts. The psychic dimension, the principle animating Adam's material body, has no real autonomy. As in Adam the pneumatic reality that proceeds from the upper world is opposed to his carnal dimension, thus the two irreconcilable realities coexist in humankind. More generally, there are two classes, two groups of people: the elect, the pneumatic, destined for salvation, and the material, the hylic, doomed to perdition.

At first sight it seems that the Gnostic has mercilessly plundered Genesis material to construct his various anthropogonic accounts.[2] More than the cosmogonic accounts, the anthropogonic texts seem to provide an exegesis, however unique, of the first chapters of Genesis. But this is only partly true. It is no surprise that some Gnostics regarded these as a privileged source. Classical mythology is poor in anthropogonic accounts, and those that did exist were unable to compete with the fascination and richness of detail found in the Biblical account. In addition to which one might mention the familiarity of these anonymous reporters with the Old Testament and the apocryphal and legendary traditions, as well as with speculations on the celestial Adam.[3] These and other particulars must not, however, obscure a specific element of the Sethian anthropogonic accounts. Far from being exegeses (however much they claim to be) of the Biblical text, they are put forward as the true Bible, containing the new, or rather the only true, myths of origins, while the Biblical accounts are merely false, deceptive distortions.[4]

THE CREATION OF ADAM AND EVE

Here too, as for cosmogony, we shall prefer to use the two Sethian texts for their narrative continuity and richness of detail: the *Apocryphon of John* and the *Hypostasis of the Archons*. Here and there we shall take into account important similarities and variants provided by other Sethian texts. Finally, we shall compare them with the Valentinian interpretation.

That these Sethian accounts deal with an actual myth is shown by the way in which the two basic Genesis texts on the creation of humankind are used: Gen. 1:26 and 2:7. Exegesis of these texts in Jewish and Christian circles has given rise to many different interpretations. Philo, for example, in accordance with his Biblical Platonism, interpreted the text of Gen. 1:26–7 ('Then God said, "Let us make man in our image and likeness . . . and God created man in his own image; in the image of God he created him; thus he created male and female') as the creation of the ideal archetypal human, who as such is androgynous and perfect.[5] Gen. 2:7 ('Then the Lord God formed man from the dust of the ground and breathed into his nostrils a life-giving breath, and man became a living creature') came, as a result, to be referred to the later formation of material, distinct and particular man.[6] Moreover, and this is an important detail, Philo interpreted the plural of the Septuagint translation (*poiēsōmen*: 'let us make') to refer to the angels, celestial co-workers whose job is to perform the lower demiurgic functions of giving form to corruptible mud.[7]

The Christian exegetical tradition remained for the most part faithful to Philo's foundation of dual creation,[8] even if in the interpretation of Gen. 1:26 it saw, according to a typological scheme, the formation 'in the image' as the starting-point of a spiritual progress that should culminate, for Christians, in their most complete spiritual formation as children of God in the likeness of the Father.[9]

Our Gnostics move along different lines. The anthropogonic phase is introduced by the arrogant assertion of the Demiurge: 'I am God, and there is no other beside me.' Stupid blasphemy and likewise a provocative challenge that seem to have been prearranged by the puppeteer above who manipulates the invisible strings that move the actors in this event. Thus, a voice from above is suddenly heard crying to the Demiurge: 'There exists Man and the Son of Man.' The voice proceeds from Incorruptibility; and this is not surprising in systems where the Voice is a hypostasis of the same divine triad.

This voice has the task of preparing the way for the manifestation of the supreme divinity, Anthropos. This is the central moment of Gnostic anthropogony: the epiphany of a luminous image.[10] In the longer recension of the *Apocryphon of John*:

> And a voice came forth from the exalted aeon-heaven: 'The Man exists and the Son of Man.' And the chief archon [Ialdabaoth] heard (it) and thought that the voice had come from his mother, and he did not know from where she (or it) came. And the holy Mother-Father taught them, and the perfect, complete foreknowledge, the image of the invisible one who is the Father of the all through whom everything came into being, the first Man, for he revealed his appearance in a human form.
>
> And the whole aeon of the chief archon trembled, and the foundations of the abyss shook. And of the waters which are above matter, the underside was illuminated by the appearance of his image which had been revealed. And when all the authorities and the chief archon looked, they saw the whole part of the underside which was illuminated. And through the light they saw the form of the image in the water.[11]

In this way the higher Anthropos reveals his appearance, not directly, but in a distorting mirror, through the waters of chaos, thus providing the Demiurge with the external form that will be the model for the formation of Adam.

The reaction of the Archons to this appearing of light is varied. It might be a reaction of amazement, as we have already seen; in other cases it comes in the form of lustful desire or greed for the beautiful forms of the higher Anthropos. In the *Hypostasis of the Archons*, when the likeness of Incorruptibility appears in the waters: '. . . the Authorities of the Darkness became enamored of her. But they could not lay hold of that Image, which had appeared to them in the waters, because of their weakness – since beings that merely possess a soul cannot lay hold of those that possess a Spirit; for they were from below, while it was from above.'[12]

That the Archons in this treatise desire to be united with the Anthropos is not surprising. They are depicted as having the bodies of women – that is, they incarnate sexual desire in the pure state: and the appearance of the beautiful male forms can only arouse their greed. When they see the image escaping them, the Archons hold a council and decide to form a creature 'in the image and likeness'. At this point the various editors have indulged in jokes over the possible interpretations offered by the ambiguous nature of the verse in Genesis. The Archons model Adam according to their body and according to the image of the Anthropos seen in the waters. Given Adam's androgynous nature and taking into account the fact that this text deals with Adam's creation out of mud and earth, one must conclude that they form the female part of Adam in the image of their bodies, while the male dimension is formed in the likeness of the beautiful male parts of the higher Anthropos. The progenitor therefore brings concupiscence into himself right from the beginning: this is to be identified with his female dimension, of demonic origin. Accordingly, his salvation is possible only through rejection of this female source.

The longer version of the *Apocryphon of John* is different: the text does not deal with the hylic, but the psychic, formation of Adam, and the verse from Genesis is therefore interpreted as follows: 'Let us make a man [say the Archons in their council] according to the image of God and according to our likeness, that his image may become a light for us.'[13] The higher Anthropos here provides the model for the androgynous Adam in his completeness, not only in his male part. What the Archons contribute is their likeness, their natural identity and their psychic substance itself.

The longer recension of this same text reveals a particularly pessimistic conception of the nature of the First Man. In a long digression (NHC

II.1. 15.14–19.10) the account inserts a detailed description of the formation not only of the psychic, but also of the material body of Adam.[14] It supplies us with the most precise example of Gnostic anatomy. It is therefore worth considering it in order to understand more fully how a Gnostic actually regarded the body, which he was inclined to see as the seat of every evil.

The seven Archons, placed in relation to the planetary spheres, form a psychic hypostasis in accordance with a widespread conception that each planet intervenes in the formation of the human psyche, adding its own particular contribution.[15] Despite some variations in the names of Archons,[16] both recensions contain an identical list of the seven parts that make up Adam's psychic hypostasis: soul out of bone, nerves, flesh, marrow, blood, skin and eyelids.[17] After the Archons, then come the demon-angels: it is their task to form the material body. Thus a first list catalogues the names of those demons responsible for the formation of the parts of the body from the head to the toe-nails:

> The first one began to create the head: Eteraphaope-Abron created his head; Meniggestroeth created the brain; Asterechme the right eye; Thaspomocha the left eye; Yeronumos the right ear; Bissoum the left ear; Akioreim the nose; Banen-Ephroum the lips; Amen the teeth; Ibikan the molars: Basiliademe the tonsils: Achchan the uvula; Adaban the neck; Chaaman the vertebrae; Dearcho the throat; Tebar the left shoulder; Mniarchon the left elbow; Abitrion the right underarm; Evanthen the left underarm; Krys the right hand; Beluai the left hand; Treneu the fingers of the right hand; Balbel the fingers of the left hand; Kriman the nails of the hands; Astrops the right breast; Barroph the left breast; Baoum the right shoulder joint; Ararim the left shoulder joint; Areche the belly; Phthave the navel; Senaphim the abdomen; Arachethopi the right ribs; Zabedo the left ribs; Barias the left hip; Abenlenarchei the marrow; Chnoumeninorin the bones; Gesole the stomach; Agromauma the heart; Bano the lungs; Sostrapal the liver; Anesimalar the spleen; Thopithro the intestines; Biblo the kidneys; Roeror the sinews; Taphreo the spine of the body; Ipouspoboba the veins; Bineborin the arteries; Atoimenpsephei, theirs are the breaths which are in all the limbs. . .[18]

The list continues as far as the demons who have formed the toe-nails. Of this long, tedious survey of diabolical anatomy the most interesting passage comprises the intervention of the demons in charge of the formation of the genital organs. Bedouk forms the right womb,[19] Arabei the left penis, Eilo the testicles, Sorma the *aidoia*,[20] a Greek term commonly used to indicate the pudenda, both male and female. The presence of the left penis leaves no room for doubt that the demon Sorma is in charge of the formation of the female parallel to the penis, the clitoris. For students and those interested in Hermaphroditism, this is another example to be added to the iconographic and literary collection the ancient world has bequeathed to us on this difficult, but suggestive, topic.

Androgynous Adam therefore has an entirely demonic body. But there is more to come in a second anatomical list.[21] It catalogues the demons who activate these parts of the body. Apart from certain differences the two lists recount the anatomical areas in the same way: head, neck, shoulders and upper extremities, chest and torso, genitals and lower extremities. It is followed by a list of the demons that govern perception, reception, the capacity for representation, and the impulses of the body: 'And the origin of the demons that are in the whole body is ordained to be [divided into] four: heat, cold, wet and dry. But the mother of all of them is matter.'[22]

At this point the author supplies another detailed catalogue of the various demons in charge of these elements. The mother of all the demons, Onorthocrasi, sits in the middle of them; she has no defined limit[23] and is mingled with all of them. She is truly matter, which here has acquired demonic traits. She nourishes the four chief demons: Efememphi, who belongs to pleasure; Iocho, who belongs to greed; Nenentophni, who belongs to pain; Blaomen, who belongs to fear. The special mother of these latter is Estensisonch-Epiptoe. And from each of these demons originate the various passions that unceasingly rend the human body. Ennoia, the Thought of their Truth, is 'the head of the material soul'.[24]

The demonization of the body could not be more radical or total. In the particular microcosm that man represents, the error and the horror of the formation of the macrocosm are repeated. A hierarchy of demons, servile and ready, is continually at work in everyone's body, transformed into a remorseless inferno in miniature. Far from being a passive, secondary element vis-à-vis the spiritual, the demonic represents an active power, charged with negative energy. Over and above the cosmos, humanity has become the true place where the battle is fought, decisive for every individual, between the forces of good and evil.

Thus, there is a varied account, if not various accounts, of the formation of Adam's body. He lies prostrate on the ground, incapable of standing up straight.[25] It is now time to animate him. In Gen. 2:7 the Gnostic exegesis finds material for a rich, diversified interpretation that conforms with the presuppositions about the generation of the Demiurge.

According to the Apocryphon of John, when the Mother decided to take possession of what she had given to the First Archon, she sent him five luminaries to advise him, if he wanted Adam's body to rise, to breathe part of his spirit upon the progenitor's face.[26] In this way, however, the Mother's power passed from Ialdabaoth to Adam's body. The First Man thus became the instrument with which the Mother (and through her the celestial kingdom) succeeds in tricking the Demiurge. Adam can now rise, shining with light.[27] The Archon Powers realize that they have made a mistake: they have created a being superior to them. Their countermove is to relegate Adam again to the lower regions to be imprisoned in the material body.

In the *Hypostasis of the Archons*, in which we have already encountered the Adam of mud and earth, the breathing of the Demiurge corresponds in turn to his psychic, not to his pneumatic formation. The latter will be achieved directly by the upper world when it introduces spiritual force into him later on.[28]

The narrative now proceeds, adhering more strictly to the stages of the account in Genesis: the formation of Eve, the 'sin' of the progenitors, the birth of Cain and Abel and the birth of Seth.

The *Apocryphon of John* recounts that the Metropator, seized with compassion[29] for the power of the Mother imprisoned in the progenitor's body, decides to send help to Adam, lost in the lower regions of matter and prey to the jealousy and envy of the Archons, in the form of a divine hypostasis, the Epinoia of Light,[30] also called Zoe or Vita (Life). She hides in Adam's body, a power waiting to fulfil her work of salvation. In fact, she 'works on all creation, taking trouble with it and establishing it at its own perfect temple and instructing it about the descent of its deficiency and teaching it about its ascent.'[31] The moment of her entrance, however, has not yet arrived.

Meanwhile, in response to the divine act of mercy, the Archons imprison Adam in the body of death and then place the mortal result of their work in Paradise. They then send him to eat of the Tree of Life. But this is a trap. This tree is an archontic creature, distilling the bitter liquid of their life:

> Its fruit is poison, and against it there is no remedy; it promises death for [Adam]. But their tree has been planted as the tree of life. I shall tell you the secret of their life: it is the counterfeit spirit, which originates in them, so as to make him deviate from his path and not recognize his perfection. This tree is made thus: its root is bitter; its branches are the shadow of death; its leaves are hatred and deception; its sap (resin) is the unction of evil and its fruit is the wish for death; its seed drinks from those who taste it; its resting place is the lower world.[32]

And now we have the creation of Eve.[33] The Epinoia of Light is hidden in Adam. The Demiurge would like to extract it, by removing Adam's rib. She then flees, but pursuit is hopeless. The Chief Archon is thus obliged to compromise. He decides to form another creature in the likeness of the Epinoia that he had seen: terrestrial Eve. When Adam sees the woman next to him, the luminous Epinoia appears to illuminate him. She frees him from the veil of ignorance covering his mind and from the intoxication of darkness. It is the moment to taste of the Tree of Knowledge. Adam is instructed by an eagle which appears on the tree (a further manifestation of Epinoia) to eat of it and attain knowledge. Ialdabaoth then metes out his punishment: Adam and Eve are driven out of Paradise.

The following scene is dedicated to the birth of Cain and Abel. In the Gnostic interpretation, they are the fruit of a purely carnal union, regarded by Gnostics as an act of impurity: the union of Ialdabaoth and Eve.[34] The higher powers, which had foreseen that act, had removed the spiritual life from her in anticipation. The product of this spiritless carnal union are Elohim and Jahweh. The first, corresponding to the Biblical Cain, has the face of a bear and is a just God who presides over fire and wind; the second, corresponding to Abel, has the face of a cat, is unjust and presides over the two lower elements, earth and water. It is the aim of Elohim and Jahweh alike to deceive mankind.[35]

Contrasted with the carnal birth of Cain and Abel, sons of concupiscence and the counterfeit spirit, is the spiritual birth of Seth. Adam, in generating him, unconsciously interprets the celestial script assigned to the pleromatic generation of Adamas and Seth. In fact there is a union with Epinoia–Zoe, the mother of spiritual life who has returned for the occasion in Eve.[36] In this way the Seth of the Sethians appears from the outset as a fully spiritual reality, called upon with his purity to found the race of the spiritual beings *par excellence*: the Sethians.

THE UNWAVERING RACE: SETH AND HIS DESCENDANTS

Even the reader who is not entirely familiar with the Biblical texts will be struck by the way in which the Gnostic editors manipulate the sacred text in order to make it suit their purposes.[37] In certain cases, it is a simple matter of retouching. However, this can change the sense of a passage profoundly. Consider just one example: the editor of the *Hypostasis of the Archons* states of Adam and Eve, 'they recognized that they were naked of the Spiritual Element',[38] deliberately adding to the Biblical 'and they understood that they were naked.' In other cases the author interferes directly with the text and chooses a different translation from the 'canonical' Septuagint.[39] In others again, the order of events is changed[40] or new actors are introduced.[41]

These interventions, however, are only corrections and necessary patches put onto a garment that is too narrow. The unique God of Genesis is replaced by the cohort of Archons whose tasks sometimes give rise, as we have seen in the anatomical list of the *Apocryphon of John*, to an impressive increase in the strength of this angelic bureaucracy. Among them, as in any self-respecting hierarchy, there is a rigid distinction of roles. It is the task of the Protarchon to breathe into Adam the vital, and in certain cases the spiritual, principle; that of the seven planetary Archons is to prepare the framework of the human machine; that of the angels is to set in motion the assembly line destined to produce Adam's body.

In certain cases, moreover, the same character is duplicated. Thus, there are two Eves: the carnal Eve, mother of Cain and Abel, and the spiritual one, mother of Seth and of the race of the spiritual beings. But, in fact, the two Eves are merely the garments employed, in a constantly changing game, which comes dangerously close to deceiving not only the Demiurge, but also the modern reader, by the true protagonist in the account: the hypostasis of the light, the envoy from the light world. In the human world the developments and chains of events that characterize the pleromatic world are in fact repeated. A single entity of light, variously named, enters upon the scene of history, with a single task: to recover the spiritual substance dispersed in matter. For this it is ready to run risks and undertake adventures, from time to time assuming the guise of different characters, but never quite managing to conceal her own features successfully.

We shall deal more fully with the soteriological powers of this entity in chapter 7. We must now resume the story of Seth and his line. With Seth's birth the second period in sacred Gnostic history is concluded. The following period is dominated by a cataclysm: the flood.[42] It is the age of the Sethian patriarchs, a period of ignorance and terror. Indeed, the Demiurge, having established a plan with the Archons, first creates *heimarmenē*, blind fate and necessity, producer of all sin and injustice.[43] But that is not enough to exterminate the race of the elect. Warned by the light of the flood to which Ialdabaoth has recourse, Noah and the elect manage to survive, but not in the ark; covered by a luminous cloud, they take refuge in a preordained place.[44] The Demiurge then devises another plan:

> He sent his angels to the daughters of men, that they might take some of
> them for themselves and raise offspring for their enjoyment. And at first
> they did not succeed. When they had no success, they gathered together

again and they made a plan together. They created a despicable spirit, who resembles the Spirit who had descended, so as to pollute the souls through it. And the angels changed themselves in their likeness into the likeness of their [the daughters' of men] mates, filling them with the spirit of darkness, which they had mixed for them, and with evil. They brought gold and silver and a gift and copper and iron and metal and all kinds of things.[45]

The effects of this action are deception, sickness and death. In this way 'the whole creation became enslaved forever from the foundation of the world until now.'[46]

This last deception of the Demiurge concludes the third period of the history of Sethian salvation. The stage is now set for the entrance of the Saviour, the incarnation of Seth himself, who inaugurates and also concludes the fourth age, the present one, in which the potential Gnostic lives. But this will be dealt with in chapter 7.

The Epinoia of Light, Adam's teacher, his spiritual companion, the one sent from the kingdom of light to save the ancestors of the elect in emergency situations, is compared in the *Hypostasis of the Archons* with another typically Gnostic heroine, Norea.[47] She is the spiritual daughter of Eve, the female counterpart of Seth. She too appears at the crucial moments in this particular version of the history of Sethian salvation. Sent into the world after the birth of Seth, she helps men to multiply and to adorn themselves.[48] When the Archon tries to enslave the Sethian Noah and his children, she intervenes to free him, but the Archon seems to emerge victorious from this first stage of the battle.[49] She continues to struggle, without any apparent success, against the Archons who want to oppress her.[50] But when she calls for help, the angel Eleleth, in accordance with the divine plan and will, manages to bring her the knowledge of salvation.[51]

That this heroine is actually of divine origin is confirmed elsewhere by a short, but important, text (NHC IX.2), in which she invokes the celestial Triad to grant her revelations and promises of salvation.[52] The historical roots of this mythical figure, which are to be found in the legendary heritage of the Judaic Haggadah,[53] ill fit their Gnostic transformation, which tends to make her substantially a parallel to Sophia, in her double role of saviour of the elect line and also the one who is saved, female spiritual substance awaiting her consort, the Illuminator.[54]

The Illuminator is also the protagonist of that particular interpretation of the history of Sethian salvation, the *Apocalypse of Adam* (NHC V.5). A composite work, in which various traditions of Iranian and Jewish origin are gathered and distilled, it represents a typical document of Sethian Gnosis devoid of significant Christian influence.[55] Of the different apocalypses contained in the Nag Hammadi library, it is certainly the closest in form and content to the late-Judaic apocalyptic genre. It contains the revelations that Adam, at the age of 700, is supposed to have made to his son Seth.

Adam and Eve originally lived in a spiritual condition similar to that of the eternal angels, who were superior to their Creator by virtue of the Gnosis that Eve is supposed to have communicated to her companion.[56] But the Demiurge's wrath is aroused; he divides the androgynous aeon. The glory that was in their hearts abandons them, together with Gnosis. Having become mortal and forgetful of their true nature, they serve the Demiurge like slaves: 'We became darkened in our hearts. Now, I slept in the thought of my heart.'[57]

The following scenario is a familiar one: the moment in which the enemy seems to triumph is actually the moment in which his defeat begins to show. Three celestial creatures appear to Adam, to announce Gnosis to him and to reveal to him the destiny of the elect seed of Seth.[58] These are the revelations, containing the future history of the Sethians, that Adam undertakes to transmit as his testament to Seth before dying.[59]

The first revelation concerns the way in which the people of Gnosis were saved from the flood. While Noah (in this case, excluded from the Sethian race) saves himself and his family in the ark, great angels of light bring the elect to safety in a secure place where the spirit of life is.[60] In the sequel, the people of Gnosis return with Noah. But the Demiurge becomes angry with Noah, accusing him of having created a generation to ridicule his power. Noah reassures him, but the people of Gnosis will have to find themselves another safe place, a holy place where they will live for 600 years.[61]

The earth, meanwhile, has been divided among Noah's sons, who respectfully serve the Demiurge. But 400,000 descendants of Shem and Japheth join the people of Gnosis. Saklas (the 'fool'), the Demiurge, then tries a second time to exterminate the elect in an act of destruction reminiscent of that of Sodom and Gomorrah. Humankind will be saved this time from the fire, sulphur and asphalt by the intervention of Abrasax, Sablo and Gamaliel, who will descend on great clouds of light and carry them to higher aeons, where they 'will be like those angels, for they are not strangers to them, but they work in the imperishable seed.'[62] At this point, a third intervention is introduced, that of the Illuminator of Knowledge,[63] the soteric entity in this text. He 'will redeem their [the descendants' of Noah] souls from the day of death.

For the whole creation that came from the dead earth will be under the authority of death. But those who reflect upon the knowledge of the eternal God in their hearts will not perish.'[64] At the same time he works miracles and prodigies to defeat the Demiurge and his powers.

There follows a digression on the thirteen earthly kingdoms.[65] But only the generations without a king, the Gnostic descendants of Seth, will know the true Illuminator: 'God chose him from all the aeons. He caused a knowledge of the undefiled one of truth to come to be [in] him. [He *or* It] said, "[Out of] a foreign air, [from a] great aeon, the great illuminator came forth." '[66]

With the fourteenth kingdom the time of the End has arrived, coinciding with the repentance of sinners and the judgement of the responsible angels. Only the Gnostics will be saved.[67] The *Apocalypse* ends with these words: 'These are the revelations which Adam made known to Seth his son. And his son taught his seed about them. This is the hidden knowledge of Adam, which he gave to Seth, which is the holy baptism of those who know the eternal knowledge through those born of the word and the imperishable illuminators.'[68] It is worth pointing out that, behind the *mise en scène* of the various illuminators, the fundamental conception of the uniqueness of the illuminator principle is also at work here and is probably to be identified with Seth himself.[69]

THE ANTHROPOGONY OF THE VALENTINIAN SCHOOL

Valentinus too regards the human body as the home of demons:

> For many spirits dwell in it and do not permit it to be pure; each of them brings to fruition its own works, and they treat it abusively by means of unseemly desires. To me it seems that the heart suffers in much the same way as an inn: for it has holes and trenches dug in it and is often filled with filth by men who live there licentiously and have no regard for the place because it belongs to another.[70]

Only by the revelation of the Son can the human heart return to a state of purity and sanctification. In the individual the process experienced by Adam, the first man, is repeated. The demiurgic powers had created him according to their own image. But that creature said things above its own condition, because a spiritual force had been introduced into it, 'the seed of higher substance'. The fragment of Valentinus states, in fact, that 'Adam, formed in the name of Man, aroused the fear of pre-existent Man.'[71]

This detail is not unimportant. Here too the model for the creation of Adam is supplied by the higher Anthropos, the celestial archetype of terrestrial humankind. But it is no longer the image of the Anthropos that manifests itself to the Archons.

The anthropogonic account of the Ophites in Irenaeus helps towards an understanding of how the Valentinian expression 'in the name of Man' is to be interpreted. When Ialdabaoth, at the end of his demiurgic activity, exclaims, 'I am the Father and God, and there is no other beside me', Sophia the Mother, hearing him, cries out:

'Do not lie, Ialdabaoth, for there is above you the Father of all, the First Man, and the Man the Son of Man.' When all were thrown into confusion at the new voice and the unexpected proclamation, and were asking where the cry came from, to divert them and keep them with him, they say that Ialdabaoth said: 'Come, let us make a man in our image.' When the six powers heard – their mother gave them the thought of man, so that through him she might empty them of their original power – they came together and fashioned a man, of enormous length and breadth.[72]

The reaction of the Archons is merely to listen, for the theme of the appearing and the luminous image is missing. What now disturbs them is not seeing the forms, but hearing the name of the higher Anthropos. Thus, every possibility of anthropomorphism, which inevitably accompanies the theme of God–Anthropos is avoided. The Archons form psychic Adam. The purpose of this formation does not conceal within it (unlike the Sethian anthropogonic texts) any intention of attack or capture of the light that has appeared.[73]

The true, if not the only, protagonist has now become the Mother. The Demiurge appears, guided, so to speak, from within: as in a technically sophisticated robot, the 'program' of creation is put into him via the abstract symbol of the idea. Thus, the way is open for a still purer and more immaterial creation 'in the name of Man'.

Valentinus' disciples pushed to its limits this tendency to remove the inner mythical content from the anthropogonic account. In their attempt to arrive at a clear, unequivocal exegesis of the myth, they had to sacrifice to the clarity of the *logos* typical features of the Sethian anthropogonic accounts: the effective tonal quality of the chief characters, the correlative emotional dynamic, the dramatic vitality of the scene, the multiplicity of symbols. This is how Ptolemy presents the creation of man, in a precise but dry, pedantic fashion:

When [the Demiurge] had formed the world, he made the choice man, not out of this present dry land, but out of the invisible substance, the liquid and flowing part of matter, and into him he breathed the psychic man, and this is he who came into being 'after the image and likeness': 'after the image' means the material similar to God, but not of the same substance; 'after the likeness' is the psychic man, whose substance is also called 'spirit of life', deriving from spiritual emanation.[74]

That this is not simply a distorted view of the heresiological source is confirmed by a brief comparison with parallel passages of the *Tripartite Tractate*. The Logos–Sophia uses the Demiurge like a hand, to beautify and to make the things of the lower world ready.[75] The Demiurge pronounces the things, and they come into existence as images of spiritual beings.[76] The same procedure is repeated in the creation of man. The Demiurge is moved invisibly by the spiritual world, which in this way brings its plan to fulfilment.[77] 'Those of the right' and 'those of the left', the psychic and hylic elements, participate in the formation of man, while Adam's spiritual soul is added by the breath of the unwitting Demiurge.[78] The first man is therefore a mixed creation, a deposit of 'those of the right' and 'those of the left'. But at the same time, with the substance from which he derives his being, he possesses a spiritual reality.

7

Mysterium Coniunctionis: The Gnostic Saviour

In the *Gospel of Philip* the Lord invites the disciple to Gnosis with these words: 'Go into your chamber and shut the door behind you and pray to your Father who is in secret, the one who is within them all. But that which is within them all is the fullness. Beyond it there is nothing else within it.'[1] The fullness of Gnosis is, therefore, within reach of the Gnostic, provided that he is able to close the door behind himself, that is, to abstract himself from the senses, the preoccupations, the deceptive, illusory, daily battles, immersing himself in that inwardness in which the secret of his true nature and origin is hidden.

The *Book of Thomas the Contender* (NHC II.7),[2] a dialogue between the resurrected Jesus and Judas Thomas, contains an invitation from Jesus to Thomas[3] to Gnosis, which symbolizes the process whereby every Gnostic is to be illuminated:

> Examine yourself that you may understand who you are, in what way you exist, and how you will come to be. Since you are called my brother, it is not fitting that you be ignorant . . . you have already come to know, and you will be called the 'one who knows himself'. For he who has not known himself has known nothing. But he who has known himself has . . . already achieved knowledge about the Depth of the All.[4]

An interior process, Gnosis appears in these passages at the same time as a process of self-redemption. In a text transmitted by Hippolytus, the *Epistle to Theophrastus*, which he attributes to a certain Monoimus the Arab, a typical representative of the so-called triadic systems and a lover of arithmetical speculation, we read:

Cease to seek after God and creation and things like these, and seek after yourself of yourself and learn who it is who appropriates all things within you without exception and says, 'My God, my mind, my thought, my soul, my body'. And learn whence comes grief, and rejoicing and love and hatred, and waking without intention, and sleeping without intention, and anger without intention, and love without intention. If you consider these things carefully, you will find yourself within yourself . . . and will find the outcome of yourself.[5]

Monoimus could not have been clearer. Like the Saviour to Thomas, he recalls to the Gnostic that salvation depends on oneself. The same revelation is made to Zostrianos (in the text of that name) during his celestial voyage by Ephesek, a pleromatic entity who describes the confused situation and obscurity in which the Gnostic finds himself before interior illumination.[6] The true being of Zostrianos is, in fact, dispersed in the thousand streams of becoming: 'instead of becoming one, he assumes many forms once again.'[7] To turn to the existent means to seek things that do not exist in reality and to undergo a process of reification: 'When he falls down to these in thought and, being powerless, knows them in another way, unless he receives the light, he becomes a product of nature.'[8] In this way, though having in himself an eternal power, the Gnostic becomes a slave of the body: 'he is always bound with cruel and cutting chains, through every evil breath, until he acts again and approaches being in himself.'[9]

The soul of the Gnostic, who lives and suffers the pains and sufferings known to every soul, to every believer, seems therefore to possess a distinctive trait which lies in its potentiality to find in itself that power and those wings that will enable it to transcend the illusory passions of this world. Gnosis, cultivated therefore in its constituent soteriological potentiality, seems not to be unaware of the need for the redeemer figure of a Saviour.

Thus we come to perhaps the most difficult, delicate and complex problem in the entire Gnostic dossier: the nature, functions and origin of the Gnostic Saviour. That a Saviour figure appears in many texts (as we have mentioned already and shall see later) is not surprising. It is clear from the Valentinians that the figure has his origins in the Christian Saviour. But in the case of non-Christian or only superficially Christian texts, the question is a little more difficult.

The question is far from having found a clear, satisfactory answer.[10] If Gnosis is a form of saving knowledge, such as to render superfluous the figure of a Saviour, Gnostic knowledge can certainly appear as a variant, though perhaps the most radical and logical, of a cognitive ethos typical of Hellenistic thought, the most complete expression of its mystique of inwardness.[11]

The figure of a personal Saviour, which was introduced later, would therefore not belong to the original nucleus of the system and so ought not to obscure the original outlines of the structure.

This argument, put forward on several occasions, some years ago found a particularly effective formulation in A. Nygren's *Agape and Eros*.[12] The point of departure was a lively polemic against those tendencies of the history of religions that, at the beginning of the century, had interpreted Christian origins in the light of the religious traditions contemporary with and prior to them, immersing the specific features of the Gospel, by means of parallels that were too often mere guesswork or superficial, in the great magma of Hellenistic religions. Nygren attempted to recover the peculiar nature of the Christian message by means of the conceptual pair *erōs* and *agapē*, erotic and spiritual love. Only the second type of love was properly Christian, while the first revealed, in its most complete Platonic expression, the pagan conceptions of divine love. Gnostic soteriology was now characterized by *erōs*, not by *agapē*. It is true that for Gnostics Jesus Christ is the only Redeemer:

... and so they can lay claim to be reckoned as Christians. On the other hand, the Christian element would be overestimated, if the part played here by Christ the Saviour were supposed to indicate a Christian conception of salvation. The whole Gnostic doctrine is built upon the Eros scheme, and the thought of Christ is introduced without destroying this scheme. Salvation means nothing but the deliverance of the spirit from the toils of matter ... Power to ascend to the divine life exists already in the imprisoned human spirit; it only needs to be awakened and made more effective.[13]

Nygren has gone straight to the heart of the problem. Gnosis appears to him to be a kind of typically erotic knowledge, directed above, as it were from below, able to provide itself with the wings, the passion and force necessary to raise it up to the kingdom of the divine.

But who will reawaken and activate this potentiality? Here theological prejudice played a cruel trick on Nygren (and on many other interpreters). The primacy and uniqueness of the Christian Saviour did not allow contrasts or possible rivals. But do Gnostic texts really go in this direction?

As in many other histōriographical controversies, the problem of the Gnostic Saviour may well be a false problem. From a methodological point of view, it is above all a problem of definition. What exactly should we understand by the term 'saviour'? If this entity is defined in purely Christian terms, i.e. how God became incarnate to redeem mankind of its sins, one obtains a definition able to fit only into a Christian situation or one deeply influenced by Christianity. But this situation is too narrow for the historical reality under discussion. Indeed one cannot ignore the fact that, in the historical-religious context in which Gnosticism arose and developed, various *sōtēr*, or saviour, figures existed that were not assimilable to the Christian *sōtēr*. And non-Christian Gnosticism possessed its own soteric figures too.[14] To these we must now turn our attention, once again allowing the texts to speak for themselves.

It will be remembered that Ephesek had revealed to Zostrianos that he had to become Gnostic in order to free himself from the cruel bondage of evil, i.e. to reach genuine being by an inner process of his own. The invitation extended to Zostrianos must not, however, be considered in isolation: doesn't Zostrianos perhaps receive revelations coming from a higher being? Doesn't the rapport with Ephesek exemplify perhaps that between the Gnostic and his Revealer–Saviour? And indeed, Ephesek continues, recalling to Zostrianos the existence of powers responsible for saving the Gnostics:

> ... these same powers exist in the world. Within the Hidden Ones corresponding to each of the aeons stand glories, in order that he who is in [the world] might be safe beside them. The glories are perfect thoughts living with the powers; they do not perish because they are models of salvation by which each one is saved when he receives them. He receives a model and strength through the same (power), and with the glory as a helper he can thus pass out from the world.[15]

This is the hidden part of the Gnostic soteriological iceberg. The process of salvation, which is revealed in the very heart of the Gnostic through the acquisition of a knowledge that is certainly in itself salvific, is placed in being, if, and only if, a revealing, illuminating force intervenes from outside. For Gnosis is principally a cry from above, light from the light world of the Pleroma. By himself the Gnostic is incapable of salvation. Gnosis is revealed knowledge, divine *charis*, or love, charity, which springs from the compassionate heart of the Father. It therefore requires a Revealer, the Gnostic *sōtēr*.

All this will become clearer if we turn briefly to the existential situation of the Gnostic. By their anthropological constitution they are prisoners of demonic powers. Equally, one can say of their cosmic *Dasein*, or existence: cast down to live, not only in a body, but also in a cosmos dominated by hostile, clever forces continually seeking their destruction, how could they escape from this closed universe except through the intervention of an external power? The *Authentikos Logos* relates that the soul is food for malevolent, diabolical powers. How could it be freed from the net in which it is enmeshed unless the Father's pity intervened?[16] Using the image of spiritual matrimony, the *Exegesis of the Soul* (NHC II.6) recounts this particular myth. The soul repents of having prostituted itself to the powers and passions of this world:

> But since she is female, by herself she is powerless to beget a child. From heaven the Father sent her her man, who is her brother, the first-born. Then the bridegroom came down to the bride. She gave up her former prostitution and cleansed herself of the pollutions of the adulterers, and she was renewed so as to be a bride. She cleansed herself in the bridal chamber; she filled it with perfume; she sat in waiting for the true bridegroom.[17]

The descent of Nous Illuminator is the necessary counterpart of the ascent of the soul. The Gnostic concept of soteriology is the result of these two vectors and these two poles in continuous tension; of a will predisposed, longing for salvation, and of a soteriological function destined to realize it.

These two components make up Gnostic soteriology and at the same time enable it to remain distinct from contemporary ideas of salvation.[18] The movement from above, mythologically expressed in the theme of the call and the descent of a Revealer, helps to distinguish it from the typical features of Hellenistic soteriology, in which the gods did not intervene except at the request of humans:

> In his misfortune he sought gods who were able to bring him good fortune; no longer good fortune due to chance, but that which was acquired by personal merit. A man had to be able to follow the divine example, otherwise he would be excluded from salvation; he must have complete faith and trust in the deity who, in his turn, demanded service from a slave or soldier, certain ethical standards and, from the intellectual, the knowledge necessary to enter into closer contact.[19]

Even in a case like this, which may appear privileged and more spiritualized, the relations with the divine world did not tend for this reason to become personalized, or the content to change in substance. We have seen that the period was bursting with revelations. But these continue to develop in a quite earthly horizon, helping, as they do, towards the liberation from contingent evils and not from evil as such. And also in the case of a purer religiosity, such as that of the mysteries, the relations of the initiate with God 'do not differ in their nature from traditional relations. The gift of God is not God himself.'[20]

Even where pagan wisdom, as in Epictetus, seems to reach its most conscious, profound expressions in its submission to the divine, it is always a conception of salvation dominated not by a personal God, who is compassionate to humankind and willing to descend among them, but by an abstract, impersonal philosophical principle.[21] The God of the Gnostics is different from the God of Epictetus and Marcus Aurelius. And this difference is the reason for the divergent soteriological conceptions. Even in the Neoplatonic doctrines, which develop a concept of salvation as liberation from matter and ascent to the higher world through successive stages of psychological 'stripping', exemplified in the celestial journey of the soul, there remain essential differences.[22] For the Gnostic the ascent is made necessary by the fall into matter of the spiritual substance that now has to be recovered. The sending of a Revealer and Saviour is necessary for this.

Moreover, the predisposition of the spiritual substance to be saved[23] and its natural affinity with the substance of the Saviour constitute as many differences between Gnostic and Christian soteriology. The Gnostic Saviour does not come to reconcile humankind with God, but to reunite the Gnostic with himself. He does not come to pardon a sin that the Gnostic cannot have committed, but to rectify a situation of ignorance and deficiency and to re-establish the original plenitude. The Gnostic Saviour comes to save himself.[24]

In the opening scenes of *Pistis Sophia* the Apostles surrounding Jesus find themselves in a special relationship with him. Jesus has come to save them. But how? And why? The reply is given by Jesus himself: because they are originally part of his own strength. This is what the Gnostic Saviour reveals to the astonished disciples, after ascending to heaven to put on the garment of light that contains all the mysteries of the Supreme Being, the Ineffable One, a garment he had been obliged to abandon in order to become incarnate in the earthly Jesus.[25] The Revealer had in fact from the beginning chosen the Apostles as assistants in his mission of salvation, in accordance with the will of the First Mystery.[26] Thus, when he had come down into the world, he had brought with him twelve forces (which come from the twelve pleromatic saviours) and introduced them into the bodies of the earthly mothers of the Apostles:

These forces were given to you before all the world, because it is you who will save the world and so that you may be able to bear the threat of the archons of the world and the sufferings of the world and its dangers and persecutions that the archons above will bring upon you . . . All men

who are in the world have received souls from the strength of the archons
of the aeons, but the strength which is in you comes from me.[27]

Enlightening his disciples and forming in them the pneumatic reality
that represents the Man of Light,[28] the Gnostic Saviour of the *Pistis
Sophia* does no more than recover that part of himself, his spiritual
substance, that had fallen prisoner to the darkness.[29]

If this example helps to clarify the nature of Gnostic soteriology, it
still leaves unsolved the question of the relationship between the Gnostic
sōtēr and his Christian counterpart. To find an answer to this problem,
we must now turn to the *Poimandres*, the first treatise in the Hermetic
corpus, a typical example of pagan Gnosis devoid of Christian influence,
with which the *Corpus Hermeticum* opens.

THE CASE OF POIMANDRES

We have already mentioned the typically Gnostic structure of thought
that underlies the opening vision. The revealer, Poimandres, is the
general and archetypal Nous, to whom Hermes' *nous* is only a particular
manifestation. What Hermes sees in his mind is therefore a reality that
he possesses potentially within himself, the world of divine powers that
now appears to him unfolded in all its richness. This vision is the source
of a truly mythical account, as evocative as it is original.

The first God, Nous or Intellect, is androgynous. Light and Life, male
function and female substance, coexist in him. His goodness itself makes
him generate a second God, a most beautiful Anthropos, with whom
he falls in love and to whom he entrusts all his creatures.[30] This is the
preface to the later anthropological drama. As to cosmology, the use of
certain creation themes[31] conceals typically Gnostic elements. The ideal
world of the divine powers, analogous in this respect to the world of
Platonic ideas, though differing from it in the dynamic character of the
powers that form it, will supply the exemplar of the cosmos. Matter
originates in an internal process of schism.[32] A gloomy, terrifying
darkness, like a serpent, is formed and occupies the lower regions. It is
primordial matter; it is damp, hurled about in an unspeakable way,
exhales smoke and utters inarticulate cries; it is proof of the irrationality
of the *physis*, or the natural, awaiting the *logos*, to make order, and
the intervention of a demiurge.[33] And in fact the cosmogonic process is
entrusted to two divine hypostases: the Logos, representing and synthesizing the rationality of the divine plan, and the Demiurge, the instrument
entrusted with its fulfilment.

As heir to this Platonic tradition, the Hermetic Demiurge is not burdened with the same negative traits as his Gnostic counterpart. First, he forms the seven governors, the seven planetary spheres, ruled by *heimarmenē*, or fate. Set in motion, these spheres in their turn are responsible for later generations in the lower elements: irrational animals, birds, fish, wild and domestic beasts.[34] Thus the kingdom is ready to receive its ruler: the man.

The creation of the man is the outcome of the fall of Anthropos from the celestial spheres into the seductive, but mortal, embraces of *Physis*, lower Nature. But why does he abandon the kingdom of light? The answer to this basic question is both simple and complex: because this was his role in the divine plan and because he could not help falling. Like the heroes in magical fables, the Hermetic Anthropos has a bundle of obligations written into his script: leaving the family home, meeting the adversary, seduction and oblivion. Only when all is lost, when the hero appears to have reached the depth of despair, can the machine that will save him be set in motion.

In the *Poimandres*, characteristically, what sets off the process of the fall of Anthropos is his desire to imitate the Demiurge. Thus from the outset his natural propensity towards the cosmic sphere is clear. When he arrives among the seven governors, they fall in love with him and each one gives him part of his own state. The planetary qualities he has assumed meanwhile have the inevitable effect of making his descent possible.[35] Cosmogonic *erōs*, which animates him, is at this point fatal to him. He then

> leant out across the celestial spheres, after having pierced the outer covering that envelops them and showed lower nature the beautiful form of the god. When nature saw the Man, who had in himself the beauty that can never satisfy and all the active force of the ministers of the heavens, together with the divine form, she smiled with love, because she had discerned in the water the form of the marvellous beauty of Man and the shadow of it on earth. Man, in his turn, having seen this form like himself, present in nature and reflected in the water, fell in love with it and wanted to live there. In the same moment that he wanted something, it happened. He descended thus to live in the form without reason. Nature, having welcomed the loved one, enveloped him completely and they became one, for they burned with love for each other.[36]

Eros, the hidden protagonist of the story, thus transformed himself imperceptibly from the positive strength that had bound the Father to the Anthropos, through a series of falls, into the potentially negative element that binds immortal Anthropos to Nature. Rather, the *erōs* that pushes Anthropos down seems to be a narcissistic *erōs*. And, in fact, the seduction scene that takes place before our eyes conceals various motifs that are interwoven to the extent that they merge into the symbolic multiplicity and the pregnancy of mythical images.[37] Man shows to the lower powers his image reflected in the waters; it is the theme, already known to us, of an epiphany of an image of the Anthropos. Even now it performs an anthropogonic function; the outcome of this epiphany will, in fact, be union with Nature and the generation of seven primordial androgynes, founders of the human race. After them that fundamental unity of androgyny will be broken to which from now on man will have to aspire to return.

Enter the narcissistic motif. Anthropos seems to want to unite with himself: or rather, to the female part of himself that he sees projected in the waters, a symbol of the female generative capacity. He thus becomes present and absent in Nature; present, because part of him is now prisoner here; but absent, in that his divine reality is not compromised by it. On the other hand, in this strange game of mirrors, Nature receives only the reflected forms of Man. And their embrace seems to recall the embrace of Amor and Psyche, who were allowed to unite, but only on condition that Psyche did not see directly the radiant beauty of her lover, for she was unable to cope with it. This is the contradictory situation of humanity after the Fall. Though humans are immortal and have dominion over everything, they suffer from the mortal condition, subject as they are to destiny. Their intellect, which comes from the Light of the Father, is male; their psyche, which comes from Life, is female; their body, which is a product of Nature, is mortal.[38]

In this tripartite anthropology the soul functions as the seat of free will. On the one hand are humans, capable of recognizing themselves and rediscovering in themselves the presence of *nous*, an intellect of divine origin, which everybody, according to a line of thought typical of the Greek philosophical tradition, is potentially capable of possessing. On the other hand, those who have preferred the body instead, the product of love's error; they are destined to remain in the darkness, 'wandering and suffering in their senses what is associated with death'.[39]

But how is it possible to recognize in oneself the presence of *nous*, the source of knowledge? The reply to this question contains the solution to the problem that concerns us: is there a Saviour figure in the *Poimandres* and what is his nature? At first the reply appears too obvious. Who is Poimandres if not the very intellect of Hermes caught in its archetypal nature? What is the vision of Hermes if not the projection onto the auxiliary screen of myth of a process of inner excavation, in which the intellect of the individual succeeds in recognizing that it belongs to a more general reality, the universal and archetypal Intellect? Accordingly, is not the movement of Gnosis a mechanism of inner self-recognition, in which the figure of Poimandres is a narrative copy and not a concrete soteriological reality? This reasoning, however, is only partly convincing.

The basic revelation received by Hermes is not only a subjective experience, as might appear to a modern psychological interpretation. The meeting with the self is always, for the ancient Gnostic, a meeting with the Other Than Me. If it is true that the general Intellect comprises the particular intellects, the opposite is not true. Only by encountering a reality that transcends them (as they believe, and find by experiment) are the Gnostics in turn able to transcend this world of contingency, starting with the particularity and individuality of their intellect. Therefore Poimandres appears to Hermes to be, and really is, a soteric figure.

He is a special type of *sōtēr*. We are certainly not dealing with a historical person seen in the richness of his concrete humanity. Poimandres' soteric virtues are quite different from those of the Christian Saviour. But is it necessary to define the Saviour figure only in terms of Christianity?

The case of the *Poimandres* teaches us that, in a religion of salvation such as Gnosis, the figure of the Saviour can also be presented in more or less abstract forms, figures and functions that correspond better to requirements that may be purely intellectual, but are not without their mythical concreteness or ability to affect the life of the individual Gnostic. And it is with this hypothesis that we can now try to broach the intricate question of the Saviour in the mythical accounts of the Sethians.

SETH THE SAVIOUR

The first chapters of the book of Genesis in which Seth is mentioned come from two sources, according to modern criticism: P (Priestly Codex) and J (Jahweh Codex).[40] P comprises Gen. 1:1–2: 4a, which deals with the creation of heaven and earth in six days; chapter 5 contains the genealogy of Seth from Adam, who fathered a son in his image and likeness after 130 years, to the birth of Shem, Ham and Japheth, the sons of Noah; finally, chapter 6:9ff. tells the story of Noah the Just. P does not mention Cain and Abel, but speaks instead of Seth as the only son of Adam, whose descendants end with Noah and his sons. J comprises chapter 2:4b–4:26: it is the story of Adam's life in Paradise, the origin of Eve, the Fall, the expulsion from Paradise, the birth of Cain and Abel and the death of Abel. Gen. 4:25 adds that God then gave Adam a new seed with the birth of Seth. Both traditions seem to attribute an important role to Seth. And this must also have been true of the ancients, who knew nothing of modern Biblical criticism.

There are various indications of the privileged position that Seth must have occupied in the theological reflections and speculations of certain groups of so-called inter-testamental Judaism, both Palestinian and of the Diaspora.[41] The origins of the Gnostic Seth are to be found in this world.[42] The importance of this figure in the present line of enquiry obliges us to consider one or two more points.

It is clear from the anthropogonic accounts that ancient interpreters too had some difficulty with the discrepancies and contrasts in the text of Genesis, which modern Biblical criticism has assigned to two sources. There are similar difficulties also about the interpretation of Adam's descendants. We must now consider both these and the special nature of Seth.

While the Greek translation of the Septuagint rendered the original text literally with *sperma heteron* (other seed), certain *Targumim* contrast the genealogies of Cain (Gen. 4:17–24) and of Seth (Gen. 5:6–32). This creates significant differences of interpretation. For example, *Targum Jonathan* 5.1–3 does not consider Cain to be a son of Adam and seems to regard the genealogy of Seth as the only true one. This interpretation seems to be confirmed further in some passages of *Genesis Rabbah*, according to which Cain and Abel were really the sons of the Devil and Seth was the only true son of Adam.[45] In the *Pirkē of Rabbi Eliezeer* it is further maintained that Samael was joined to Eve, who then conceived. Cain, the fruit of this marriage, was the father of a wicked race.[46] Rabbi Simeon says that 'from Seth were born and descended all the generations of the just. From Cain were born and descended all the generations of the wicked.'[47] There seems to be a similar conception underlying 1 Enoch 85–90. It is the description of a vision in which Enoch sees the beginning of history, from the time of the creation of the world to the coming of the Messiah. In the symbolism typical of the apocalyptic genre, animals represent humans. In the antediluvian period, which concerns us here, Seth is described as a white bull and the people of Israel as nation of white bulls, and the Messiah too is a white bull. But the rest of humanity is symbolically represented as a collection of black oxen,[48] which 'suggests that Seth is regarded as the Father of the chosen race and, ultimately, of the Messiah.'[49]

Elsewhere Seth is also considered to have had special knowledge of the events preceding the expulsion of Adam from Paradise. This is what the *Books of Adam and Eve* tell us. It must, however, be remembered that, according to the texts, this knowledge was not transmitted to Seth's generation.[50]

It is not surprising that echoes of these traditions recur in a typical representative of Hellenistic Judaism such as Philo of Alexandria. Several times in *De posteritate Caini* he touches upon the nature of Seth and the generation that follows him. From Cain only the wicked could have descended. Therefore (a typical allegorical interpretation) all lovers of virtue are descendants of Seth.[51] Indeed, he is the 'seed of human virtue', sown by God.[52] Thus, the descendants of Seth are not confined merely to the antediluvian, but in fact include the whole of humanity. This interpretation seems in some way to anticipate, even if on a purely ethical level, the divisions of caste within humanity favoured by the Gnostics.

The *Apocalypse of Adam* is a good example of how Gnostic reflections on Seth are based on traditions like those of so much Jewish apocryphal literature, in which Seth appears as the repository (but not yet the revealer) of esoteric knowledge.

But in the *Apocryphon of John* hierarchical promotion has already taken place. It will be recalled that Christ created four luminaries. Adamas, prototype of Adam, is placed in the first; Seth in the second; his descendants in the third. Only in the *Gospel of the Egyptians*, however, does Seth rise to a role of the first rank and is clearly identified with the Saviour. This text, represented in the Nag Hammadi collection by two versions,[53] is a typical mythological treatise in which, after the description of the pleromatic world, the history of the salvation of a Sethian group is outlined. It was the divine Seth himself who composed this esoteric work:

> The great Seth wrote this book with letters in one hundred and thirty years. He placed it in the mountain that is called Charaxio, in order that, at the end of the times and eras, by the will of the divine Autogenes and the whole pleroma, through the gift of the untraceable, unthinkable, fatherly love, it may come forth and reveal this incorruptible holy race of the great savior, and those who dwell with them in love, and the great invisible eternal Spirit and his only begotten Son, and the eternal light and his great, incorruptible consort, and the incorruptible Sophia and the Barbelon and the whole pleroma in eternity. Amen.[54]

The place occupied by Seth in the pleromatic hierarchy of the text is not unlike that assigned to him in the *Apocryphon of John*. What the text specifies and emphasizes is his salvific role. After the initial triad of the Father, Mother/Barbelo, Son (each of whom has an ogdoad of powers, all of them surrounded by Domedon Doxomedon, an aeon that envelops the world of light) comes from Christ, the thrice male; then the male virgin, Youel, and the child Esephech. Finally, the Logos, the son of the great Christ, appears. He generates Mirotheo, who in his turn produces Adamas of Light: 'The incorruptible man Adamas asked for them a son out of himself, in order that he (the son) may become father of the immovable, incorruptible race.'[55] Then Manifestation appears, the aeon whose job it is to generate the four luminaries Harmozel, Oroiael, Davithe, Eleleth and the 'great incorruptible Seth, the son of Adamas, the incorruptible man'.[56]

Among the events that will mark the stages of the history of the salvation of the group, the text specifies those events that pose a threat to the seed of Seth. A flood will be sent

> for the consummation of the aeon. But it will be sent into the world because of this race. A conflagration will come upon the earth. And grace will be with those who belong to the race through the prophets and the guardians who guard the life of the race. Because of this race famines will occur and plagues. But these things will happen because of the great, incorruptible race. Because of this race temptations will come, a falsehood of false prophets.[57]

The great Seth, aware of these dangers to his seed, calls upon the higher powers to give him guardians to protect the ancestry of the elect. Four hundred angels are sent, with the great Seth himself at their head. He endures the three *parousiae*, or presences (flood, conflagration and judgement of the Archons) 'to save her [the race] who went astray, through the reconciliation of the world and the baptism through a Logos-begotten body which the great Seth prepared for himself, secretly through the virgin.'[58] Seth, thus represented as the living Jesus, is ready for the Passion. By the crucifixion of Jesus he defeats the archontic powers of the thirteen aeons and equips his followers with an invincible Gnosis.

The figure of the Saviour here is clearly influenced by Christian soteriology, but at the same time the idea that Jesus could be only one of the manifestations of Seth confirms the statements, however confused, recorded by the heresiologists.[59] The idea of a saving power of pleromatic origin, which assumes various forms throughout the history of salvation, is not specifically Christian.[60] On the contrary, it is traceable in other Sethian texts, thus confirming a soteric dynamism written into the very logic of the system and independent of possible Christian influence.

An example of this is found in the *Apocryphon of John*. The real protagonist of the Genesis story is substantially the Epinoia of Light.

Both Adam and the Archons appear as puppets whose strings are manipulated by this heavenly messenger of the Father's mercy. She is Epinoia, an intellectual hypostasis responsible for carrying out the project conceived by the Father in his *pronoia*, or forethought, before all time and applying it to humankind. Is it any wonder that some Gnostics once again invested with divinity the mental functions and faculties through which the process of Gnosis is realized and which they conceive as the reflection in the human mind of all that happened at that time in the mind of God? And more: the Epinoia in our text moves simultaneously on two levels: as *salvator*, or Saviour, and as *salvanda*, or the one to be saved. As *salvator* she witnesses the whole of creation. But whom else does she awaken to Gnosis if not herself? The Tree of Knowledge, in fact, is Epinoia herself. Eating of it, Adam learns of his superiority to the Demiurge. Thus, Epinoia has a countermove to every attack made by the Archons on the First Formed and the spiritual substance in him. Epinoia is a quick-change artist, able to assume the most diverse roles, from eagle to Eve. She also conceals herself in Adam as his spiritual substance in its female dimension of life.

This last characteristic confirms her androgynous nature. As *salvanda*, as the spiritual dimension and substance present in man, she is passive in the female sense, the bride awaiting the arrival of her spiritual bridegroom, that is, her male dimension responsible in his illuminating function for the recovery of the scattered spiritual substance.

The treatise, in its longer recension, concludes deliberately with a doxology on Epinoia, which deserves to be quoted: 'I, therefore, the perfect Pronoia of the all, changed myself into my seed, for I existed first, going on every road. For I am the richness of the light; I am the remembrance of the pleroma.'[61] She therefore came down to the kingdom of darkness, the prison of the Archons, which ultimately coincides with the body. Reawakening the First Man, she has fulfilled the original revelation, of which those that follow are only repetitions scattered in time:

And I said, 'He who hears, let him get up from the deep sleep.' And he wept and shed tears. Bitter tears he wiped from himself and he said, 'Who is it that calls my name, and from where has this hope come to me, while I am in the chains of the prison?' And I said, 'I am the Pronoia of the pure light; I am the thinking of the virginal Spirit, he who raised you up to the honored place. Arise and remember that it is you who hearkened, and follow your root, which is I, the merciful one, and guard yourself against the angels of poverty and the demons of chaos and all those who ensnare you, and beware of the deep sleep and the enclosure of the inside of Hades.'[62]

We could give more examples, but the substance would be the same. In the Sethian texts there are different figures of the Revealer–Saviour called upon to perform an identical function: to illuminate that part of the spiritual substance fallen into the world of darkness. In the *Hypostasis of the Archons* the great angel of light, Eleleth, introduces himself to Norea with these words: 'I . . . am Eleleth, sagacity, the Great Angel who stands in the presence of the Holy Spirit. I have been sent to speak with you and save you from the grasp of the Lawless. And I shall teach you about your Root.'[63] Equally, Zostrianos is illuminated by the messenger of the Knowledge of Eternal Light, which reminds him of his origin as father of the elect race and invites him to make the celestial journey.[64]

This idea finds its most evocative expression in one of the most interesting of the Coptic texts, the *Trimorphic Protennoia* (NHC XIII.1).[65] The Protennoia is none other than that primordial thought, the first Ennoia, as a reflection of which the Father thought and conceived his plan. Thus she is invisible and visible at the same time: invisible, because concealed in the thought of the Invisible; visible, because, as the spiritual breath that moves and activates every creature, she represents the most complete manifestation of the Father:

> I am the life of my Epinoia that dwells within every power and every eternal movement and (in) invisible Lights and within the Archons and Angels and Demons and every soul dwelling in [Tartaros] and (in) every material soul. I dwell in those who come to be. I move in everyone and I delve into them all. I walk uprightly, and those who sleep I [awaken]. And I am the sight of those who dwell in sleep . . . Within my Thought, it is I who am laden with the Voice. It is through me that knowledge comes forth. [I] exist in the ineffable and unknowable ones. I am perception and knowledge, uttering a Voice by means of Thought. [I] am the real Voice. I cry out in everyone, and they know that a seed dwells within [me]. I am the Thought of the Father and through me proceeded [the] Voice, that is, the knowledge of the everlasting things. I exist as Thought for the [All]. I am joined to the unknowable and intangible Thought. (It was) I (who) revealed myself within all those who know me, for I am the one joined with everyone within the hidden Thought and in an exalted Voice.[66]

The Protennoia descends moreover into 'the world of mortals for the sake of my portion that was in that place'[67] and completes the work of salvation:

I shall tell you an ineffable and indivulgeable mystery from my Forethought: Every bond I loosed from you, and the chains of the Demons of the underworld I broke, these things which are bound on my members as restraints. And the high walls of darkness I overthrew, and the secure gates of those pitiless ones I broke, and I smashed their bars. And (as for) the evil Force and the one who beats you, and the one who hinders you, and the Tyrant, and the Adversary, and the one who is King, and the real Enemy, indeed all these I explained to those who are mine, who are the Sons of the Light, in order that they might nullify them all and be saved from all those bonds and enter into the place where they were at first.

I am the first one who descended on account of my portion which is left behind, that is, the Spirit that (now) dwells in the Soul, but which originated from the Water of Life. And out of the immersion of the mysteries I spoke, I together with the Archons and Authorities. For I went down below their language and I spoke my mysteries to my own – a hidden mystery – and the bonds and eternal oblivion were nullified. And I bore fruit in them, that is, the Thought of the unchanging Aeon, and my house, and their [Father].[68]

The various metamorphoses of the Protennoia also end in the meeting with the earthly Jesus, whom she impersonates, freeing him from the accursed cross and re-establishing him in the Father's mansion.[69] As in other Sethian texts, this trespassing into the territory of Christian soteriology is deceptive. Jesus is only one of many manifestations of a revealing power, an illuminating *dynamis*, a soteric entity whose names can change, whose epiphanies can vary, but whose substantial reality remains the same in its structure. This structure is not Christian, because its base is a God whose female dimension and spiritual substance (scattered through the darkness) are waiting to be impregnated, enlightened, regenerated by a saving male power. By uniting with his power, the female dimension will be able to recover its own identity.

THE VALENTINIAN JESUS

The Sethian myths, then, reveal soteric functions and entities that arise independently of any Christian influence and are embedded in the very logic of a system that has arisen and established itself outside Christianity. If there has been Christian influence, the meeting with the figure of the Christian Saviour seems to have provided an opportunity to add one more name to the list of soteric manifestations. Thus, the celestial Christ, his pleromatic prototype, has been superimposed on the earthly Jesus. Only in some cases has the influence been more profound and produced effects that betray a major eschatological tension,[70] a deepening of the Saviour figure whose relations with the disciples acquire more purely personal value.[71]

The impression left by the Sethian texts is therefore one of radically dualistic soteriology. Only the unwavering race,[72] the race that knows no king,[73] the seed of Seth[74] has the promise of salvation from the beginning. On the other hand, there is the anonymity of the psychics and the hylics, the *massa perditionis*, or doomed mass, which has no chance of escape. The intervention of different soteric figures has a unique function in this context: to save the seed of the elect, the spiritual descendants of Seth, from the irrevocable condemnation awaiting the Demiurge and his creatures.

The encounter with the Christian Saviour, however, has profoundly influenced the soteriology of other Gnostic groups: in particular, the Valentinians. We learn from Hippolytus that a vision of the Logos Christ is supposed to be fundamental to the teachings of the group's founder, Valentinus.[75] Hippolytus also reports a famous Valentinian psalm: 'Harvest.[76] I see that everything is suspended for the spirit. I observe that everything is transported through the spirit. Flesh is suspended from the soul. The soul is transported by air. The air is suspended from the ether. Fruits come forth from the abyss. An infant comes forth from the uterus.'[77]

This reverse chain of being, against a typically Stoic background,[78] imagines the various elements of the sublunar world ('flesh', i.e. hylic elements) and the Hebdomad ('soul', i.e. the psychic element, 'air', i.e. the spiritual element outside the Pleroma, from which it is separated by the limit, which is ether) chained to each other by the *pneuma* and dependent on the pleromatic world. The fruits coming from the Abyss and its matrix are none other than the Saviour, the perfect fruit of the Pleroma, the *nēpios*, or infant, who spoke to Valentinus in his fundamental visionary experience.

The figure of Jesus appears from time to time in the few extant Valentinian fragments.[79] But how very important he was in Valentinian thought can be seen clearly in the Christological speculations of his disciples.[80]

Let us consider the structure of the Valentinian Pleroma. It is pervaded by a key notion. The thirty aeons represent none other than the complex personality of the Son in his articulations: the intellectual as Nous, the logical as Logos, the anthropological as Anthropos. A manifestation of the unknown, infinite, simple, formless Father, the Son, is distinguished from him by his character of 'person'. The aeons, psychologically distinct and hierarchically ordered, reveal the real wealth of his perfections.

Their development, according to a rigorous order in rank, reveals from the start the paradigmatic nature of the life of the higher Christ, which will be made manifest in the life of the earthly Jesus.

The pre-existent Christ is the nerve centre, the heart of the secret life of Valentinian Christology. It is guided by a basic idea, which must always be taken into account if one is to pinpoint its most important difference (beyond or beneath the countless analogies and various points of contact) from the Christological speculations of the second-century church Fathers: the earthly life of Jesus is a visible manifestation of a *mysterium magnum*, or great mystery, the clues to which are hidden in the pleromatic myth. But there is also a fundamental difference with regard to the ideas of salvation examined above. Valentinian Christology, with its theological issues and psychological acuteness, is the product of mature reflection, guaranteed by a brilliance in the sphere of Biblical exegesis unparalleled in the second century. His is the Jesus of the Gospels, the Jesus already foretold to some extent by the Old Testament.[81]

This interpretation naturally presupposes that for the Valentinians the Old Testament does not have to be rejected as the work of a blind, malevolent Demiurge, even if, unlike that of other Gnostics, their view of Holy Writ does not extend to an altogether positive evaluation of it.[82] In a letter to Flora, a Gnostic follower, Ptolemy speculates:[83] Who is the author of the Law? The Supreme God, as some Christians would have it, or the Devil? Neither, he replies. To prove this he adduces, as is typical of his exegesis as that of a Christian Gnostic, 'our Saviour's words, which alone permit us to approach without error the knowledge of things'.[84] If we leave the parts attributable to Moses and human legislation, the author of the Law is the Demiurge, the just God, who has given us a Law divided into three parts:

> the pure legislation which is not mixed with evil, which is therefore properly called 'law', which the Saviour came not to destroy but to fulfil [Matt. 5:17] . . . the law which is intertwined with baseness and injustice, which the Saviour destroyed because it was not consonant with his nature. The third division is that law which is exemplary and symbolic, that which is ordained according to the image of the spiritual and transcendent things. This the Saviour changed from being perceptible (to the senses) and phenomenal into the spiritual and invisible.[85]

In the perspective of the Valentinian history of salvation, the phase of the Old Testament dispensation represents the psychic moment in which the plan of salvation is still transmitted to humanity indirectly, through images and symbols, a phase that will be replaced by the coming of Jesus which will institute the beginning of the pneumatic dispensation. But actually in the Old Testament one can already find hints and foreshadowings of the coming of the Saviour. The Jesus of the New Testament, however, is not simply one of the many manifestations of impersonal pleromatic entities, but the only true definitive Saviour. Only with him does the pneumatic dispensation begin.

On this point the Valentinians were certainly not far from contemporary positions held in the True Church. The New Testament offered them the framework of the principal external and historical events in the life of Jesus within which to assemble Christological reflections, even if, as we have seen, the premises from which they started and the consequences of their exegesis were different from those of the Fathers.

Only Christ, the Son of God, appeared in their eyes to be capable of liberating humanity and revealing Gnosis to them. This was the task preordained for him by the Father. It was also a mission beyond the competence of Sophia. Matter, however spiritual, being typically female and therefore passive, was quite unable to perform the active, formative, dynamic role of the Saviour. As the moon is confined to receiving the sun's rays, Sophia Achamoth had received in her encounter with the Saviour-Sun his rays of light, the seeds of light that he had transmitted to her. As for the satellite angels accompanying him, like the rays of the sun, they are far from representing individuals or self-sufficient entities, but they symbolize the dynamic richness of Jesus. They contain within themselves the multiple celestial male images with which the female spiritual substance, disseminated within Gnostics, was invited to reunite, following the example of Sophia, in order to reconstitute the original androgynous unity.[86]

The Son therefore descends into the world to save the Church of the Spiritual ones. He comes to struggle against the powers of evil,[87] to correct a situation of fundamental disorder,[88] to triumph once and for all over destiny. Indeed, *heimarmenē*, or fate, rules over humankind:

> [It] is the meeting of many, opposing powers. These are invisible and do not appear; they regulate the course of the stars and govern through them ... through the fixed stars and the planets the invisible powers, which are transported on them, administer and survey births ... Every being is born at a precise moment of its own through these powers, since the dominant element fulfils the conditions of nature either at the beginning or within sight of the end.[89]

Theodotus, a Valentinian whose teachings have been preserved by Clement of Alexandria in his *Excerpts from Theodotus*, does not diverge in his astrological beliefs from common opinion: the stars regulate human life through the coming together of occult powers. But he is not a fatalist. In fact 'the Lord offers us peace and frees us from such strife and conflict between the powers. . . .For this the Lord came down, to bring the peace of heaven to those on earth.'[90]

The first definitive defeat of the powers of destiny thus coincides with the descent of the Saviour. The theme of the descent through the seven heavens was very widespread in contemporary mythology and philosophy.[91] The Valentinians brought something new to it: he who arrived, descending through the seven heavens, was the Saviour of the world. The theme also helped, from the Valentinian point of view, to underline the complex nature of the Saviour. To come down through the various spheres necessarily involved (according to the pagan model of the descent of the soul, of which we have already seen clear traces in the psychology of the *Poimandres*) the assimilation of the powers and qualities symbolized by the various planets, whose nature he assumed. In the case of the Gnostic Jesus, this dynamic meant that he, passing through the Ogdoad (the spiritual world of Sophia Achamoth), the Hebdomad (the psychic world of the Demiurge and his planets) and the sublunar zone (corresponding to the kingdom of matter), took upon himself the elements that were supposed to make up his body.

'Totum redemptum quod assumptum' (all that is assumed is redeemed). This golden rule of Christian soteriology applied also to Valentinian soteriology. But with a fundamental difference. In his journey to the world Jesus became a perfect microcosm, encapsulating in hierarchic order the three elements that are mingled and confused in the world. He came to save them, indeed to separate them, eliminating the confusion and medley, in order to re-establish every element in the place assigned to it by the laws of nature.[92] The *mysterium coniunctionis*, or mystery of union, that was thus celebrated in the person of the Saviour did not, however, prejudice his unity. It was a unique and identical Saviour who, conceived in the bosom of the Father as the Only Begotten, sent forth as the First Begotten of creation, took it upon himself to be born of Mary and become man. There is thus a return to the triadic rhythm popular in Gnostic thought. The Saviour, one person in three distinct forms, possesses both in his cosmic dimension and in his anthropological constitution a triple nature: pneumatic, psychic and hylic.

But, it might be asked, what relations could there ever have been between the Saviour and matter? In reality, the various directions of the Valentinian school, though diverging on many individual points, were agreed in maintaining that the Saviour had assumed a body able to render him visible, like earthly beings. But there was still the question of what particular kind of body. Some thought that the body of Jesus was psychic in nature. Thus Ptolemy: 'For the fulfilment [of the dispensation] he assumed a body that is psychic in substance, but made with ineffable skill so as to be visible, perceptible and capable of suffering. He assumed nothing hylic, however, for matter cannot receive salvation.'[93] But others who belonged to the oriental branch of the school (according to Hippolytus) considered that Christ's body was purely spiritual:[94] a further echo of the potential devaluation of the psychic element, which is, however, a positive factor in the reflections of thinkers of the western branch.

At the end of his descent from the heavens, the Saviour was ready to be born of Mary. In some sense, he became incarnate. But behind the term 'flesh', as is true of other terms the Gnostics shared with the True Church, there are profoundly different conceptions. In the Valentinian perspective the incarnation was not the goal, the culmination of a mysterious divine process, but a part (and not even the most important part) in the global mystery of the assumption, distinction and conservation of substance and nature. So when the Gnostics spoke of Christ's *sarx*, or flesh, they simply meant his becoming human and making himself a visible man. This process was not, however, an end in itself. In the Valentinian dispensation of salvation it was rigidly and hierarchically subordinate to the two more important moments of the spiritualization of the Saviour – that is, of the assumption of spiritual substance; and of his animation – that is, of the appropriation of the soul or rational psyche.

In this way the Christian conception of the incarnation was finally overturned. The end became the means of a more complex spiritual dispensation. 'And the Word was made flesh' of John 1:14 did not mean of course that Jesus was also made of a body and will of flesh, but more simply that he assumed the visible body necessary for the earthly phase of the saving dispensation of the Logos. From the Gnostic point of view then, the problem of the incarnation was not posed as a mystery of the personal communion of the Logos with human nature. Before the virginal conception, which takes place in Mary's womb, the Logos was already united personally with psychic and spiritual substances, at the same time making itself spiritual and psychic man.[95]

The crucial passage in Luke 1:35, in which the angel of the Lord, announcing the birth of a son to Mary, adds, 'The Holy Spirit will come upon you and the power of the Most High will overshadow you', merely confirmed this interpretation. The Most High was none other than the God of the Old Testament, the Demiurge; he provided the Saviour with the psychic dimension, while the intervention of the Holy Spirit guaranteed him the assumption of the pneumatic nature.[96]

Thus the curtain could be raised on what to the Gnostic appeared not the first, but the last, act of a cosmic drama: the assumption of a visible body. By itself the problem of the Virgin Birth did not raise special difficulties. Gnostically, the factor of virginity emphasized, in both the pleromatic and the human worlds, the assumption of typically male functions and qualities.[97] More delicate and bound to provoke discussions and controversies was the evaluation of Mary's contribution. For some (and this can be said of most Christian Gnostics) Jesus was truly born of Mary.[98] If he had appeared in human form on earth with the aim of saving man, he did so by assuming a real body and nature, even if they were *sui generis*. As a result, his passion and death were equally real, though they affected only the physical Jesus. This conception, contrary to what the heresiologists maintained, was not docetist; Jesus had not suffered in appearance only.[99] However little the human element in itself interested the Gnostics (for it was always doomed to be lost because of its nature as adjunct and instrument), the carnal nature of their Saviour was not the less real, even though it may have been fleeting and transitory. But Jesus had not come to redeem it, but to restore it to its true origin.

Some Valentinians, like Ptolemy, in contrast, did not accept the physical birth of Jesus. Making use of an image from folklore traditions,[100] the Valentinian doctor maintained that Christ 'passed through Mary as water passes through a tube.'[101] Thus Jesus' human nature came to be devalued. His body was not material, like that of the Virgin. His human nature was therefore apparent and bound to deceive the Archons.

This disharmony between the various tendencies of the school did not apply to the event in Jesus' life that became central to the Gnostic reinterpretation: the baptism in the waters of the Jordan. Only then did the Saviour, whatever the true nature of his body was, assume in its fullness the nature of Gnostic Redeemer.

Let us return to the events related of the pleromatic Son. They describe the progressive fall of the higher Christ; in Gnostic terms, the systematic triumph of his female dimension, which is celebrated by the sin of Sophia. Jesus instigates a movement in the opposite direction which aims to restore the original equilibrium. Thus if the movement in the Pleroma starts from the virginal *pneuma* of the Father (essentially male) and leads to the abortive movement of Sophia (exclusively female), the life of Jesus will unfold in reverse order of perfection *a minore ad maius*, or from the smaller to the greater. In the virgin birth Sophia intervenes as the Holy Spirit; this is the formation in substance. In the baptism in the Jordan the Spirit of the Father will appear in the form of a dove; it is the moment of formation according to Gnosis.[102] After the thirty years of private life corresponding to, and modelled upon, the thirty aeons of the Pleroma, Jesus is now ready to fulfil his work of redemption.

Thus baptism assumes a strategic importance in the Gnostic perspective: 'Jesus revealed [on the banks of the Jordan] the fullness of the kingdom of heaven.'[103] 'The Saviour was a bodily image of the unitary one. He is the totality in bodily form.'[104] Upon Jesus the dove, a symbol of the Son descends – Nous, who alone knows the Father and henceforth can fulfil the task of salvation assigned to him: to transmit the knowledge of the Father, for only the Son knows him.

The scene on the Jordan becomes a typical example of illumination. Once again, in the heart of Jesus, the ideal Gnostic *anthrōpos*, there is a repetition of the enlightening process already familiar to us. Before the Jordan he is in a typically female state of passivity, weakness, without form. The dove that descends on him illuminates him, forming him and enabling him to acquire the 'male' dimension that will henceforth determine his actions.

Seen in this perspective, the passion and death that crowned his earthly life appear less important. What counts once again is the fact that the Valentinians regard these events symbolically. The passion of Jesus is not important either in itself or in its redemptive value, but rather in the pleromatic reality it reflects, i.e. the passions of the Mother, Sophia. Thus too the Cross is significant inasmuch as it reflects and repeats the functions of the pleromatic Cross: the function of limit, belonging to its horizontal dimension, which is also the function of saving the human nature of Christ, which has been given back to its destiny of death and corruption; and the opposing function, belonging to its vertical dimension, of reuniting the lower with the higher *pneuma*.[105]

This was also the Gnostics' response to a possible objection. Had the Saviour suffered? He had both suffered and not suffered. The physical, human Christ died a real death on the Cross. But the higher Christ had left him before that death. The pneumatic part of the Saviour had thus become uniform with the rhythm of *systolē* and *diastolē*, or contraction and dispersion, animating the spiritual circulation of the pleromatic Anthropos. Having spread over Jesus at the time of the Jordan, the pneumatic power now becomes concentrated and withdraws, receding from the physical Christ abandoned to his mortal fate. Not that the *pneuma* is separated substantially from Jesus; as the rays of the sun at evening return to their source, ready to illuminate the earth again on the following day, so the spiritual rays of the pleromatic world, having withdrawn from Jesus at the moment of his passion and death, are now ready to shine on the Resurrected One.[106]

The Resurrection thus conceals the final mystery of the Valentinian Saviour. With the various natures restored to their origin, he who now speaks to the disciples (the Valentinians liked to extend this period to eighteen months) is the Gnostic Saviour in his spiritual purity and perfection. If during his earthly ministry he still spoke in parables, in keeping with his complex nature, from now on he will speak openly and without any concealment. The *mysterium coniunctionis* is finally dissolved.

OTHER GNOSTIC CHRISTOLOGIES

The Valentinian conception of the Saviour is imposing in its coherence, profundity and systematization. The Valentinian texts at Nag Hammadi have simply enriched and filled in the details of a design already known in outline.[107]

Some of the other groups of Christian Gnostics, such as the Ophites of Irenaeus, opened the way, with their speculation to the Christological conceptions of the Valentinians themselves;[108] others, like Basilides, took an independent, but, as we shall see, substantially parallel, line; others, finally, are clearly indebted to Valentinian ideas.[109] Given the wealth of evidence here, the analysis will be confined to some important texts now taking into account the variety of schools and tendencies and adopting a more analytical approach.

The *Apocalypse of Peter* (NHC VII.3)[110] is of particular importance. The Gnostic work, which has nothing to do with the second-century Christian apocalypse of the same name, is a typical apocalypse,[111] containing the report of a revelation to Peter while he was with the Saviour, who interpreted it to him. Like the other texts found at Nag Hammadi, the apocalypse directs a lively polemic not only against the psychics of the True Church 'who name themselves bishops and deacons',[112] but also against other Gnostic groups, 'blind ones who have no guide'.[113]

The first scene deals with the groups of hostile priests and with the people who want to kill Jesus.[114] The Saviour had come down to this world without the knowledge of the Archons (and without forewarning from the other prophets) to bring Gnosis to Peter, whom he had chosen,[115] and to the other disciples. He had also come to warn him of the traps that the Adversary, the Counterfeiter of Justice, had laid for them. Peter is thus warned so that he can understand the tragic events that are about to take place. The second scene[116] describes Peter's vision of the crucifixion. Those who come to kill Jesus do not actually touch him. Peter asks who it is that is smiling on the Cross and who is the other being tortured instead. The Saviour explains to him that the one who is mocking is the living Jesus,[117] while he who is crucified is a substitute, he who was born in the likeness of the living Jesus, but whose body is doomed to death and corruption. The third, final vision[118] concerns the Resurrection of Jesus in the Gnostic reinterpretation. Peter now sees someone approaching the Apostles who resembles the one smiling at the Archons from the Cross. He is the Saviour, filled with the Holy Spirit, surrounded by a great, ineffable light, blessed by ranks of invisible angels. Jesus interprets this text too, as follows:

> Be strong [he says to Peter], for you are the one to whom these mysteries have been given, to know them through revelation, that he whom they crucified is the first-born, and the home of demons, and the stony vessel (?) in which they dwell, of Elohim, of the cross which is under the Law. But he who stands near him is the living Savior, the first in him, whom they seized and released, who stands joyfully looking at those who did him violence, while they are divided among themselves. Therefore he laughs at their lack of perception, knowing that they are born blind. So then the one susceptible to suffering shall come, since the body is the substitute. But what they released was my incorporeal body. But I am the intellectual Spirit filled with radiant light. He whom you saw coming to me is our intellectual Pleroma, which unites the perfect light with my Holy Spirit.[119]

Although it is not Valentinian, the Christology in this apocalypse is a clear confirmation of the Valentinian view. Far from being docetist, this Christian Gnostic emphasizes the reality of the sufferings of Jesus' physical body, but of a Jesus who was momentarily abandoned by the spirit of his Father.[120] The Son as such has not suffered, nor could it be otherwise; for his nature is distinguished by impassibility and therefore does not know the material laws of *pathos*, or suffering.

A variant of this scheme, in itself not theologically important, but indicative of the solutions that Gnostic schools were able to provide for the same problem, is already known to us from Irenaeus on Basilides. Christ is also for him the Intellect of the Father, sent on earth to save man:

> ... to liberate those who believe in him from those who made the world. To their [the angels'] nations he appeared on earth as a man and performed miracles. For the same reason also he did not suffer, but a certain Simon of Cyrene was compelled to carry his cross for him. And this [Simon] was transformed by him [Jesus] so that he was thought to be Jesus himself,

and was crucified through ignorance and error. Jesus, however, took on the form of Simon and stood by laughing at them.[121]

This interpretation is confirmed today in the *Second Logos of the Great Seth* (NHC VII.2).[122] This text, whose Sethian nature is disputed,[123] is presented as a typical revelation dialogue, in which Jesus tells a group of 'the perfect and incorruptible' his true story, from the celestial origin to the death, resurrection and return to the Pleroma. Coming down without allowing himself to be recognized by the Archons, he fought them with their own weapon: deceit. When they crucified him, they believed that they had defeated him once and for all. In fact, Simon of Cyrene was the one to carry the Cross and wear the crown of thorns: 'But I was rejoicing in the height [of Heaven] over all the wealth of the archons and the offspring of their error, of their empty glory. And I was laughing at their ignorance.'[124]

The conception underlying these accounts does not change. It is not the Saviour in his spiritual dimension who suffers, but his carnal nature, which is not an illusion. The Saviour's physical body or that of his substitute is, from the Gnostic point of view, a decoy, a trap set for the Archons. Hence the Saviour's liberally triumphant laughter: laughter of both joy and ironic derision at the powers who believed that they had imprisoned the Redeemer and who now persist in tormenting the outer wrapping of the body.

Examples of this kind might be multiplied. The *Letter of Peter to Philip*[125] (NHC VIII.2) is a short treatise, the work of a Christian Gnostic, which, in the form of a letter from Peter to Philip, makes certain revelations that Peter is supposed to have received from the Resurrected One, Christ the Illuminator: 'Our illuminator, Jesus, [came] down and was crucified. And he bore a crown of thorns. And he put on a purple garment. And he was [crucified] on a tree and he was buried in a tomb.'[126] But 'Jesus is a stranger to this suffering, but we are the ones who have suffered at the transgression of the mother.'[127]

The reality of the Gnostic Jesus is therefore only apparently paradoxical. He was both true man and at the same time true God. His human dimension cannot be denied, but at the same time it cannot be forgotten that it did not join the divine nature to the point where it could no longer be recognized distinctly, but, according to a typical Stoic doctrine,[128] it only mingled with it, and at a suitable time and place these natures separated.

This is clearly the teaching of Basilides as reported in Hippolytus. The gospel, the cognitive, generative power of the higher Son, descends upon Jesus, the son of Mary. Thus illuminated, he receives 'the power of separation'. His task is in fact to separate the elements. Illuminating the third sonship, the Church of the Spiritual ones, dispersed in the world, he purifies it and forms it in accordance with Gnosis. It is thus able finally to ascend on high, returning to its celestial home, the Pleroma. But the intervention of the Saviour also has a cosmic dimension. Indeed, he is 'the first fruits of a division, according to their kind, of the elements that were confused in the world'.[129] And the passion took place for no other reason than 'in order to separate the confused elements according to their kind. In the same way that all sonship, which had been left shapeless to give and receive benefits, had to be divided according to its kind, so also Jesus was divided according to his kind.'[130]

In Christ therefore not only is the mystery of the joining of the various elements celebrated, but also of their final separation, of their return, each to its own nature 'so that every creature may remain in its natural condition and none desire anything that is against nature.'[131]

8

Waiting for the End

THE NATURE OF GNOSTIC ESCHATOLOGY

In the presentation of the great themes and motifs of Gnostic 'myth', we have so far given pride of place to Sethian texts and those of the Valentinian school, at the risk of paying less attention to a historically more complex fabrication, whose subtle variations and shades are becoming more evident from the increasingly deep analysis of the Nag Hammadi texts. On the other hand, if there is a moment in the mythical account in which the various Gnostic traditions appear not only to run parallel, but almost to converge in the same doctrinal stream that, if it does not impede them, renders minute and detailed distinctions superfluous, that moment is the 'end of time'.[1]

It is true that eschatological beliefs *per se* tend to constitute a doctrinally homogeneous complex. In the myths about the end, more than in those about the beginning perhaps, cultural sterotypes and models emerge that in a sense are obligatory, rigidly codified by tradition and reinforced, for every generation, by the suffering and inescapable experience of the individual. Here the rule seems to be one of repetition. What could be more monotonous than certain eschatological doctrines? Death liberates a spiritual principle able to survive its challenge. A destiny of rewards and punishments, more or less ethically distributed, awaits him. The world too has its own goal: destruction, renewal and return.

And yet from this slight amount of material various religions have been able to derive an impressive number of variations.[2] The traditional motifs of every eschatology (destiny of the individual after death, destiny of humanity, places and nature of retribution, destiny of the world), which appear at first sight substantially identical in the most diverse religious traditions, in fact undergo profound inner changes. These are revealed in all their importance only in the long term as the result of repeated minute shifts in emphasis.[3]

Gnostic eschatology is no exception to this rule. On the whole, it is the child of Roman imperial eschatology[4] (of which we have already mentioned some important aspects). The changes in celestial geography were paralleled by changes in the society of the elect. Religious democracy, which had opened the way to Paradise for everyone, though it may have achieved its most complete expression in Christianity, had known indicative parallels in the eschatological beliefs of the mystery religions.[5] In contrast, in other cases, one sees an aristocratic type of exclusion: only the noble in spirit can get through the gate of Heaven, the most convinced ascetics, the experts in the 'inner search'. Neoplatonism is, in this connection, a clear example of how eschatological beliefs and problems of social prestige and cultural differentiation, typical of aristocratic elites in decline, could proceed in parallel.[6]

An aristocratic concept of merit also seems to characterize individual Gnostic eschatologies. One is born better; one does not become better. Perhaps Max Weber[7] was right to see the Gnostic teachers as representative of a marginalized intelligentsia of the Roman provinces, without effective political power and in search of effective ideological alternatives through new forms of redemption and flight from a world that had become increasingly alien to them. Eschatological beliefs, if they also reveal a more general sociological situation, nevertheless appear to be constructed according to the individual's view of the fundamental imperative of Gnostic propaganda: disengage yourself from the mass doomed to perdition; disengage yourself from those groups, the psychics, who claim to regulate the salvation of the masses; become one of us, join this club of elect souls predestined to salvation. For certain social groups therre could be no more religiously effective invitation.

The blood of syncretism also runs through the body of the eschatological beliefs. Consider the doctrine of metempsychosis. This concept, of Indian origins,[8] had found an important Greek parallel in Orphism[9] and was widespread in the imperial period.[10] Some Gnostics took it over and adapted it to the particular needs of their systems. Basilides, for instance, believed in it. Origen reports that in his commentary on the Pauline passage 'I died ... indeed sin began to be imputed to me' (Rom. 7:9) Basilides is said to have understood it not as a reference to the dispensations of the law, but rather to metensomatosis, or incarnation: 'He says, "Indeed the Apostle said: Once I lived without the law' [ibid.]. That is, before I came into this body, I lived in a sort of body that did not come under the law, the body of a beast or bird."'[11] The beings of the world are united by a sort of cosmic bond. To reach the summit of the ladder of evolution necessarily involved overcoming the different grades of being. As a microcosm, humankind combines within itself all levels of reality tested in different rebirths. Only Gnosis will allow it, according to one of Basilides' ideas (as Hippolytus reports), the definitive separation of the natures acting within it.

Without Gnostic features, the doctrine of metempsychosis could thus assume different functions. According to Irenaeus, the Carpocratians are said to have used it as the basis and explanation of their depravity. Their guiding principle is a radical antinomianism, a contemptuous rejection of all law, both divine and human:

> They say that conduct is good and evil only in the opinion of men. And after the transmigrations the souls must have been in every kind of life and every kind of deed (if a man does not in *one* life do at one and the same time all that is not merely forbidden for us to speak or hear but may not even enter into the thoughts of our minds, nor may one believe if men in our cities do anything of the sort) so that, as their scriptures say, their souls have been in every enjoyment and when they depart from the body they are deficient in nothing; but they must labour lest perchance, because something is lacking to their freedom, they be compelled to be sent again into their bodies.[12]

For the Carpocratians metempsychosis therefore became the means of asserting their own freedom from the Demiurge and his laws. Only by violating the law does one demonstrate its inconsistency and emptiness.

The Gnostic syncretistic way is also clear in the descriptions of the places of punishment in the Underworld, typical of the inexhaustible stock of folklore of Hellenistic *nekyiai*,[13] or funeral ceremonies, that were to reappear in the horrific scenes of infernal punishment that enliven some Christian apocalypses. It is no accident that one of these scenes is to be found in the *Apocalypse of Paul* (NHC V.2).[14] The first of the four apocalyptic texts in Codex V, this writing describes Paul's journey through the ten heavens[15] (developing the famous Pauline reference to the ascent to the third heaven in 2 Cor. 12:2–4), accompanied by an infant, a symbol of the Spirit of the Son, depicted in his virginal purity. In the fourth heaven Paul witnesses a scene of judgement and punishment, recalling similar descriptions in Jewish apocalyptic texts.[16] In the fifth heaven 'I saw a great angel . . . holding an iron rod in his hand. There were three other angels with him, and I stared into their faces. But they were rivalling each other, with whips in their hands, goading the souls on to the judgment.'[17]

Still more traditional in its gloom is the picture of destiny awaiting the condemned, outlined by the Saviour in the *Book of Thomas the Contender*:

... he will be handed over to the Ruler above who rules over all the powers as their king, and he will turn that one around and cast him from heaven down to the abyss, and he will be imprisoned in a dark narrow place. Moreover, he can neither turn nor move on account of the great depth of Tartaros and the [heavy bitterness] of Hades that besets [him. They are imprisoned] in it in [order that they might not escape] – their [madness] will not be forgiven. [And the Rulers who will] pursue you [will] deliver [them over to the] angel Tartarouchos [and he will take whips of] fire, pursuing them [with] fiery scourges that cast a shower of sparks into the face of the one who is pursued. If he flees westward, he finds the fire. If he turns southward, he finds it there as well. If he turns northward, the threat of seething fire meets him again. Nor does he find the way to the East so as to flee there and be saved, for he did not find it in the day he was in the body, so that he will find it in the day of Judgment.[18]

The threat could not but be felt by all those insecure people unable to resist the animal pleasures of the body and the seductive enticements of woman. In Gnostic terms it might refer to those who were somehow predestined by their nature to the eternal fire. There was therefore no need to waste time in constructing new types of dwelling places and infernal pleasures for them, when the popular religious traditions of the time offered such refined, attractive products!

A similar tendency to borrow is the basis of certain apocalyptic scenes of the end of the world. Themes recur, such as the signs of the end, the judgement, the punishment of the condemned who had been hurled into the abyss, typical of Jewish apocalyptic.[19] In the *Trimorphic Protennoia* the Gnostic divinity has the task of revealing, among other things, the end of this aeon to the Sons of Light: 'And I shall tell them of the coming end of this aeon and teach them of the beginning of the aeon to come, the one without change, the one in which our appearance will be changed. We shall be purified within those aeons ...'[20]

This typical doctrine of the two aeons involves almost inevitably an equally widespread reflection on time: the present aeon is complete; its times, hours, days and months have passed.[21] To this belief there is added the following speculative elements, more properly Gnostic: the Archons, who have achieved knowledge, through the voice of the Protennoia, of the imminent end of this aeon, realize that they have been deceived by their Lord. The Demiurge is not the only God. In reality he is condemned to perdition. The Archons weep bitterly over the inexorable conclusion of the aeon. The times have been cut back, the days shortened. The moment of the end is approaching for the Archons too.[22]

The destiny of the Archons, of the Demiurge and of the world cannot give rise to doubt. They are destined to defeat and destruction. It is not important, from the doctrinal point of view, if this end is described in gloomy apocalyptic terms or, as in Valentinian teaching, by means of the Stoic theory of universal conflagration.[23] On the contrary, what matters to the Gnostic is not so much the destiny of the conquered as the reward awaiting the victors and the eventual obstacles that stand in the way of their final victory. But to reveal all this, to tell of the luminous blessedness of the future aeon, not even the suggestive descriptions in Jewish apocalyptic were sufficient. It was necessary to make up an eschatological product that would allow a glimpse of the reality of the final promises and unleash the fascination of unknown horizons of happiness.

The first element in the newness and also in the unity of individual Gnostic eschatology is reflected in the very activities of the Saviour. Whether it is a question of an anonymous, impersonal function, like the Sethian Saviour or the Jesus Christ of Christian Gnostic groups, in the activities of the Revealer and Illuminator there appears in some way the eschatological quintessence of Gnostic myth. We have already mentioned that the Protennoia reveals to the Sons of Light the ineffable secret of her descent: the final liberation of those who belong to her. This is echoed by the Christian Saviour in the *Psalm of the Naassenes*, a masterpiece of Gnostic hymnology on the fate of the soul and recorded by Hippolytus.[24]

> First-born Nous was the law that engendered all
> Next to the first-born was the outpoured chaos
> Thirdly the soul received a law as it worked [?as it was made]
> Hence clad in the form of a stag(?)
> It labours captive, as a spoil for death.
> Now with royal (honour) it sees the light,
> Now cast out into misery, it weeps.
> Now it is wept for, it rejoices,
> Now it is judged, it dies,
> . . . and without escape the wretched soul
>   enters a labyrinth of evils in its wanderings [text uncertain].
> But Jesus said, 'Father behold:
> Pursued by evils here upon earth
> There roams the (work) of thine own breath.
> It seeks to escape the bitter chaos
> But knows not how it shall win through.
> Therefore send me, Father.
> Bearing the seals I will descend,

I will pass through all the Aeons,
I will disclose the mysteries
I will show the forms of the Gods
And the hidden things of the holy way,
Called Gnosis, I will impart.'[25]

On the other hand, if it is true that the 'way of ascent is like that of the descent', as the editor of the *Three Stelae of Seth* crisply puts it,[26] the model of this double movement is offered precisely by the activities of the Saviour. Jesus had received Gnosis at the moment of baptism, but only with passion and death had he truly closed the cycle of his earthly actions. Death was therefore a passage, perhaps for the Gnostic not altogether threatening, but always necessary. One must not forget that only at the moment of death could one achieve *discretio naturarum*, the definitive decision and separation of substances that conceals a fundamental aspect of Gnostic soteriology.

That individual Gnostic eschatology is built on a typical tension between 'already' and 'not yet', between the acquired possession of a Gnosis that cannot, however, be total and definitive, is confirmed by other elements.

For many Christian Gnostics the world too has its own function in the divine dispensation of salvation; a purely negative function, if you like, of an element destined to purify the Church of the Spiritual ones, but necessary none the less. Basilides maintains this, as will be noted. The Naassenes maintain it in their interpretation of the Pauline passage (1 Cor. 10:11): 'We are the publicans "who have been overtaken by the end of the world". Indeed the end is the seed sown in the world by the being without shape, thanks to which the whole world is perfected. Indeed it was through them that it began to come into existence.'[27]

By means of a pun (the Naassenes call themselves 'publicans', i.e. *telōnai*, because they are able to understand the *telē*, the last things), these Gnostic Christians reveal a fundamental idea. The world, as the area in which the seeds of the Spiritual Church have been put, becomes an element necessary to the dispensation of salvation, like the winter soil which receives the seed. The Valentinian author of the *Gospel of Philip* is thus able to assert: 'Those who sow in winter reap in summer. The winter is the world, the summer the other aeon.'[28] Only with the end of the world, therefore, can the drama of Gnostic salvation be fulfilled. On the other hand, the end of the world coincides with the end of the mingling of light and darkness, of the collection of particles of light scattered in matter that constitutes the collective dimension of an eschatology at first sight purely individualistic.[29]

These themes are brought together in the eschatological passages in

On the Origin of the World. At the completion of the aeon the revealers will appear and reveal the type of incorruptibility that has risen from the murky mass of matter, descending into the very inside of the cosmos and of humanity, an invisible form of what is visible, a dimension hidden, but the more true, of what is clear, though apparent and transient.[30] Then

> the light will [cover the] darkness and it will wipe it out. It will become like one which had not come into being. And the work which the darkness followed will be dissolved. And the deficiency will be plucked out at its root (and thrown) down to the darkness. And the light will withdraw up to its root. The glory of the unbegotten will appear and it will fill all the aeons ...[31]

Projected onto the cosmic, collective scale, the fraction of time that lies between the reception of Gnosis and the death of the individual is now extended to acquire the dimension of the 'time of the Church'.

THE TIME OF THE CHURCH

The Church of the Spiritual beings, exiled in this world, suffers the birthpangs of which the beginning is known and the end, one hopes, is imminent. The arc of this time thus helps, by delimiting it, to constitute the Church.

How is this possible? Isn't time a creation, a trap and a trick of the Archons? Shouldn't the Gnostic rather break this chain of minutes, hours and days, which binds him as a prisoner in the cosmos? 'The birth cries [out; hour] begets hour, [and day [begets day]. The months made known [the month. Time] has [gone round] succeeding [time].'[32]

To break the bars of this invisible cage, shouldn't the Gnostic be ready to renounce time? There is much evidence for this. The time of the Gnostic, his real time, seems to be mythical time *par excellence*.[33] A ray of light falls from above into the darkness. The sequence of moments, monotonous and repetitive, is unexpectedly broken. Gnosis presents itself in the guise of illumination – an unexpected, instantaneous, total flash of lightning, breaking the connected thread of cosmic time to propel the Gnostic into that particular wavelength: timeless, mythical time.

And yet an interpretation that gave precedence to this vertical dimension of time in Gnosis, breaking as it does the historical continuum, would be too one-sided. For mundane time is still a copy, however pale and deceptive, of pleromatic time. Eugnostos[34] says that cosmic time is a type, a copy of the First Generator. Thus, the twelve months are modelled on the twelve aeons; the 360 days of the year on the 360 powers revealed by the Saviour. Finally, the hours and minutes find their pleromatic counterparts in the countless angels populating these worlds.

Rather than eliminate time and break this continuous line enveloping them with its threatening silence, Gnostics must learn to understand what is really happening behind the temporal organism. The time of the divine will shall then be revealed to him, the salvific line measured out by *kairoi*, moments of revelation, whose reassuring succession directs the Gnostic to a safe landing: first individual, then collective, salvation which is final.[35]

Gnostic eschatological tension may appear as tension towards an end that, in fact, coincides with the beginning. According to the *Tripartite Tractate*,[36] *arché* (beginning) and *telos* (end) perhaps coincide to form not so much a progressive straight line of *kairoi* as a curved line that tends to end in a circle. However, this is merely an appearance. Even where, as in the Sethian systems, Christian influence of a particular conception of time seems lacking or indecisive, according to the original formation of their history of salvation, the texts clearly point to a linear, and not to a cyclical, view of time.[37] The 'not yet' is the period of the assembly of the seeds of light dispersed in the world. The end will coincide, thus, with the *restitutio*, or restoration, of the original spiritual body, whose members are dispersed in the darkness. But this *apokatastasis*,[38] this re-establishment of original fullness, is also a *renovatio*, or renewal, of the initial condition. Gnostic nostalgia for origins is not satisfied by the simple return to the original Paradise. What would have been the point of the exile of the Gnostic Church? Was it not perhaps aiming at the elimination of that potential deficiency and congenital incontinence in the very life of the Pleroma, expressed in the sin of Sophia? And in fact, in its trials of exile, crossing the frightful threshold of evil, experiencing and suffering the pangs of spiritual birth, the Gnostic Church matures individually and collectively. Evil can be defeated finally only if it is objectified in the work of creation. And when the Pleroma is renewed internally, it will know true repose. And not only that. Some thinkers, such as Ptolemy, who had revalued the psychic element as the seat of free will, consequently were unable to drive it back into no man's land, non-being, which awaited matter as a result of the final conflagration. Though it may not guarantee a privileged place, even the Demiurge and the psychics have their ticket to watch the spectacle of eternal beatitude. While Sophia enters the Pleroma to celebrate her eternal nuptials with the Saviour, followed by the Church of the Spiritual beings, which is finally reunited with its male counterpart, the angels of the Saviour, 'the Demiurge will also be transferred to the place of the Mother Sophia – that is, the Intermediate Region. The souls of the just will also find repose in the Intermediate Region. Indeed, nothing psychic can enter the Pleroma.'[39]

The time of the Church is, therefore, important for the Gnostic, especially for the Christian Gnostic. It is a time of trials, conflicts and decisions. Gnosis does enable the Gnostic to revive somehow, but this inner illumination prefigures and anticipates, but does not replace, the final liberation, which will take place for the individual only at the moment of death and, for the great body of Gnostics, at the moment of their final reconstitution.

The *Pistis Sophia* affords an important, singular interpretation of this theme. Jesus has come to save souls. The psyche is in fact subject to the influence of two forces, equal, but opposite: divine luminous power and its antagonist, the *antimimon pneuma*, the counterfeit spirit, the cup of forgetfulness that the Archons, after forming the soul, forced it to drink.[40] The soul would therefore appear to find itself in a situation of perfect free will, of risky, but tempting, equilibrium. In fact, the power of the counterfeit spirit seems to have the upper hand. Thus, the intervention of the Saviour is necessary. He is the bringer of a Gnosis understood as knowledge and possession of the supreme mysteries, celebrated by Gnostic mythology: pleromatic hierarchies, the dualism of light and darkness, the origin of the mingling. Characteristically, however, possession of these mysteries does not conclude the process of salvation: final, complete knowledge is actually deferred until the end.[41]

We have already mentioned, apropos of the Apostles, a typical feature of our text: the theme of the Saviour saved. But the subject is common to all the Gnostics. The supreme mystery of the Ineffable is none other than the mystery of Jesus. The soul that possesses him is liberated at the moment of death from the material body made by the Archons; it is transformed into a flow of light, which quickly returns to its source; the Saviour himself.[42]

Possession of the mysteries is therefore decisive. They 'are merciful and forgive at all times.'[43] Salvation is not, however, a mechanical process, nor is it decided once and for all. Not for nothing is the third book of the *Pistis Sophia* devoted almost entirely to a case study in minute detail of the possibility of relapse. Possession of the pleromatic mysteries does not cancel out individual responsibility. There is the extreme case of the one who receives them and continues to sin and dies without repentance. For that individual there is no salvation, but only damnation (though not a final damnation). There is always the possibility of escape, even if only through the intervention of a friendly soul already saved. At worst, the impenitent soul, which does not succeed in clinging to any of the spiritual life-belts, will once again be cast into a body where new possibilities of salvation will be offered to it.[44]

But even the patience of the First Mystery, apparently infinite, has a limit. The time in which the mysteries can be received, the time of the salvation of the Gnostic Church of the *Pistis Sophia* is, in fact, limited. This apparently inexhaustible series of possibilities will finally come to an end with the completion of the 'number of perfect souls'.[45] This is a limit that cannot be passed. When this number is complete, the gates of the Kingdom of Light will finally be closed, and no one will be able to enter.

Thus Jesus repeatedly invites his disciples to be missionaries, so that they may communicate to everybody those mysteries that are not the inheritance of a restricted elite.[46] And it must be done quickly. No one knows the exact number of perfect souls and so it cannot be foreseen when it will be complete. There is need for vigilance so as not to miss what might be the last chance of eternal salvation.

This is one of the many possible examples of how New Testament themes and motifs have been added and adapted to a mythological, typically Gnostic theological scheme.[47] Not only is the apostle consubstantial with his Saviour, who reveals to him his celestial origin, but also the mission, however open and ecumenical, is written in a programmed logic in which the closed number with access to the higher world is determined by the typical requirements of the Gnostic system. But above all, as in most Gnostic texts, this prolix treatise helps to emphasize an important idea for a more exact evaluation of eschatological conceptions. The Gnostic Church too has its own time, a time of mission, dangers, threats and decisions. Not everything in fact is decided together with the acquisition of Gnosis. Indeed, interior illumination requires confirmation and proof up to the final decisive challenge, which even the Gnostic will sooner or later be called upon to face: death.

GNOSTIC ACCOUNTS OF THE ASCENT OF THE SOUL

With his death and resurrection, Christ showed the Gnostic the definitive way of liberation. But death had been preceded by the Passion. For the Gnostic this meant abandonment, however momentary, of the Spirit. It was a frightening test on the threshold of final victory: the ultimate, distressing, but unavoidable, rite of passage.

There is a great deal of talk in modern society about death. This may be an unconscious, subtle defence mechanism for a society that no longer understands 'experienced death'.[48] Death has been banished, forbidden and, in daily life, has become an unmentionable subject. Its domestication has passed through a funereal conspiracy of silence. Where it appears and is not to be suppressed, it is exorcized through the filters of the television screen or dressed up in the substantial garb of official ceremonies. It is not 'my' or 'your' death, but anonymous death, at most a death spectacle. It is pointless to insist on the differences in the theories about death in archaic and pre-modern societies.[49] It may be interesting to emphasize some themes in this brief reawakening of interest in a world of experiences and thoughts once familiar and commonplace. One has only to think of a recurrent motif in modern literature on the subject of death, especially in America, of medical origin.[50] What happens to the person in a coma? Is it possible to photograph (or, in more fortunate cases, to interview those who have experienced) the moments before the great irretrievable step and to understand the state of mind and the thoughts that accompany them? Reduced to arid scientific curiosity, or worse, to the publicity hype of a new 'bestseller', it may appear simply as a further act of cruelty to an invalid who has become a guinea pig. But in terms of religious history it takes on a more human light and a different cultural dimension. It is the theme of the *Zwischenzustand*, the twilight zone, those eternal moments, the fine bridge between time and its cessation, an area explored and wonderfully described by so many religious spirits.[51] It is enough to glance through that extraordinary volume, the *Tibetan Book of the Dead*, to detect some surprising aspects, of relevance to the contemporary situation.[52] The central theme is that of the bard: a minute, lucid, almost obsessive, analysis of the representative states violating inexorably and mercilessly the aseptic moment of transition. Buddhist meditation has rigorously analysed them and ordered them hierarchically in a sort of spiral; and it is necessary to ascend this spiral, with all its menace, in order to reach the desired goal: the final abandonment of those illusions (however vivid and resistant) against which humans are called to fight, and the resulting dissolution of those representations (menacing, but captivating) that, in the Renaissance Books of the Dead, are translated into endless struggles between devils and angels on the bed of the dying, the lost and the helpless.[53]

Even our Gnostics recognized this singular challenge. Their ascents of the soul, the celestial journeys awaiting the souls immediately after death, are the most illuminating example of how they experienced the problem of the intermediate stage. They constitute their reply to the problem confronting every society: how to institutionalize and to regulate, how to make socially tolerable, if not productive, an event in itself so dangerously destructive.

Roman imperial society offered a surprisingly wide range of answers to this inevitable question. They include the exasperated individualism of some Stoic philosophers and the universalism typical of mystery and salvation religions, which altered the intellectual, mythical and architectural geography (one thinks, e.g. of the catacombs or Christian cemeteries).[54] The Gnostic response, as far as we know, represents a middle way. Indeed, it celebrated the 'victory over death', typical of redemptive religions. Cerberus had been tamed and domesticated. Death, even though able to cast one into the caves of hell, could now, more importantly, open the way to the irresistible seductions of a promised land where an eternal life of happiness triumphed. From being an end, it had become a means, a docile instrument that could be acquired by means of ascetic disdain or unthinking indulgence in pleasure, an instrument that would accelerate the process of embracing everlasting happiness.

But it was not a mechanical, painless event. Or, at least, death should not always be regarded as a moment that had been already resolved. We deduce this from the fact that some groups practised a sort of reassuring rite of extreme unction: they poured over the head of the dying or the dead oil and water or a special perfume mixed with water, accompanied by invocations, so that the soul of the dying might be able to withstand the final test: the ascent through the menacing heavens of the Archons.[55]

A Nag Hammadi text contains a prayer that seems to be representative of the prayers to be said by the dying or by those watching over them at the moment of death. It is recited by James just before his martyrdom.[56] In its all-consuming invocations anxiety about the imminent test and joyful confident abandon are merged poetically:

> My God and my Father, who saved me from this dead hope, who made me alive through a mystery of what he wills, do not let these days of this world be prolonged for me, but the day of your [light . . .] remains in [. . .] salvation. Deliver me from this [place of] sojourn. Do not let your grace be left behind in me, but may your grace become pure. Save me from an evil death. Bring me from a tomb alive, because your grace–love is alive in me to accomplish a work of fullness. Save me from sinful flesh, because I trusted in you with all my strength! Because you are the life of the life, save me from a humiliating enemy! Do not give me into the hand of a judge who is severe with sin! Forgive me all my debts of the days (of my life)! Because I am alive in you, your grace is alive in

me. I have renounced everyone, but you I have confessed. Save me from evil affliction! But now is the [time] and the hour. O Holy [Spirit], send [me] salvation [. . .] the light [. . .] the light [. . .] in a power [. . .].[57]

The individual soul, encouraged in this way, was ready to approach the great journey. This was organized in a scheme that we find fully illustrated in the *Poimandres*. Hermes asks how the soul ascends to heaven and Poimandres replies:

First, at the dissolution of the material body you surrender this same body to change, and the form you have disappears, and you surrender your character to the demon, now ineffectual. And the bodily senses return, each to their own sources; they become separate parts and are compounded again for effectiveness. And passion and desire go into the irrational nature. And so the creature then goes upwards through the harmony of the spheres; and in the first circle it gains the capacity to grow and to diminish; in the second evil machinations, guile, unexercised; in the third the deceit of lust, again unexercised; in the fourth the ostentation of command . . . not exploited; and in the fifth impious boldness and the rashness of audacity; in the sixth the evil urges for riches, unexercised, in the seventh the lurking lie.[58]

In Christian Gnostic texts this passage of instructions assumes a more menacing aspect. Unlike the Hermetic planetary governors, the Archons are implacable customs officials and border guards. One needs special passports to get across the various planetary borders. In certain situations the proud self-awareness of the Gnostic seems to be enough to overcome the truculent arrogance of the Archons. This is true of certain Marcosians. They have a formula, which they are obliged to recite after death in front of every power:

'I am a son of the Father, the pre-existent Father, and now a son in the pre-existent Father.[59] I have come to behold all things, both what is strange and what belongs to me. But they are by no means totally strange, but belong to Achamoth, who is female and who has made these things for herself. I derive my being from him who was pre-existent, and I go again to that which is my own, whence I came forth.' And according to them, when he says this, he eludes and escapes from the powers. He then comes to those who are about the Demiurge and says, 'I am a precious vessel, more precious than the female which made you. If your mother does not know her origin, I know myself and am aware whence I am, and I invoke the incorruptible Sophia, who is in the Father, mother of your mother, who has neither father nor any male consort. A female sprung from a male made you, and she did not know her mother, but believed that she existed all alone. But I call upon her mother.' When those around the Demiurge hear this, they become greatly confused and pass judgement on their origin and the race of their mother. But he proceeds to his own, after casting away his chain, the soul.[60]

Elsewhere the malevolent power of the Archons is defeated by more open recourse to mysterious seals and magical passwords. In the *Second Book of Jeu* Jesus patiently instructs his disciples how to behave on their celestial journey. When they leave the body and reach the First Aeon:

> The Archons of this aeon come before you; they seal you with this seal. Their name is *zōzezē*. They hold the number 1119 in both hands. When they have finished sealing you with this seal and have given their name once only, do you say these words of protection: 'Away with you, Proteth, Personiphōn, Chous, Archons of the First Aeon, for I call upon Eaza, Zēōzaz, Zōzeōz.' But when the Archons of the First Aeon have heard these names they will be greatly terrified and will retreat and flee to the west leftwards and you will be able to continue.[61]

This scene is repeated up to the Eleventh Aeon (only the seals and the Archons change). At the Twelfth Aeon the Pleroma of the Invisible and Ungenerated God begins. But even here the Gnostic soul will have to continue to provide the angels with heavenly seals, numbers and magical names, until he reaches the Fourteenth Aeon, the *sancta sanctorum*, or holy of holies, of this system, which can be entered only by the possessor of the mystery of forgiveness of sins.

Thus the Gnostic reaches the end of his long, perilous journey. What awaits him is the last repose, the final conquest of struggles, dissensions and lacerations. To express this concept, the various traditions of the Gnostic movement employ different themes and images. Whether it is the spiritual marriage of the Valentinians or the motif of the celestial garment, the underlying idea is the same. The individuals, reconstructed in androgynous unity, can now rest in themselves, because the soul 'has found her rising. She came to rest in him who is at rest. She reclined in the bridechamber. She ate of the banquet for which she has hungered. She partook of the immortal food. She found what she had sought after. She received rest from her labors.'[62] Then finally there will be 'penetration into what is silent, where there is no need for voice nor for knowing nor for forming a concept nor for illumination, but (where) all things are light which does not need to be illuminated.'[63]

9

Simon Magus and the Origins of Gnosticism

GNOSIS AND GNOSTICISM

'The perfect conceptual definition cannot stand at the beginning, but must be left until the end of an enquiry . . . that is, inherent in the very essence of the formation of historical concepts, which as its goal does not seek to classify reality in abstract generic concepts, but rather to fit it into generic patterns of a specific individual colours.'[1] With this statement Max Weber, in his *Protestant Ethic*, undertook a complex work of historical research and reconstruction, the thankless task of delimiting the difficult concept of the 'spirit of capitalism'. Having completed our survey of the principal Gnostic myths, we too must now address the inescapable problem of definition.

Anyone unwilling to consider methodological questions can skip this paragraph. But anyone who, on the other hand, likes to pursue these intricate paths that all too often are in danger of becoming labyrinths with no exit or, worse still, intellectually narcissistic mirror games; or anyone who, more commonly, considers them an unpleasant, but indispensable, part of historical research, will have to agree with the judgement of the great sociologist. However, whether, following his suggestion, the definition of historical concepts is placed only at the end of a long, complex journey of discovery or, in contrast, is postulated, still partially and provisionally, at the beginning of the research as an indispensable working hypothesis, the object of research has always to be identified.[2] The advantages of a correct definition certainly outweigh the disadvantages.

What then do we mean by the terms 'Gnosis' and 'Gnosticism'? In an earlier chapter we traced the principal stages in the history of *gnōsis* and recalled the particular significance that this term had acquired in the world of the Gnostics. So to speak of 'Gnosis' (and of 'Gnostics')[3] means using terms and employing concepts made by the very builders and inhabitants of this particular conceptual world. The margin of difference between our perspective and the ancient one should be minimal. According to some scholars, this way is a faithful reflection of historical reality and is the only possible one within the framework of a terminological analysis.[4]

The origins of the term 'Gnosticism' are, however, different. As in the case of similar linguistic formations,[5] we are dealing here too with a term coined by modern scholars.[6] There is no linguistic equivalent in the vocabulary of the ancients. The procedure, which may at first seem incorrect, is in fact quite legitimate in terms of the formation of historical concepts. For these are not simply lifeless photographic frames of the past, but are nurtured by awareness of the difference, the consciousness of a gap, an empty space in which historical intelligence can delineate itself. And the historical concepts of this 'drama' are an indispensable factor, provided of course that one knows how to respect the rules of historical writing. But they must be used with appropriate finesse, because only in this way is it possible to identify and delimit the continuous magmatic, transitory reality of history.

The Congress of Messina (1966), on the theme of the origins of Gnosticism,[7] formulated a terminological proposal that still retains a nucleus of validity. In the final protocol it was decided to use the term 'Gnosis' to mean 'knowledge of the divine mysteries reserved for an élite'.[8] In contradistinction to this extended use of 'Gnosis' is the restricted term 'Gnosticism', chosen to indicate a specific historical phenomenon and, in particular, the Gnostic systems of the second century, which appear historically well documented. The document continues:

> The Gnosticism of the second-century sects involves a coherent series of characteristics that can be summarized in the idea of a divine spark in man, deriving from the divine realm, fallen into this world of fate, birth and death, and needing to be awakened by the divine counterpart of the self in order to be finally reintegrated. Compared with other conceptions of a 'devolution' of the divine, this idea is based ontologically on the conception of a downward movement of the divine whose periphery (often called Sophia or Ennoia) had to submit to the fate of entering into a crisis and producing, even if only indirectly, this world, upon which it cannot turn its back, since it is necessary for it to recover the pneuma, a dualistic conception on a monistic background, expressed in a double movement of devolution and reintegration.[9]

Second-century Gnosticism is therefore characterized by a particular

Gnosis (inasmuch as this is not detectable in other Gnostic forms), based on the divine communal nature of the divine spark, the luminous, pneumatic element, which must be reawakened and reintegrated into the divine world. It is a circularity that implies identity of substance between the subject of knowledge (the Gnostic), the object (the divine substance of their ontological ego) and the means by which the subject knows, Gnosis as a revelation in the form of a call from above effected by a Saviour figure or a particularly esoteric, divinely guaranteed tradition.

The definition proposed by the protocol of the Congress of Messina undoubtedly refers to a particular type of system, such as the Sethian or the Valentinian, a dynamism that develops in a crisis in the Pleroma. There is a danger that other systems may be excluded from this definition; though undoubtedly Gnostic, they may be considered from other doctrinal perspectives.[10] But it would be even more perilous to aspire to a definition that claimed to embrace all the elements characterizing the various second-century systems. It would be easy to prove that none of these systems possesses all the elements at the same time.

The clear merit of the Messina proposal consists rather in having recalled an elementary truth, with its definition based on a typology that belongs to the historically concrete. The Nag Hammadi documents have not substantially altered the nature of the question,[11] and up to now most of our information is in fact about systems that can for the most part be dated to the second century. All the documents labelled 'Gnostic' and assigned to earlier periods owe this definition to more or less established hypotheses.

Thus emerges the most delicate, controversial question. What do we know of the origins of Gnosticism? Is it actually possible, and to what extent, to speculate on the origins of this phenomenon? This last question, which theoretically precedes the first, is not otiose. Many scholars have maintained that the origins of Gnosticism cannot be located. Indeed, this point of view has quite a lot to be said for it. Gnosticism is not a multicoloured Harlequin costume whose patches can be taken apart to reveal the origin of each one, but a historical constellation endowed with an internal principle and equipped with direction, coherence and autonomy. Thus the problem of origins becomes one of determining its essence. To grasp the specific, identifying element of this historical world means in fact to approach the problem of origins on a new basis, because, as an independent historical quantity, Gnosticism could not but have in itself its own origins. To adopt this criterion does not, however, mean that we have to give up the search for motifs and traditions that might have, if not anticipated, in some sense prepared the way for the great second-century systems. They must have started somewhere. This research, then, instead of being the ultimate objective of the enquiry, merely becomes a dependent variable.

Whatever the value of this line of enquiry, its importance is undeniable, for it has overturned the traditional principle of interpretation in favour of the questions that seek to recover the 'structure', the internal patterns in the Gnostic system.

How productive this position can be even today, compared with research into origins that is too often simply directed at itself, will become clear from the following example. Many scholars propose a Jewish origin for Gnosticism,[12] a position that has many distinguished champions[13] and a great deal to be said in its favour. The Nag Hammadi texts have confirmed the importance of Jewish influence, which is clearly present in the reinterpretation of the events in Genesis, the speculations on Adam in Paradise and the connections with the world of the apocalypse and with wisdom speculations. These and other probable influences have induced divers scholars to see the historical origins of second-century Gnostic systems in a particular Jewish world on the fringes of official Judaism and identified in a variety of ways.[14]

This hypothesis, which today appears historically more reliable in the light of the new documents, is not, however, without certain weaknesses. The scholars who defend it presuppose that, in the variegated world of inter-testamental Judaism, there were currents and thinkers who, as a result of subsequent intellectual development or violent religious and political crises such as the destruction of the Temple,[15] had worked out a religious vision that was permanently at odds with official Rabbinical Judaism, in which the relations between God and the world were so markedly dualistic that they implied a radical critique of the Old Testament God in some irritable language. But what precisely do 'heterodox' and 'official' Judaism mean, when the religious world in the centuries that straddle the Christian era is characterized by the absence of a genuine orthodoxy and by a shadowy, ambiguous ideological universe, complex and still not sufficiently understood in its most characteristic features? There is once again a danger of trying to explain obscure matters in obscure terms. Or, what is worse, of projecting the concepts of the second-century Gnostic systems onto texts and fragments of earlier centuries that themselves have nothing that is certainly Gnostic. 'There are many stones scattered all over the Jewish field, and when the mason gathers them, he will be able to build any house he likes with them.'[16] The same may be said of those particular stones that comprise Old Testament material. The mere use of them proves nothing.[17] In some cases they have been used by Christian Gnostic groups as polemic against the positive value given to the Old Testament by the True Church.[18] As for other texts – the *Apocalypse of Adam*[19] explains – the date (hotly disputed) has been brought down by some to the third century AD. Thus their connection with Judaism becomes much more tenuous and fleeting.

However, all these interpretations face one obstacle that is difficult to overcome. In fact, Gnosticism took shape in an atmosphere of violent, total rejection of Judaism, a characteristic of certain anti-Jewish Christian circles rather than of any Jewish group known to us. Moreover, if it is true that radical 'anti-cosmism' and 'anti-somatism' are distinctive features of the Gnostic world, how is one to explain the fact that these are almost entirely absent from the Jewish texts known to us?[20] As for the supposed influence of traumatic events such as the destruction of the Temple, it is too easily forgotten that, after its destruction in AD 70, the Jewish world continued to believe that it would be rebuilt and this new hope nurtured obedience to the Law. Even those who see the wisdom schools and the scepticism that characterized them, and the cosmopolitan intellectuals who attended them as a likely Jewish milieu for the sources of Gnosticism are unable to point to passages in Gnostic texts where the influence of these schools can be proved definitively.

We do not wish to bore the reader with these arguments. If we have dwelt on the case of Judaism, it is because of the value of its example. To argue that inter-testamental Judaism contains elements leading to Gnosticism (arguments of pre-Gnosticism) or, absolutely, to already independent forms of pre-scriptural Gnosticism (proto-Gnosticism) seems to infer too much from too little. These conclusions may be applied, with greater reason, to hypotheses that argue a Greek or Iranian origin for Gnosticism.

However it may be delimited or defined, what appears to be a constituent element of Gnosticism in its various forms and systems is that new mental focus, the *katēgoriales novum*, or new category, that emerges with it on the religious scene at the beginning of late antiquity (whether expressed as the meeting with the self, radical anti-cosmism, the Saviour saved, or the pleromatic crisis). Far from being the parasitic aspect of a movement lacking in originality, its striking feature is that it cannot be reduced to pre-existing motifs. If it is true that 'the history and connection of individual motifs can be investigated from a philological point of view, the origin of genuine Gnosis cannot be explained.'[21]

Though it might in some sense owe much to the complex, shifting background of Hellenistic syncretism; though it might have been influenced in various ways, not always easy to assess, by other cultural traditions; though it might be related in some (as yet unknown) way to certain circles that, like the Judaism of the Diaspora, came to act as a receptacle or, like the classical philosophical tradition (in particular, the Platonic), provided the indispensable analytical tools and conceptual framework to organize and explain the divine world, nevertheless second-century Gnosticism in all its variety appears as the original fruit of a plant rich in numerous vital juices.

IN SEARCH OF THE ORIGINS: SIMON MAGUS AND THE MYTH OF HELEN

Perhaps the best example of the methodological and interpretative problems concealed behind the quarrel about the origins of Gnosticism is Simon Magus, the forerunner of Goethe's Faust.[22] Simon and his mythical companion, Helen, were destined to become the model of every ideal Gnostic couple. In fact, he is a somewhat shadowy, elusive, historical figure.

The ancient defenders of the Christian faith regarded him as the heresiarch *par excellence*, the incarnation of evil, who in his own way succeeded in spreading the discord of heresy,[23] according to a cliché that was to endure for centuries.[24]

When modern historians have tried, with the help of original source criticism, to reconstruct a historical Simon from the lifeless figure of heresiological interpretation, theological controversy and legendary embellishment, they find themselves confronted with a thankless task.[25]

The available sources are now few, of disputed interpretation and sometimes difficult to date. The most ancient is the short notice in the Acts of the Apostles 8:9–12. Composed towards the end of the first century,[26] it bears witness to the existence in Samaria of 'a man called Simon, who performed magic and amazed the people of Samaria, claiming to be a great man. Everybody, great and small alike, paid attention to him, saying: "This man is the power of God that is called great." They paid attention to him because for quite a long time he had amazed them with magical tricks.'

Converted and baptized by Philip, he is full of wonder at the sight of prodigies and miracles performed by the Apostles. He is particularly struck by the laying on of hands performed by Peter and John. He offers them money in an attempt in turn to acquire the power of transmitting the Spirit. Peter curses him and, we must deduce, expels him from the community. From this brief report derive both the sin of simony and the age-long tradition of Simon the Magician.

By itself the report tells us nothing of possible Gnostic aspects of Simon's teaching. That a person called Simon existed in Samaria about the middle of the first century AD may be taken as historical fact. The description 'magician' is not necessarily to be regarded as an editorial addition.[27] Simon appears with the typical attributes of the divine man. He practises magic arts and is generally known by the widely attested title 'Great Power'.[28] Some would regard him as the object of a syncretistic cult in which he was linked with Zeus.[29] It is, however, difficult (and methodologically incorrect) to read this brief report in the light of the Simonian system, Gnostic in type, which developed in the second century, attributing to the Simon of the Acts the nature of a Gnostic Saviour in competition with the Christian Saviour and regarding the Lucan text as confirmation of the existence of a non-Christian, pre-Christian Gnosis, an alternative to (if not indeed an influence upon) nascent Christianity.[30]

The two later reports of Justin and Irenaeus bear witness to a profoundly different situation. Justin[31] confirms the existence of a certain Samaritan Simon, native of a village called Gitton, who is said to have performed his miracles in the reign of Claudius (AD 41–54). But he also introduces a very new element: the myth of Helen. Adored by practically all Samaritans as the paramount God, Simon wanders about with a certain Helen, a whore who claims to have been redeemed by him and whom the followers of Simon called the First Thought emitted by him.

If therefore the Simon of Justin is transformed into the Supreme God, his companion, Helen, is the earthly counterpart of the Gnostic entity already known to us: Ennoia or the First Thought of the Father. That she is called Helen is clear evidence of the syncretistic character now assumed by the cult. There is also archaeological evidence of this.[32] Helen, the female Eternal One, is also a Greek designation of a female divinity of obviously oriental provenance. Like Selene, the Moon, companion of the Sun, Simon's companion bears witness to the androgynous nature of the First Principle.[33] But she is also the female dimension of the divinity fallen into the world of matter, the soul cast down to prostitute itself before repenting and being saved by Nous, her intended bridegroom and consort (according to certain Nag Hammadi texts that would seem to show echoes of Simonian Gnosis).[34]

Irenaeus' longer report[35] deals with the most properly Gnostic phase in the development of the Simonian system. A cult originally probably Samaritan in origin and linked with the figure of the divine man, Simonianism is transformed into a typical Gnostic system under the decisive influence of Christianity.

The pre-existent God emits a Thought, the First Ennoia, 'the Mother of All, by means of whom he had planned at the beginning, in His mind, to create angels and archangels'.[36] This Thought, knowing the will of the Father, descends to generate the creative powers of this world. Thus, Simon's Ennoia performs a dual function, but already attested by Justin: she is the partner of the pre-existent God and is Sophia *Anima mundi*. There is no mention, at least in this report, of a more articulated division of the pleromatic world, nor is there any concept of an internal crisis in the Pleroma or of a Demiurge who is the monstrous product of the sin committed by the last aeon.

After creating angels and archangels, Ennoia is imprisoned by them out of envy, because they did not wish to be considered descendants of anyone; they are unaware of the existence of a God superior to them. This is a theme typical of the Gnostic cosmogonies already examined. Falling prisoner thus to the powers that she herself has generated, Ennoia is enclosed in a human body. Journeying across the centuries from one female body to another (among them that of Helen of Troy), she experiences every kind of suffering. Finally she becomes a whore in a brothel in Tyre, in Phoenicia. And here the pre-existing God, in the guise of Simon, descends to redeem her for ever.

The pre-existent God of the Simonians, according to their reinterpretation of the Christian Trinitarian mystery, descended first as the Son among the Jews. He later appeared, in the guise of Simon, as the Father in Samaria. Finally, as the Holy Spirit, he descended on other nations. Simon is the universal Saviour and Redeemer. In liberating Helen, he actually liberates the soul dispersed in matter and reveals himself as he really is: the True God. Moreover, he also descends to re-establish the world situation, which is badly governed by the angels. The message that he is said to have announced, at first as Jesus (a Jesus who, among other things, is supposed not to have really suffered), then as Simon, is one of total liberation. Whoever believes in him is safe from this world, which is destined for destruction. The Gnostic is now free to act in accordance with the criteria of a sovereign liberty, no longer subject to mundane norms and conventions.

Even if the Simonian system, in what might be called the second (or third) phase, seems to be unaware of typical Gnostic elements such as the Demiurge or self-knowledge, there can be no doubt of its structure. In the background can be seen themes such as the breaking of the unity of the archetypal androgyne; the progressive estrangement of its female dimension, whose duty is characteristically that of *genetrix mundi* or World Mother; the fall of this principle into a world in dualistic opposition to the upper world; the consequent need for redemption and liberation by means of a Saviour figure who, in this case coincides with the pre-existent God Himself. The story of Helen and Simon symbolizes the story of the soul fallen into this world of darkness and ignorance, a whore, but ready to be converted and to receive her heavenly spouse, her liberator and Saviour. The charms of the eternal female and the magic arts of the male counterpart combine so cleverly as to produce a model and a legend destined to last for centuries.

It is difficult to establish a connection between this report in Irenaeus and the system attributed to the Simonians by Hippolytus, who derives it explicitly from the *Megalē Apophasis*, or Great Revelation.[37] The concept of the divine that characterizes this work is monistic. An infinite Divine Power pervades and gives form and life to everything. Initially upright, since the divinity is absolutely transcendent, it then unfolds, in a series of hypostases, into the realities of the microcosm and the macrocosm. Everyone has an image of this power in themselves. It is their job to become an image, to realize the divine potential that is within them, to recover the ontological fullness of their being. There is no doubt about the Gnostic nature of the system. Consider, for example, the following passage from Hippolytus:

> To you then I say what I say and write what I write, this writing (that follows): there are two offshoots of all the aeons, which neither begin nor end, proceeding from a single root, the power of which is silence, invisible, incomprehensible. One of these appears on high, namely the great power which is in the universe, which governs all things, (which is) male; and the other below, a great conception, which is female, which generates all things. Therefore being each other's counterparts they form a pair and exhibit the space between them, the intangible air which has neither beginning nor end. Within it is the Father who upholds all things and nourishes the things that begin and end. This is he who stands, took his stand and will stand, being a male-and-female power like the pre-existing infinite power, which neither begins nor ends, existing in isolation.[38]

The pre-existent principle produces as an image of itself an entity that is also androgynous. According to its male dimension, it is Nous or Intellect, which governs everything; according to the female dimension, it is the Thought whose responsibility it is to give birth. Thus we find a duplication of the functions attributed by the Simonians of Irenaeus to Ennoia: cognitive power within the Father of his own mystery and generative power towards the world. Together these functions reconstitute the perfect image of the Father, whose direct intention is to save the created world and Man. This entity, which is, was and will be upright, offers the ideal model for the perfect Gnostic. To become an image: that is, in the particular language of this revelation, to achieve Gnosis means in fact to make straight the true human, the essential human who still lies supine within us.

By virtue of its decidedly syncretistic nature, its strongly monistic tendency and its deep debt to the tradition from which it draws a long series of *topoi*, or topics, the *Megalē Apophasis* is an important witness to the third (or fourth) phase of the Simonian movement, which is by now detached from the figure, historical or legendary, of Simon. Having abandoned the symbolism hidden behind the Ennoia–Helen myth, the Simonian of this generation appears to reflect more optimistically and rather more universally on the very essence of the Gnostic myth: the meeting with the self as an attempt to reconstruct the original androgynous unity.[39]

The final phase of the Simon story is given in the *Apocryphal Acts of Peter* and the pseudo-Clementine romance.[40] By now legend has taken over. According to the rules of the narrative romance typical of these narratives, Simon, who has become Peter's enemy *par excellence*, engages in a series of contests with the apostle to demonstrate their respective magic powers and is inevitably defeated, having become possessed by a ceaseless, masochistic delirium for power which results in tragi-comic self-destruction.[41] The biographical details contained in these sources are as follows: his parents were called Anthony and Rachel; he received a classical education at Alexandria and a Christian education with John the Baptist.[42] The details, on the whole, are unreliable. This may not, however, be the case regarding his connection with Dositheus, a shadowy figure who appears to have had some part in the beginnings of a Gnostic movement in Samaria.[43] Similarly the statement that insists on his Roman travels may have some claim to historical veracity. Even if Simon was not active towards the middle of the second century in Rome, a Simonian community certainly was (as we know from Justin), in lively competition with (and dependent upon) the local Gnostic communities.

What conclusions can we draw from this brief analysis of the principal testimonies concerning the Simonian movement? There appear to have been different phases of development. From a local cult of Jewish origins, but syncretistic in tendency and lacking specifically Gnostic features, revolving around a Samaritan holy man, it became in the second century a typical Gnostic movement. The impact of Christianity was decisive in the sense that Simon was transformed into a Gnostic Saviour. The encounter with pagan philosophy provided further elements of confirmation and added depth to the mythological nucleus. This nucleus has features in common with (though not necessarily derived from) the myth of the archetypal Androgyne and his Ennoia, which we know from other sources. Simonianism demonstrates the ability to adapt and change, typical of certain mythical themes in the course of a long history. Even if it tells us little (and that much of questionable value) about the origins of Gnosticism, its internal development raises a problem to which we must now direct our attention: the history of the Gnostic movement itself.

10

Visionaries, Prophets and Divines: Towards a History of Gnosticism

ECSTASY, POSSESSION AND REVELATION

Simon Magus is an emblematic figure. Whatever his historical reality may have been (and this is now lost to us), the features accorded to him by the heresiologists are so many indicators of the way in which his opponents perceived and experienced the dangers of Gnosticism. Irenaeus accuses the Simonians of practising exorcism and incantations, singing erotic hymns, confecting love potions, invoking those demon companions (typical of Greek magic) who send dreams, and generally making use of every sort of magic.[1] The purpose of this sort of accusation is clear: to discredit the opponent in whatever way. The history of opposition to sectarian movements furnishes so many examples of this sort that the historian must be on his guard against them. Indeed, Christians themselves were liable to be the victims of similar accusations.

And yet it is permissible to ask whether the easy cliché of the accusation of magic does not conceal, at least in this case, a significant nucleus of historical truth. This does not mean literally trying to establish the value, the function and the nature of magic in Gnosticism[2] (a problem made more difficult by the fact *inter alia* that magic in the late antique world was more widespread and less easy to define than one is now inclined to believe[3]). Identical actions were subject to opposing ideological interpretations. Celsus regarded the miracles of Jesus as an example of negative magic. Origen objected to them in that those thaumaturgical acts could never be regarded in this way, because they had been performed for good by a man of exceptional, irreproachable morality, who would certainly not stoop to using evil demons.[4] Equally ambivalent are the miracles performed by Apollonius of Tyana. Philostratus,[5] his biographer, is anxious to demonstrate, with arguments not unlike those of Origen, that his enemies' accusations of his practice of diabolical arts are unjustified, because Apollonius seeks to do good and his hero's thaumaturgical power originates in a divine source.[6]

Against this background the case of Simon Magus deserves further consideration. We have already mentioned the profound religious revolution in the marketing of religious goods at the dawn of the Christian era. In an age of prophets and holy men who had pushed back the frontiers of the sacred world, one had to adapt oneself to the new cultural models if one wished to make a success in that particular profession. But what were the distinctive signs that the public, with its insatiable appetite for novelty, expected from these *novi viri*, or new men? They had to be signs capable of proving them, both socially and religiously, to be representatives of the world above, at the same time increasing sources of their fortune.

Weber intentionally used the phrase 'charismatic power' to define the leaders of every sacred cosmos, attributing to them a divine origin. The ancient world endorses this view. The most striking example in the area of the Fertile Crescent, where ancient civilizations sprang up, consists in the so-called phenomenon of sacred kingship,[7] which has significant parallels in politico-religious phenomena investigated by anthropologists among pre-literate societies, especially in Africa.[8] If the king is, by birth or election, the legitimate source of a power that derives from the divinity, the priestly caste, in its various historical manifestations, is the mediator *par excellence* of this power. Ancient societies, including Greek and Roman, display a tendency towards strict regulation of the use of sacred power. Such power is vested in well-defined, hierarchically ordered institutions; regulated by rites enveloped in the protective cocoon of inviolable traditions and immobilized by subtle codification worthy of the most refined casuistry, whose secret is possessed by restricted elites; wisely administered in temples and sacred places erected to the glory of the divinity and frequently inclined to become genuine centres of political and economic power and to confer prestige on those who run them; controlled in this way, the sacred had finally become domesticated. The collective phenomena of the 'undomesticated sacred' that do not conform to this picture are rare indeed. As the case of the Dionysiac religion shows, they are for the most part mere functional cracks in an edifice that preserves its secular solidity intact.

The traditional boundaries between human and divine were well garrisoned, even in the most difficult frontier zones. Take, for example, the case of ancient prophecy.[9] There are certainly profound differences between the Biblical and the pagan prophet. The Biblical prophet does not lose his personality in the will of God, but speaks in his place, announcing to the chosen people a divine message, now of liberation, now of ruin.[10] The pagan prophet or prophetess, e.g. the Pythian, empties him- or herself of their own personality to become a vehicle of the divine power, which uses the person to transmit not ethical messages, but all sorts of announcements and promises.[11] Nevertheless, the Biblical prophet and the pagan prophet share a fundamental attribute: they both underline the difference between human and divine.

Thus the *theios anēr*, the holy man, from this perspective, testifies to a decisive change in attitude, as we have already seen. The stereotype of Simon Magus is excellent corroboration of this. He is a fusion of human and divine. And this difficult union, whose subtle balances are bound to vary, but of which there can be no doubt, is actually his strength. Humanity is no longer the temporary, but the permanent, residence of the divinity. Indeed, they actually are the divinity. And the leader is merely the example of a process that every one of the elect can verify and realize within him- or herself.

Was the inner conviction of the holy man or woman enough to provide reassurance of their acquisition of this new divine dimension? They were confronted by a public eager for concrete proof and used to men and women prepared to legitimize the proper *cursus* of religious honours by means of visions and trances. Isn't success measured in some degree by its effects? So weren't the magical practices of certain Gnostic groups perhaps the inevitable price to pay for confirming, on a psychological, but also objective, level, the success achieved by the acquisition of this new benefit?

The exclusive, uncontrolled possession of sacred power can, however, play cruel tricks. The Apostle Paul was well aware of this when in his letters he castigated the Corinthians, the same community that he had founded himself a few years earlier.[12] Religious enthusiasm – and Paul knew very well what he was talking about – could lead to unfortunate conclusions. The Corinthians regarded themselves as 'pneumatic' and 'perfect',[13] and took pride in a 'knowledge' that allowed them to do anything. Possessors of the Spirit, they considered themselves already resurrected.[15] The very membership of the community became proof and evidence that they belonged to the Spirit.[16]

The recipients of these letters do not betray any sort of improbable Gnostic leanings,[17] but they are an important sign of the times; they bear witness to a charismatic spirit, to which the Gnostic leaders will also lay claim.

That the psychological origins of Gnosticism cannot be detached from phenomena of possession and religious enthusiasm typical of the period is also confirmed by the sparse evidence available to us. Some Valentinian leaders experienced a fundamental vision. We have already mentioned the case of Valentinus. Irenaeus tells us that one of his disciples, Marcus the magician, had a similar experience. In a vision the Supreme Tetrad descended from invisible, unnameable places in the Pleroma in female form to reveal to him something never before revealed to God or man, who he really was and how he came into being.[18]

Marcus' visionary experience, akin to that of Valentinus, displays some interesting features. The vision is a means of divine revelation. Full detailed studies of its importance, diffusion and typology are now available.[19] Ancient literature, Biblical and classical, contains many examples,[20] but there is no space to examine them here. In the Hellenistic period, in step with the process of the individualization and spiritualization of religion, the vision tended to acquire a new status and a different function. It is transformed from a means of attaining definite goals of material benefits[21] (through incubation, astrology or magic) into an internal spiritual experience, which proves a decisive turning-point in the life of the individual. In this sense Valentinus' vision is not unlike that of Paul; it is a meeting with Christ, which radically transforms the life of the visionary. The *epopteia*, or vision, thus becomes an end in itself. The vision loses its thaumaturgical function and acquires a redemptive one.

In the case of Valentinus and Marcus, he who appears to the visionary is not immersed in sleep, but awake and alert, the Supreme Divinity himself in his role as Saviour of humanity. Unlike the apocalyptic visions, whose Sybilline allegory inevitably features a particular intermediary (usually an angel), in these Gnostic visions the divinity is revealed directly, because this is the only way in which it can reveal to the Gnostic the umbilical cord that unites the Gnostic to himself, his own ontological reality. The vision proper is followed by an explanation in the form of the recital of a myth,[22] a paradigm with which we are already familiar. It is at the root of the visionary experience of Hermes in the *Poimandres*. Its 'Gnosticism' consists in the fact that, as a result of this particular pneumatic vision, Gnostics become what they see.

We find indirect confirmation of this strange mystical union in the *Sitz im Leben*, or situation implied in a certain Gnostic literary genre of revelation discourse. We have already often encountered this genre in documents such as the *Pistis Sophia* or the *Apocryphon of John*. With only one or two variations, the scene is always the same. The perfect Saviour, the risen Jesus, reveals to the circle of chosen disciples total, definitive *gnōsis*. In many cases the means of revelation is the vision. This happens to Mary Magdalene in the *Gospel of Mary*[23] and to the disciples in the *Wisdom of Jesus Christ*.[24] The experience of John in the eponymous *Apocryphon* is significant. The Supreme Triad[25] appears to him. The vision of the divine in many forms[26] enables him thus to understand and to grasp intuitively the very nucleus of the system. The resulting explanation, in the form of a mythical account, is intended merely to express and, as it were, to unfold, on the level of logical-discursive and spatio-temporal co-ordinates, a reality already perceived and possessed in its constituent nucleus.

So if a particular psychological origin for Gnosticism is required, it must be located in experiences like those of Valentinus, events that moreover had to be widespread, as the experiences concealed in a literary genre such as the revelation discourse confirm. 'The Spirit blows where it will.' But the Gnostics now knew that this liberty was in deep knowledge and intuition of the Father's will itself, of which the Spirit was the most complete manifestation.[27]

SECOND-CENTURY GNOSTIC DOCTORS

But who really were the Gnostics? It has taken so long to arrive at this inevitable question for the simple reason that the documents, though they tell us much about their doctrines and ideas, only tell us a little about the personalities and biographical data on the founders and heads of the schools. For the most part, we have to rely for this on information provided by the heresiological sources. The picture that emerges, though fragmentary and partial, covers the second century. In addition to the names of Basil and Valentinus, already mentioned, there are others who deserve closer attention.

Irenaeus (who, together with Clement of Alexandria, is our principal source for Gnostic prosopography) tells us that Simon's successor was one Menander, also a Samaritan accused of magical practices.[28] Like Simon, he preached the existence of a First Power, an unknown and absolutely transcendent God, said to coexist with Ennoia, who brought forth the angels who created this world. Unlike his presumed master, however, Menander, who also identified himself with the Saviour sent by the Invisible Ones for the salvation of humankind, is said not to have identified himself with the Supreme Power. A new, interesting feature is that his disciples can obtain resurrection, and hence immortality, in this life by means of baptism in the name of the founder. This seems to indicate, in the earliest forms of Gnosticism, the existence and the importance of certain ritual practices.

The information given by Irenaeus about Menander is difficult to assess. It is unique in the mass of heresiological literature. If taken literally, it would bring us forward to the generation after Simon

158   *Visionaries, Prophets and Divines*

(*c.* AD 80). Irenaeus seeks to show Menander's dependence upon Simon and attributes to him doctrines similar to those of the arch-heretic himself. But we saw in chapter 9 above that Simonianism as known to the Bishop of Lyons has to be placed in the middle of the second century, not of the first. On the other hand, the simplicity of this system may be seen as an indication in favour of an earlier date. The Gnostic myth seems to be reduced to a few essential elements: a Supreme God, Ennoia–Sophia the mother of the angels who create this world, a Saviour figure who promises a Gnosis drenched in magic, and baptismal practices that aim to reassure and confirm the proselyte. The most likely hypothesis is that Menander represents one of the first links in the Gnostic chain. It is significant that the area in which this Gnostic teacher was active was Antioch, for this would confirm the probable Jewish origins of his teaching and the function of Jewish Christianity as a privileged channel of its diffusion.[29]

Menander is said to have been succeeded by Saturninus (or Satornilus, an Antiochene from Daphne) and Basilides, in Syria and Alexandria respectively.[30] Like Menander, Saturninus is said to have taught the existence of an unknown God, himself the creator of the archangels, angels, power and dominions.[31] The world was created by seven angels, who also made humankind, for

> When a shining image appeared from the supreme power above, which they were not able to detain, he says, because it immediately sped back upwards, they exhorted one another, saying, 'Let us make a man after the image and likeness.' When this was done, he says, and their creation could not stand erect because of the powerlessness of the angels, but crept like a worm,[32] then the power above took pity on him because he had been made in his likeness and sent a spark of life which raised the man up, equipped him with limbs and made him live.[33]

We are now in full Gnostic myth and in a period that can probably be dated between AD 120 and 130 (Saturninus is contemporary with Basilides). The many Gnostic parallels with Saturninus' anthropogony remove any doubt about the reliability of Irenaeus' report. Saturninus taught a typical Gnostic theory of dual creation. Fashioned on the physical plane according to the forms of a luminous divine image (an interpretation of Gen. 1:26), Adam is nevertheless unable to stand upright. The Supreme God infuses into him directly the spark of life that constitutes his spiritual principle (an interpretation of Gen. 2:7). In this version there is no mention of the Ennoia–Sophia myth theme or that of Demiurge. The spark of life, at the moment of death, will return to the divine reality consubstantial with it, while the body will disintegrate.

Clearly Jewish in origin, the movement, perhaps in a second phase known to Irenaeus, seems to have been influenced by Christianity. Hostile to the God of the Jews, who was identified with one of the seven creator angels, Saturninus taught that Christ the Saviour – for him ungenerated, incorporeal and with no form, in accordance with the rules of a rigorous docetism – had come to destroy the God of the Old Testament and to save those who had the spark of life, which comes from him. To speed up the process of salvation, his disciples practised extreme asceticism, abstaining from meat and sexual intercourse. They considered that matrimony and procreation were of Satanic origin.[34]

In Basilides we encounter for the first time the embodiment of a truly profound and original Gnostic thinker.[35] It is quite unlikely that he was a disciple of Menander or that his dualism was Persian in origin.[36] But it is certain that he was dependent upon the tradition of Greek thought, and his residence in Alexandria may be considered confirmation of this.[37] He lived in the first half of the second century. Of his enormous output (including twenty-four books of *Exegetics* on the Gospels and on odes and psalms) only a few fragments survive in the works of Clement of Alexandria. There are also two notices about him in Irenaeus and Hippolytus, but they disagree with each other. His work was continued by his son (perhaps in the spiritual sense), Isidore, about whose works (*Ethics, A Treatise on the Temporary Soul, An Interpretation of the Prophet Parchor*) we know something from Clement.

Basilides was a Christian Gnostic. According to Hippolytus he derived his teaching from oral, esoteric traditions going back to the Apostle Matthew,[38] or (according to Clement) to Glaucias, a disciple of Paul.[39] He began a tradition that is found again in other Christian Gnostic writers.[40] He sought to relate his teachings to eyewitness accounts of the life of Jesus, the privileged generation of Apostles and first disciples. In an age in which oral tradition still retained its prestige intact,[41] there was perhaps no more authoritative method, in Christian circles,[42] of legitimating their own doctrines.

From the fragments of Clement and Origen there emerges an impressive, if somewhat partial, picture of the person, and it reinforces the originality and vigour of Basilides' thought. The starting-point seems to have been the problem of evil.[43] And the fragments are imbued with a profound pessimism about the intrinsic sinfulness of the human soul. Even the child who has not sinned has in itself the inclination to sin; and even the perfect human being does not escape this paradoxical situation.[44] Isidore explained this congenital tendency to evil by the doctrine of the appendages of evil:[45] 'The desire for evil things is born as a result of the stength of the appendages.' To explain this one might think of the widespread conception (already mentioned) according to which the soul, in its descent to the world through the planetary spheres, receives specific negative characteristics. Or, even better, a doctrine like that of the *antimimon pneuma*, or counterfeit spirit, in the *Apocryphon of John* or the *Pistis Sophia*. However that may be, the doctrine of the attachments of the soul is merely a variant of dualist anthropology typical of Gnosticism. Evil is innate, dwells in human beings and lives and acts in them. Far from the detailed and horrifying descriptions of the demons at work in the human body provided by the *Apocryphon of John*, Basilides' anthropology, equally pessimistic, finds in the redemptive action of Jesus (interpreted in a profoundly ethical way) the means of liberating the soul from the cycle of reincarnation. The first precept 'of the will of God [is] to love everything, for everything is interrelated; and the second is not to desire anything; the third is not to hate anything.'[46] This ethic of compassion and non-violence, whose evident similaries have led some to consider (improbable) Buddhist influence,[47] must be seen against the background of the information about Basilides presented by Irenaeus and Hippolytus.

In fact, it is difficult to reconcile the two reports. We have already mentioned Basilides' original system as described by Hippolytus, which revolves around the idea of a non-existent God from whom the seed of the world comes and who contains a triple Sonship. The tendency towards monism and optimism in this system makes one think (rightly) of a later phase in Basilides' thought,[48] in opposition to the original dualistic pessimistic nature of the system, as it appears in Clement's fragments and Irenaeus' report. Indeed the Basilides of Irenaeus is said to have made a greater division between the cosmos and the pleromatic world.[49] Apart from the ungenerated Father, the divine universe of Basilides' system is said to come ready made from the Nous, Logos, Thought or Phronesis, Wisdom and Power. From the last two aeons come virtue, Archons and angels, which form the various heavens, up to a total of 365, so as to make a perfect correspondence between celestial space and the cycle of the year.[50] The angels that are in the Last Heaven are those that created everything that is in the world, including humankind. Their king is the God of the Jews. Among them is a continual struggle for predominance. This explains the evils that afflict the world and its peoples.

The ungenerated Father then sends his own Nous, also called Christ, to liberate 'all who believed in him from the power of the angels who had created the world.'[51] His suffering, however, is only apparent. It will be remembered that Simon of Cyrene really suffered in his place.

None of the theories proposed to reconcile these two statements is very convincing. As we have said, that of Hippolytus represents an optimistic, universalistic phase in the development of the master's thought, a phase that should be attributed to a Basilidian school at the beginning of the third century, in keeping with a general tendency in the Gnostic movement of that century.

Carpocrates was also a contemporary of Basilides.[52] Some doubt has been expressed (wrongly) about this person's historicity,[53] for the simple reason that almost no details of his life have come down to us. Clement of Alexandria does tell us a little about his son, Epiphanes, whom he actually identifies as the true founder of the movement. Born at Same, in the island of Cephalonia, he is said to have died there at the age of seventeen. A temple was built there in his honour and he was worshipped in it as a god.[54] Still, Clement records a few extracts from his *On Justice*;[55] they do not prove it to be a Gnostic work, though they indicate that it belongs to the utopian, libertarian tradition. Appealing to the ancient opposition between nature and law, already posed by the Sophists, Epiphanes affirms the natural community of material wealth, repudiating the concept of private property as a product of human law. The inevitable consequence of this antinomianism is typically depraved behaviour:

> In common for all he made the vines which refuse neither sparrow nor thief, and likewise the corn and the other fruits. Fellowship and what belongs to equality when violated gave birth to a thief of creatures and of fruits. In that God made all things in common for man and brought together the female with the male in common and united the animals likewise, he declared righteousness to be fellowship with equality. But those thus born rejected the fellowship which had brought about their birth and say: 'Who marries one, let him have her', when they could all share in common, as the rest of the animals show.[56]

Epiphanes was thus obliged to attack the Mosaic Law also, whose injunction not to desire the goods or the wife of one's neighbour 'turned what was communal into private property'.[57] This veiled attack, not against the God of the Old Testament (Epiphanes recognizes a single providential God), but against his legislator, seems to be the only point of contact with Gnosticism.[58]

Irenaeus' statement on the Carpocratians provides a picture of a more expressly Gnostic system.[59] There is the figure of Marcellina, otherwise

unknown. Irenaeus says only, however, that she came to Rome during
the papacy of Anicetus (c. AD 160). One wonders if in this case too
Irenaeus' statement does not reflect a later stage of development in the
Carpocratian system, whose early embryonic phases are said to go back
to Epiphanes.

The importance of the doctrine of metempsychosis for these Gnostics
has already been mentioned. The soul, of divine origin and cast down
into this world, a prisoner of the body created by the malevolent
Archons, had to try every kind of sin to be able to aspire to liberation.
Here too antinomianism and libertinism are bound inextricably together
in confirmation of the superiority of the Gnostic compared with human
and demiurgic laws.

Jesus the Saviour is actually only a man. The son of Joseph, he was
the most just of men. At a specific moment the ungenerated God instilled
into him a superior power. It was this power that spoke with the
disciples, revealing to them the secrets of Gnosis in private converse. To
be the possessor of Gnosis is to be equal, if not superior, to Jesus. This
Christology presents characteristics typical of certain groups of Jewish
Christians, who regarded Jesus merely as a man (albeit a superior one).[60]
It underlines the presence and the importance of the Judaic element. On
the other hand, the Carpocratians known to Irenaeus had assumed
purely syncretistic features, according to him. In addition to practices
such as that of branding the back of the right earlobe, they worshipped
images, some of them painted, including that of Christ (they believed it
went back to the time of Pilate, who is said to have had it made during
the trial), which they displayed together with those of the great
philosophers Pythagoras, Plato, Aristotle and others. This confirms the
link with the Greek philosophical tradition that appears in the fragments
of Epiphanes.

Marcion, also a contemporary of the Gnostic thinkers of the first half
of the second century,[61] deserves a special section to himself. It was his
destiny to be born in a land of great religious traditions: Asia Minor,
at Sinope (modern Sinop) on the Black Sea. His father was a bishop
and his family must have belonged to the highest social class in that
lively, important commercial city. In his life, in his original profession
as shipowner and merchant (*nauklēros*), he travelled widely; his
geographical travels tended to merge with his spiritual ones (as they did
for other religious leaders of the time). We do not know the date of his
birth, but it must be placed towards the end of the first century AD. It
was not ancient custom to profile childhood or adolescence, as modern
writers do, and the Christian polemicists[62] tended to concentrate on the
acme of Marcion's career, the time when his personality came to

maturity. This was the time of his arrival in the Rome where Valentinus was carrying out his mission as a teacher. He had grown up in the Christian tradition, driven out perhaps by the rivalry of his father, perhaps by disagreements with his own community,[63] probably after spending some time in the coastal cities of Asia Minor, such as Ephesus and Smyrna.[64] Polycarp of Smyrna calls him the 'firstborn of Satan'.[65] Marcion made his way to Rome, an almost obligatory goal in his wanderings (*c.*139–40).[66] There, according to Irenaeus,[67] he became the disciple of Cerdon the Syrian,[68] who lived in Rome during the papacy of Hyginus (136–40). Marcion learned from him that 'the God proclaimed by the Law and the prophets is the Father of Our Lord Jesus Christ, for the one is known and the other is unknown, one is just and the other is good.'[69]

In addition to having a strong personality, Marcion possessed a lively ambition, a quality that was compatible with an intense, radical religiosity like his. More than a prophet, he seems to be a logical believer, a sort of Occam whose razor-sharp reasoning exposes contradictions and rejects every possibility of compromise.

At first he joined the community of Roman believers and sought to expound his doctrines at a synod. But they were rejected, and he was expelled in 144,[70] a decisive date for the Marcionite church, which later was to take it as that of its own *hegira*, or expulsion. He must have regarded the expulsion as a sign from destiny. It was time to replace the false church with the real one. Thus, after his estrangement from the Roman church, he founded his own, with a hierarchy of bishops, priests and deacons, in competition with the model of the True Church, from which it diverged by virtue of the possibility of a career in the priesthood, which it offered to women.[71]

The vision of an opportunity to establish an ecclesiastical organization as an alternative to the True Church was evidently successful. A few years later Justin bears witness to its success,[72] and Tertullian, his fierce adversary, was compelled to admit that Marcion's church had 'filled the entire world.'[73] While Gnostic schools and conventicles began to disperse in later centuries as a result of internal disputes and under pressure from the triumph of both Christianity and Manichaeism, Marcionite churches diffused throughout Italy, Egypt, Mesopotamia and Armenia were still flourishing in the fourth and fifth centuries, according to the lively polemic of the great Syrian father, Ephraem.[74]

Before Mani, Marcion had understood that if one wanted to compete with the True Church or to replace it, it was necessary to beat it at its own game: organization. This meant an efficient, functional hierarchy, a lively, attractive liturgy, as well as clear and precise doctrines. In support of his doctrine Marcion therefore compiled a corpus, a sort of embryonic canon of New Testament texts uniquely valid for his church, including the Gospel of Luke and ten Pauline letters. He had also exerted a form of censorship, to remove all Jewish elements from these texts.[75]

His reasons for this censorship were dictated by his theological system, about whose interpretation there has been some lively controversy. We now propose, therefore, to examine his doctrine.

Its distinctive feature is that, though it is not strictly within the Gnostic system, it is difficult to understand it without reference to this religious area. In one way Marcion follows the path opened up by Paul. What struck him about Pauline teaching and what he sought to explore more deeply was the mystery of grace and its relation to divine justice. The unavoidable dialectical polarization, which constitutes the originality and profundity of the Apostle's thought left Marcion perplexed and dissatisfied. He saw justice and grace not as two aspects able to coexist in one God, but as irreconcilable modalities of two different gods. Theological dualism thus led him to a ditheistic formula with its resultant anti-cosmism, both strongly bound up with Gnostic doctrines. 'The Marcionites impudently turn up their noses at creation and reject the work of the Creator. "This world? A truly magnificent piece of work, well worthy of its creator," they say', is what Tertullian has to say about them.[76]

The Creator and his world reflect and condition each other. If the body is doomed to perdition and the world is the seat of evil, its Creator, the Spirit of this world, cannot be positive. Not that the Demiurge is arrogant or malevolent, as in many Gnostic systems. He simply has nothing in common with the Good God, the alien God accessible only to the Son.

In a lost work, the *Antitheses*, Marcion systematically laid out the points of opposition between the two Gods.[77] One is the artisan, the God of creation and generation, the ruler of this Aeon; he can be predicated, because he is known, and known from his own real work, the world. The other is the hidden God, unknown and incomprehensible. In the latter case the predicates typical of contemporary apophatic theology recur, but with a different emphasis. Marcion's God, an alien *par excellence* to this world, is above all the New God, the Good God. In contrast to the Gnostic systems, humankind and the world are utterly alien to him. It is an important point: the nature of God is quite different from that of man, just as it is different from that of the world. The human is made of corruptible body, and of soul, but this soul is not a spark of the same substance as the divinity. Marcion's God, therefore, is not the Gnostic God, who is obliged in some way (even in his infinite liberty and unknowable will) to reveal himself to the elect, because by saving the elect he saves himself. The revelation made by the Son of God to humanity is an act of pure, total and unfathomable grace: 'This single work is sufficient for our God, Who has liberated man through His supreme, superlative goodness.'[78] This statement conceals the nucleus of Marcionite theology. The intervention of divine grace cannot in any way be conditioned by humans. God does not intervene to liberate them from sin or guilt or misfortune, as Paul taught; still less, to recover his own parts, which have been dispersed in matter, as the Gnostics required. Marcion's grace is 'a grace that has no past ... the paradox of an incomprehensible grace, unsought, unprecedented ... a profound mystery of divine goodness as such.'[79]

It is against this background that his Christology must be interpreted. It is not docetist. Christ really did suffer, even if it was in a particular body. It teaches that the Saviour redeemed men as strangers 'because no one ever buys those who belong to him.'[80] And the price of the redemption was his blood. It was not offered for the remission of sins or in vicarious expiation, but to cancel the Demiurge's claim on his creatures once and for all.[81] The adopted souls that listen to, and accept, the message of the Stranger God are saved by their own experience of faith, not because they receive some sort of Gnosis.[82]

So is Marcion a Biblical theologian or a Gnostic doctor? The answer to this question depends largely, of course, on what is meant by Gnosticism. If anti-cosmism is regarded as its essence, it is difficult to deny Marcion the hallmark of Gnosticism. This position has been argued authoritatively by Jonas,[83] but nevertheless contradicts the evidence of all the factors that point in the opposite direction. Marcion does not have the actual concept of Gnosis as a doctrine of the meeting with the self. Accordingly, its necessary mythological correlate is absent, that is to say, the minute anatomy of the self projected onto the mythical screen of the mental processes that take place in the pleromatic Anthropos by means of the action of his cohort of hypostases. Even where clearly analogous elements can be seen, as in the figure of the Demiurge, these actually function and can be explained in different ways. It is true that in Marcion the polemic against the Old Testament, its God and its prophets reappears. But this treatise alone is not enough to label a system of thought as Gnostic. Even Marcion's asceticism has its own roots:

> Not wanting to help to populate the world made by the Demiurge, the Marcionites declare their refusal to marry, challenging their Creator and hastening towards the Unique Good, which has called them and which

(they say) is God in a different sense. Therefore, not wanting to leave anything of themselves here, they become continent, not for any moral principle, but out of hostility to their maker and because they do not want to avail themselves of his creation.[84]

This refusal is therefore not dictated by an ethical principle, but rather by the wish not to collaborate in any way with the work of the Demiurge, in a 'metaphysical alignment', which is a distinctive feature of Marcionite thought: a radical Paulinism carried to its extreme, whose presuppositions are far from both the tradition of the True Church and the Gnostics.[85]

That there is a profound difference, though not an insuperable one, between Marcion and Gnosticism (though they are in some ways linked) may also be deduced from what we know of his disciple, Apelles.[86] He probably came into contact with Alexandrian Gnosticism and broke the fascinating, but very delicate, doctrinal balance of the master. He resolutely explored the Gnostic possibilities virtually embedded in his system. The Demiurge became explicitly a creature of the Supreme God.[87] The Old Testament, which Marcion considered to be simply a religiously worthless document, becomes a work of deception, whose lies Apelles sets out to refute in his *Syllogisms*.[88] Unlike Marcion, who put himself forward in the guise of an exegete and theologian, Apelles (according to Eusebius) adapted himself to the genetic model of Gnostic knowledge and allowed himself to be convinced 'by the oracles of a virgin possessed, Philomena',[89] and he wrote down these revelations in a (no longer extant) work, the *Revelations*. But a more significant feature, which also represents a radical departure from the psychology of the master is that Apelles recognized in souls a pre-existence with the Good God, that is, a divine origin, which predestined them to salvation, according to the model of the *viri novi* of Arnobius.[90]

The second half of the century is dominated by the Valentinian school, whose mythological and theological systems have been fully treated. We now have to confine ourselves to the few biographical data that we have of its founder and his most important disciples.

We know that Valentinus came to Rome during the papacy of Hyginus (136–40), but rose to the peak of his teaching career in the time of Pius (150–5).[91] Egyptian by birth, he received his education at Alexandria, where he probably came into contact with the Gnostic writings and mythological stories that he used as the basis of his own Christian Gnostic system. We know of his success as a teacher in Rome from Tertullian. He was put up for the papacy, but passed over in favour of Pius the Martyr. He then broke with the community, which later rejected him as a heretic.[92] But he must have continued his activity in Rome for many years, because he was still active under Anicetus (154–65).[93]

Even his enemies concede that he had an outstanding personality,[94] a religious genius, visionary and mystic (his initiation into Gnosticism is an example), a poet and a shepherd of souls. The extant fragments of his work seem to reflect the impetus and depth of the founder of the religious community. He addresses his disciples in a prophetic tone in a homily:

> From the beginning you are immortal and children of eternal life. You wished to take death to yourselves as your portion in order that you might destroy it and annihilate it utterly and that death might die in you and through you. For when you destroy the world, you yourselves are not destroyed, but you are lords over the whole creation and over all decay.[95]

Critics have taken pains to reconstruct the system probably devised by Valentinus.[96] The almost insurmountable difficulty has been that heresiological literature presents it in such diverse and irreconcilable ways. Moreover, some of the Valentinian texts from Nag Hammadi have been attributed (on rather flimsy evidence) to Valentinus himself.[97] The hypothesis (though not admitted) of many of these reconstructions is that the Gnostic systems developed from the simple to the complex. Accordingly, one must hypothesize that the original founder's system was extremely simple. On the other hand, Valentinus was active for a long time during which he probably introduced variations and corrections into his own system.

Hippolytus tells us that Valentinus' disciples were divided into two schools: the western or Italian, with Ptolemy and Heracleon; and the eastern or Anatolian, with Theodotus, Assionicus and Marcus.[98] The reason for this schism was, as we have already explained, a Christological controversy about the nature of the body of Christ, considered by the western branch to be psychic, and by the eastern one to be pneumatic. The former continued the work of the master in Rome and extended it to south Gaul. A central feature of this Italian branch seems to have been, if the Christological controversy is any indication, the positive evaluation of the psychic element. We have already mentioned this in connection with Ptolemy, the author of the *Epistle to Flora* and the deviser of the system expounded by Irenaeus in the long account he devotes to the Gnostics: 'It rivals the system of Mani in [its] conceptual compactness and is superior to it in depth of thought.'[99]

The same tendency is evident in Heracleon,[100] according to Clement of Alexandria, the most esteemed of Valentinus' disciples.[101] He was the author of a commentary on St John's Gospel of which Origen quotes many passages in order to refute them in his own commentary on the same work. It is the first known continuous commentary on a Gospel. Heracleon uses the technique of allegory to discover the underlying principles of Gnostic anthropology, on which he concentrates his attention. The importance of this work is confirmed by the fact that Origen himself, in his meticulous rebuttal of it, is actually influenced by it, especially in its exegetical technique.

We know nothing of Theodotus. Clement of Alexandria composed a work called *Excerpta ex Theodoto*[102] or, more precisely, *Extracts from the Work of Theodotus and the Oriental School at the Time of Valentinus*. But it is actually a complex work, in which it is not always easy to distinguish Clement's observations from the quotations from Theodotus and in which the doctrines of the western and eastern schools are intermingled. The work is an indispensable document for the study of the Valentinian system.

We are better informed about Marcus the magician.[103] An oriental from Asia Minor, or perhaps even Egypt, he moved to the West, as far as the Rhône Valley, where his activities came to the attention of Irenaeus, who hastened to pour scorn on what he considered to be Marcus' real motives: 'He is especially interested in women, particularly in wealthy, elegant women, whom he frequently attempts to seduce.'[104] The fascination with which certain types of women regard some religious leaders is certainly not an invention of Irenaeus, who makes an easy game of being ironical about the adventures of this Gnostic Casanova. But the comments he makes in his report help us to understand the Gnostic aspect of this seduction.[105] Marcus interprets the symbolism of spiritual matrimony in a quite literal way. By means of the material seed, Marcus, the envoy of the Supreme Tetrad, transmits the seed of light to his victim in turn. In this way the reunion between male and female is anticipated, as is that of angel and image, intellect and psyche, that will finally take place in the Bridal Chamber of the Pleroma.

Against this background it is easy to understand the spate of cultic activity that took hold among some groups of Marcosians. Another feature of Marcosian Gnosis is the predilection for arithmetical speculation and number mysticism, widespread in contemporary culture, which the Marcosians used in order to reinterpret the mysteries of the pleromatic world.[106]

Beyond the most representative exponents of the Valentinian school, we must admit once again that we know little or nothing of other Gnostic figures. Hippolytus has left us an intriguing document: the *Book of Baruch*, by the Gnostic Justin.[107] The text expounds a typical triadic system: a transcendent principle, the Good; a second principle inferior to it, the Father of All, or Elohim; a female principle inferior to both, Eden, or Earth, who is half woman and half beast, because she participates in both upper and lower worlds. Humans are the fruit of the union of Elohim with Eden, from whom they receive spirit and soul, respectively. But then Elohim returns to the Good. Eden, angry and jealous, scatters her angels, especially Naas (the serpent), against what remains of her lover in the world, the Spirit. The redemptive process then breaks forth. Baruch, an angel of Elohim who opposes Naas, sends liberators (Moses, some prophets, including a pagan one, Heracles, whose presence confirms the syncretistic nature of the system), who nevertheless fail in their mission. Only Jesus will succeed in the work of redemption, ensuring the return of the human spirit to its original principle.

An original document, even in the variety of its borrowings (especially from Judaism),[108] the *Book of Baruch* in its compactness reveals the intervention of a creative figure. But the heresiologist's discretion has left us only the name of this figure.

Hippolytus also mentions the system of a certain Monoimus the Arab, in which arithmetical speculations are prominent.[109] We are now at the end of the second century, a period to which the activities of Prodicus, a libertine Gnostic mentioned by Clement of Alexandria, should probably be referred.[110]

RESISTANCE AND SURRENDER

The statements of heresiologists allow us to reconstruct the visible part of an iceberg. We have some idea of the complexity and vastness of the submerged part, but we cannot be specific about it. What are the spatio-temporal co-ordinates that we have to use to assess many of the Nag Hammadi texts? How can we arrange them without resorting to convenient labels that will help us to classify their content but not to assess their historical value? Take the case of the texts we have defined as Sethian. The theological systems illustrated by them undoubtedly present structural affinities and analogies. But to conclude from these affinities that there were certain groups who called themselves 'Sethians' is historically quite a long step, and it is not always possible to be certain about it.[111]

What can be documented historically is, rather, the gradual disappearance or the slow submersion into third- and especially fourth-century society of groups and communities that had played an important social and religious role in second-century society. The very structure of Gnostic associations contributed significantly to this phenomenon of gradual dissolution – their character as clubs, confined and restricted to intellectuals, to esoteric communities programmed to exclude the external world, often in conflict with each other, lacking organization or institutions.[112] What appeared in the second century as strongly binding elements had been changed into points of weakness.

Second-century Gnosticism was the expression of an economically expanding and socially mobile provincial society. Its cosmopolitan aspects, with its syncretistic tendencies, its cultural flexibility, its ability to realize an aristocracy of the spirit on the religious level, its use of mythological, symbolic languages to satisfy popular and intellectual taste (it was both profoundly theological and speculative) were able to contain the tensions of the newly emerging social groups and to provide an outlet for the uprooting and social-religious crisis experienced by traditional groups as a result of acute economic and social change. In this situation the openness of the communities, their internal fluidity and egalitarianism were strong points, but they proved to be short-lived. They were to pay dearly for the absence of real organization and the rejection of institutional roots.

When Gnostics adhered to more traditional structures or created their own alternatives, they developed and lasted longer. We have already mentioned the case, albeit anomalous, of Marcion's church. The fortunes of the Valentinian school afford a more relevant example.[113] Divided as it was internally by doctrinal disputes, it nevertheless had the advantage of being able to graft itself on to existing and widely tested structures. The organizational tradition of *Schulbetrieb*, or schooling, and the elite school revolving around the figure of a recognized master and attended by select, faithful pupils,[114] though not perhaps a strong, cohesive element, enabled it to survive. It was a not inconsiderable life-support to be grasped in the treacherous, dangerous crises of the third century. The subsequent history of Valentinianism, however relative, for several centuries is proof of this.

The hostile attacks of Plotinus[115] and Origen[116] prove that the Valentinian tradition was still thriving in the third century. There is even more significant evidence of its survival after the Diocletianic revolution. Epiphanius mentions Valentinian groups in Egypt in the second half of the fourth century when he records in his *Panarion* that 'the seed of Valentinus is still in Egypt today,'[117] a statement confirmed by the privilege the curators of the Nag Hammadi corpus have afforded, within it, to the school's writings. Even Didymus the Blind (d. 398), active in Alexandria, bears witness to the survival of Valentinian anthropology and Christology. He attacked both them and their 'many' adherents repeatedly.[118]

At Antioch John Chrysostom, in a series of works at the end of the fourth century, directly attacked the Valentinians, who continued to enjoy a certain prestige, on the subject of asceticism.[119]

Imperial policy also has provided us with an important document. An edict of 362 (of Julian the Apostate) tells us that there were disagreements between Arians and Valentinians[120] at Edessa under Constantius. Ambrose tells of reprisals *c*.388 against Valentinians at Kallinikon,[121] an important Roman fortress and commercial city on the Euphrates in Osrhoene. At the instigation of the local bishop, monks had attacked first the synagogue and then the Valentinian cult centre. They were also the target of imperial religious policy. They are especially mentioned in the anti-heretical law of Constantine in 326.[122] That this is no mere cliché (Valentinians are constantly found in lists of heretics) is clear from the fact that under Theodosius they enjoyed a tolerant and protective silence. For the axis of religious policy has shifted against more immediate dangers, such as Arianism on one side and Manichaeism on the other. But under Theodosius II the edict of 30 May 428 once again reveals the Valentinians as heretics 'forbidden to assemble and to pray on Roman territory.'[123]

This evidence is enough to provide a picture of how enduring and widespread the school was. Isolated traces survive into the seventh and eighth centuries, but only a pale echo of the great flowering of the second century. These fleeting references should not, however, deceive us. If the third century was a period of resistance, the fourth century was one of surrender. The previous century testifies to a discreet florescence of texts and treatises. Many of the Coptic texts must have been composed during this period in their original Greek: e.g. the texts of the Askew and Bruce codices and the speculations of Arnobius' *viri novi* can be assigned to the third century.

Some scholars have posited a devolutionary phase in Gnosticism, whose beliefs are marked by a proliferation of entities and pleromatic worlds and whose cultic practices show a significant increase in magic.[125] It is difficult to support this hypothesis. Moreover it requires a more certain dating of many of the Nag Hammadi treatises. In any case one must remember that some second-century systems (e.g. the 365 heavens of Basilides) had begun to multiply the intermediaries and that magical formulas and arithmetical speculation were already being cultivated by some groups, such as the Marcosians.

Rather, if there is a tendency evident in the third-century texts, it is that the monistic aspect implicit in second-century dualist systems[126] becomes more marked by a process of reaction (and adaptation) *vis-à-vis* the increasing success of the Neoplatonic theory of emanation and the optimism and universalism of the True Church.

Epiphanius is almost our only source for the pockets of fourth-century resistance, provided by groups of Archontics (a type of Gnosis like that of the Sethians)[127] or libertine Gnostics, whom we shall discuss in chapter 11. But by now the evidence is isolated and historically irrelevant. The Gnostic adventure was coming to an end.

11

Ascetics and Libertines

TOWARDS A SOCIOLOGY OF GNOSTICISM

Tertullian's caustic pen gives a rare glimpse of the internal life of a Gnostic community:

> First, one does not know who is a catechumen or a believer. They enter on equal terms, they listen on equal terms, they pray on equal terms . . . they do not care if they profess different doctrines, provided that they all help to destroy the truth. All are proud, all promise knowledge. The catechumens are perfect before being instructed. And heretical women, how brazen they are! They dare to teach, to dispute, to exorcize, to promise cures, even perhaps to baptize. Their ordinations are improper, superficial, changeable. Now they appoint neophytes, now those attached to secular life, now apostates from our faith [Christianity], so as to bind with vainglory those whom they cannot bind with the truth. Nowhere is it easier to obtain promotion than among the enemy, where simply being there is considered an achievement. And so, today one man is a bishop, tomorrow another. Today one is a deacon who tomorrow will be a lector. The presbyter of today is the layman of tomorrow. Even members of the laity are charged with the duties of a priest.[1]

Even if in this polemic the African writer associates the practices and behaviour that seem to belong to different groups, to Marcionites as well as Valentinians, his sardonic, lively group portrait is still valid. Tertullian is an institutionalist. What he finds intolerable is the anti-institutional aspect of the Gnostic movement. The existence of roles, which are apparently observed, is continually subject to discussion by the implicit possibility of changing them at will. The protective umbrella of a hierarchical order is constantly threatened by an indiscriminate egalitarianism, which makes catechumens and initiates equal, while traditional male superiority is threatened by the snares of impudent, uncontrolled feminism.

Tertullian's description, however, confines itself to the external and generic data of a fundamental sociological problem: the nature, internal structures and mechanisms of co-opting and exclusion that are central to Gnostic communities.[2] With the available data the problem appears almost insoluble: difficulties of internal order, such as the esoteric nature of the groups in question, the absence of direct, or at any rate easily usable, references, the lack of epigraphical or archaeological material, which usually helps to fill in the lacunae of the literary documentation, and the scarcity of heresiological evidence all seem to militate against a purely sociological investigation.

Various elements seem, nevertheless, to emphasize the probable egalitarian structure that must have characterized the community in the awareness of its members and in its daily life. Gnostics were brothers and sisters,[3] a generation and a race of the perfect,[4] children of the same Father. They live in a house of ideal peace, where dissension is unknown.[5] The same caste structure, distributed in more or less rigid anthropological hierarchies, helped to confirm the egalitarianism of the group of the elect.

On the other hand, some exhortations raise the question of what these images conceal. Are they not perhaps ideal representations, which seek to portray the opposite of what is actually the case? Dissension and polemic within and between the various schools are well known.[6] And it is unlikely that egalitarianism was rigid and absolute. Irenaeus speaks of the *inexpertiores*, 'somewhat inexperienced' in connection with those who were first to fall into the Gnostic trap, the *rudes*, or 'simpletons'.[7] It may be inferred from this that there were different levels of followers in certain cases. Of course, this also depended on the consistency of the group. There did not, however, have to be many members; as Basilides warns, one in a thousand is capable of attaining the Gnostic mysteries.[8] Within these small groups self-consciousness was also a cohesive element. To define onself as the 'seed of Seth', 'the unwavering race', 'the race that knows no sovereign', earthly or heavenly, implied, at least, theoretically, a group that was more rigid and compact internally, in total retreat from the surrounding world.[9] This is proved indirectly by the more ambiguous, flexible encounter of the Valentinians with the world. They glimpsed the possibility of mediation. They reached out to the psychics of the True Church. All in all, they did not have the rigid, intolerant, exclusive conception of salvation typical of the average Gnostic conventicle, which was closed to the world.

The relations of the group with the outside world were influenced by their adopted model of aggregations and associations. A scholastic type of structure, such as that of the Valentinians, placed the initiate in a particular teaching tradition at a high level, which, while creating an intellectual type of hierarchy, at the same time encouraged a special spiritual communion between disciples and master, the sort that existed between Plotinus and his disciples (in a very different context).

But in other situations the prevailing model must have been that of the *thiasoi* of the mystery cults, clubs of those who adhered to particular initiations, mostly recognized in or tolerated by law.[10] These were especially widespread in the Hellenistic period. They exude the same cosmopolitan atmosphere; they contain individuals looking for religious well-being as a personal possession; they practise rites of passage that guarantee the initiate a new religious and social licence.

It would, however, be dangerous to overdo the comparison. While we are reasonably well informed about, for example, the Mithraeans, and their structure, initiation rites and hierarchical scale,[11] we know little or nothing about analogous Gnostic cult places and what we do know must be treated cautiously.[12]

We shall say a little more about cult practices in the next section. But we must emphasize the difficulty of drawing an outline of the Gnostic communities. It is not unlikely that there were certain levels of spiritual perfection (as, for example, among the later Manichaeans), but this differentiation on the basis of the nature of the members must not be forced or interpreted solely in the sense intended by Irenaeus. There are different sources of evidence of a certain cultural homogeneity in the Gnostic communities. Whoever uses their writings will become the possessor of an elementary scholastic baggage full of the sort of philosophical notions to be found in handbooks (at least).[13] Their compilers, with good reason, betray the influence of the Hellenistic school.[14] Even the existence of genuine translation schools is a valuable piece of evidence.

To support these little translation schools was no small economic undertaking. Eusebius[15] tells us that a Valentinian called Ambrose, later converted to Christianity, was able to finance the costly work of stenography and calligraphy for his master Origen, simply because he was very wealthy. This significant detail in turn raises two questions.

The first concerns the social background and economic status of the initiates. Here too the sources are obstinately scarce. We have already mentioned Marcus the magician, who liked the company of rich, beautiful women. It would, however, be misleading to generalize on the basis of this isolated fact. It is true that, at least in the case of leaders like Basilides and Valentinus, they probably were of a wealthy socio-economic origin. They must have completed their entire study course, an accomplishment that in those days involved considerable expense and required a large fortune, with its travels and residence in the most famous schools. It is significant that Marcion (though not strictly Gnostic) belonged to a wealthy Sinope family. But it is unlikely that the well-to-do classes were the only ones to be recruited. Gnostic Christians exploited the same territory as the Christian missionaries, whose activity is widely attested in the principal economic and commercial centres of the Empire. Only rarely did they recruit from among the well-to-do classes. It is true that they were active among a socially stratified group, but this was largely the petit bourgeoisie (to use an equivalent modern term).[16]

This is not surprising. The Hellenistic *polis*, with its varied markets, its racial crossroads, cultural outlets and the myriad possibilities of openings for upward social mobility and religious and cultural change, became a melting pot for old and new religious movements. It had already encouraged a certain expansion in Judaism. Paul's mission had also passed through the synagogues. And Christian communities (as in the case of Valentinus) might shed their skin to reveal a Gnostic serpent.

That women occupied a privileged place in Gnostic communities can be deduced from several sources.[17] The egalitarian and anti-institutional nature of the Gnostic communities is one indication: they sought to reinforce the new social prestige of women emerging in society or to mitigate, if not to abolish, their traditionally subordinate role in society and the family. True society now became the spiritual one, composed of brothers and sisters; the other society was merely a pale imitation or, worse, a degenerate illusion.

The burial inscription of Flavia Sophē, a Gnostic, reads:[18]

> You who long for the Fatherly light, sister and spouse, my Sophē, anointed in the baths of Christ with incorruptible, pure oil, you hasten to look upon the divine faces of the heroes, the great angel of the great council [the Saviour], the true son, as you enter the bridal chamber and rise [immortal] to the bosom of the Father.

One thinks immediately of the privileged role of Mary Magdalene, revamped in the esoteric Gnostic tradition. She occupies a prominent position in the revelation discourses.[19] In the *Pistis Sophia* she is, apart from the Saviour, the principal actor. Conscious of her superior nature, she continually intervenes to question Jesus or reply to his most difficult questions. All this bears witness to her pneumatic superiority.[20] A Gnostic gospel is directly connected with her revelations.[21] And in the *Gospel of Philip* she appears as the Saviour's terrestrial companion, the counterpart of celestial Sophia.[22]

Thus Tertullian's picture of heretical, impudent women who 'dare to teach, debate, carry out exorcisms and promise cures' was not far from the truth. Marcellina was a Carpocratian leader. Apelles received revelations from the prophetess Philomena. The women who agreed to sexual intercourse with Marcus received the gift of prophecy denied to them by the True Church. The circle closes.

Here too, however, one must not force these data too much. The *Gospel of Thomas* finishes with this lapidary verdict, which should discourage any interpretation trying to be too 'modern': 'Simon Peter said to them, "Let Mary [Magdalene] leave us, for women are not worthy of Life." Jesus said: "I myself shall lead her in order to make her male, so that she too may become a living spirit resembling you males. For every woman who will make herself male will enter the Kingdom of Heaven." '23

The invitation, couched in a gentle, persuasive form, as here and in parallel cases,24 or in contrast in a brusque, threatening way and in openly, violently misogynistic language,25 nevertheless conceals the same thought: women as such cannot enter the kingdom of heaven. This conviction underlies both the inscription of Flavia Sophē and the relationship of Marcus with his prophetesses. Some Valentinians, as we shall see later, instituted a sacrament, spiritual matrimony, to confirm a central feature of their theology on the level of ritual practice. The female function is essentially generative, and generation inevitably means a progressive ontological impoverishment. Therefore the female element is the cause, however indirect, of the creation of the world and of humankind. By itself, however, it is incapable of aspiring to the heights. The process of salvation, in this sense, is essentially male; a process, as it were, of masculinization. The final equilibrium re-established in the bosom of the archetypal Androgyne will therefore be an equilibrium in which the male is destined to triumph. Indeed, this was inevitable in a society still profoundly patriarchal, which had not experienced the boldness of modern feminism.

The second question raised by Eusebius' statement about the Valentinian Ambrose concerns the economic bases of Gnostic communities. This is a matter likely to remain unresolved. It is a subject about which we know, unfortunately, almost nothing; the sources of income, the amounts involved, the use of resources, payment of taxes and the means of internal distribution are all unknown. Were there common funds that paid for missionary activity, translations, upkeep? Or were these purely spiritual communities, whose members did a normal job in the outside world to support themselves? The absence of internal information makes any comparison with possible parallels useless, whether with, e.g. the self-sufficient communities like those of the Essenes described by Philo (who lived on the edge of cities) or the 'spiritual clubs', like the Hellenistic *thiasoi*.

We must therefore leave to one side this intriguing question, which is likely to remain hypothetical, and examine another aspect about which we are better informed: the cult.

RITUAL PROCESSES

For the ancients religion was primarily cult observance and ritual practice. Even at the beginning of the second century the devout Plutarch expressed this deeply rooted conviction in the *Moralia*:

> When travelling you can find cities without walls, writings, kings, houses, property, that have no need of money, without any idea of a gymnasium or theatre. But a city without a sacred place or gods, that has no prayers, oaths, oracles, sacrifices for thanksgiving or rites to ward off misfortune, has never been or ever will be seen by any traveller.[26]

The Gnostic tendency to undermine the traditional religious institutions of the *polis* was also at work in the cult. A 'left' wing of the Valentinians, consistent with its uncompromising logic of genuine theological and political dualism, considered that true perfection had no need of any external ceremony:

> . . . one ought not to celebrate the mystery of the ineffable and invisible power by means of visible and corruptible created things, the inconceivable and incorporeal by means of what is sensually tangible and corporeal. The perfect redemption is said to be the knowledge of the ineffable 'Greatness'. From ignorance both deficiency and passion derived; through knowledge will the entire substance derived from ignorance be destroyed. Therefore this knowledge is redemption of the inner man. And this is not corporeal, since the body perishes, nor psychic, because the soul also derives from the deficiency and is like a habitation of the spirit. The redemption must therefore be spiritual. The inner spiritual man is redeemed through knowledge. Sufficient for them is the knowledge of all things. This is the true redemption.[27]

This perfect 'pneumatic equation', distinguished by its radical nature, helps to illuminate a profound change in religious behaviour at the beginning of the Christian era. In pagan mystery cults theology develops from ritual. In the new religious movements, however, unless it is expressly rejected, ritual becomes an expression of theology. The change is quite important, even if historical reality has amused itself by weaving, from the traditional situation depicted by Plutarch and the radical solutions of certain Valentinians, a more variegated and faded texture reflecting the complexity of human reality more accurately.

Gnostic ritual might be classified according to three types.[28] There were the rites that had acquired an exclusively symbolic value and did not require external verification. A typical example is provided by the fourth treatise in the *Corpus Hermeticum, The Crater*, which belongs to the pessimistic dualistic trend. It describes the acquisition of intellect (which means that it is not a natural possession) as being immersed in a *kratēr*, or mixing bowl (in which wine was mixed with water). The messenger of Gnosis announces in fact to humans: 'Immerse yourself, you who can, in this *kratēr*, you who believe that you will return to him who sent the *kratēr* here, you who know why you were born.'[29] In this way all those who heard the message and immersed themselves in the *kratēr* 'were made to participate in knowledge and became perfect.'[30]

Is it possible, as some interpreters think, that this symbolism conceals genuine practising of ritual immersion?[31] It seems most improbable: 'The Hermeticists occupied the position among the ancient religiously minded distinctive of the Quakers today, inasmuch as their faith necessitated no fixed cult and dispensed with sacraments and their concomitant sacerdotalism', is an observation made, not without a certain anti-catholic irony, by Angus in 1929.[32] His remark is still valid today as far as Hermetic ritual practice is concerned. This Hermetic ritual is an *Idealritual*,[33] which takes shape in an atmosphere of mystical participation in the mysteries of personal rebirth and solitary encounters (requiring no external apparatus) with the divinity. Against this background some of the statements in Gnostic treatises, in which the act of Gnosis is seen as a baptism[34] or an unction,[35] can be better understood. It is a mistake to want to see in them more or less veiled hints of genuine cult practices – and also because the texts are quite specific when they discuss actual rites.

The second type of ritual is marked by the presence of a specific ceremonial. In some cases the rites preserve a strong symbolic value; in others they are simply reduced to the gestural act.

Many of these rituals had been taken up by various contemporary institutions, both the True Church and the mystery cults. Baptism is attested among the Valentinians,[36] who evidently derive it from the Christian cult. Those like Marcus,[37] who believed in the usefulness of a tangible rite, appealed to the baptism of Christ. There were two baptisms: the first, imperfect and used by members of the Church in connection with the remission of sins, was the baptism of the earthly

Saviour, the visible Jesus, announced by John the Baptist for repentance; the second, the Gnostic type, was spiritual baptism, the redemption brought by Christ for perfection.[38] In this second case, the neophyte was led to the water and baptized with these words: 'In the name of the Father unknown to all, in the Truth, Mother of All, in the One Who came down upon Jesus, in the union, redemption and communion of powers.' In order to impress the listener, others added Hebrew words, meaning: 'Through all the power of the Father I invoke you, you who are called light, good spirit and life, because you have reigned in the body.'[39] Forms of unction and of the eucharist are also attested[40] as sacraments (as we have already seen) that were to attend the demise of the believer.

But the Gnostics also invented new ritual forms: for instance two parallel, but opposing, rites: the ceremony of the bridal chamber, a Valentinian conceit, and the orgiastic cults of some libertine groups, mentioned by Epiphanius. The first in particular deserves our attention. Its rich symbolism, with its mixture of the themes of continence, matrimonial sexuality and the function of woman, throws a penetrating light on a certain type of Gnostic mentality.

The Coptic version of the Hermetic *Asclepius* depicts the mystery of sexual union as follows:

> And if you wish to see the reality of this mystery, then you should see the wonderful representation of the intercourse that takes place between male and female. For when the semen reaches its climax, it leaps forth. In that moment the female receives the strength of the male; the male for his part receives the strength of the female, while the semen does this. Therefore the mystery of intercourse is performed in secret, in order that the two sexes might not disgrace themselves in front of many who do not experience that reality. For each of them [the sexes] contributes its (own part in) begetting. For if it happens in the presence of those who do not understand the reality, (it is) laughable and unbelievable. And, moreover, they are holy mysteries, of both words and deeds, because not only are they not heard, but also they are not seen.[41]

The sexual union that is consummated in marriage between gods or between gods and humans is at the heart of the rituals belonging to many religions.[42] In the ancient world the ceremonial *hieros gamos*, or sacred marriage, is widely attested in Egypt and Mesopotamia.[43] Even ancient Israel was not unaware of its mythological nuances, but significantly retraces and sublimates the relationship between Jahweh, the husband, and Israel, the unfaithful wife, even if in texts such as the

Song of Songs the mystical background continues to be filled with ancient erotic imagery.[44]

In the Hellenistic world the theme returns in the mysteries, even if the interpretation of certain passages remains disputed.[45] As for primitive Christianity, the New Testament itself is rich in nuptial images that concentrate on the relationship between Christ and his Bride, the Church.[46] The image is susceptible of various interpretations. And in the ascetic Christian tradition it tended to legitimate both the ideal of chaste marriage or the spiritual ideal of a woman and of a church, a virgin and a new Eve, able to make up for the sin of the mother.[47]

It is not surprising that the theme of spiritual marriage had, for the Valentinians, a significant function not only in myth, but also in cult. Reasons of general and specific order combined. The millennial history of ascetic movements, of Christian heresies and generally of nonconformist religions presents as an underlying theme polemic against, criticism and rejection of, the institution of marriage, which in the medieval and modern period, eventually came to be identified with Christian matrimony. The great variety of solutions proposed (complete rejection of marriage by the Encratites,[48] unconsummated marriage among certain Christian ascetics,[49] mystical celibacy,[50] Mormon patriarchal polygamy,[51] 'marriage' with several partners, as practised in certain nineteenth-century American settlements,[52] and the matrimonial Nicodemism of certain Russian sects[53]) converges, however, on one point: criticism of the institution of marriage, with its regimentation and its sexual hierarchy, its cultural models and, not least, its economic bases. The official microcosm contained in it and the genetic code imposed on it by society must be replaced by other embryonic germs of the new world.

We have often mentioned that the theme of the union of Nous and Psyche, of the angel and its image, to restore the original androgynous unity, is central to the Valentinian myth. It constitutes a bond between the beginning and the end of this great mythological epic. On the other hand, if one considers the risks implicit in an individual ritual practice of a purely spiritual kind unconstrained by social control, it will come as no surprise that the Gnostics had found in this myth support for a genuine ritual. Indeed, it is not given to everyone to control his/her sexuality alone without some residual danger. There is always the lurking risk that rejection of a public ritual may be transformed into a menacing display of obsessive, neurotic and ultimately destructive private ritual. The ritual process therefore imposes itself with all its force. It is true that one might still resort to the seductive strategy of Marcus the magician: the private realization of the act. But, apart from other considerations, it was a matter of individual practices, not easy to codify, of an art of seduction not always available to everyone. Those who denied themselves and were thus not able to pursue this avenue had to resort to periodical social control of their instincts, intentions and acts; and, more precisely, to the social force of the ritual process, which was able to adapt and periodically to refashion the individual biopsychic being in accordance with the norms of the behaviour code that the group imposed on itself.[54] Only in this way was it possible to tame, to control and to channel those dark, savage forces of sexuality identified (significantly) by Gnostics with the bestial side of human nature – in general with its female dimension. An event such as matrimony, charged with the mysterious sacredness of sexual intercourse, might open itself to various possibilities, from its denial to the socially controlled sublimation of the individual libido. The dangers of perilous, inevitable temptation and deviation were avoided by the force of the symbolic process. The energies and impulses, both sexual and aggressive, unleashed in the clear symbolism of the ritual kiss,[55] became embroiled in new pregnant symbols representing the values and virtues on which the structural order (and hence the community itself) depended.

Thus, Irenaeus tells us, some Valentinians 'prepare a bridal chamber and perform a mysterious initiation with invocations for the initiates and define these actions of theirs as spiritual marriages in imitation of higher unions.'[56] The *Gospel of Philip* helps us to understand the sense of this restraint by means of symbolism and this religious control of sexuality. Indeed, 'the bridal chamber is not for the beasts or for slaves or for impure women, but for free men and virgins.'[57] The author refers several times to his model of matrimonial relationship. Adultery must be rejected.[58] To achieve this, control over one's impulses is essential:

> The children a woman bears resemble the man who loves her. If her husband loves her, then they resemble her husband. If it is an adulterer, then they resemble the adulterer. Frequently if a woman sleeps with her husband out of necessity, while her heart is with the adulterer with whom she usually has intercourse, the child she will bear is born resembling the adulterer.[59]

Thus spiritual matrimony is not dictated by pleasure, but by the will.[60]

Underlying these statements is a typically Valentinian concept: the truth is not present in this world naked and pure, but in types and images. The Gnostic therefore has to pass through an image of the ideal celestial reality. This image, stripped of its most material features, is in fact spiritual matrimony, anticipation of the perfect, definitive spiritual union that will take place in the Bridal Chamber of the Pleroma. Then 'the wedding feast, common to all who have been saved, will take place, until all are made equal and know each other.'[61] Then 'the souls put to one side, the spiritual elements, accompanied by the Mother who leads the bridegroom, will themselves lead in the bridegrooms (that is, their angels) and enter the Bridal Chamber within the Limit. They will come in sight of the Father, having become intellectual Aeons, for the intellectual, eternal marriage of the syzygy.'[62]

However one interprets the cult, it helps to illuminate the internal history of Valentinianism. Unlike the first generation, the second 'seemed able to attain the intellectual act too easily and not with enough certainty. That which is concrete, the gesture, the sign, the words, the formulas, all of this acquires greater certainty.'[63] This tendency will become clearer in some third-century documents. The *Pistis Sophia* and the *Books of Jeu* affirm clearly that 'it is no longer Gnosis, but sacramental practice that is decisive for salvation.'[64]

What can happen when ritual control of sexuality is no longer practised is clear from the spermatic, orgiastic cults described by Epiphanius. The future bishop of Salamis, at the happy age of twenty (*c*.335) decided to go to Egypt, the chosen land of monasticism and asceticism, where he was overtaken by misfortune. We do not know exactly how he came into contact with a Gnostic sect which openly rejected asceticism and paradoxically exalted those dark forces that he wanted to learn how to control and suppress. Lascivious women tried to seduce him, initiating him into the rites and written works of the group. It apparently took him some time to realize what was going on. Frightened by the abyss opening up before him, he betook himself to the bishops of the city, denounced the Gnostics and engineered the excommunication of ninety Gnostic converts masquerading as Christians.[65]

Despite all this, Epiphanius' account seems reliable. However coloured it might be, the very prudishness of the account guarantees the substantial truthfulness of the picture of the heretics that he presents:

> First, they have their women in common. And if a stranger comes to their sect, they have a sign of recognition, the men for the women and the women for the men: when they stretch out their hand, by way of greeting, they make a tickling stroke beneath the palm of the hand, indicating that the new arrival belongs to their cult. After this recognition of each other the proceed to a feast at once. They serve up lavish helpings of wine and meat, even if they are poor. When they have had their drink and filled their veins, as it were, to bursting point, they give themselves over to passion. The husband withdraws from his wife and says to her: 'Rise up, make love with your brother.' The miserable wretches then indulge in promiscuous intercourse. And, though it truly shames me for the disgraceful

things they did (as the Apostle said, 'it is shameful to speak of them'), nevertheless I shall not recoil from saying what they did not recoil from doing, so as to arouse in my readers a shuddering horror of their scandalous behaviour.

After copulating, as if the crime of their whoredom were not enough, they offer up their shame to heaven. The man and woman take the man's sperm in their hands and stand looking up to heaven. With this impurity in their hands, they pray in the manner of the Stratiotici and Gnostics, offering to the natural Father of the Universe what is in their hands, saying, 'We offer you this gift, the body of Christ.' And so, they eat it, partaking of their own shame and saying, 'This is the body of Christ, and this is the Passover. And so our bodies suffer and are compelled to confess the passion of Christ.' Similarly with the woman's emission at her period: they collect the menstrual blood which is unclean, take it and eat it together, and say, 'Behold the blood of Christ . . .' And while they fornicate, they deny that it is for procreation. They practise the shameful act not to beget children, but for mere pleasure, while the Devil is playing with them and dishonouring the divine creature. They take their pleasure to its conclusion and take for themselves sperm of their impurity so that it will penetrate no further and produce children, then they eat the fruit of their shame. If one of them happens to allow the sperm to penetrate the woman and make her pregnant, listen to the outrage that they dare to perform. At the right moment they extract the embryo with their fingers and take this aborted infant and crush it with pestle and mortar; when they have mixed in honey, pepper and other spices and perfumed oils to lessen their nausea, they all assemble to the feast, every member of this troop of swine and dogs, each taking a piece of the aborted child in the fingers. And so, when they have finished their cannibal feast, they end with this prayer to God: 'We have not been deceived by the Archon of lust, but we have retrieved our brother's transgression.' And this they consider the perfect Passover.[66]

The ideological presuppositions of these practices must be sought in the myths of these groups, who, apart from a few variants, are substantially very similar.[67] There are two opposing forces in the world: the power of the Supreme God who generated Barbelo, the cause of everything, and then made her fertile; and the power of the Lord of this world. A part of the divine substance fell into the world; it had to be gathered together and set free. This classic scheme was reinterpreted by Epiphanius' Gnostics in the light of a particular concept of the *pneuma*. According to these Gnostics, 'all that was stolen from the Higher Mother (Barbelo) by the Archon who made this world and by all the other gods who are with him and angels and demons must be gathered together by the power which is in the bodies by means of the emissions of seed by men and women.'[68]

This myth is based on a conception of the *pneuma* also found in contemporary medicine,[69] in which it was the carrier of the *semen vitae*, or seed of life, in Gnostic terms the *semen luminis*, or seed of light, and so the bearer of spiritual life. Human sperm thus transmits that of the divine. 'To gather up the *membra* [parts]', the typical Gnostic theme at the root of the *Gospel of Eve*,[70] one of the group's texts, involves the emission and recovery of all the generative matter that contains and transmits the seeds of light.[71] At the same time, it implies the attempt to put an end to the generative cycle that contributes to the dispersion of the luminous substance.

Epiphanius' statement, though it refers only to isolated groups living in Egypt in the first half of the fourth century, raises a question that goes to the heart of Gnostic ethics: were the Gnostics ascetics or libertines?

ASCETICS OR LIBERTINES? THE DILEMMA OF GNOSTIC ETHICS

'The history of religion in general, even of Christianity for all its predominant asceticism, offers too many instances in virtually every century of the combination of cultic rites with sexual activities not acceptable in ordinary society.'[72] The nineteenth-century Catholic priest, Boullan, of Lyons, taught his women and his disciples that, if they wanted to ascend the spiritual ladder, they would do well to sleep with him. This was clearly one of the many reincarnations of Marcus the magician. Boullan performed obscene ceremonies and pornographic rites, in which the host was combined with male sperm and menstrual blood. They seem to be a spontaneous, unconscious echo of the orgiastic rites of Epiphanius' Gnostics.[73]

Early Christianity had, however, often been threatened by movements of this sort in its anxious search for a more rigid asceticism. In the fourth century the Messalians of Syria and Asia Minor, a spiritual movement of ascetic tendency, were accused of wild promiscuity. There is a revealing passage in the homilies of pseudo-Macarius. The author warns the faithful Messalian[74] against taking the image of the soul as a wife too literally. The flesh is weak: and the text seems to suggest that, at least in certain cases, the excitement caused by excessive spiritual exaltation might run the risk of resulting in nothing but carnality.

Irenaeus accuses the Valentinians of depravity. His reasoning presupposes that the Gnostics are, in modern terms, amoral, if not nihilistic. They are allowed to do everything, to violate every norm, for they are

above every legal and ethical convention: 'the spiritual element ...
cannot be corrupted, whatever it may be involved in.'[75] He notes three
practices: eating flesh consecrated to idols; participating in every pagan
festival, including the theatre and the circus; corrupting the women to
whom they teach their doctrines. The first two accusations are clearly
specious. As far as we are concerned, it is only the third that qualifies
as depravity. This type of classification, however, highlights Irenaeus'
methodology (and his belief in it): everything that violates Christian
standards is a sign of the Gnostics' antinomianism and anti-legalism.
Depravity is merely a logical consequence.

This procedure is certainly not isolated. Plotinus also adopts it in his
critique of Gnostic ethics.[76] Having established correct ethical positions,
he then draws the logical conclusions, accusing the Gnostics of
immorality.[77]

Are the criticisms of these external observers about Gnosticism justified
by the original texts? However surprising and paradoxical it may be,
the answer is 'No'. Not a single Gnostic Nag Hammadi text contains
any hint of immoral behaviour or, even worse, of any incitement to
immoral behaviour. There could not be a more radical contrast between
external sources and direct documentation. To return to Irenaeus, the
charge of sexual depravity is made not only against the Valentinians,
but also against the Simonians, the Basilidians, the Carpocratians and
the Cainites. If we consider other heresiologists, the list inevitably
becomes longer.[78] This may indicate merely heresiological prudishness
born of mistrust, inadequate critical acceptance of oral tradition or
inventions pure and simple, whose purpose it was to warn the disoriented
flock of impending danger.

If it is true that the original sources confirm the hypothesis of a
militant asceticism in the Gnostic groups, it would nevertheless be
mistaken to deny the heresiological evidence any historical value.
Independently, authors otherwise reliable, such as Irenaeus and Clement
(not to mention the particularly youthful experience of Epiphanius),
adequately prove the existence, in the ethical Gnostic pendulum, also
of depraved attitudes and behaviour, which must have run counter to
the prevailing sexual ethic. However, that this is not simply a matter of
a merely heresiological *topos*, is sufficiently shown by the actual internal
disputes in Gnostic groups, an example of which is provided by the
accusations in the *Pistis Sophia* against immoral practices of some
Gnostics, not to mention more general reasons, which may be ascribed
to the very logic of human behaviour (and of which we have already
given examples).[79]

Rather, if the Nag Hammadi texts have shown an important new aspect of Gnostic ethics, it is that their nature is susceptible to control and is not wholly deterministic. It is significant that non-Gnostic texts such as the *Sentences of Sextus* are found in the library.[80] The *Sentences* are a collection of wisdom sayings, which were very popular in Christian circles in the early centuries, extremely ethical and ascetic in tendency. The dominant theme is control of the passions as a means of approaching God and becoming his children. One must avoid the temptations of this world and its overlord and live a pure life illuminated by reason in order to turn to the Good. It is the traditional theme of the two ways, presented here in ascetic and Encratite terms. The soul should always be alert when confronted by bodily passions (95 and 391), whose demands may be satisfied only in so far as they are conducive to good health (78). All sexual impulses should be repressed by the soul that aspires towards God (230–3), even when the believer is married (239). If one should then become aware of not being able to overcome them, it is better to castrate oneself, for only in this way will one escape the fires of hell (13 and 273). Accordingly, it is advisable not to marry: it will be easier to approach God (230a).

The practice of continence (*enkrateia*) was then made to apply to other perils apart from sex (which was identified with woman, and was the enemy) such as greed, luxury and wealth. Not of themselves Gnostic, it is nevertheless understandable that these prohibitions proved acceptable to certain Gnostic groups who had made rejection of this world and its pleasures their ethical imperative and their normal daily conduct. Other features of the *Sentences* too, the proud consciousness of belonging to an intellectual elite or the privileged rapport with God reserved for the continent,[81] must have appealed to Gnostic mentality, especially if, as some think, the collector of these books belonged to a monastic or ascetic movement.[82]

The same might be said of the *Teachings of Silvanus*,[83] which contain exhortations to lead a life of abstinence (employing the style of Greek wisdom literature) and to reject the passions, especially the sexual ones. The author advocates struggle in the name of reason and with the help of Christ, the Light who illuminates the mind.

This situation of a struggle of the senses, which requires a conscious choice, is similar to that found in other Gnostic texts in the library. Rigid determinism is followed by a more elastic, malleable freedom of choice. In the *Authentikos Logos* the soul, a prey to continual tension, finds itself having to face up to a fundamental decision: to choose the life or the death of the spirit. Night and day it is attacked remorselessly by many enemies because it is their inextinguishable desire not to allow them any peace, constantly goading them. The author compares the

Adversary *par excellence*, the Devil, to a fisherman. He casts his nets as traps. To be caught in one of them is to be damned: 'And we will be taken down into the dragnet, and we will not be able to come up from it because the waters are high over us, flowing from above downward, submerging our heart in the filthy mud.'[84] The nets that the Adversary casts into this world are interwoven with desires:

> First he injects a pain into your heart until you have heartache on account
> of a small thing of this life, and he seizes (you) with his poisons. And
> afterwards (he injects) the desire of a tunic so that you will pride yourself
> in it, and love of money, pride, vanity, envy that rivals another envy,
> beauty of body, fraudulence.[85]

Of these dangers the most treacherous is ignorance, accompanied by a certain spiritual apathy. But the soul can escape these traps and recognize that passions are transient and illusory.

It will then adopt a new way of life: 'Afterwards she despises this life, because it is transitory. And she looks for those foods that will take her into life.'[86]

This open situation of liberty and responsibility, which is not resolved into a single act, but requires continual reassurance, has its parallels in the *Apocryphon of John* and the *Pistis Sophia* and is also documented in other Gnostic writings.[87]

At the end of our Gnostic odyssey, we find ourselves confronted by a final question frequently asked, but difficult to answer exhaustively or definitively. Isn't the Gnostic saved by nature?[88] Isn't it precisely the awareness of this eternally preordained salvation that makes possible its ambivalent ethics, torn between two extremes: an asceticism that seeks to cancel out the very root of our desires and a depraved antinomianism that mocks the laws of this world and its rulers?

Perhaps Jonas was right to emphasize the anarchic and nihilistic character of a naturally rebellious ethic in search of a metaphysical liberty, which exists absolutely, in itself.[89] It is legitimate to ask, however, if this fascinating modern interpretation really catches the variety, the richness and (why not?) also the contradictory nature of ethical behaviour that appears to us, in concrete terms, more complex and variegated. If a modern enquiry were possible, it would be even more interesting to know how self-aware the average Gnostic was. This person, who is not simply a statistical ghost, free from the excesses of the orgiastic cults and the heroism of the virtuous in death, sensitive to the subtle, exhilarating fascination of predestination, but also more inclined in behaviour to live with the perception of a situation still fluid and open, was perhaps content with simpler motivations than those assigned to him or her by modern interpreters: '. . . return to your divine nature',[90] is the message in the teachings of *Silvanus*, 'Live according to the mind. Do not think about the things pertaining to the flesh.'[91] 'You shall be man.'[92]

Only by living to the full his human adventure was the Gnostic able to realize his dream of freedom.

Notes

INTRODUCTION

1. This happened to traditionalists such as René Guénon, Frithjof Schuon and Aldous Huxley. Underlying their work is an idea of 'Gnosis' as a mystery reserved for elites (see ch. 9), a mystery revealed at the dawn of history and handed down through the centuries in different religious traditions via esoteric channels; see A. Huxley, *The Perennial Philosophy* (London, 1947) and É. Schuré, *Les Grands Initiés* (Paris, 1954).

2. For example, the great German exegete and theologian Rudolf Bultmann was subjected to accusations of being a 'new Gnostic'; see G. L. Borchert, 'Is Bultmann's theology a new Gnosticism?', *Evangelical Quarterly* 36 (1964), 222–8; J. E. Burkhart, 'Gnosis and contemporary theology', *McCormick Quarterly* 18 (1965), 43–9; K. Prümm, *Gnosis an der Wurzel des Christentums?* (Salzburg, 1972), pp. 24ff.

3. On Jung's relationship with Gnosis see G. Quispel, 'Jung und die Gnosis', *ErJ* 37 (1968), 277–98. In many of his works, beginning with the fundamental *Symbols of Transformation* (1911), Jung used materials taken directly from Gnostic sources. In this respect *Aion* (1951) is especially important; after examining a number of Gnostic documents, Jung came to the conclusion that many Gnostics were no less than psychologists (p. 222). His memoirs are very informative about the period (1918–26) when he not only studied ancient Gnostics, but also underwent 'Gnostic' experiences and wrote the *Septem Sermones ad Mortuos*. For details of Jung's works in English see R. F. Hull (trans.), *The Collected Works of C. G. Jung* (London, 1902ff.), 20 vols.

4. The conferences, beginning in 1933, are published in *Eranos Jahrbücher*. Among the scholars of the various types of Gnosis, ancient and modern, who have taken part in them, one might mention H. Corbin, G. Scholem and E. Benz. Mircea Eliade has written vividly about the atmosphere of these meetings in his *Journal* (London, 1978).

5. *Gnosis als Weltreligion* (Zurich, 1951).

6. He has written a lively, interesting autobiographical account in 'A

retrospective view' in G. Widengren (ed.), *Proceedings of the International Colloquium on Gnosticism. Stockholm, August 20–25 1973* (Stockholm–Leiden, 1977), pp. 1–15, Jonas's bibliography is presented in B. Aland (ed.), *Gnosis, Festschrift für Hans Jonas* (Göttingen, 1978). See also I. P. Culianu, *Gnosticism e pensiero moderno: Hans Jonas* (Rome, 1985). On the relationship between Heidegger and Gnosis see S. A. Taubes, 'The Gnostic foundation of Heidegger Nihilism', *Journal of Religion* 34 (1954), 155ff.

7. 'Gnosticism and modern Nihilism', *Social Research* 19 (1952), 430–52 and *The Gnostic Religion*² (Boston, 1963), pp. 320ff.

8. According to E. Benz, *Les Sources mystiques de la philosophie romantique allemande* (Paris, 1968), ch. 1, the four mystical sources of Romantic German philosophy are: German mysticism from Meister Eckhart; the thought of Jacob Böhme; the work of Emanuel Swedenborg; the discovery of Indian thought. For different reasons all these strands of thought contain, from a phenomenological point of view, important Gnostic themes. Swedenborg (1688–1772) should really be treated separately; he is a central figure in the eighteenth-century esoteric theosophical tradition, a complex amalgam of scientist and mystic, whose visions are replete with Gnostic themes. He had a profound influence on contemporaries noted for their contribution to cultural life: 'No other mystic had such a profound influence on nineteenth-century French literature as Swedenborg. Balzac, Baudelaire, Nerval and Georges Sand owe him much, as do Strindberg and many other great writers' (A. Faivre, *L'Ésotérisme au XVIIIe siècle* (Paris, 1973), p. 104). With Louis de St Martin, the 'unknown philosopher', he represents one of the most important links in historical transmission through the esoteric and generally theosophical medium of the doctrines of Böhme and the Cabbala, which in their turn constitute a further source of speculative idealism.

9. At the beginning of the last century F. C. Baur (1792–1860), a disciple of Hegel and founder of the Tübingen School, began to see the speculative theology of German Idealism as a sort of superior Gnosis; see *Die christliche Gnosis* (Tübingen, 1835), pp. 668–735. Lügert too regarded Hegel as a 'conscious Gnostic'; see G. Krüger, 'Die Aufgabe der Hegelforschung', *ThRu* (1935), 294–318. As for Schelling, see Baur, *Christliche Gnosis*, pp. 611ff., and E. Benz, 'Theogonie und Wandlung des Menschen bei F. W. J. Schelling' in his *Urbild und Abbild* (Leiden, 1974), pp. 69ff.

10. There are not many attempts: H. Cornelis and A. Léonard, *La Gnose éternelle* (Paris, 1959), who examine the theosophy of Mme Blavatsky, the traditionalism of Guénon, Jung and westernized Hinduism; J. Zandee, 'Oude en niuewe vormen van Gnostiek', *Neederlandish Theologish Tijdschrift* 22 (1968), 161–84, who examines Böhme, the Rosicrucians, theosophy, the anthroposophy of Rudolf Steiner, and contemporary theologians such as J. A. T. Robinson and Paul Tillich; E. Samek Lodovici, *Metamorfosi della gnosi* (Milan, 1979), who examines Hans Küng and various currents of contemporary thought; G. Hanratty, 'Gnosticism and

modern thought', *Irish Theological Quarterly* 47 (1980), 3–23 and 119–32; ibid. 48 (1981), 80–92, who examines Hegel and Marx, Nietzsche and Heidegger's existentialism, Jung and Simone Weil, etc. It is clear that Christian esotericism offers an obligatory and historically solid channel through which certain Gnostic traditions have been metamorphosed and transformed: see A. Faivre, 'L'ésotérisme chrétien' in H. C. Puech (ed.), *Histoire des religions*, vol. 2 (Paris, 1972), pp. 1304–62.

11. In addition to the picture provided by Baur, *Gnosis*, pp. 544ff., see also E. H. Schmitt, *Die Gnosis*, II *Die Gnosis des Mittelalters und der Neuzeit* (Leipzig, 1907), and S. Hutin, *Les Gnostiques* (Paris, 1963). On the persistence of Gnosticism in the Middle Ages, including Bogomils, Paulicians and Cathars, see H. C. Puech and A. Vaillant, *Le Traité contre les Bogomiles de Cosmas le Prêtre* (Paris, 1945); S. Runciman, *The Medieval Manichee* (Cambridge, 1947); M. Loos, *Dualist Heresy in the Middle Ages* (Prague–The Hague, 1974); G. S. Gasparro, 'Sur l'histoire des influences du gnosticisme' in Aland (ed.), *Gnosis*, pp. 316–50.

12. F. Secret, *Les Kabbalistes chrétiens de la Renaissance* (Paris, 1964).

13. W. E. Peuckert, *Das Rosenkreuz*² (Berlin, 1973); S. Hutin, *Histoire de Rose-Croix*³ (Paris, 1971); F. A. Yates, *The Rosicrucian Enlightenment* (London, 1972).

14. G. Wehr, *Alle Weisheit ist von Gott* (Gütersloh, 1980).

15. A. Koyré, *Mystiques, spirituels alchimistes du XVIe siècle allemand* (Paris, 1971).

16. Id., *La Philosophie de Jacob Böhme* (Paris, 1929).

17. 'The history of the influence of Jacob Böhme on European philosophy is one of the most exciting chapters in the history of the European spirit', according to Benz, *Sources mystiques*, p. 17. See also S. Hutin, *Les Disciples anglais de Jacob Böhme* (Paris, 1960). For a list of the translations of Böhme's works into various European languages see W. Buddecke, *Die Jacob Böhmes Ausgaben. Ein beschreibendes Verzeichnis*, II *Die Übersetzungen* (Göttingen, 1955).

18. G. Quispel, 'Faust: symbol of Western Man', *ErJ* 33 (1966), 241–65; R. G. Zimmermann, *Das Weltbild des jungen Goethe* (Munich, 1970).

19. Hegel's Dutch friend, P. G. van Ghert, offered the philosopher a complete edition of the works of Böhme, two folio volumes (*Theosophia Revelata*, Amsterdam, 1715), acknowledged in a letter of thanks by Hegel from Nuremberg, 15 Oct. 1810.

20. E. Benz, *Swedenborg in Deutschland* (Frankfurt, 1948).

21. On Baader see E. Susini, *Franz von Baader et le romantisme mystique*, II–III *La Philosophie de Franz von Baader* (Paris, 1942); on the relationship with Böhme see Benz, *Sources*, pp. 19ff.

22. Benz, *Sources*, pp. 7ff.

23. K. Marx and F. Engels, *On Religion* (New York, 1964; repr. from Moscow, 1957), pp. 24, 291 and n.

24. E. Topitsch, *Sozialphilosophie zwischen Ideologie und Wissenschaft²* (Luchterhand, 1966), pp. 261–96.

25. L. Pellicani, *I rivoluzionari di professione. Teoria e prassi dello gnosticismo moderno* (Florence, 1975); A. Besançon, *Les Origines intellectuels du léninisme* (Paris, 1973); R. Aron, 'Remarques sur la gnose léniniste' in *The Philosophy of Order*, ed. P. J. Opitz and G. Sebba (Stuttgart, 1981), pp. 263–74.

26. The paraphrase comes from E. Vögelin, *Order and History*, IV *The Ecumenic Age* (Baton Rouge, 1974), p. 19. See also his *New Science of Politics* (New York, 1952) and 'Marx: the genesis of Gnostic socialism' in J. Hallowel (ed.), *From Enlightenment to Revolution* (Chapel Hill, NC, 1975), pp. 273–302. On Vögelin see G. Sebba, 'History, modernity and Gnosticism' in Opitz–Sebba *Philosophy*, pp. 190–241.

27. S. Givone, *William Blake. Arte e religione* (Milan, 1978), p. 16. On the relations with ancient Gnosis see ch. 1. On Blake's sources, which range from Hermetism to Orphism, from Neoplatonism to theosophical esotericism and Hinduism see K. Raine, *Blake and Tradition* (Princeton, 1968), 2 vols. See also J. Roos, *Aspects littéraires du mysticisme philosophique: W. Blake, Novalis, Ballanche* (Paris, 1951). On the fate of Blake in modern culture see Givone, *Blake*, pp. 17ff.

28. On Novalis see H. J. Mahl, *Die Idee des goldenen Zeitalters im Werk des Novalis* (Heidelberg, 1965).

29. P. Heller, *Dialectics and Nihilism* (Cambridge, Mass., 1966), p. 289.

30. B. Juden, *Traditions orphiques et tendances mystiques dans le romantisme français* (Paris, 1971).

31. J. Richer, *Gérard de Nerval et les doctrines ésotériques* (Paris, 1947).

32. Hutin, *Gnostiques*, pp. 121–2; A. Viatte, *Victor Hugo et les illuminés de son temps* (Paris, 1943).

33. Faivre, *Ésotérisme*, p. 190.

34. M. Carrouges, *André Breton et les données fondamentales du Surréalisme* (Paris, 1950).

35. Hutin, *Gnostiques*, p. 125. A recent example of how ancient Gnostic myths can directly inspire contemporary narrative is H. Bloom, *The Journey to Lucifer* (New York, 1979), who takes his inspiration from Valentinus and Nag Hammadi texts. See P. Perkins, *The Gnostic Dialogue* (New York–Toronto, 1980), pp. 209ff.

36. Hanratty, 'Gnosticism' (1980), II. 129ff. See G. Quispel, 'Hermann Hesse und die Gnosis' in Aland (ed.), *Gnosis*, pp. 492–507. Other examples are given by C. Colpe, 'The challenge of Gnostic thought for philosophy, alchemy and literature' in B. Layton (ed.), *The Rediscovery of Gnosticism*, 2 vols (Leiden, 1980–1), 1. 32–56 (Proust, Joyce, Musil, Mann).

37. S. Pétrement, *Le Dualisme chez Platon, les gnostiques et les manichéens* (Paris, 1947), p. 129.

38. R. Ruyer, *La Gnose de Princeton. Des savants à la recherche d'une religion* (Paris, 1974); and the proceedings of the colloquium held at Paris in June

1978, *Les Yeux de chair et les yeux de feu. La science et la Gnose* (Cahiers Univ. St Jean Jérusalem, 5 (1979), 1–244).

39. Cornelis–Léonard, *Gnose éternelle.*

40. e.g. the Conference, *Rediscovery of Gnosticism* (1978).

41. J. Delumeau, *Le Catholicisme entre Luther et Voltaire* (Paris, 1971), pp. 293ff.

42. G. Filoramo, 'Nuove religioni: problemi e prospettive' *RSLR* 15 (1979), 445–72.

43. On the concept of the 'religious field' see P. Bourdieu, 'Génèse et structure du champ religieux', *Revue française de sociologie* 12 (1971), 295–334.

44. T. Roszak, *Where the Waste Land Ends. Politics and Transcendence in Post-Industrial Society* (New York, 1972), p. 262; see F. W. Haack, *Geheimreligion der Wissenschaft. Neugnostische Bewegungen* (Stuttgart, 1966); P. H. Hartman, 'Social dimensions of occult participation: the Gnostica study', *British Journal of Sociology*, 27 (1976), 169–83; J. M. Robinson in the introduction to his edition of *The Nag Hammadi Library in English*[3] (Leiden etc., 1988), p. 1.

45. G. Arnold, *Unparteiische Kirchen- und Ketzerhistorie* (Frankfurt, 1729). On Arnold see E. Seeberg, *Gottfried Arnold, die Wissenschaft und die Mystik* (Meerane, 1927).

46. K. Rudolph (ed.), *Gnosis und Gnostizismus* (Darmstadt, 1975) and L. Cerfaux, 'Gnose', *DB Sup* III. 659f.

CHAPTER 1   FRAGMENTS OF A LOST FAITH

1. This account is based on the following works by J. M. Robinson, *Nag Hammadi Library in English*, pp. 1ff.; 'The discovery of the Nag Hammadi codices', *Biblical Archaeologist* 42 (1979), 206–24; 'From cliff to Cairo' in B. Barc (ed.), *Colloque International sur les Textes de Nag Hammadi* (Quebec–Louvain, 1981), pp. 21–58. As a result of first-hand investigations Robinson was able to improve on earlier accounts usually based on J. Doresse, *The Secret Books of the Egyptian Gnostics* (London, 1960).

2. R. A. Lipsius, *Die Quellen der ältesten Ketzergeschichte* (Leipzig, 1875); A. von Harnack, 'Zur Quellenkritik Geschichte des Gnostizismus', *Zeitschrift für die historische Theologie* (1874), pp. 143–226; A. Hilgenfeld, *Die Ketzergeschichte des Urchristentums* (Leipzig, 1884).

3. The *Liber contra omnes haereses* is mentioned by Justin himself (1 *Apol.* 26). An attempt to reconstruct it was made by P. Prigent, *Justin et l'Ancien Testament* (Paris, 1964).

4. The full title of the work is *A Scrutiny and Refutation of what is Falsely Called Gnosis*. This title, discussed by A. Rousseau and L. Doutreleau, *Irénée de Lyon. Contre les hérésies* (Paris, 1979), 1. 31ff., indicates that the work is divided into two parts: the first, contained in Book 1, discusses a series of Gnostic doctrines, especially the Valentinian; the second, contained in Books 2–4, 'overturns' them, refuting them with arguments

based on reason (Bk 2), the doctrine of the Church, God and Christ (Bk 3) and the words of the Lord (Bk 4). Book 5 deals almost exclusively with the resurrection of the flesh, denied by the Gnostics, and concludes with a profession of millenarian faith.

5. For a fuller discussion see especially ch. 10.

6. On the relationship between Irenaeus and the *Syntagma* see Hilgenfeld, *Ketzergeschichte*, pp. 21ff. and 46ff.

7. R. McL. Wilson, 'Twenty years after' in Barc (ed.), *Colloque*, p. 61.

8. P. Perkins, 'Irenaeus and the Gnostics', *VigChr* 30 (1976), 193–200; E. P. Meijering, *God Being History* (Amsterdam, 1975), pp. 31–8; R. Greer, 'The dog and the mushrooms: Irenaeus' view of the Valentinians assessed' in Layton (ed.), *Rediscovery* I. 146ff.

9. E. Hamann, 'Hippolyte', *DTC* VI. 2487–511; V. Loi, 'La problematica storico-letteraria su Ippolito' in *Ricerche su Ippolito* (Rome, 1977), pp. 9–16.

10. The Hippolytan authorship of this and other works has been contested on several occasions by P. Nautin, *Hippolyte et Josipe* (Paris, 1947); 'La controverse sur l'auteur de l'*Elenchos*', *RHE* 47 (1952), 5–43. For an assessment of his methodology see K. Koschorke, *Hippolyts Ketzerbekämpfung und Polemik gegen die Gnostiker. Eine tendenzkritische Untersuchung seiner 'Refutatio Omnium Haresium'* (Wiesbaden, 1975).

11. On the concept of 'heresy' see the classic work of W. Bauer, *Rechtgläubigkeit und Ketzerei im altesten Christentum²* (Tübingen, 1934, with additions by G. Strecker, 1964). See also H. E. W. Turner, *The Pattern of Christian Thought* (London, 1954), and H. Schlier, αἵρεσις, *TW* I. 180–2.

12. In his two works *Adversus Valentinianos* and *Adversus Marcionem*.

13. His concept of God provides the basic motif of his thought and the organizational principle of his attack; see Greer, 'Dog and mushrooms'. See also N. Brox, *Offenbarung, Gnosis und gnosticher Mythos bei Irenäus: zur Charakteristik der Systeme* (Salzburg–Munich, 1966); and B. Aland, 'Gnosis und Kirchenväter' in Aland (ed.), *Gnosis*, pp. 163ff.

14. See in general A. Orbe, *Antropología de S. Ireneo* (Madrid, 1969).

15. W. Völker, *Der wahre Gnostiker nach Clemens Alexandrinus* (Leipzig, 1952). For a discussion of the radical evangelical roots of this ideal of Gnosis see J. Dupont, *Gnosis. La Connaissance religieuse dans les Épîtres de Paul* (Paris, 1949) and I. L. Bouyer, *La Spiritualité du Nouveau Testament et des Pères* (Paris, 1960), pp. 292ff.

16. F. Bolgiani, 'La confutazione di Clemente Alessandrino', *Atti dell' Accademia Scientifica di Torino* 96 (1961–2), 537–664.

17. H. Jonas, *Gnosis und spätantiker Geist*, II.1 *Von der Mythologie zur mystischen Philosophie²* (Göttingen, 1966), 171ff.; G. Quispel, 'From mythos to logos', *ErJ* 39 (1970), 161ff., and 'Origen and Valentinian Gnosis', *VigChr* 28 (1974), 29–42. For a contrary view see J. Daniélou, *Message évangélique et culture hellénistique* (Tournai, 1961), pp. 427ff.

18. Daniélou, *Message*, pp. 103ff.

19.   W. Schneemelcher, 'Epiphanius von Salamis', *RAC* 5.909–27.

20.   The *Panarion* is the most complete ancient survey of heresies. The work is divided into three volumes containing seven books (vol. 1 contains Bks 1–3; vol. 2 has Bks 4–5; vol. 3 has Bks 6–7). The number of eighty heresies appears for the first time in *Ancoratus* 12–13, an earlier work. When Acacius and Paul, having read *Ancoratus* in AD 375, asked Epiphanius for a more detailed analysis and a refutation of the eighty heresies, Epiphanius had already begun the *Panarion* (1.2), which he must have completed during 377: see P. Fraenkel, 'Histoire sainte et hérésie chez Saint Épiphane de Salamine', *RevThPh* (1962), 175–91. On the structure of the work see J. Dümmer, *Die griechischen christlichen Schriftsteller. Geschichte, Gegenwart und Zukunft* (Berlin, 1977), pp. 74ff. On the sources of Epiphanius see R. A. Lipsius, *Zur Quellenkritik des Epiphanius* (Vienna, 1865), and, for a contrary view, J. Dümmer, 'Die Gnostiker im Bilde ihrer Gegner' in P. Nagel (ed.), *Studien zum Menschenbild in Gnosis und Manichäismus* (Halle–Saale, 1979), pp. 247ff.

21.   We are indebted to Celsus for the famous diagram of the Ophites, a systematic representation of the world of the Gnostics (Origen, *Contra Celsum* VI. 24–38). See T. Hopfner, 'Das Diagramm der Ophianer' in *Charisteria für R. Rzach* (Reichenberg, 1930), pp. 86–98; G. Bornkamm, 'Ophiten', PW XVIII. 654–8; H. Leisegang, *Die Gnosis* (Leipzig, 1924), pp. 111ff. On the polemic see N. Brox, 'Antignostische Polemik bei Christen und Heiden', *Münchener Theol. Zeitschrift* 18 (1967), 265–91. On Celsus see C. Andresen, *Logos und Nomos. Die Polemik des Celsus wider das Christentum* (Berlin, 1955), and K. Pichler, *Streit um das Christentum. Der Angriff des Kelsos und die Antwort des Origenes* (Frankfurt, 1980).

22.   The fundamental texts of Plotinus' polemic against the Gnostics are translated with commentary by V. Cilento, *Paideia antignostica* (Florence, 1971). See also D. Roloff, *Plotin. Die Gross-Schrift III, 8–V, 5–II, 9* (Berlin, 1970).

23.   C. Elsas, *Neuplatonische und gnostische Weltablehnung in der Schule Plotins* (Berlin–New York, 1975), and F. G. Bazan, *Plotino y la Gnosis* (Buenos Aires, 1981).

24.   A.-J. Festugière, *Hermétisme et mystique païenne* (Paris, 1967), pp. 261–312, and M. Mazza, 'La dottrina dei viri novi nel secondo libro dell' *Adversus Nationes* di Arnobio', *Helikon* 3 (1963), 11–169.

25.   Elsas, *Neuplatonische Weltablehnung*, pp. 41ff.

26.   W. Bauer, 'Die Oden Salomos' in E. Hennecke and W. Schneemelcher (eds), *Neutestamentliche Apokryphen*[4] II (Tübingen, 1971), 576–625. On the hypothesis that this text was written by a Gnostic author, Bauer observes (p. 577): '"Gnostic" here is to be understood in its broadest sense.' See also J. H. Charlesworth (ed.), *The Odes of Solomon* (Oxford, 1973). Charlesworth is against a Gnostic authorship; see his 'The Odes of Solomon, not Gnostic', *Catholic Biblical Quarterly* 31 (1969), 357–68.

On the Jewish-Christian nature of this composition see J. Daniélou, *Theéologie du Judéo-Christianisme* (Paris, 1961), pp. 12ff.

27. The thesis of a Gnostic origin was first formulated by R. A. Lipsius, *Die Apokryphen Apostelgeschichten und Apostellegenden* (Braunschweig, 1883–90), pp. 4ff.

28. In general see G. Bornkamm, *Mythos und Legende in den Apokryphen Thomasakten* (Göttingen, 1933). According to Bornkamm (in Hennecke-Schneemelcher, eds, *Apokryphen* II. 300), 'the view of salvation central to the *Acts* is that of Gnosis.' He believes this to be true especially of the two hymns: *Hymn of the Pearl* and *Marriage Hymn of the First Praxis* (ch. 6ff.). Here, as elsewhere, the greatest difficulty consists in defining the 'Gnostic' nature of the various motifs with an ascetic background that recur in the *Acts* and suggest Encratite rather than Gnostic influence; see the justifiable reservations of J. D. Kaestli in F. Bovon et al., *Les Actes Apocryphes des Apôtres* (Geneva, 1981), pp. 54–5.

29. See P. H. Poirier, *L'Hymne de la Perle des Actes de Thomas* (Louvain, 1981).

30. For the critical edition see A. D. Nock and A.-J. Festugière, *Hermès Trismégiste* I–IV (Paris, 1980). The studies of Festugière are basic work, in particular, *La Révélation d'Hermès Trismégiste*, 4 vols (Paris, 1944–54) and the review by H. Dörrie, *Platonica Minora*, ed. V. Buchheit (Munich, 1976), pp. 100–11.

31. Festugière, *Hermétisme*, pp. 38–9.

32. J. Kroll, *Die Lehren des Hermes Trismegistros* (Münster, 1914) suggested dividing the tracts of the corpus according to doctrine. W. Bousset, however, in an important review of Kroll republished in his *Religionsgeschichtliche Studien* (Leiden, 1979), pp. 97ff., sees religion itself as the criterion for dividing the texts and suggests two main religious influences: an optimistic one of Greek origin and a pessimistic-dualist one of oriental origin.

33. *CH* V and, in general, A.-J. Festugière, *Le Dieu cosmique* (Paris, 1949).

34. In particular, treatises IV, VI and VII.

35. Nock–Festugière, *Hermès Trismégiste*, I.vii.

36. See the collection in W. Förster (ed.), *Die Gnosis* II (Zurich, 1971). 173–418 (English trans. by R. McL. Wilson, *Gnosis*, Oxford, 1972).

37. On the sources see R. Macuch, *Zur Sprache und Literatur der Mandäer* (Berlin, 1976), pp. 147–70. On the various stages of the well-documented research see K. Rudolph, *Die Mandäer*, I *Prolegomena: Das Mandäerproblem* (Göttingen, 1961); 'Zum gegenwärtigen Stand der mandäischen Religionsgeschichte' in K. Tröger (ed.), *Gnosis und Neues Testament* (Berlin–Gütersloh, 1973), pp. 121–48 and 'Der Mandäismus in der neueren Gnosisforschung' in Aland (ed.), *Gnosis*, pp. 244–77.

38. K. Rudolph, 'Quellenprobleme zum Ursprung und Alter der Mandäer' in J. Neusner (ed.), *Christianity, Judaism and other Graeco-Roman Cults. Studies for Morton Smith at Sixty* (Leiden, 1975), pt 4, pp. 112ff., regards the third century as the period in which the earliest Mandaean texts can be dated, even if certain traditions might seem to be earlier.

39. R. Bultmann, 'Der religionsgeschichtliche Hintergrund des Prologs zum Johannesevangelium' and 'Die Bedeutung der neuerschlossenen mandäischen und manichäischen Quellen für das Verständnis des Johannesevangeliums', both republished in his *Exegetica*, ed. E. Dinkler (Tübingen, 1967), pp. 10–35 and 55–104.

40. C. Schmidt, *Koptisch-gnostische Schriften*, I *Die Pistis Sophia. Die beiden Bücher des Jeu. Unbekanntes altgnostisches Werk*, ed. W. Till (Berlin, 1962). In his preface Till sketches the principal stages in the fortunes of this text. See also H. Leisegang, 'Pistis Sophia', PW XX. 1813–21.

41. This is what happened to the English translation; the translator himself belonged to theosophical circles: G. R. S. Mead, *Pistis Sophia: A Coptic Gnostic Gospel*² (London, 1921). See also C. W. King, *The Gnostics and their Remains* (London, 1887), who studied the text as a source of mysteries and esoteric Christianity. In France Amélineau's translation (1895) underwent a similar fate; see J. M. Rivière, *Histoire des doctrines ésoteriques* (Paris, 1940), pp. 190ff.

42. The *PS* and the two books of *LJ* were republished by V. Macdermot, *Pistis Sophia* (Leiden, 1978) and *The Books of Jeu and the Untitled Text in the Bruce Codex* (Leiden, 1978); the text is that of Schmidt, the translation of Macdermot.

43. For the earlier period see H. Rossel's well-documented study published in *H. Rossels theologische Schriften*, ed. A. Neander (Berlin, 1874), pp. 179–249. On Baur see P. C. Hodgson, *The Formation of Historical Theology: A Study of F. C. Baur* (New York, 1966), and H. Harris, *The Tübingen School* (Oxford, 1975), pp. 11ff.

44. A. von Harnack, *Lehrbuch der Dogmengeschichte*,³ I (Freiburg–Leipzig, 1894), 211ff. On Harnack see K. Neufeld, *A. von Harnack. Theologie auf der Suche nach der Kirche* (Paderborn, 1977).

45. On the School see J. Hempel, 'Religionsgeschichtliche Schule', RGG V.991–4, and A. F. Verheule, *Wilhelm Bousset: Leben und Werk* (Amsterdam, 1975), pp. 271ff.

46. His fundamental work is *Hauptprobleme der Gnosis* (Göttingen, 1907, repr. 1973); and his article 'Gnosis Gnostiker', PW VII. 1503–47.

47. See the following works by R. Reitzenstein: *Poimandres* (Leipzig, 1904); *Das iranische Erlösungsmysterium* (Göttingen, 1921); and *Die hellenistischen Mysterienreligionen*³ (Leipzig, 1927). See also C. Colpe, *Die religionsgeschichtliche Schule* (Göttingen, 1961).

48. H. von Glasenapp, *Das Indienbild deutscher Denker* (Stuttgart, 1960).

49. H. Jonas, *The Gnostic Religion*² (Boston, 1963), pp. 3ff.: 'What we do witness at the period coinciding roughly with the beginnings of Christianity is an explosion of the East. Like long pent-up waters its forces broke through the Hellenistic crust and flooded the ancient world, flowing into the established Greek forms and filling them with their content, besides creating their own new beds' (p. 23). Jonas clearly states that the life-giving roots of this conception, typical of their *Lebensphilosophie*, are

attributable to the influences of Spengler, 'the clever dilettante' *Die mythologische Gnosis*³ (vol. I of his *Gnosis und spätantiker Geist* (Göttingen, 1964), p. 73). On the relationship between the two see G. Sebba, 'History, Modernity and Gnosis' in Opitz–Sebba (eds), *Philosophy of Order*, pp. 195ff.

50. See above, n. 6 to the Introduction.

51. E. Tröltsch, 'Die Dogmatik der religionsgeschichtlichen Schule' in his *Gesammelte Schriften*, 2 (Tübingen, 1912–15), 500–24. On Tröltsch see G. Cantillo, *Ernst Troeltsch* (Naples, 1979), pp. 135ff.

52. H. G. Gadamer, *Kleine Schriften*, III (Tübingen, 1972), 202–11.

53. J. M. Robinson, 'The Jung Codex', *Religious Studies Review* 3 (1977), 17–30.

54. *The Facsimile Edition of the Nag Hammadi Codices*, published under the auspices of the Egyptian Antiquities Department and Unesco in Leiden between 1972 and 1977.

55. See above, n. 44 to the Introduction.

56. M. Krause, 'Die Texte von Nag Hammadi' in Aland (ed.), *Gnosis*, pp. 227ff., and K. W. Tröger, 'Zum gegenwärtigen Stand der Gnosis und Nag Hammadi Forschung' in K. W. Tröger (ed.), *Altes Testament-Frühjudentum-Gnosis* (Berlin–Gütersloh, 1980), pp. 11ff.

57. These figures are far from certain, given the fragmentary state of Codices XII and XIII; see Krause, 'Texte', in Aland (ed.), *Gnosis*, pp. 223ff.

58. A complete index of editions and translations is to be found in D. M. Scholer, *Nag Hammadi Bibliography 1948–1969* (Leiden, 1971) with annual supplements in *Novum Testamentum*.

59. J. Zandee, 'Die "Lehren des Silvanus" als Teil der Schriften von Nag Hammadi' in M. Krause (ed.), *Essays on the Nag Hammadi Texts* (Leiden, 1975), pp. 239–52.

60. M. Krause, 'Die Petrusakten in Codex VI' in M. Krause (ed.), *Essays on the Nag Hammadi Texts* (Leiden, 1972), pp. 36–58, and A. Guillaumont, 'Des nouveaux actes apocryphes: les Actes de Pierre et des Douze Apôtres', *RevHR* 196 (1979), 141–52.

61. J. P. Mahé, *Hermès en Haute Égypte. Les Textes hermétiques de Nag Hammadi et leurs parallèles grecs et latins* (Quebec, 1978).

62. M. Krause, 'Das literarische Verhältnis des Eugnostosbriefes zur Sophia Jesu Christi. Zur Auseinandersetzung der Gnosis mit dem Christentum' in A. Stuiber and A. Hermann (eds), *Mullus. Festschrift für Th. Klauser* (Münster, 1964), pp. 215ff.

63. G. Filoramo, 'Gli apocrifi gnostici: il genere letterario delle apocalissi', *Aug* 23 (1983), 124ff.

64. K. Rudolph, 'Der gnostische Dialog als literarisches Genus' in P. Nagel (ed.), *Probleme der koptischen Literatur* (Halle–Wittenberg, 1968), pp. 85–107; and Perkins, *Gnostic Dialogue*.

65. H. Nibley, 'Evangelium quadraginta dierum', *VigChr* 20 (1966), 1ff.

66. W. Bauer, *Das Leben Jesu im Zeitalter der neutestamentlichen Apokryphen* (Tübingen, 1909), pp. 258ff.

67. J. E. Ménard, *L'Évangile selon Thomas* (Leiden, 1975).

68. G. Filoramo, 'Il problema della rivelazione nel Vangelo di Verità', *Atti dell'Accademia Scientifica di Torino* 108 (1973), 607, n. 1.

69. On the title and structure see H. M. Schenke, 'Der sog. Tripartitus Tractatus und die in den Himmel projizierte gnostische Anthropologie' in Nagel (ed.), *Studien*, pp. 147ff.

70. J. M. Sevrin, 'À propos de la Paraphrase de Shem', *Muséon* 88 (1975), 66–96; D. A. Bertrand, 'Paraphrase de Shem et Paraphrase de Seth' in J. E. Ménard (ed.), *Les Textes de Nag Hammadi* (Leiden, 1975), pp. 146–57; M. Krause, 'Die Paraphrase des Seem und der Bericht Hippolyts' in Widengren (ed.), *Proceedings*, pp. 101–10.

71. Porphyry, *Vita Plotini* 16; J. Sieber, 'An introduction to the tractate Zostrianos', *NT* 15 (1973), 237ff.

72. H. M. Schenke, 'Das sethianische System nach Nag Hammadi Handschriften' in P. Nagel (ed.), *Studia Coptica* (Berlin, 1974), pp. 165–72.

73. M. Krause and P. Labib, *Die Drei Versionen des Apokryphon des Johannes im koptischen Museum zu Alt-Kairo* (Wiesbaden, 1962). In addition to the example cited above in n. 62 there is also *EvAeg*, NHC III.2 and IV.2. See R. McL. Wilson, 'One text, four translations: some reflections on the Nag Hammadi Gospel of the Egyptians' in Aland (ed.), *Gnosis*, pp. 441–8.

74. J. W. B. Barns, 'Greek and Coptic papyri from the covers of the Nag Hammadi codices: a preliminary report' in Krause (ed.), *Essays* (1975), pp. 9–17 (with an important addendum on p. 17 by E. G. Turner). This interpretation must be revised in the light of that addendum and the remarks of J. C. Shelton in J. W. B. Barns, G. M. Browne and J. C. Shelton, *Nag Hammadi Codices. Greek and Coptic Papyri from the Cartonnage of the Covers* (Leiden, 1981). On the complex problems of translation into Coptic see R. McL. Wilson, 'The trials of a translator: some translation problems in the Nag Hammadi texts' in Ménard (ed.), *Textes*, pp. 32ff., and M. Krause, 'Die Texte von Nag Hammadi' in Aland (ed.), *Gnosis*, pp. 230ff. On the original language of the text see A. Böhlig, 'Report on the Coptological work' in R. McL. Wilson (ed.), *Nag Hammadi and Gnosis* (Leiden, 1978), p. 133: 'I myself consider all the documents as translations from Greek.'

75. F. Wisse, 'Gnosticism and early monasticism in Egypt' in Aland (ed.), *Gnosis*, pp. 431–40.

76. According to T. Säve-Söderbergh, 'Holy scriptures or apologetic documentation? The *Sitz im Leben* of the Nag Hammadi texts', in Ménard (ed.), *Textes*, pp. 3–14, the codices constitute a heresiological library assembled by the 'orthodox' monks for the purposes of refutation. See also his survey of the discussion of the problem: 'The pagan elements in early Christianity' in Barc (ed.), *Colloque*, pp. 71ff., and Krause, 'Texte' in Aland (ed.), *Gnosis*, pp. 241–3.

77. For a classification of the texts according to this criterion see F. Wisse, 'The opponents in the New Testament in the light of Nag Hammadi writings' in Barc (ed.), *Colloque*, pp. 101ff.

78. A. Böhlig and F. Wisse, *Zum Hellenismus in den Schriften von Nag Hammadi* (Wiesbaden, 1975), and J. Ries (ed.), *Gnosticisme et le monde hellénistique* (Louvain, 1982).
79. R. McL. Wilson, 'Jewish "Gnosis" and Gnostic origins: A survey', *Hebrew Union College Annual* 45 (1974), 179–89, and W. C. van Unnik, 'Gnosis und Judentum' in Aland (ed.), *Gnosis*, pp. 65–86.
80. K. Rudolph, 'Gnosis und Gnostizismus: ein Forschungsbericht', *ThRu* 36 (1971), 48ff., and C. Colpe, 'Irans Anteil an Entstehung und Ausgang des antiken Synkretismus' in Tröger (ed.), *Altes Testament*, pp. 327–43.
81. K. Koschorke, *Die Polemik der Gnostiker gegen das kirchliche Christentum* (Leiden, 1978); E. Pagels, *The Gnostic Gospels* (London, 1980); M. Krause, 'Christlich-gnostische Texte als Quellen für die Auseinandersetzung von Gnosis und Christentum' in M. Krause (ed.), *Gnosis and Gnosticism* (Leiden, 1981), pp. 47–65.
82. Tröger (ed.), *Gnosis*; W. Schmithals, 'Gnosis und Neues Testament', *Verkündigung und Forschung* 21 (1976), 22–46; G. MacRae, 'Nag Hammadi and the New Testament' in Aland (ed.), *Gnosis*, pp. 144–57.

CHAPTER 2   BETWEEN DEMONS AND GODS

1. P. R. L. Brown, *The World of Late Antiquity* (London, 1971).
2. Id., *The Making of Late Antiquity* (Cambridge, Mass., 1978), pp. 27f.
3. *De def. or.* 411 Dff.
4. M. Caster, *Lucien et la pensée religieuse de son temps* (Paris, 1937), p. 26, writes: 'The taste for oracles is a dominant feature of second-century society. It is to be found among philosophers (except Epicureans and Sceptics, of course) and was rife among both upper and lower classes.' See M. Nilsson, *Geschichte der griechischen Religion*[2] (Munich, 1961), II.467ff. *POxy* 1477 (end of 3rd cent. AD) provides us with a series of typical questions put to oralces: '(72) Shall I receive my salary? (73) Shall I remain in the place where I am going? (74) Shall I be sold? (75) Shall I receive favours from my friend? (76) Am I allowed to make a contract with so and so? (79) Shall I obtain money? (80) Is the wanderer still alive? (87) Shall I be made ambassador? (88) Shall I become a senator? (89) Will there be any obstacle to my flight? (90) Must I divorce my wife? (91) Have I been poisoned?' It is clear that the questions come from the most diverse social strata. In a time of political insecurity, when the performance of honorific offices such as ambassador or senator required considerable financial outlay, it is not surprising that the oracles were consulted about one's personal *cursus honorum*, or career.
5. J. Ferguson, *Religions of the Roman Empire* (London, 1970), p. 107.
6. The principal source book of Hellenistic magic is K. Preisendanz (ed.), *Papyri Graecae Magicae* (Leipzig, 1928). An English version of these and the principal Egyptian Demotic texts has recently been published: H. D. Betz (ed.), *Greek Magical Papyri in Translation, Including Demotic Spells* (Chicago, 1986). See also A.-J. Festugière, *L'Idéal religieux des grecs et*

l'Évangile (Paris, 1932), pp. 280ff.; M. P. Nilsson, *Die Religion in den griechischen Zauberpapyri* (Lund, 1948); A. D. Nock, 'Greek magical papyri' in his *Essays on Religion and the Ancient World*, ed. Z. Stewart (Oxford, 1972), 1. 176–94.

7. Caster, *Lucien*.

8. See the interpretation of E. R. Dodds, *Pagan and Christian in an Age of Anxiety* (Cambridge, 1965).

9. F. Boll, C. Bezold and W. Gundel, *Sternglaube und Sterndeutung*[4] (Leipzig, 1931), pp. 44ff.

10. The assimilation of the infernal world to the sublunar region has been attributed to various philosophical trends and to more or less controversial figures such as Heracleides Ponticus or Poseidonius. See I. P. Culianu, '"Démonisation du cosmos" et dualisme gnostique', *RevHR* 120 (1979), 16ff.

11. A famous Pythagorean *akousma*, or oral instruction, recorded in Iamblichus, *Vita Pythagorei* 18, says that the Islands of the Blessed are connected with the sun and the moon. See Culianu, '"Démonisation"', p. 12, n. 50.

12. E. Norden, *P. Vergilius Maro Aeneis Buch VI*[4] (Stuttgart, 1957), pp. 270ff.

13. J. Kroll, *Gott und Hölle* (1932, repr. Darmstadt, 1963), pp. 58ff.

14. A.-J. Festugière, *Personal Religion Among the Greeks* (Berkeley, 1954).

15. Nilsson, *Geschichte*, pp. 534ff.

16. H. Wolfson, *Philo*[3], I (Cambridge, Mass., 1962), 26ff.

17. There is a full collection of texts with commentary in A.-J. Festugière, *Le Dieu inconnu* (Paris, 1954), pp. 225–41.

18. H. D. Betz, 'The Delphic maxim *gnōthi seauton* in Hermetic interpretations', *HThR* 63 (1970), 465–84, and J. Haussleiter, 'Deus internus', *RAC* III.799ff.

19. R. Bultmann, 'ζάω', *TW* II. 833ff.; H. Conzelmann, φως, *TW* IX. 343, n. 328.

20. Brown, *Making of Late Antiquity*, p. 25.

21. The so-called 'celestial journey' of the soul. See W. Bousset, 'Die Himmelsreise der Seele', *ARW* 4 (1901), 136ff. and 229ff., and C. Colpe, 'Die Himmelsreise der Seele ausserhalb und innerhalb der Gnosis' in U. Bianchi (ed.), *Le origini dello gnosticismo* (Leiden, 1967), pp. 421ff.; I. P. Culianu, *Psychanodia* I (Leiden, 1983), and *Expériencees de l'extase* (Paris, 1984).

22. W. R. S. Schödel, '"Topological" theology and some monistic tendencies in Gnosticism' in Krause (ed.), *Essays* (1972), pp. 88ff.

23. H. Dörrie, 'Die Frage nach dem Transzendenten im Mittelplatonismus' in *Entretiens sur l'antiquité classique*, V (Geneva, 1960), 191–223.

24. M. Harl, 'Le langage de l'expérience religieuse chez les Pères grecs', *RSLR* 13 (1977), 5–34.

25. R. McL. Wilson, *The Gnostic Problem*[2] (London, 1964), and W. D. Hauschild, *Gottes Geist und der Mensch* (Munich, 1972), pp. 259ff.

26. H. Dörrie, 'Hypostasis, Wort- und Bedeutungsgeschichte' in his *Platonica Minora*, pp. 13–69; H. Köster, ὑπόστασιϛ, *TW*, VIII.571ff.

27. Wilson, *Gnostic Problem*, pp. 42ff.; M. Simon, 'Éléments gnostiques chez Philon' in Bianchi (ed.), *Origini*, pp. 366ff.; R. Arnaldez, *Philon d'Alexandrie: De opificio mundi* (Paris, 1961), pp. 122ff.

28. Apart from Iamblichus there is also Porphyry; see F. Romano, *Porfirio di Tiro* (Catania, 1979), pp. 131ff.

29. H. M. Kleinknecht, λόγοϛ, *TW* VI.1220ff.; Daniélou, *Message*, pp. 335ff.; R. A. Norris, *God and World in Early Christian Theology* (London, 1966).

30. Philo is a typical example. Two elements are combined in his notion of *Logos*: both the revealed divine word and, as the Stoics taught, the force that drives the world. See E. Bréhier, *Les Idées philosophiques et religieuses de Philon d'Alexandrie* (Paris, 1925), p. 101.

31. This is the case with the angels of Philo in *De opificio mundi* 72ff., to whom the plural *poiēsōmen* ('let us make') of Gen. 1:26 in the Septuagint translation is applied. See Wolfson, *Philo* 1.272ff.

32. H. Happ, *Hyle* (Berlin–New York, 1971).

33. *Asclepius* 16 and the observation on the passage by Festugière, *Hermès* II.371, n. 135.

34. P. Merlan, 'Greek philosophy' in A. H. Armstrong (ed.), *The Cambridge History of Later and Early Medieval Philosophy* (Cambridge, 1970), pp. 26–7, on the theory of reduplicated matter in Plotinus. For a genetic explanation of his theory see H. C. Puech, *Plotin et les gnostiques* (Paris, 1958), p. 184.

35. C. Andresen, 'Erlösung', *RAC* VI.54ff.

36. A. D. Nock, *Conversion* (Oxford, 1961), pp. 122–3.

37. Festugière, *L'Idéal*, pp. 142ff.

38. F. Cumont, *Oriental Religions in Roman Paganism* (London, 1911), pp. 27–8.

39. Cumont, *Oriental Religions*, pp. 21ff.

40. Nock, *Conversion*, p. 7.

41. Ibid., pp. 18ff.

42. M. Simon and A. Benoit, *Le Judaisme et le christianisme antique* (Paris, 1968), pp. 75ff.

43. G. Maier, *Mensch und freier Wille* (Tübingen, 1971), pp. 165ff.

44. Whether among the Essenes or at Qumran there were, as frequently happens in sectarian groups, different grades of initiation that might last for years. Only at the end did one become a fully fledged member of the community of 'saints'. See M. Simon, *Les Sectes juives au temps de Jésus* (Paris, 1960), pp. 42–73 and 105–13; M. Hengel, *Judentum und Hellenismus*[2] (Tübingen, 1973), pp. 394ff.; E. Schürer, *The History of the Jewish People in the Age of Jesus Christ*, ed. G. Vermes, F. Millar and M. Black (Edinburgh, 1979), II.555ff. The sources on the Essenes have been collected by A. Adam, *Antike Berichte über die Essener* (Berlin, 1961). For a guide to the enormous literature on Qumran see B. Jongeling,

A *Classified Bibliography of the Finds of the Desert of Judah* (Leiden, 1971).

45. O. Betz, *Offenbarung und Schriftforschung in der Qumransekte* (Tübingen, 1960), pp. 96ff.

46. See ch. 3.

47. G. Wetter, *Charis* (Leipzig, 1913), and H. Conzelmann, χάρις, *TW* IX.363ff.

48. On ancient demonology see J. Tambornino, *De antiquorum demonismo* (Giessen, 1909); W. Bousset, 'Zur Demonologie der späteren Antike', *ARW* 8 (1915), 134ff.; P. Boyancé, 'Les dieux démons personnels dans l'antiquité' *Revue Philologique* 61 (1935), 189ff.; S. S. Jensen, *Dualism and Demonology: The Function of Demonology in Pythagorean and Platonic Thought* (Copenhagen, 1966); Daniélou, *Théologie*, pp. 146ff.

49. T. Hopfner, *Griechisch-ägyptischen Offenbarungszauber* (Leipzig, 1921), p. 4.

50. M. Detienne, *De la pensée religieuse à la pensée philosophique: La notion de 'Démon' dans le pythagorisme ancien* (Paris, 1963).

51. 'With the demons late antique men found themselves flanked by an invisible society that shared with them all the incongruities and the tensions of their own visible world', says Peter Brown in *The Making of Late Antiquity*, p. 20. On the particularly important demonological thought of Plutarch see G. Soury, *La Démonologie de Plutarque* (Paris, 1942), and Nilsson, *Geschichte*, pp. 401ff., 407ff. and 446ff.

52. T. Hopfner, 'Mageia', PW XIV.301ff.

53. On theurgy see T. Hopfner, 'Theurgie', PW VI.258ff.; S. Eitrem, 'La théurgie chez les Néoplatoniciens', *Symbolae Osloenses*, 22 (1942), 49ff.; E. R. Dodds, 'Theurgy and its relationship to Neoplatonism', *JRS* 37 (1947), 55ff.

54. J. Michl, 'Engel', *RAC* VI.60ff. and 109ff., and A. Szabo, 'Die Engelvorstellungen vom Alten Testament zur Gnosis' in Tröger (ed.), *Altes Testament*, pp. 143–52.

55. Daniélou, *Théologie*, p. 143, and I. P. Culianu, 'Les anges des peuples et la question du dualism gnostique' in Ries (ed.), *Gnosticisme*, pp. 133–7.

56. D. S. Russell, *The Method and Message of Jewish Apocalyptic 200 BC–AD 100* (Philadelphia, 1974), pp. 244ff.

57. The angelology of the Dead Sea Scrolls is important in this sense. See L. Moraldi (ed.), *I manoscritti di Qumran* (Turin, 1971), pp. 313–14, on the subject of I QS XII.1ff.

58. G. Quispel, 'Das ewige Ebenbild des Menschen' in his *Gnostic Studies* (Istanbul, 1974) I.140ff.

59. e.g. Enoch is transformed into an angel and identified 'with the angel Yahoel or Yoel, who occupies an important and sometimes dominant position in the earliest documents of throne mysticism and in the apocalypses. The most important characteristics of this angel are now transferred to Metatron' according to G. Scholem, *Major Trends in Jewish*

Mysticism (Jerusalem, 1941), p. 67. For other examples see Michl, 'Engel', pp. 243ff. Perhaps the most characteristic example of hierarchical promotion is the identification of Christ as an angel; see J. Barbel, *Christos Angelos* (Bonn, 1941), and Daniélou, *Théologie*, p. 167.

60. H. Wey, *Die Funktionen der bösen Geister bei den griechischen Apologeten des zweiten Jahrhunderts nach Christus* (Winterthur, 1957).

61. The crypto-teleological use of the term is rightly criticized by W. Bätke, 'Aufgabe und Struktur der Religionswissenschaft' in G. Lanczowski (ed.), *Selbstverständnis und Wesen der Religionswissenschaft* (Darmstadt, 1974), pp. 134–5.

62. T. Hopfner, 'Traumdeutung', PW VI.2233–45; D. del Corno, 'I sogni e la loro interpretazione nell'età dell' Impero' in *Aufstieg und Niedergang der römischen Welt* 16.2.1605–18, and *Artemidoro. I Libri dei Sogni* (Milan, 1975). Artemidorus' book is the most famous ancient work of dream interpretation. See also Dodds, *Pagan and Christian*, pp. 38ff.

63. A. D. Nock, 'A vision of Mandulis Aion' in *Essays* 1.371ff. A good example is Thessalus: having tried to acquire medical knowledge by following the traditional schools of dialectic doctors or leafing through books of magical and astrological medicine, Thessalus receives, thanks to a priest belonging to an Egyptian temple, and in a private revelation from Asclepius, the medical expertise that will make him outstanding among men. See Festugière, 'L'expérience religieuse du médecin Thessalos' in *Hermétisme*, pp. 141ff.

64. Festugière, *Hermétisme*, pp. 13ff.

65. *Ion* 533 dff. and *Phaedrus* 254 a and 265 b; H. Lewy, *Sobria Ebrietas* (Giessen, 1929), pp. 45ff.

66. Nilsson, *Geschichte*, pp. 527–8.

67. P. Volz, *Die Eschatologie der jüdischen Gemeinde im neutestamentlichen Zeitalter* (Tübingen, 1934), pp. 147ff.

68. W. Bousset and H. Gressman, *Die Religion des Judentums im späthellenistischen Zeitalter*[3] (Tübingen, 1926), pp. 147ff.

69. XLI 1ff. P. Scacchi, *Apocrifi dell'Antico Testamento* (Turin, 1981), p. 449, observes: 'Enoch is essentially an intermediary between the transcendent God and other beings, whether they live in or out of time ... indeed he is a man (XII.1–2), but he lives in the world of the spirit. He can therefore see invisible reality and reveal it to men with a "tongue of flesh" (XIV.2).'

70. Russell, *Method and Message*, pp. 107ff.; L. Koep, *Das himmlische Buch in Antike und Christentum* (Bonn, 1952); Daniélou, *Théologie*, p. 150.

71. W. Schmithals, *Die Apokalyptik* (Göttingen, 1973).

72. Dodds, *Pagan and Christian*, pp. 39ff.

73. 'We have plenty of illustrations for the desire to be informed of something by a vision', says A. D. Nock, 'Mandulis Aion', p. 372. Festugière, *Hermétisme*, pp. 23–4, makes a useful distinction between a self-referential vision and a vision as a means of achieving a purpose. For a list of visions of the first type in the ancient world see F. Pfister, 'Ekstasis', *RAC* I.971ff.

In general see J. Lindblom, *Gesichte und Offenbarungen. Vorstellungen von göttlichen Weisungen und übernatürlichen Erscheinungen im ältesten Christentum* (Lund, 1968), and E. Benz, *Die Vision. Erfahrungsformen und Bilderwelt* (Stuttgart, 1969).

74. *Met.* XI.6.
75. Oracles 1–4 in K. Aland, *Kirchengeschichtliche Entwürfe* (Gütersloh, 1960), and the comment on pp. 111–12. On the fundamental vision of Priscilla see K. Froelich, 'Montanism and Gnosis' in *Essays in Honour of Florowski* (Rome, 1973), pp. 104–5.
76. J. Dey, *Palingenesia* (Münster, 1937).
77. Brown, *Making of Late Antiquity*, ch. 1.
78. M. J. Vermaseren, 'Hellenistic religions' in C. J. Bleeker and G. Widengren (eds), *Historia Religionum* (Leiden, 1969), I.495.
79. J. Leipoldt, *Die Frau in der antiken Welt und im Urchristentum* (Leipzig, 1953); K. Thräde, 'Frau' *RAC* VIII.197–269; S. A. Pomeroy, *Goddesses, Whores, Wives and Slaves* (New York, 1975).
80. L. J. Swidler, 'Greco-Roman feminism and reception of the Gospel' in B. Jaspert (ed.), *Traditio-Krisis-Renovatio* (Marburg, 1976), pp. 41ff. The process of women's emancipation had begun, in the great urban centres, with the first Hellenism (see C. Schneider, *Kulturgeschichte des Hellenismus* (Munich, 1967) 1.78ff.) and continued throughout the Empire; see J. Carcopino, *Daily Life in Ancient Rome* (London, 1947), p. 106.
81. Cumont, *Oriental Religions*, p. 41.
82. E. S. Fiorenza, 'Word, spirit and power: women in the early Christian communities' in R. Ruether and E. McLaughlin (eds), *Women of Spirit* (New York, 1979), pp. 39ff.
83. L. Zscharnack, *Der Dienst der Frau in den ersten Jahrhunderten der christlichen Kirche* (Göttingen, 1902); P. Labriolle, *La Crise montaniste* (Paris, 1913), pp. 23ff.
84. On Apuleius see A. Pennacini, P. L. Donini, T. Alimonti and A. Monteduro Roccavini, *Apuleio letterato, filosofo, mago* (Bologna, 1979).
85. On Apuleius and Middle Platonism see Donini in Pennacini et al., *Apuleio*, pp. 103–11.
86. J.-P. Mahé, 'Quelques remarques sur la religion des Métamorphoses et les doctrines gnostiques contemporaines', *RevSR* 46 (1972), 1ff.
87. Alimonti in Pennacini et al., *Apuleio*, esp. p. 125.
88. G. F. Gianotto, 'Reductio ad fabulam. Sintesi e mediazione culturale nelle *Metamorfosi* di Apuleio' in *I canoni letterari* (Trieste, 1981), p. 61.
89. *Dial c. Tr.* 1–2; N. Hyldahl, *Philosophie und Christentum* (Copenhagen, 1966), pp. 88ff.

CHAPTER 3   THE GNOSTIC IMAGINATION

1. R. Bultmann, γινώσκω, *TW*, I.688ff.
2. Heracl. fr. 101a; Herod. 1.8; Plato, *Phaedr.* 250 d and *Republic* VI. 507 c.

3. *Gorgias* 508 a.
4. *Excerpta ex Theodoto* 78.2
5. Kroll, *Lehren*, pp. 350ff.
6. Irenaeus, *AH* 1. 21.4.
7. NHC I.3.22.3. All Nag Hammadi texts are cited with reference to codex, tract, page and line; the translation is that of J. M. Robinson, *Nag Hammadi Library*.
8. *Apol.* 38 a.
9. For what follows see H. C. Puech, 'Doctrines ésotériques et thèmes gnostiques dans l'Évangile selon Thomas', *Annuaire. Collège de France*, 63 (1963), 199ff.; 66 (1966), 259ff.; 68 (1968), 292.
10. As *syzygos*, or partner, image and angel. In the *Hymn of the Pearl* it is the celestial garment that the prince puts on in his father's kingdom before going to Egypt. The theme of the garment recurs in the *Pistis Sophia*. See Bousset, *Hauptprobleme*, p. 303, and G. Quispel, *Makarius, das Thomasevangelium und das Lied von der Perle* (Leiden, 1967), pp. 57–8.
11. Plato, *Laws* 716 c. See A. Schneider, 'Der Gedanke der Erkenntnis des Gleichen durch Gleiches in antiker und patristischer Zeit' in *Festgabe für Cl. Bäumker* (Münster i.W., 1923), pp. 65–76.
12. J. Wach, *Das Verstehen* (Tübingen, 1926) 1.38, n. 2.
13. Festugière, *Dieu inconnu*, pp. 131–2.
14. E. R. Dodds, *The Greeks and the Irrational* (Berkeley, 1951), pp. 236ff.
15. *Ethica Nichomachea* 1177[b]–1178[a].
16. Fr. 61.
17. H. von Arnim (ed.), *Stoicorum Veterorum Fragmenta* (Leipzig, 1903), 1.146.
18. *Leg. All.* 1.31ff.
19. *Fug.* 133.
20. *Leg. All.* 3 161.
21. *Mut.* 223.
22. On the *topos* in Hellenistic literature see J. Pépin, *Idées grecques sur Dieu et sur l'homme* (Paris, 1981), p. 86, n. 3.
23. *Praem.* 45.
24. *Rer. div.* 55; *Spec. leg.* 4.123 *Op. mundi* 135–44.
25. F. N. Klein, *Die Lichtterminologie bei Philon von Alexandrien und in den hermetischen Schriften* (Leiden, 1962), p. 42.
26. P. Sacchi, *Storia del mondo giudaico* (Turin, 1976), pp. 156–7.
27. E. Schweitzer, πνεῦμα, *TW* VI.387ff.; R. J. Mortley, 'Gnosis', *RAC* X.485–6.
28. 1 QS XI.5–6.
29. 1 QS XI.3–4.
30. J. Dillon, *The Middle Platonists* (London, 1977), pp. 231ff.; P. L. Donini, *Le scuole l'anima l'impero: la filosofia antica da Antioco a Plotino* (Turin, 1982), pp. 100ff.
31. Festugière, *Dieu inconnu*, pp. 128ff., 134ff.

32. É. des Places, *Oracles chaldaïques* (Paris, 1971), p. 43.
33. Festugière, *Dieu inconnu*, p. 133.
34. Des Places, *Oracles*, p. 43, fr. 2.
35. For possible Gnostic influences see A. H. Armstrong, 'Gnosis and Greek philosophy' in Aland (ed.), *Gnosis*, p. 109.
36. G. Filoramo, *Luce e gnosi* (Rome, 1980).
37. R. Bultmann, 'Zur Geschichte der Lichtmetaphysik im Altertum' in his *Exegetica*, pp. 323ff.
38. G. P. Wetter, *Phos* (Uppsala, 1915), pp. 7–8, 12ff.
39. *CH* I.4.
40. *CH* I.6.
41. *CH* I.7.
42. For the Coptic tract see Mahé, *Hermès*; for *CH* XIII W. C. Grese, *Corpus Hermeticum XIII and Early Christian Literature* (Leiden, 1979).
43. *CH* XIII.1.
44. *CH* XIII.8–9. See Festugière, *Dieu inconnu*, pp. 221ff.
45. Filoramo, *Luce*, 25–6.
46. *CH* XIII. 8.
47. *CH* XIII.9.
48. *CH* XIII.10: 'You have known, my son, the manner of regeneration in us [says Hermes to Tat]. Spiritual regeneration has taken shape in us . . . and we have become divine, thanks to this birth.'
49. The traditional thesis according to which the *logos* of the Ionian philosophers broke with earlier mythological tradition and opened the way to later scientific, rational thought is supported by, among others, W. Nestle, *Vom Mythos zum Logos* (Stuttgart, 1940), and B. Snell, *Entdeckung des Geistes. Studien zur Entdeckung des europäischen Denkens bei dem Griechen*[4] (Göttingen, 1975). A radical critique, which illuminates the more complex relationship between *mythos* and *logos* is given by F. M. Cornford, *Principium Sapientae: The Origins of Greek Philosophical Thought*[2] (New York, 1965); cf. W. Jaeger, *The Theology of the Early Greek Philosophers* (Oxford, 1947). Fundamental to the understanding of the transformations of *mythos* are the works of J.-P. Vernant, *Les Origines de la pensée grecque* (Paris, 1962), and *Mythe et pensée chez les grecs* (Paris, 1965). In general see G. S. Kirk, *Myth. Its Meaning and Function in Ancient and Other Cultures* (Cambridge, 1970), and the anthology of interpretations edited by M. Detienne, *Il mito greco. Guida storica e critica* (Rome–Bari, 1975).
50. *Republic* II. 377 b–378 c.
51. *Poetics* VI.6–IX.5.
52. J.-P. Vernant and M. Detienne *Les Ruses de l'intelligence. La mètis des grecs* (Paris, 1975).
53. For a radical critique of this structuralist scheme see V. di Benedetto and A. Lami, *Filologia e marxismo. Contro le mistificazioni* (Naples, 1980).
54. *Def. or.* 421 A.

55. K. Koch, *Ratlos vor der Apokalyptik* (Gütersloh, 1970), p. 23.
56. J.-P. Vernant, *Mythe et société en Grèce ancienne* (Paris, 1974), pp. 196ff.
57. E. R. Dodds, *The Ancient Concept of Progress* (Oxford, 1973), pp. 1–26.
58. See the anthology edited by G. F. Gianotti, *Mito e storia nel pensiero greco* (Turin, 1976), pp. 183ff.
59. Ibid., p. 185.
60. Vernant, *Mythe*, p. 213; Kirk, *Myth*, p. 187.
61. Nilsson, *Geschichte*, pp. 56ff.
62. D. Sabatucci, *Lo stato come conquista culturale* (Rome, 1975).
63. J. Pépin, *Mythe et allégorie* (Paris, 1958).
64. F. Buffière, *Les Mythes d'Homère et la pensée grecque* (Paris, 1956), pp. 392ff.
65. R. A. Baer, *Philo's Use of the Categories 'Male' and 'Female'* (Leiden, 1970), p. 10.
66. *Dec.* 156.
67. P. Frutiger, *Les Mythes de Platon* (Paris, 1930); W. Hirsch, *Platons Weg zum Mythos* (Berlin–New York, 1971).
68. Vernant, *Mythe et pensée*, pp. 51–78.
69. For what follows see Y. Vernière, *Symboles et mythes dan la pensée de Plutarque* (Paris, 1977), ch. 2.
70. Ibid., p. 118.
71. The three myths are in Plutarch's mature works *De fac.*, *De sera num.*, *De gen.* See the apposite analysis of Vernière, *Symboles*, ch. 2.
72. Vernière, *Symboles*, p. 267.
73. Pépin, *Mythe*, p. 73; Frutiger, *Mythes de Platon*, p. 223.
74. Nock, *Conversion*, pp. 120ff.
75. Vernière, *Symboles*, p. 75.
76. Ibid., p. 173.
77. *De fac.* 994 E and *De Is.* 367 CD.
78. See in general Festugière, *Dieu cosmique*.
79. *De fac.* 943 EF.
80. A.-J. Festugière, *L'Astrologie et les sciences occultes* (Paris, 1944), pp. 90 ff.
81. Such is the case of the dualistic myths related in *De Iside*.
82. On the origins, fate and limits of this category see F. Bolgiani, 'Il concetto di "religione popolare" in F. Bolgiani (ed.), *Strumenti per richerche delle classi popolari* (Turin, 1981), pp. 11–30, and 'Religione popolare', *Aug* 21 (1981), 7ff.
83. W. K. C. Guthrie, *Orpheus and Greek Religion*[2] (London, 1952), and Nilsson, *Geschichte* 1.678ff.
84. M. Detienne, *Dionysos mis à mort* (Paris, 1977), pp. 161ff.
85. G. Carchia, *Orfismo e tragedia. Il mito trasfigurato* (Milan, 1979), pp. 15ff.
86. Detienne, *Dionysos*, pp. 166f.

CHAPTER 4   IN THE WORLD OF THE PLEROMA

1. NHC II.3.75.3ff. On the history of the term 'dualism' see J. Duchesne-Guillemin, 'Dualismus', *RAC* IV.334–50, and 'Gnosticisme et dualisme' in Ries (ed.), *Gnosticisme*, pp. 89ff.

2. Dodds, *Pagan and Christian*, pp. 3ff.

3. A. E. Taylor, *Plato* (London, 1926), pp. 436ff. On the different interpretations of the Platonic Demiurge see H. Schwabl, 'Weltschöpfung', PW suppl. IX.1540; W. Theiler, 'Demiurg' *RAC* III.694–711. On the fate of this interpretation see M. Baltes, *Die Weltentstehung des platonischen Timaios nach den antiken Interpreten* (Leiden, 1976).

4. See the famous passages condemning the body in *Phaedo* 66 c, 67a, 94 e and *Cratylus* 400 c, 414 a. On dualism in Plato see U. Bianchi, *Prometeo, Orfeo, Adamo* (Rome, 1976), pp. 42ff.

5. In *De Iside*, 'the first treatise of comparative religion that was at the same time a treatise on dualism' (Bianchi, *Prometeo*, p. 46). See also J. Ries, 'Plutarque historien et théologien des doctrines dualistes' in Ries (ed.), *Gnosticisme*, pp. 146–63.

6. J. Bidez and F. Cumont, *Les Mages hellénisés* (Paris, 1938), 1.3–163.

7. See in general U. Bianchi, *Zaman i Ohrmazd. Lo zoroastrismo nelle sue origini e nella sua essenza* (Turin, 1958); R. C. Zaehner, *The Teachings of the Magi: A Compendium of Zoroastrian Beliefs* (London, 1975); M. Boyce, *Zoroastrians. Their Religious Beliefs and Practices* (London, 1979).

8. Bianchi, *Prometeo*, pp. 95ff., 108ff.

9. P. Moreau, *L'Âme du monde de Platon aux stoïciens* (Paris, 1939, repr. Hildesheim, 1965).

10. Merlan, 'Greek philosophy', pp. 25–6.

11. F. Cumont, *L'Égypte des astrologues* (Paris, 1937), pp. 204ff., and W. Gundel, 'Astrologie', *RAC* I. 817.

12. See above, ch. 2, n. 55.

13. *De somn.* II.114. On the term 'angels of the nations' see E. Peterson, *Frühkirche, Judentum and Gnosis* (Rome, 1959), pp. 51ff. On the number, seventy or seventy-two, see Bousset, *Hauptprobleme*, pp. 358–60, and H. Bietenhard, *Die himmlische Welt im Urchristentum und Spätjudentum* (Tübingen, 1951), pp. 109ff.

14. *Enn.* III. 2.3.

15. *Enn.* III. 2.12.

16. On the nature of these Gnostics see Filoramo, *Luce*, p. 69, n. 8.

17. *Enn.* II. 6.

18. *Enn.* II. 13–16.

19. *Enn.* II. 5.

20. W. Beierwaltes, 'Die Metaphysik des Lichtes in der Philosophie Plotins', *Zeitschrift für philosophische Forschung* 15 (1961), 334ff.

21. *Enn.* II 9. 12 and 30–9.

22. V. Macdermot, 'The concept of the Pleroma in Gnosticism' in Krause (ed.), *Essays* (1981), pp. 76–81.
23. In the terminology proposed by Jonas, *Gnostic Religion*, pp. 236–7, this type of Syrian dualism is contrasted with the Iranian variety (Mazdaism or Manichaeism), in which evil exists *ab aeterno* as the principle opposed to good.
24. *Ref.* V.12.1ff.
25. NHC II.3.69.9ff.
26. NHC II.4.87.10–11. On the theme of examplarism see J. Zandee, 'L'exemplarisme du monde transcendant par rapport au monde visible dans le Tractatus Tripartitus du Codex Jung', *Revue d'Égyptologie* 24 (1972), 224–8.
27. On this entity see J. H. Sieber, 'The Barbelo Aeon as Sophia in Zostrianos and related tractates' in Layton (ed.), *Rediscovery* 2.788–95, and M. Scopello, 'Youel et Barbelo dans le Traité de l'Allogène' in Barc (ed.), *Colloque*, pp. 374–82. On the etymology see H. M. Schenke, 'The phenomenon and significance of Gnostic Sethianism' in Layton (ed.), *Rediscovery* 2.624.
28. F. T. Fallon, 'The Gnostic Apocalypses' *Semeia* 14 (1979), 123ff.
29. NHC XI. 3.60.13ff. 'Silence', as we shall see, plays a central role in Valentinian mythological accounts: see A. Orbe, *En los albores de la exegesis iohannea* (Rome, 1955), p. 31, n. 73, and *Hacia la primera teología de la procesión del Verbo* (Rome, 1958), p. 65, n. 36; p. 349, n. 23. As a condition of the initiate see Des Places, *Oracles*, no. 132 with comment on p. 143. See also H. Schlier, *Religionsgeschichtliche Untersuchungen zu den Ignatiusbriefen* (Giessen, 1929), pp. 38ff., and in general O. Casel, *De philosophorum graecorum silentio mystico* (Giessen, 1919). For ethnological parallels see M. Detienne, *Les Maîtres de Vérité dans la Grèce archaique* (Paris, 1967), p. 22, n. 69. See also G. Mensching, *Das heilige Schweigen* (Giessen, 1926).
30. Koschorke, *Polemik*, pp. 152ff.
31. On the subject of Anthropos, central to Gnosticism, see Bousset, *Hauptprobleme*, pp. 160–223; K. Rudolph, 'Ein Grundtyp gnostischer Urmensch-Adam Spekulation', *ZRGG* 9 (1957), 1–20; H. M. Schenke, *Der Gott 'Mensch' in der Gnosis* (Göttingen, 1962). For an overall view of the problem see F. Borsch, *The Christian and Gnostic Son of Man* (London, 1970).
32. J.-E. Ménard, *L'Évangile de Vérité* (Leiden, 1972), p. 175. On the concept of *aiōn* in Hellenism see Kroll, *Lehren*, pp. 67–71, and Festugière, *Dieu inconnu*, pp. 152, 176ff. On the law of development of the aeons of the Gnostic Pleroma see A. Orbe, *La teología del Espiritu Santo* (Rome, 1966), pp. 130ff.
33. On the term *prosōpon*, or face, in Gnostic texts see R. Kasser et al., *Tractatus Tripartitus* (Berne, 1973), pp. 330–2; in Manichaeism see *PCol* 17.7ff.; F. Altheim, 'Persona', *ARW* 7 (1929), 36–52; M. Nédoncelle, 'Prosopon et persona dans l'antiquité classique', *RevSR* 22 (1948), 277–99; Vernant, *Mythe et pensée*, pp. 233ff.

34. On Gnostic pneumatology, apart from the basic work of Orbe, *Teología*, see Hauschild, *Gottes Geist*, pp. 151ff., 224ff.

35. On the Gnostic concept of emanation and how it differs from Neoplatonic emanation see K. Kremer, 'Emanation', *Historisches Wörterbuch der Philosophie* II. 445–8.

36. H. Jonas, 'Delimitation of the Gnostic phenomenon' in Bianchi (ed.), *Origini*, pp. 94–104.

37. K. Koschorke, '"Suchen und Finden" in der Auseinandersetzung zwischen gnostischen und christlichen Christentum', *Wort und Dienst* 14 (1977), 51ff.

38. NHC I.5.109.3ff. In Gnostic texts there is frequently polemic against worldly wisdom, which is occasionally contrasted with the simplicity of Gnostic wisdom; see NHC VIII.1.2.25ff.; X.6.17ff.; VIII.2.134,19ff.; I.3.19.21ff.; II.7.140.9ff.; I.4.43.25ff. See also H. Martin, Jun. 'The anti-philosophical polemic and Gnostic soteriology of the Treatise on the Resurrection' *Numen* 20 (1973), 20–37.

39. Cf. NHC III.3.70.1ff.

40. NHC I.5.110.3ff.

41. NHC I.5.110.11f.

42. BG.22.19ff.; see also NHC XI.3.61.32ff.

43. NHC I.5.51.8ff.

44. NHC XIII.1.45.2–3.

45. E. L. Dietrich, 'Der Urmensch als androgyn', *ZKG* 55 (1939), 297ff; R. A. Bullard, *The Hypostasis of the Archons* (Berlin–NY, 1970), pp. 75ff. See also W. A. Meeks, 'The image of the androgyne: some uses of a symbol in earliest Christianity' *HR* 13 (1970), 165ff. In Valentinian and Sethian texts androgyny is a basic element of the pleromatic world. Thus, in accordance with the theory of the image, in which the Demiurge and his cohort of Archons are images, however abortive, of the Upper World, these too appear as androgynous entities: NHC II.1.5.4–11; BG 27.4 and 18–28; NHC II.5.102.1–11; BG 94.9–11 for the primordial Anthropos, and NHC II.4.94.18/33–5; 95.3ff.; II.5.100. 5–7; 101.10–12. 22–5 (see also 102.1–11) for the androgyny of the Archons and the Demiurge. This androgyny is typical, as we shall see, also of the First Man, Adam; it is also an attribute of the soul, which before its fall into this world 'was virgin and androgynous' (NHC II.6.127.19ff.). The myth of the androgyne is typical of various esoteric Christian hymns; see E. Benz, *Adam. Der Mythus vom Urmensch* (Munich, 1955). On the Platonic origins (in the famous myth in the *Symposium*) and fate of the androgyne and the related motif of the hermaphrodite see O. Jessen, 'Hermaphroditos', PW VIII.714–21; M. Delcourt, *Hermaphrodite. Mythes et rites de la bisexualité dans l'antiquité classique* (Paris, 1958), and 'Utrumque-neutrum' in *Mélanges Puech* (Paris, 1974), pp. 117–23. On contemporary biological theories that explained the phenomenon see E. Lesky, *Die Zeugungs- und Vererbungslehren der Antike und ihre Nachwirken* (Wiesbaden, 1951),

pp. 86ff. On the diffusion of the theme in the history of religions
see A. Bertholet, *Das Geschlecht der Gottheit* (Tübingen, 1934), and
H. Baumann, *Das doppelte Geschlecht* (Berlin, 1955).

46. M. Eliade, *Méphistophélès et l'Androgyne* (Paris, 1962), pp. 121ff.
47. Baer, *Philo's Categories*, pp. 34ff.
48. J. Heldermann, 'Isis as Plane in the Gospel of Truth?' in Krause (ed.),
Essays (1981), p. 39.
49. On the text and its apocalyptic content see M. Tardieu, 'Les trois stèles
de Seth: un écrit gnostique retrouvé à Nag Hammadi' *RSPhTh* 57
(1973), 545–73. On Dositheus see Hilgenfeld, *Ketzergeschichte*, pp. 155ff.;
R. McL. Wilson, 'Simon, Dositheus and the Dead Sea Scrolls', *ZRGG* 9
(1957), 21–30; E. Yamauchi, *Pre-Christian Gnosticism* (London, 1973),
p. 57; Tardieu, 'Trois stèles', p. 551, n. 36.
50. NHC VII.5.122.8ff. On the theme of the Triad see Bousset, *Hauptprobleme*,
pp. 333–4; K. Beyschlag, *Simon Magus und die christliche Gnosis*
(Tübingen, 1974), p. 164, n. 70; J. M. Robinson, 'The Three Stelae of
Seth and the Gnostics of Plotinus' in Widengren (ed.), *Proceedings*,
pp. 133ff.; Tardieu, 'Trois stèles', pp. 562–3; A. Böhlig, 'Triade und
Trinität in den Schriften von Nag Hammadi' in Layton (ed.), *Rediscovery*
2.617–34.
51. This is the famous distinction that underlies the reflections on the Logos
of Philo and many other Church Fathers between *logos endiathetōs*
(residing in the mind) and *logos prophorikos* (uttered): see H. A. Wolfson,
The Philosophy of the Church Fathers[3] (Harvard, 1970), pp. 177ff., and
M. Pohlenz, *Stoa*[4] (Göttingen, 1970), index II.
52. NHC XIII.1.35.32ff.
53. Irenaeus, *AH* I.1.1. Cf. a parallel passage of another Valentinian document,
Epistula dogmatica (Epiph. *Panarion*, 31.5.5), from which we learn that
Ennoia, wishing to break the eternal chains that bound her to the male
principle, *ethēlyne* his *megethos*: 'magnitudinem libidinis illecebris ad sui
consuetudinem inflexit', i.e. she seduced him). If the initiative has passed
from the male element to the female in this document, in other Valentinian
texts there is a tendency (third possibility) to eliminate the female dimension
of the Father altogether: 'Indeed, some wish to preserve the Pythagorean
purity of the Valentinian doctrine and to maintain that the father lacks a
female element and alone.' (*Ref.* VI.29.3)
54. BG 91.4ff.
55. On the theme of the mirror see G. Filoramo, 'Dal mito gnostico al mito
manicheo' in *Trasformazioni della cultura nella Tarda Antichità* (Turin,
1984).
56. BG 26.15.
57. Orbe, *Teología* (index).
58. Ibid., p. 126. On Ennoia in Gnosticism see G. Lüdemann, *Untersuchungen
zur simonianischen Gnosis* (Göttingen, 1975), pp. 65–71.
59. Filoramo, *Luce*, p. 57, n. 48. See also M. A. Williams, 'Stability as a

soteriological theme in Gnosticism' in Layton (ed.), *Rediscovery* 2.819ff., and B. Aland, 'Gnosis und Philosophie' in Widengren (ed.), *Proceedings*, pp. 54–6.

60. NHC XI.3.60. 19ff.; 59.14–16.
61. NHC XIII.1.35.2–3; 12ff.
62. NHC I.5.72.1ff. On the nature of this sigh or breath see G. Filoramo, 'Pneuma o conoscenza in alcuni testi gnostici' in Ries (ed.), *Gnosticisme*, pp. 236–44.
63. The female element performs a similar function in certain cabbalistic traditions; see Scholem, *Major Trends*, pp. 283ff., and *Sabbatai Sevi* (London, 1973), pp. 61–2.
64. NHC VII.5.120.26ff.
65. On *autogennētos*, or self-generated, see J. Whittaker, 'Self-generating principles in second-century Gnosticism' in Layton (ed.), *Rediscovery* 1.176–89.
66. On the Gnostic parallels of this name, which deliberately recall the triadic nature of the primordial entity, see Y. Janssens, *La Prōtennoia Trimorphe* (Quebec, 1978), p. 63.
67. In certain texts he is called the 'First-Appearing One' (NHC VIII.1.13.4 and 15.9ff.) or 'Protophanes' (NHC XI.3.45.36ff.)
68. A central theme, particularly developed in the *Gospel of Truth*: see S. Arai, *Die Christologie des Evangelium Veritatis* (Leiden, 1964), pp. 67ff., and J. D. Dubois, 'Le contexte judaïque du "nom" dans l'Évangile de Vérité', *RThPh* 24 (1974), 188–216. In general see F. G. Untergassmair, *Im Namen Jesu. Der Namensbegriff im Johannesevangelium* (Stuttgart, 1974), pp. 188ff.
69. Orbe, *Teología*, pp. 126ff.
70. Irenaeus, *AH* 1.2.1.
71. NHC I.5.66.8ff.
72. BG 91.14ff.
73. G. Verbeke, *L'Évolution de la doctrine du pneuma des stoïciens à St Augustin* (Paris–Louvain, 1945), pp. 18ff., and H. Saake, 'Pneuma', PW suppl. XIV.393ff.
74. 1 *LJ* 44.
75. Filoramo, 'Pneuma' in Ries (ed.), *Gnosticisme*, pp. 240–1.
76. A typical theory of ancient psychology: the soul, *psychē* (whose name is thought to derive from *psychos*, 'cold'; see A. Dihle, ψυχή, *TW* IX.606) is the result of a gradual process of 'cooling' (*anapsyxis*) of the spirit, the breath of life, which was originally warm: see Tertullian, *De anima* 25.2 and 27.5 and the comment by J. H. Waszink, *Tertulliani De anima* (Amsterdam, 1947), pp. 321, 329–30, 351. See also A.-J. Festugière, *Les Doctrines de l'âme* (Paris, 1953), pp. 186ff.
77. NHC I.3.34.1ff. and the comment by Ménard, *Évangile*, pp. 158ff. See also P. Meloni, *Il profumo d'immortalità* (Rome, 1975), pp. 44ff.
78. NHC I.3.35.25ff.

79. The texts used by Schenke to create his 'Sethianische System' in Nagel (ed.), *Studia Coptica*, are *Allog, AJ, HA, EvAeg, ApcAd, StelSeth, Zostr, Melch, Nor, Prot*. For further details see Filoramo, *Luce*, p. 43, n. 1, and, in general, the papers on Sethianism in Layton (ed.), *Rediscovery 2* . If we accept the division proposed by Krause, 'Texte von Nag Hammadi' in Aland (ed.), *Gnosis*, pp. 238ff., we find (1) non-Christian texts (which does not mean pre-Christian): *Zostr, Allog, Nor*; (2) Gnostic-Christian texts that were originally not Christian: *HA, AJ, ApcAd* or already regarded as Gnostic-Christian: *Melch, Prot*, StelSeth.

80. On these four lights see G. Filoramo, '*Phoster* e salvatore in alcuni testi gnostici' in U. Bianchi and M. J. Vermaseren, *La soteriologia dei culti orientali* (Leiden, 1982), p. 869.

81. BG 34.19ff.

82. On this latter aspect, which is a little odd for Gnostic eschatology, see Hauschild, *Gottes Geist*, pp. 225ff., and my observations on *Pistis Sophia* in ch. 8.

83. Schenke, 'Sethianisches System', 168.

84. Apart from Orbe, *Teología*, see also F. M. Sagnard, *La Gnose valentinienne et le témoignage de S. Irénée* (Paris, 1947).

85. Irenaeus, *AH* I.1.1.

86. On the problem in general see H. Hegermann, *Die Vorstellung vom Schöpfungsmittler im hellenistischen Judentum und Urchristentum* (Berlin, 1961); U. Wilcken, σοφία, *TW* VII.465–528; B. L. Mack, *Logos und Sophia. Untersuchung zur Weisheitstheologie im hellenistischen Judentum* (Göttingen, 1973). On the origins of Gnostic Sophia there are disagreements, and these are related to the question whether Sophia or Anthropos comes first; Bousset, *Hauptprobleme*, p. 217, believes that Sophia is later than the *Urmensch*, or original man, whereas G. Quispel, 'Der gnostische Anthropos', *ErJ* 22 (1953), 223, believes that Sophia is a central figure, of Jewish origin. In general, see Wilson, *Gnostic Problem*, pp. 197ff.; C. Colpe, 'Gnosis II', *RAC* XI.574; G. W. MacRae, 'The Jewish background of the Gnostic Sophia myth', *NT* 12 (1970), 86–101; K. Rudolph, 'Sophia und Gnosis' in Tröger (ed.), *Altes Testament*, pp. 221–37; I. P. Culianu, *Feminine versus Masculine*, in H. G. Kippenberg, *Struggles of Gods* (Berlin–New York, 1984).

87. Cf. A. Orbe, 'Spiritus Dei ferebatur super aquas', *Greg* 44 (1963), 717.

88. NHC II.1.9.25ff.

89. On the recurrence of the term in Gnostic texts see N. A. Dahl, 'The arrogant Archon and the lewd Sophia' in Layton (ed.), *Rediscovery* 2.708, n. 47. Dahl disputes the interpretation of M. P. Nilsson, 'Sophia-Prunikos', *Eranos* 45 (1947), 169–72, and argues that the term possesses 'clearly sexual connotations (lewd, unchaste, lascivious, voluptuous or something of the sort), but it is not a term for a prostitute or a promiscuous woman.' On the other hand, G. Quispel, 'Jewish Gnosis and Mandaean Gnosticism' in Ménard (ed.), *Textes*, pp. 82–122, relates the term to the myth of the Simonian Ennoia

who was found in a brothel and in this way reconstructs a background of sacred prostitution of the variety known in the Near East.

90. R. Unger, 'Zur sprachlichen und formalen Struktur des gnostischen Textes "Der Donner: vollkommener Nous"'. *Oriens Christianus* 59 (1975), 78–107. On this title see M. Tardieu, 'Le titre du deuxième écrit du Codex VI', *Muséon* 87 (1974), 523–30; 88 (1975), 365–9; and H. M. Schenke, 'Die Tendenz der Weisheit zur Gnosis' in Aland (ed.), *Gnosis*, p. 352, n. 5. On the Gnostic character of the text see G. W. MacRae, 'Discourses of the Gnostic revealer' in Widengren (ed.), *Proceedings*, pp. 121–2.

91. MacRae, 'Discourses', pp. 111ff.

92. NHC VI.2.13.1ff.

93. G. Quispel, 'Hermann Hesse und Gnosis' in Aland (ed.), *Gnosis*, pp. 494ff.

94. *AH* I.29.4. On the connection between this statement and the system described in *AJ* see C. Schmidt, 'Irenäus und seine Quelle in Adv. Haer. I,29', *Philothesia P. Kleinert dargebracht* (Berlin, 1907), pp. 315–36; H. C. Puech, 'Gnostische Evangelien' in Hennecke–Schneemelcher (eds), *Neutestamentliche Apokryphen* 1.229ff.; H. M. Schenke, 'Das literarische Problem des Apokryphon Johannis', *ZRGG* 16 (1962), 56–63.

95. *AH* I.30.1–2.

96. *Panarion* 21.2.

97. *Panarion* 31.5.

98. On the difference between *thelēma* and *boulēma* see A. Orbe, 'Teología bautismal de Clemente Alejandrino', *Greg* 35 (1955), 423, n. 50.

99. See above, n. 61.

100. *AH* I. 12.1. Cf. the *noïkē boulēsis*, or intellectual wish, of the *Epistula dogmatica* in Epiphanius, *Panarion* 31.5.9. The theme recurs frequently in the Coptic texts: NHC II.3.82.7–8; VII.1.1.4–6; 4.15 *et passim*; VII.5.126.30–2; 3.80.24–6. In general, see E. Benz, *Marius Victorinus und die Entwicklung der abendländischen Willensmetaphysik* (Stuttgart, 1932); Wolfson, *Philosophy*, pp. 197ff.; Beyschlag, *Simon Magus*, pp. 141ff.

101. According to Hippolytus, *Refutatio* VI.30.7, Sophia is moved by the desire to imitate the Father and, like him, to generate alone.

102. *AH* I.2.2.

103. On the limit see Sagnard, *Gnose valentinienne*, pp. 254ff., and Orbe, *Teología*, pp. 276ff., 603ff.

104. *Refutatio* VI.30.8.

105. *AH* I.2.5.

106. Orbe, *Teología*, p. 400.

107. *AH* I.2.6.

CHAPTER 5 THE ARROGANCE OF THE DEMIURGE

1. NHC I.5.75.35ff.: 'Indeed, this free-will which was generated with the Totalities [the aeons] ensured for this one [the Logos-Sophia] that

he accomplished everything he wanted without there being any obstacle in his way.'

2. On the etymology of Achamath see Colpe, 'Gnosis', p. 573. On the Valentinian myth of Sophia see G. C. Stead, 'The Valentinian myth of Sophia', *JTS* 20 (1969), 75–104.

3. M. Tardieu, *Trois mythes gnostiques* (Paris, 1974), p. 57, n. 48, for other Gnostic parallels. See also Q. Hofius, *Der Vorhang vor dem Thron Gottes* (Tübingen, 1972), pp. 28–48, for the Jewish background; Detienne and Vernant, *Ruses*, pp. 67ff. for the Greek parallels; R. Eisler, *Weltenmantel und Himmelszelt* (Munich, 1910), for religious and historical parallels.

4. NHC II.5.98.11ff. and BG 118.18ff.

5. That is, if various elements in the celestial world are formed 'in the image' of the model, the archetype or *Urbild*, in accordance with a law of exemplarism by which they reproduce the quintessential image of original man (if not distorted, then increasingly faded). When he leaves the Pleroma, he takes part in a different process: the cosmos, from the Demiurge downwards, is a reverse (and therefore negative) image of the perfection of the Upper World; see J. Jervell, *Imago Dei* (Göttingen, 1960), pp. 122–70. On the law of exemplarism see Sagnard, *Gnose valentinienne*, pp. 244f.

6. Sophia's androgyny is understood by Philo, *De fuga et inv.* 51: Sophia is female in name, male in nature.' See Bréhier, *Idées philosophiques*, pp. 115ff. and Baer, *Categories*, pp. 62–3. Evidently her male function consists in sowing the *logoi* of the world in chaotic and shapeless matter.

7. Lesky, *Zeugungs- und Vererbungslehren*, and Filoramo, *Luce*, pp. 48ff.

8. *Enn.* II.9.11.

9. Lesky, *Zeugungs- und Vererbungslehren*, pp. 129ff.

10. The technical term is *aporrhoia*, or effluence, from astrology (see Reitzenstein, *Poimandres*, p. 16, n. 14) and is widespread in magical texts (see Hopfner, 'Mageia', p. 321, and Festugière, *Idéal religieux*, pp. 296–7), indicating, within the more general law of universal sympathy, the influences exercised by the different forces, especially those of astral origin, on the terrestrial world and man. For the Gnostic contexts see Filoramo, *Luce*, p. 76, n. 103.

11. Orbe, *Teología*, pp. 313ff.

12. *AH* I.4.1.

13. *AH* I.4.2.

14. Orbe, *Teología*, pp. 399ff.

15. *AH* I.4.5.

16. Ibid.

17. Ibid.

18. This is true of Simonian systems (cf. ch. 9) and those of Menander and Saturninus (cf. ch. 10).

19. e.g. in the so-called triadic systems, about which Hippolytus tells us; see

Bianchi (ed.), *Origini*, p. 18.

20. 'He is always a problematical and never a venerable figure', says Jonas in 'Delimitation', p. 96. This figure is unlikely to originate in a single tradition of thought, consisting as it does of Jewish elements (see Wilson, *Gnostic Problem*, pp. 191–2; A. F. Segal, *Two Powers in Heaven* (Leiden, 1977), pp. 244ff.; Dahl, 'Arrogant Archon', pp. 690–1; B. Barc, 'Samael-Saklas-Yaldabaoth. Recherche sur la genèse d'un mythe gnostique' in Barc (ed.), *Colloque*, pp. 123–50); of Orphic elements (see G. Quispel, 'The Demiurge in the *Apokryphon of John*' in Wilson (ed.), *Nag Hammadi*, pp. 1–33); or, more generally, of Graeco-Hellenistic elements (see Theiler, 'Demiurg', p. 708: Demiurge = *anima mundi*; see also G. Quispel, 'Gnostische Anthropos', *Gnostic Studies* I.210ff.) But, in this matter of origins, it ought to be borne in mind always that 'the Valentinian and, generally speaking, the Gnostic Demiurge is a *metabasis eis allo genos* (transition to another genus)', according to U. Bianchi, 'Religio-historical observations on Valentinianism' in Layton (ed.), *Rediscovery* I.109.

21. V. Goldschmidt, *Le Système stoïcien et l'idée de temps*[2] (Paris, 1969), pp. 146ff.

22. *Met.* Z 9. 1034^a 20ff.

23. *Pol.* III. 1277^b 28–30; 1282^a 17ff.

24. Vernant, *Mythe et pensée*, pp. 196ff.

25. *AH* I.30.3.

26. J. H. Waszink, 'Abtreibung', *RAC* I.57.

27. Plutarch, *De Iside* 19.65. On the Valentinian *ektrōma*, or untimely birth, see Schlier, *Relig. Untersuchungen*, p. 156, and K. Müller, *Beiträge zum Verständnis der valentinianischen Gnosis* (Göttingen, 1920), pp. 230ff. The theme becomes central in Manichaean anthropogony, indicating the rejection of procreation; see H. C. Puech, *Le Manichéisme* (Paris, 1949), p. 173, n. 236.

28. *BG* 37.12ff.

29. Quispel, 'Demiurge', p. 22.

30. Dahl, 'Arrogant Archon', p. 690.

31. Various etymologies have been proposed for the name; see G. Scholem, 'Ialdabaoth reconsidered' in *Mélanges Puech*, pp. 405–21; Barc, 'Samael', pp. 141ff.; F. T. Fallon, *The Enthronement of Sabaoth* (Leiden, 1978), pp. 29ff.

32. *BG* 38.14ff.

33. *NHC* II. 4.94.11ff.

34. Orbe, *Teologia*, p. 268.

35. *NHC* VII. 5.121.3ff.; 124.2ff. In general, see V. W. van der Horst, 'Der Schatten im hellenistischen Volksglauben' in M. J. Vermaseren (ed.), *Studies in Hellenistic Religions* (Leiden, 1979), pp. 23–6.

36. *AH* I.4.1; see I. P. Culianu, 'La femme céleste et son ombre' in his *Iter in silvis* (Messina, 1981), pp. 77–96.

37. *Leg. All.* III. 96.
38. B. Barc and M. Roberge (eds), *Hypostase des archontes et Noréa* (Quebec, 1980), p. 31.
39. M. Scopello, 'Le mythe de la chute des anges dans l'*Apocryphe de Jean*' *RevSR* 54 (1980), 220–30.
40. H. Schlier, 'Das Denken der frühchristlichen Gnosis' in *Neutestamentliche Studien für R. Bultmann*[2] (Berlin, 1957), p. 71.
41. NHC II.5.99.17ff.
42. NHC II.5.100.2ff.
43. *AH* I.5.1.
44. NHC I.5. 100.19ff.
45. NHC II.1.10.20ff.
46. K. Rudolph, *Die Gnosis* (Göttingen, 1978), pp. 75ff. (Eng. version ed. R. McL. Wilson, 1983.)
47. BG 39.6ff.
48. R. M. Grant, *Gnosticism and Early Christianity*[2] (NY–London, 1966), pp. 46ff.; W. Fauth, 'Seth-Typhon, Onoel und eselköpfige Sabaoth. Zur Theriomorphie der ophitisch-barbelo-gnostischen Archonten', *Oriens Christianus* 57 (1973), 79–120; A. J. Welburn, 'The identity of the Archons in the "Apocryphon Johannis"', *VigChr* 32 (1978), 241–54.
49. BG 39.16–18.
50. BG 44.14–15.
51. A list of the Gnostic texts is given by H. G. Bethge, 'Die Ambivalenz alttestamentlichen Geschichtstraditionen in der Gnosis' in Tröger (ed.), *Altes Testament*, p. 94, n. 16; Schenke, *Gott 'Mensch'*, pp. 87–92; Dahl, 'Arrogant Archon', pp. 693–8.
52. The Demiurge's task is to breathe *psychē* (i.e. breath of life) into the body of Adam, which is incapable of standing up straight. On the status of the psychic element, which does not enjoy real autonomy and therefore tends to be either absorbed into the spiritual or, as here, into the hylic, see Jonas, *Mythologische Gnosis*, p. 212, and M. Simonetti, '*Psychē* e *psychikos* nella gnosi valentiniana', *RSLR* 1 (1961), 1ff.
53. *AH* I.5.3.
54. *AH* I.5.1.
55. *AH* I.5.4.
56. Hegesippus, *Acta Archelai* 67.7–8, on the subject of Basilides; Orbe, *Hacia la primera*, pp. 246ff.
57. *Refutatio* V.19.1–22.
58. NHC VII. I.1.7ff.
59. *Refutatio* V.19.1ff.
60. F. Wisse, 'The redeemer figure in the Paraphrase of Shem', *NT* 12 (1970), 130–40; M. Roberge, 'Le rôle du *nous* dans la Paraphrase de Sem' in Barc (ed.), *Colloque*, pp. 328–9. On the meaning of 'paraphrase' see B. Aland, 'Die Paraphrase als Form gnostischer Verkündigung' in Wilson (ed.), *Nag Hammadi*, pp. 75–90.

61. *Refutatio* V.19.1–13.
62. On Manichaean darkness see Puech, *Manichéisme*, p. 164, n. 298.
63. *Refutatio* V.8.1.
64. *Refutatio* V.17.2.
65. Leisegang, *Gnosis*, p. 19.
66. *Refutatio* V.7.38.
67. *Refutatio* VI.9.3–18; see also ch. 9.
68. *Refutatio* VI.17.1.
69. Ibid.
70. Ibid. VI.13.
71. Ibid.
72. On the God (*ouk ōn*, who does not exist, of Basilides see Orbe, *En los albores*, pp. 302–3; H. A. Wolfson, 'Negative attributes in the Church Fathers and the Gnostic Basilides', *HThR* 50 (1957), 145–56; J. Whittaker, 'Basilides on the ineffability of God', *HThR* 62 (1969), 367–71.
73. On the system of Basilides according to Hippolytus and its connection with the statements of other heresiologists see J. H. Waszink, 'Basilides', *RAC* I.1217–25; G. Quispel, 'L'homme gnostique (la doctrine de Basilide)', *ErJ* 16 (1948), 89–139; W. Foerster, 'Das System des Basilides', *NTS* 9 (1969), 233–55.
74. *Refutatio* VII.22.16.
75. Ibid. VII.23.3.
76. Ibid. VII.27.1.
77. NHC X.1.5.22–6.
78. B. A. Pearson, 'The tractate Marsanes (NHC X) and the Platonic tradition'

CHAPTER 6   AND GOD SAID, 'LET US MAKE MAN ...'

1. Quispel, *Gnosis als Weltreligion*, p. 29.
2. P. Nagel, 'Die Auslegung der Paradieserzählung in der Gnosis' in Tröger (ed.), *Altes Testament*, pp. 49–70.
3. E. Peterson, *Frühkirche, Judentum und Gnosis* (Rome–Freiburg–Vienna, 1959), pp. 107ff.; J. E. Ménard, 'Le chant de la Perle', *RechSR* 42 (1968), 291, n. 5; Daniélou, *Théologie*, pp. 382–3.
4. G. Filoramo and C. Gianotto, 'L'interpretazione gnostica dell'Antico Testamento', *Aug* 22 (1982), 69ff.
5. *Op. mundi* 72–5; *Conf. ling.* 168ff.; *De fuga* 68ff.; R. McL. Wilson, 'The early history of the exegesis of Gen. I.26' in *Studia Patristica* (Berlin, 1957), 1. 423.
6. *Leg. All.* I.38, and L. Schotroff, *Der Glaubende und die feindliche Welt* (Neukirchen–Vlyn, 1970), pp. 4ff. See also Hauschild, *Gottes Geist*, pp. 256ff.
7. The plural was explained in various ways in Rabbinic circles; see Schenke, *Gott 'Mensch'*, pp. 124ff.

8. C. Kannengiesser, 'Philon et les Pères sur la double création de l'homme' in *Philon d'Alexandrie* (Paris, 1967), pp. 272–96.

9. P. Schwanz, *Imago Dei* (Halle, 1970).

10. On the concept of 'epiphany' see E. Pax, *Epiphaneia* (Munich, 1955). Of the various ways in which the phenomenon can happen, the most common here seems to be *actio* and *reactio*; these are due to the particular concreteness and 'reality' that one wishes to attribute to the scene.

11. NHC II.1.14.13ff. (BG: 47.14ff.).

12. NHC II.4.87.14ff. This is the theme of the 'seduction of the Archons'. It is no accident that one finds it among the libertine sects; see Epiphanius, *Panarion* 21.2.5 (Simonians); 25.2.2–4 (Nicolaites); 26.1.3 (Phibionites). On the theme of cosmogonic *erōs* in *OrigMund* see Tardieu, *Trois mythes*, pp. 144–65; on the Manichaean parallels see F. Cumont, *Recherches sur le Manichéisme*, 1 *La Cosmogonie manichéenne* (Brussels, 1908), pp. 54–68.

13. NHC II.1.15.2–4. The parallel text in BG 48.1–4 merely says: 'Let us make a man according to the image and likeness of God.' In the long version the purpose of demiurgic creation emerges more clearly: to capture the elusive light by means of sympathetic magic.

14. P. Nagel, 'Anatomie des Menschen in gnostischer und manichäischer Sicht' in Nagel (ed.), *Studien*, pp. 67–94.

15. J. Flamant, *Macrobe et le néo-platonisme latin, à la fin du IVe siècle* (Leiden, 1977), pp. 557ff., and J. Dillon, 'The descent of the soul in Middle Platonic and Gnostic theory', in Layton (ed.), *Rediscovery* 1. 357–64.

16. S. Giversen, *Apokryphon Johannis* (Copenhagen, 1963), pp. 243–5.

17. Nagel, 'Anatomie', pp. 70–1.

18. NHC II.1.15.29–17.6.

19. The meaning of the Coptic *tete* is uncertain.

20. NHC II.1.16.28–30 = NHC IV.1.26.3–5.

21. NHC II.1.17.8–29 = NHC IV.1.26.20–27.12.

22. NHC II.1.18.2ff. Cf. *Test. Reub*, II–III, in *Testaments of the Twelve Patriarchs*.

23. NHC II.1.18.3; *attošs*, which corresponds to the Greek *aoristos* (see W. E. Crum, *A Coptic Dictionary* (Oxford, 1939), 449B) is the equivalent of the Neopythagorean and Middle Platonist 'unlimited' matter.

24. NHC II.1.18.33–4.

25. According to a model widespread in late Judaism, the Adam of earth is gigantic and creeps like a worm; see G. Scholem, 'Die Vorstellung von Golem', *ErJ* 22 (1953), 240ff., and Jervell, *Imago Dei*, pp. 99ff.

26. BG 51.1ff.

27. On the importance of the *status erectus*, or standing upright, see M. Simonetti, 'Note sull' 'interpretazione gnostica dell' Antico Testamento', *VetChr* 9 (1972), 358–9.

28. NHC II. 4.88.10ff.

29. The theme of 'compassion' is linked with the female dimension of God; see Orbe, *Teología*, pp. 199ff.
30. Epinoia is of central importance in Gnostic 'mythology of reflection', indicating the externalization of internal thought (see C. A. Baynes, *A Coptic Gnostic Treatise Contained in the Codex Brucianus* (Cambridge, 1933), p. 11, n. 11). In NHC XIII.1.35.13ff. and 39.19, etc. she is one of the manifestations of Ennoia (to be precise, the second), when she appears as a woman (see Janssens, *Prōtennoia*, p. 60). See also NHC IX.2.28.2 and *Refutatio* VI.18.6–7. Plotinus criticizes this concept of 'reflection', which he considers typically Gnostic; according to him, in the formation of the world nothing comes from logical consequence or reflection, but everything is before it (*Enn.* V.8.7 and 41ff.). For Origen's use of the term see H. Crouzel, *Origène et la 'connaissance mystique'* (Brussels, 1961), pp. 389–91.
31. BG 53.10ff.
32. BG 56.7ff.
33. BG 59.6ff.
34. Bethge, *Ambivalenz*, pp. 90–2.
35. BG 62.8ff.
36. BG 63.14ff.
37. Barc–Roberge (eds), *Hypostase*, pp. 26–7.
38. NHC II.4.90.17.
39. e.g. NHC II.4.90.16, where in the phrase, 'their eyes will be opened' (Gen. 2:7) the word *ophthalmoi* (eyes) is replaced by *kakia* (evil). There is some doubt in this passage as to whether the verb after *kakia* means 'be opened', 'become manifest' or 'arise from'; see Barc–Roberge (eds), *Hypostase*, p. 100.
40. The presentation of animals to Adam takes place before the entry into Paradise.
41. Or the existing ones reduplicate, as the history of the Gnostic Eve shows.
42. For Gnostic parallels see Bethge, *Ambivalenz*, pp. 94–8.
43. BG 72.3ff.
44. BG 73.2ff.
45. NHC II.1.29.17ff.
46. NHC II.1.30.4–7.
47. B. A. Pearson, 'The figure of Norea in Gnostic literature' in Widengren (ed.), *Proceedings*, pp. 143–152.
48. NHC II.4.92.3ff.
49. NHC II.4.92.8ff.
50. NHC II.4.92.18ff.
51. NHC II.4.92.32ff. On Eleleth see Barc–Roberge, *Hypostase*, pp. 115–16; Janssens, *Prōtennoia*, pp. 68–9; A. Böhlig and F. Wisse, *Nag Hammadi Codices III,2 and IV,2. The Gospel of the Egyptians* (Leiden, 1975), pp. 196–7.
52. Barc–Roberge, *Hypostase*, pp. 151–71.

53. Pearson, 'Norea', pp. 147ff.
54. On this distinction see K. M. Fischer, *Tendenz und Absicht des Epheser-briefes* (Göttingen, 1973), pp. 182ff.
55. For a survey of the principal interpretations of this controversial text see K. Rudolph, 'Forschungsbericht' *ThRund* 34 (1969), 161ff., and E. Yamauchi, 'Pre-Christian Gnosticism in the Nag Hammadi texts', *Church History* 48 (1979), 130–5.
56. According to a model found in other texts; see Barc–Roberge, *Hypostase*, pp. 91ff.
57. NHC V.5.65.21ff.
58. See the model in Gen. 18:1ff.
59. G. W. E. Nickelburg, 'Some related traditions in the *Apocalypse of Adam*, the *Book of Adam and Eve* and 1 Enoch' in Layton (ed.), *Rediscovery* 2.519.
60. NHC V.5.69.19ff.
61. NHC V.5.71.10ff.
62. NHC V.5.76.3ff.
63. On the term *phōstēr* see A. Böhlig, *Mysterion und Wahrheit* (Leiden, 1968), pp. 150–60.
64. NHC V.5.76.15ff.
65. NHC V.5.77.27–83.4.
66. NHC V.5.82.21ff.
67. L. Schotroff, 'Animae naturaliter salvandae' in W. Eltester (ed.), *Christen-tum und Gnosis* (Berlin, 1969), pp. 65–97.
68. NHC V.5.85.19ff.
69. B. A. Pearson, 'The figure of Seth in Gnostic literature' in Layton (ed.), *Rediscovery* 2.496ff.
70. Clem. Alex. *Stromateis* II. 114.3–6.
71. Ibid. 36.4.
72. *AH* I.30.6.
73. Unlike what happens in *AJ*. See n. 13 of this chapter.
74. *AH* I.5.5.
75. NHC I.5.100.31ff.
76. NHC I.5.100.36; 101.6ff.
77. NHC I.5.101.3ff.
78. NHC I.5.104.31ff.

CHAPTER 7   *MYSTERIUM CONIUNCTIONIS*

1. NHC II.3.68.10ff.
2. J. D. Turner, *The Book of Thomas the Contender* (Missoula, 1975), and Perkins, *Gnostic Dialogue*, p. 100. Essentially this is an encratite text: the mysteries revealed by the Saviour to his favourite disciple are the mysteries of the eternal fire that punishes licentious malefactors and the mysteries of the pleromatic light that will be enjoyed by the elect.

3. On the figure of Thomas, who does not have a central role in the New Testament (see John 9:16; 15:14; 20:24–9; and Acts 1:13), but is important in later traditions, e.g. the apocryphal *Acts of Thomas*, in which he appears as Judas Thomas Didymus; see J. Doresse, *L'Évangile de Thomas* (Paris, 1959), pp. 38–40, and Ménard, *Évangile selon Thomas*, p. 76.

4. NHC II.7.1.138.8ff. See R. Kuntzmann, 'L'identification dans le Livre de Thomas l'Athlète' in Barc (ed.), *Colloque*, pp. 278–87.

5. *Refutatio* VIII.15.1–2.

6. NHC VIII.1.45.9ff.

7. NHC VIII.1.45.24ff.

8. NHC VIII.1.45.27ff.

9. NHC VIII.1.46.10ff.

10. There is still no comprehensive treatment of the delicate, complex, and decisive problem of Gnostic soteriology; see Andresen, 'Erlösung'; W. Förster σωτήρ, *TW* VII.1005–21; Wilson, *Gnostic Problem*, pp. 218ff.; Rudolph, *Gnosis*, pp. 130–48; Colpe, 'Gnosis', pp. 613ff.

11. A. D. Nock, 'The milieu of Gnosticism', *Gnomon* 12 (1936), pp. 611–12; Quispel, 'Gnostische Anthropos, pp. 224–34 (on the background of his interpretation there are analyses of Jung; see *Aion*, pp. 184ff.); Ménard, *Évangile de Vérité*, pp. 17ff. Ménard, 'La gnose et les textes de Nag Hammadi' in Barc (ed.), *Colloque*, pp. 16–17, observes: 'External salvation and the doctrine of *Heilsgeschichte*, where God reveals Himself and leads His people to salvation and the Saviour, are quite alien to the Gnostic.'

12. A. Nygren, *Agape and Eros* (London, 1938).

13. Ibid., p. 85.

14. H. M. Schenke, 'Die neutestamentliche Christologie und der gnostische Erlöser' in Tröger (ed.), *Gnosis*, pp. 211ff.; Fischer, *Tendenz und Absicht*, p. 190, n. 45; Rudolph, *Gnosis*, pp. 141–2. This position is based on an acute observation of Bousset, *Hauptprobleme*, p. 238.

15. NHC VIII.1.46.16ff.

16. Some doubt has been expressed as to the Gnostic nature of this text; see F. Wisse, 'On exegeting the Exegesis of the Soul' in Ménard (ed.), *Textes*, pp. 68ff.; R. van den Broeck, 'The Authentikos Logos: a new document of Christian Platonism', *VigChr* 33 (1979), 260ff. For a contrary opinion see Koschorke, '"Suchen und Finden"', p. 51, n. 3 and p. 57, n. 37; S. Arai, 'Zum "Simonianischen" in Authentikos Logos und Bronte' in Krause (ed.), *Gnosis* (1981), p. 9, n. 19.

17. NHC II.6.132.6ff. See W.C. Robinson, 'The Exegesis on the Soul', *NT* 12 (1970), 102–17.

18. Andresen, 'Erlösung', pp. 119ff.

19. Vermaseren, 'Hellenistic Religions', p. 505.

20. Festugière, *Idéal religieux*, p. 135.

21. Nilsson, *Geschichte*, p. 399.

22. Ibid., pp. 727–8.

23. On the traditional interpretation (e.g. that of Clement of Alexandria),

which defends the deterministic interpretation of the three natures see W. Förster, *Von Valentin zu Herakleon* (Giessen, 1928), pp. 22–3; Sagnard, *Gnose valentinienne*, pp. 387ff., 567–8 and 606–7. For a contrary viewpoint see H. Langerbeck, *Aufsätze zur Gnosis* (Göttingen, 1967), pp. 38ff.; Schotroff, 'Animae', pp. 92–3; Rudolph, *Gnosis*, pp. 134–5.

24. The theme of the 'Saved Saviour' is central to Manichaeism and Mandaeism, but it is rare in the Gnostic texts: NHC II.3.54.35ff.; 72.34ff. and the comment of Ménard, *L'Évangile selon Philippe*, p. 201; NHC I.3.42.37 and, in general, the soteriology of the *Pistis Sophia*.

25. See ch. 6.

26. For an analysis of the *Pistis Sophia* system see Leisegang, 'Pistis Sophia'.

27. See ch. 7.

28. Filoramo, *Luce*, pp. 28ff. The 'man of light' (*prōme mpouoein*) is a technical expression, which indicates the new reality generated in man as a result of illumination; see *Pistis Sophia* 113, 125 and 132; BG 71.11–12 = NHC III.1.36.25; NHC II.5.151.19; 155.26–7; NHC V.5.83.1–8; NHC I.2.10.4; NHC II.2 = POxy 655.24, and the comment of Puech, 'Doctrines ésotériques', lxix (1969), 272ff. Puech recalls other contexts that are not specifically Gnostic (the alchemist Zosimus). See also Schenke, *Gott 'Mensch'*, p. 7. According to J. Munck, 'Bemerkungen zum koptischen Thomasevangelium' *Studia Theologica* 14 (1960), 142–3, the Gnostic theory derives from a 'democratization' of the speculations about the Adam of Light.

29. In contrast to other conceptions of the Apostolate held by Gnostic groups like the Valentinians, this theory presupposes that the Apostles are perfect from the outset; Rousseau-Doutreleau, *Irénée de Lyon. Contre les Hérésies III* (Paris, 1952), 46–9; W. Schmithals, *Das kirchliche Apostelamt* (Göttingen, 1961), pp. 103ff.; M. Krause, 'Der "Dialog des Soter" im Codex III' in Krause (ed.), *Gnosis* (1977), pp. 29ff.

30. CH I.12. For an overall view of the text see H. Gundel, 'Poimandres', *PW* XXI.1193ff.; E. Hänchen, 'Aufbau und Theologie des Poimandres', *ZThK* 53 (1956), 149–91; Jonas, *Gnostic Religion*, pp. 147–63.

31. C. H. Dodd, *The Bible and the Greeks*[2] (London, 1954), pp. 99–209.

32. CH I.4. and the observations of Festugière, *Dieu inconnu*, 41–2, on the interpretation of *en merei gegenēmenon*.

33. CH I.4.

34. CH I.9–11.

35. CH I.13. On the Platonic theme of the fall of the soul underlying this myth see Festugière, *Doctrines de l'âme*, pp. 63ff.

36. CH I.14.

37. Jonas, *Gnostic Religion*, pp. 156ff.

38. CH I.15.

39. CH I.19.

40. The sources on Seth have been collected by A. F. J. Klijn, *Seth in Jewish, Christian and Gnostic Literature* (Leiden, 1977).

41. Klijn, *Seth*, pp. 4–32.
42. Ibid., p. 112; Pearson, 'Figure of Seth', pp. 496 and 503.
43. Klijn, *Seth*, pp. 4–5.
44. Ibid., p. 6.
45. *Genesis Rabbah* 24.6: 'Rabbi Shimon said: "In the 130 years since Eve separated from Adam, male spirits became passionate for her, and she generated from them; female spirits became passionate for Adam, and generated from him."' (See A. Ravenna, *Commento alla Genesi* (Turin, 1978), p. 193).
46. In *PRE* 22 it is stated explicitly, in reference to Gen. 5:3, that Cain is not the seed of Adam, either in his likeness or image. It is therefore nor surprising that the generation of Cain has been identified by some (see Klijn, *Seth*, p. 9, about Rabbi Meir = *PRE* 22) with an immoral generation or by others with the 'daughters of men' of Gen. 6:2, who had (sexual) relations with the 'sons of God' of Gen. 6:1; see P. S. Alexander, 'The Targumim and early exegesis of "Sons of God" in Gen. 6' *Journal of Jewish Studies* 23 (1972):60–71. As for Samael (the etymology of which is disputed; see Klijn, *Seth*, p. 3, n. 6), he appears in various Jewish, Christian and Gnostic apocrypha (see Bullard, *Hypostasis*, pp. 52–4, and Barc–Roberge, *Hypostase*, pp. 34–5). The figure who, according to *Ps. Jon. Gen.* 3.6, was the angel of death and, according to *Genesis Rabbah* 10.110, was the leader of all the devils, from the third century AD was to become 'the main figure in Jewish demonology, both Rabbinic and Cabbalistic, who embodies all previous demonological traditions' (Barc, 'Samael', p. 136). On the fate of Samael in Bogomilism see Loos, *Dualist Heresy*, p. 92, n. 7.
47. *PRE* 22 (see Klijn, *Seth*, p. 8).
48. Enoch 85:8ff.: 'And, after this, she bore another white bull and, after it, she bore black bulls and cows. I saw in my sleep that white bull, how it likewise grew and became a large white bull, and from it came many white bulls; and they were like it. And they began to beget many white bulls, which were like them, one following the other' (H. D. F. Sparks (ed.), *The Apocryphal Old Testament* (Oxford, 1985)).
49. Pearson, 'Seth', p. 491.
50. Klijn, *Seth*, pp. 16–18; see also M. E. Stone, 'Report on Seth traditions in the Armenian Adam books' in Layton (ed.), *Rediscovery* 2.468–9.
51. *De post. Caini* 42.
52. *De post. Caini* 173; see R. Kraft, 'Philo on Seth' in Layton (ed.), *Rediscovery* 2.457–8.
53. The critical edition is that of Böhlig–Wisse, *Gospel of the Egyptians*. See also Wilson, 'One text'.
54. NHC III.2.68.10ff.
55. NHC III.2.51.5ff. = NHC IV.2.62.30ff. On Adamas see Böhlig–Wisse, *Gospel of the Egyptians*, p. 173 and Barc–Roberge (eds), *Hypostase*: 154.
56. NHC III.2.51.20ff. = NHC IV.2.63.15ff.

57. NHC III.2.61.3ff. = NHC IV.2.72.11ff.

58. NHC III.2.63.8ff. = NHC IV.2.74.22ff.

59. Ps. Tertullian *Adv. omnes haer.* 2 (Christ is 'tantummodo [virtually] Seth'. For an overall view of the heresiological statements see Klijn, *Seth*, pp. 82–90.

60. This concept, of Jewish origin, is due to the fusion of eschatological expectation of one prophet only and the theological reflection that since all the prophets basically announced the same truth, there was only one who became incarnate in a succession of various people (see O. Cullmann, *The Christology of the New Testament* (London, 1963), pp. 38–50; and John 1:21, in which the Jews asked the Baptist: 'Are you the prophet?'). It re-emerges in the so-called *Gospel of the Hebrews* (see Jerome, *In Isaiam Prophetam* 11.2: the Holy Spirit says to Jesus when He comes out of the water after baptism: 'I have waited for you in all the prophets, that you should come and I should rest in you') and especially in the *Pseudo-Clementines*; see *Hom.* III.17.1 and 20.2 and H. J. Schoeps, *Theologie und Geschichte des Judenchristentums* (Tübingen, 1949), p. 98. G. Strecker rightly insists on the Gnostic background of the concept; see Hennecke–Schneemelcher, *Apokryphen* II.67–8. It is no accident that the theory of continuous revelation is present in Manichaean, as well as in Sethian, Gnostic texts; see Puech, *Manichéisme*, pp. 61–3 and n. 241.

61. NHC II.1.30.11.

62. NHC II.1.31.5.

63. NHC II.4.93.8ff. On Eleleth see Barc–Roberge, *Hypostase,* pp. 113–14 and Janssens, *Protennoia*, pp. 68–9.

64. NHC VIII.1.3.30ff.

65. For the text see Janssens, *Protennoia*. See also R. McL. Wilson, 'The "Trimorphic Protennoia"' in Krause (ed.), *Gnosis* (1981), pp. 50–4. The text has been interpreted by some as a possible *Vorlage* of the prologue of the *Gospel of John*; see C. Colpe, 'Heidnische jüdische und christliche Überlieferung in den Schriften von Nag Hammadi', *JAC* 17 (1974), 122–4, and J. M. Robinson, 'Sethians and Johannine thought' in Layton (ed.), *Rediscovery* 2.642–62.

66. NHC XIII.1.35.12ff.

67. NHC XIII.1.40.12–14.

68. NHC XIII.1.41.2ff.

69. NHC XIII.1.50.12ff.

70. Colpe, 'Gnosis', pp. 552–3.

71. G. Filoramo, 'Aspetti del processo rivelativo nel "Logos di Rivelazione" gnostico', *Atti dell'Accademia Scientifica Torino* 109 (1974), 114–15.

72. BG 22.15; 65.2; 73.9; 75.20; 88.9.

73. F. T. Fallon, 'The Gnostics: the undominated race', *NT* 21 (1979), 271–8.

74. NHC III.2.54.10 = NHC IV.2.65.30. On the other self-designation see F. Siegert, 'Selbstbezeichnung der Gnostiker in den Nag Hammadi Texten', *ZNW* 71 (1980), 129–32.

75. 'Indeed Valentinus says he saw a small child recently born and asked him who he was. The child replied that he was the Logos. Valentinus then tells a tragic myth and tries to derive it from the sect that bears his name' (*Refutatio* VI.42.2).

76. On the reading θέρος (harvest) see M. Simonetti, *Testi gnostici cristiani* (Bari, 1970), p. 130, n. 10. On the concept of 'spiritual harvest' see Heraclitus, frr 32–3.

77. *Refutatio* VI.37.6–8. The interpretation of *pneumati* is disputed; see B. Herzhoff, *Zwei gnostische Hymnen* (Bonn, 1973), pp. 41ff.

78. Herzhoff, *Zwei Hymnen*, p. 48.

79. See fr. 3 in Clement of Alexandria, *Stromateis* III.59.3: 'Jesus bore everything and was master of himself; he behaved in a divine manner, eating and drinking in a divine manner; he did not evacuate the food from his body. Such was his self-mastery that the nourishment within him did not decay, for he could not tolerate corruption.'

80. The following passage relies on the fundamental work of A. Orbe, *Cristologia gnostica*, 2 vols (Madrid, 1976). See M. Simonetti, 'Note di cristologia gnostica', *RSLR* 5 (1969), 529–53, and J. D. Kaestli, 'Valentinianisme italien et valentinianisme oriental: leur divergence à propos de la nature du corps de Jésus' in Layton (ed.), *Rediscovery* 1.391–403.

81. Orbe, *Cristologia* 1.55ff.

82. Filoramo, 'Interpretazione gnostica', pp. 58–9.

83. The letter has been preserved in *Panarion* 33. 3–7; see G. Quispel, *Ptolémée. Lettre à Flora* (Paris, 1949).

84. *Panarion* 33.3 and 8.

85. *Panarion* 33.5:1–2.

86. Orbe, *Teologia*, pp. 429ff.

87. Orbe, *Cristologia*, pp. 134ff.

88. Ibid., 153ff.

89. *Excerpta ex Theodoto* 68–71.

90. Ibid., 72.1 and 74.1.

91. C. Schmidt, *Gespräche Jesu mit seinen Jüngern nach der Auferstehung* (Leipzig, 1919), pp. 281ff.; Daniélou, *Théologie*, pp. 228ff.; Beyschlag, *Simon Magus*, pp. 172ff.; C. H. Talbert, 'The myth of descending-ascending redeemer in Mediterranean antiquity', *NTS* 22 (1975), 418–40.

92. According to the traditional meaning of *sōtēria* as 'preservation' of a certain condition; see Andresen, 'Erlösung', p. 126.

93. *AH* I.6.1.

94. *Refutatio* VI.35.7.

95. Orbe, *Cristologia* 1.322.

96. Ibid., 330ff.

97. Orbe, *Teologia*, p. 47.

98. NHC IX.3.33.11; 39.29–31; 45.9–11.

99. There are many texts in which it is stated that Christ suffered before

dying: NHC I.3.20.10–30; 31.4–6, and Arai, *Christologie*, pp. 90 and 93–4; NHC I.4.44.21–34; 45.14–15; 46.16ff., and M. L. Peel, *The Epistle to Rheginus* (Philadelphia, 1969), p. 121, n. 21, pp. 159–60, 172; NHC I.5.113.32–8; 114.33–115.11; NHC XI.1.20.10ff.; NHC IX.1.5.1–11, and H. M. Schenke, 'Die jüdische Melchisedek Gestalt als Thema der Gnosis' in Tröger (ed.), *Altes Testament*, p. 124. What these texts affirm is that the suffering of Jesus is real, but it does not affect the Saviour as such, merely the particular part of his body that is capable of suffering; see Koschorke, *Polemik*, p. 44, and E. Pagels, 'Gnostic and orthodox views of Christ's passion: paradigms for the Christian's response to persecution?' in Layton (ed.), *Rediscovery* I. 262–83.

100. M. Tardieu, ' "Comme à travers un tuyau". Quelques remarques sur le mythe valentinien de la chair céleste du Christ' in Barc (ed.), *Colloque*, pp. 151ff.
101. *AH* I.7.2.
102. A. Orbe, *La unción del Verbo* (Rome, 1961), pp. 229ff., 345ff.
103. NHC II.3.70.34ff.
104. NHC I.5.116.29–33.
105. Orbe, *Cristología* 2.294ff.
106. Ibid., 242ff.
107. This much becomes clear from an examination of such texts as *EvVer*, *Rheg*, *TracTrip*. On the Christology of *EvPh* see H. G. Gaffron, 'Studien zum koptischen Philippusevangelium unter besonderen Berücksichtigung der Sakramente' (Ph.D. thesis Bonn, 1969), pp. 202–3.
108. *AH* I.30.12–14.
109. Cf. the Christology of the *Pistis Sophia*.
110. On the structure of the text see Koschorke, *Polemik*, pp. 11ff.
111. J. D. Dubois, 'Le préambule de l'Apocalypse de Pierre' in Ries (ed.), *Gnosticisme*, p. 384.
112. NHC VII.3.79.24–6.
113. Ibid. 72.10ff.
114. Ibid. 71.15ff.
115. On the place of Peter in the Gnostic texts see J. E. Ménard, *La Lettre de Pierre à Philippe* (Quebec, 1977), pp. 6–7, and Perkins, *Gnostic Dialogue*, pp. 113ff.
116. NHC VIII.3.81.3–14.
117. G. Bröker, 'Lachen als religiöses Motiv in gnostischen Texten' in Nagel (ed.), *Studien*, pp. 111–15.
118. NHC VIII.3.82.4–16.
119. Ibid., 82.18ff.
120. Matt. 27:50.
121. *AH* I.24.4.
122. P. Painchaud, *Le Deuxième traité du Grand Seth* (Quebec, 1982).
123. Ibid., p. 21.
124. NHC VII.2.56.14ff. and Painchaud, *Deuxième traité*, p. 18.
125. Ménard, *Lettre*.
126. NHC VIII.2.139.15ff.
127. Ibid. 139.21ff.
128. Orbe, *Cristología* 1.380ff.

129. *Refutatio* VII.27.8.
130. Ibid. 27.12.
131. Ibid. 27.1.

CHAPTER 8 WAITING FOR THE END

1. On Gnostic eschatology in general see M. L. Peel, 'Gnostic eschatology and the New Testament', *NT* 12 (1970), 14ff., and Rudolph, *Gnosis*, pp. 184–219. The category 'eschatology' has recently been criticized; see J. Carmignac, *Le Mirage de l'eschatologie* (Paris, 1979), pp. 136–7. We use it to indicate the complex of final events that affect the destiny of humankind and the world.
2. E. Smiess, *Entwicklungsgeschichte der Vorstellung vom Zustande nach dem Tode* (Jena, 1887); J. G. Frazer, *The Belief in Immortality and the Worship of the Dead*, 3 vols (London, 1913–24) and *The Fear of the Dead*, 3 vols (London, 1933–6); C. Clemen, *Das Leben nach dem Tode im Glauben der Menschheit* (Leipzig, 1920); K. T. Preuss, *Tod und Unsterblichkeit im Glauben der Naturvölkern* (Tübingen, 1930); H. J. Klimkeit (ed.), *Tod und Jenseit im Glauben der Völker* (Wiesbaden, 1978); G. Stephenson (ed.), *Leben und Tod in der Religion* (Darmstadt, 1980). For a phenomenological treatment see C. J. Bleeker, 'Types of eschatology' in Bleeker (ed.), *The Sacred Bridge* (Leiden, 1963), 250ff; G. Widengren, *Religionsphänomenologie* (Berlin–NY, 1969), pp. 440–50.
3. J. le Goff, *The Birth of Purgatory* (Chicago, 1984).
4. The basic works are F. Cumont, *Afterlife in Roman Paganism* (New Haven, Conn., 1922), *Recherches sur le symbolisme funéraire des romains* (Paris, 1942), *Lux Perpetua* (Paris, 1949). See also Nilsson, *Geschichte*, pp. 543–58, and Ferguson, *Religions*, pp. 100–17; I. P. Culianu, *Psychanodia* 1 and *Expériences de l'extase*.
5. O. Kern, 'Mysterien', PW XVI.1253, and B. Gladigow, 'Jenseitsvorstellungen und Kulturkritik', *ZRGG* 26 (1974), 301ff.
6. Nilsson, *Geschichte*, pp. 147 and 457–8. He observes rightly (p. 549) that ancient 'popular' representations, linked to a concept of the survival of the body after death, continue to be widely attested under the Empire, even if scholars prefer to concentrate on the more aristocratic doctrines such as the celestial voyage of the soul.
7. *Wirtschaft und Gesellschaft*[2] (Tübingen, 1925), I. 287.
8. F. Heiler, *Erscheinungsformen und Wesen der Religion* (Stuttgart,1961), pp. 520–1.
9. Guthrie, *Orpheus*, pp. 164–71.
10. Festugière, *Doctrines de l'âme*, pp. 119ff.; H. Dörrie, 'Kontroversen um die Seelenwanderung im kaiserzeitlichen Platonismus', *Hermes* 85 (1957), 414–35.

11. Origen, *Commentationes ad Rom.* V.1; see Leisegang, *Gnosis*, p. 207.
12. *AH* I.25.4. For other references see Hilgenfeld, *Ketzergeschichte*, and Beyschlag, *Simon Magus*, p. 153 and n. 47.
13. A. Dieterich, *Nekyia*² (Leipzig–Berlin, 1913, repr. Stuttgart, 1969); L. Radermacher, *Das Jenseits im Mythos der Hellenen* (Bonn, 1903).
14. Text and translation by W. R. Murdock and G. W. MacRae, *Nag Hammadi Codices V,2–5 and VI* (Leiden, 1979), pp. 47–63.
15. On the ten heavens see G. Flügel, *Mani, seine Lehre und seine Schriften* (Berlin, 1862), pp. 218 and 220; Cumont, *Recherches* 1.28, n. 2; Bietenhard, *Himmlische Welt*, p. 6. Ten is the perfect number from the earliest reflections of the Pythagoreans; see Kroll, *Lehren*, p. 205, and Philo, *Spec. leg..* 4.105.
16. Murdock–MacRae, *NHC V, 2–5 and VI*, p. 48.
17. NHC V.2.22.2.
18. NHC II.7.142.30ff.
19. Bousset–Gressman, *Religion des Judentums*, pp. 289ff.; Volz, *Eschatologie*, pp. 147ff.; Russell, *Method*, 263ff.
20. NHC XIII.1.42.19ff.
21. Ibid. 42.27ff.
22. Ibid. 44.1ff.
23. *AH* I.7.1; see M. Spanneut, *Le Stoïcisme des Pères de l'Église* (Paris, 1957), pp. 92–3, 357ff; on cosmic Gnostic eschatology see also R. Haardt, 'Das universaleschatologische Vorstellungsgut der Gnosis' in K. Schubert (ed.), *Von Messias zum Christus* (Vienna, 1964), pp. 315–36.
24. Herzhoff, *Zwei Psalmen*, pp. 80ff.
25. *Refutatio* V.10.2.
26. NHC VII.5.127.20.
27. *Refutatio* V.8.28.
28. NHC II.3.52.25ff.
29. Peel, 'Gnostic eschatology', pp. 157ff.
30. See our observations on the dialectic between 'hidden' and 'revealed' in 'Aspetti del dualismo gnostico', *Memorie dell Accademia Scientifica di Torino* 5.2 (1978), 239–307, esp. 289ff.
31. NHC II.5.126.35ff. But see also the preceding apocalyptic description 125.32ff. See NHC VII.1.43.28–45.31 and VI.4.43.28ff. For a comparison with the parallels of Jewish apocalyptic see Russell, *Method*, pp. 271–6.
32. NHC XIII.1.42.30ff.
33. H. C. Puech, 'La gnose et le temps', *ErJ* 20 (1951), 57–113.
34. NHC III.3.83.21ff.
35. H. I. Marrou, 'La théologie de l'histoire dans la gnose valentinienne' in Bianchi (ed.), *Origini*, pp. 215–25.
36. NHC I.5.127.23–4.
37. Orbe, *Unción*, p. 407; Rudolph, *Gnosis*, p. 212. See also Jonas, 'Delimitation', p. 92. For a cyclical interpretation of Gnostic time see also J. Zandee, 'Gnostic ideas on fall and salvation', *Numen*, 11 (1964), 19, 41, 47, 49–51

and 66–8.

38. A central concept of both Gnostic and ecclesiastical eschatology; see C. Lenz, 'Apokatastase', *RAC* I.510–16; P. Siniscalco, 'I significati di "restituire" e "restitutio" in Tertulliano', *Atti dell' Accademia Scientifica di Torino* 1 (1951), 45ff. and 'ἀποκατάστασις and ἀποκαθίστημι nella tradizione della Grande Chiesa fino ad Ireneo' *Studia Patristica* (1961), pp. 380–96; N. A. Dahl, 'Christ, creation and the Church' in his *The Background of the New Testament and its Eschatology* (Cambridge, 1956), pp. 422ff., identifies seven types of relationship between the first and second creations: restitution, transformation, identity, conservation of certain aspects, perfection of the old reality in the new, and pre-existence in the mind of God of certain elements that will be revealed only at the end of time. For Gnostic circles in general see Andresen, 'Erlösung', p. 123, and G. Filoramo, 'Rivelazione ed escatologia nello gnosticismo cristiano del secondo secolo', *Aug* 18 (1978), 82, n. 13. See also A. Méhat, 'Apokatastasis chez Basilide' in *Mélanges Puech*, pp. 365–75.

39. *AH* I.7.1; see D. Devoti, 'Temi escatologici nello gnosticismo valentiniano', *Aug* 18 (1978), 47–61.

40. For the following account see C. Gianotto, 'Il processo salvifico delle anime e il loro destino finale nella Pistis Sophia' in Ries (ed.), *Gnosticisme*, pp. 377–83.

41. Ibid., pp. 379–82.

42. *Pistis Sophia* 96.

43. C. Schmidt, *Pistis Sophia* (Copenhagen, 1925), p. 304.

44. On the unlimited mercy typical of the soteriology of this text see C. Schmidt, *Pistis Sophia. Ein gnostisches Originalwerk des 3. Jahrhunderts aus dem koptischen übersetzt* (Leipzig, 1925), pp. xxix–xxx.

45. W. C. van Unnik, 'Die "Zahl der vollkommenen Seele" in der Pistis Sophia' in *Festschrift für Otto Michel* (Leiden, 1960), pp. 467–77.

46. Gianotto, 'Processo', p. 380.

47. Ibid., p. 383.

48. P. Ariès, *L'Homme devant la mort* (Paris, 1977), pp. 553ff.

49. An impressive amount of material has been collected in R. W. Habenstein and W. M. Lamers, *Funeral Customs the World Over* (Milwaukee, 1960); see also the judgement of the thanatologist L. V. Thomas, *The Anthropology of Death* (London, 1970).

50. 'Death', *Continuum* 5.3 (1976), 459–601, and G. Heuse, *Guide de la mort* (Paris, 1975).

51. See n. 2 of this chapter.

52. K. Sagaster, 'Grundgedanken des tibetanischen Totenbuches' in Klimkeit, *Tod und Jenseit*, pp. 175–89.

53. A. Tenenti, *Il senso della morte e l'amore della vita nel Rinascimento* (Turin, 1957), p. 443 and fig. 40.

54. Ariès, *L'Homme devant la mort*, pp. 41ff.

55. *AH* I.21.5.
56. W. P. Funk, *Die zweite Apokalypse des Jakobus aus Nag Hammadi Codex V* (Berlin, 1976).
57. NHC V.4.62.16ff.; Funk, *Apokalypse Jakobus* p. 211, and, for Gnostic parallels to this prayer of James, 214–17; see also M. Tardieu, 'Les Trois Stèles de Seth', *RSPhTh* 57 (1973), 557–8.
58. *CH* I.25. The order of planets that makes up the background of this ascent of the soul is the so-called 'Chaldaean' order: Moon, Mercury, Venus, Sun, Mars, Jupiter and Saturn; see F. Boll, *Kleine Schriften zum Sternkunde des Altertums* (Leipzig, 1950), pp. 183, 213 and 218; and Culianu, *Psychanodia* 1, *passim*.
59. A. Orbe, *Los primeros herejes ante la persecución* (Rome, 1956), p. 138, prefers the reading ἐν τῷ ὄντι to ἐν τῷ παρόντι, basing this on the Latin 'filius autem in eo qui ante fuit'. The accuracy of this reading is confirmed by the parallel passage of NHC V.3.32.29 – 35.25.
60. *AH* I.21.5.
61. 2 *LJ* ch. 52. Pre-Nag Hammadi Gnostic texts have been collected and studied by Bousset, 'Himmelsreise', and Colpe, 'Himmelsreise'. See also I. P. Culianu, 'L'ascension de l'âme dans les mystères et hors des mystères' in Bianchi (ed.), *Soteriologia*; and Culianu, *Psychanodia* 1, and *Expériences de l'extase*.
62. NHC VI.3.35.8ff.
63. NHC I.5.124.21ff. For a collection of Gnostic parallels see P. Pokorny, 'Über die sogenannte individuelle Eschatologie in der Gnosis' in Nagel (ed.), *Studien*, p. 128, nn. 6 and 7. On the concept of *anapausis* (rest) see P. Vielhauer, '*Anapausis*. Zum gnostischen Hintergrund des Thomasevangelium' in *Aufsätze zum Neuen Testament* (Munich, 1965), pp. 215–34; J. E. Ménard, 'Repos et salut gnostique', *RevSR* 51 (1977), 71–88.

CHAPTER 9   SIMON MAGUS

1. M. Weber, 'Die protestantische Ethik und der "Geist des Kapitalismus"', *Archiv für Sozialwissenschaft und Sozialpolitik* 20–1 (1904–5), para. 3 of 'Geist'.
2. On the complex problems of definition see R. Robinson, *Definition* (Oxford, 1950), and W. P. Alston, *Philosophy of Language* (Englewood Cliffs, 1964), ch. 6.
3. On the use of these terms by Gnostics as self-designations see M. Smith, 'The history of the term "Gnostikos"' in Layton (ed.), *Rediscovery* 2.796–807.
4. This is Smith's argument, ibid., n. 3.
5. For example, the term 'Orphism', which has been rejected by some on the grounds that it tends to create a fictitious ideological unity in quite heterogeneous documents; see the critical remarks of U. Wilamowitz-Moellendorff, *Glauben der Hellenen* (Berlin, 1931), 2.199, who prefers

the term 'Orphik' as an appropriate translation of the Greek *ta orphika* (Orphic things/matters), and does not accept a corresponding *orphismos*.

6. Smith, 'Term "Gnostikos"', p. 798. On the terminological problems and theoretical difficulties see the various articles of Ugo Bianchi, most recently 'Le gnosticisme: concept, terminologie, origines, délimitation' in Aland (ed.), *Gnosis*, pp. 33–64, and R. McL. Wilson, 'Slippery words, II: Gnosis, Gnostic, Gnosticism', *Expository Times* 89 (1978), 296–301.

7. Bianchi (ed.), *Origini*.

8. Ibid. xx.

9. Ibid. xxvi–xxvii.

10. Rudolph, 'Forschungsbericht', pp. 15ff.

11. Wilson, 'Twenty Years After', pp. 64–5.

12. Apart from the works cited in ch. 1, n. 79, see in general Tröger (ed.), *Altes Testament*, esp. pp. 155–68.

13. The nineteenth-century works are H. Graetz, *Gnosticismus und Judentum* (Krotoschin, 1846); A. Hönig, *Die Ophiten: Ein Beitrag zur Geschichte des jüdischen Gnosticismus* (Berlin, 1889); P. Friedländer, *Der vorchristliche jüdische Gnosticismus* (Göttingen, 1898).

14. The thesis put forward by H. Jonas, 'Response to G. Quispel's Gnosticism and the New Testament' in J. P. Hyatt (ed.), *The Bible and Modern Scholarship* (Nashville, 1965), pp. 279–93. He maintains that Gnosticism took shape in Samaria in circles that were Jewish in origin, but anti-Jewish in ideology. This explains the acute anti-Semitism of various Gnostic texts. On this latter aspect see K. W. Tröger, 'The attitude of the Gnostic religion towards Judaism as viewed in a variety of perspectives' in Barc (ed.), *Colloque*, pp. 86–98.

15. The argument of Grant, *Gnosticism and Early Christianity*.

16. I. Grünwald, 'Aspects of the Jewish–Gnostic controversy' in Layton (ed.), *Rediscovery* 2.714–15 and 'Knowledge and vision', *Israel Oriental Studies* 3 (1979), 63ff.

17. Van Unnik, 'Gnosis und Judentum' in Aland (ed.), *Gnosis*, pp. 80ff.

18. Koschorke, *Polemik*, pp. 109ff.

19. W. Beltz, 'Bemerkungen zur Adamapokalypse' in Nagel (ed.), *Studia Coptica*, p. 159.

20. Van Unnik, 'Gnosis und Judentum', p. 86.

21. C. Colpe, 'Gnosis', *RGG*³ II.1649.

22. P. M. Palmer and R. P. Moore, *The Sources of the Faust Tradition from Simon Magus to Lessing* (New York, 1936).

23. Hilgenfeld, *Ketzergeschichte*, pp. 163ff. and 453ff., and H. Waitz, 'Simon Magus in der altchristlichen Literatur', *ZNW* 5 (1904), 121–43.

24. E. M. Butler, *The Myth of the Magus* (Cambridge, 1979).

25. Beyschlag, *Simon Magus* (esp. pp. 79–98); Lüdemann, *Untersuchungen*; Leisegang, *Gnosis*, pp. 60ff.; E. Hänchen, 'Gab es eine vorchristliche Gnosis?', *ZThK* 49 (1952), 316ff.; L. Cerfaux, 'La gnose simonienne' in *Recueil Cerfaux* (Paris, 1954), pp. 191ff.; Grant, *Gnosticism*, pp. 70ff.;

Quispel, *Gnosis als Weltreligion*, pp. 45ff.; Jonas, *Gnostic Religion*, pp. 103ff. See also W. A. Meeks, 'Simon Magus in recent research', *RSR* 3 (1977), 137–42; K. Rudolph, 'Simon Magus oder Gnosticus? Zum Stand der Debatte', *ThRu* 42 (1977), 279–359.

26. E. Hänchen, 'Simon Magus in der Apostelgeschichte' in K. W. Tröger (ed.), *Gnosis und Neues Testament* (Berlin, 1973), pp. 267ff.

27. In the sense that he is a typical 'divine man'; see Bieler, *Theios Anēr*, pp. 83ff., and Beyschlag, *Simon Magus*, p. 122.

28. On the problems raised by this much-discussed formula see R. Bergmeier, 'Quellen vorchristlicher Gnosis?' in G. Jeremias (ed.), *Tradition und Glaube* (Göttingen, 1971), p. 204; Lüdemann, *Untersuchungen*, pp. 42ff.; Beyschlag, *Simon Magus*, pp. 106ff.

29. Lüdemann, *Untersuchungen*, pp. 49ff.

30. The thesis of Hänchen, 'Vorchristliche Gnosis?'

31. 1 *Apol.* 26.1–3.

32. L. H. Vincent, 'Le culte d'Hélène à Samarie', *RevBib* 45 (1936), 221ff.

33. Quispel, *Gnosis als Weltreligion*, pp. 61ff.

34. S. Arai, 'Simonianische Gnosis und die "Exegese über die Seele"' in M. Krause (ed.), *Gnosis and Gnosticism* (Leiden, 1977), pp. 185–203, and 'Zum "Simonianischen"', pp. 3–15.

35. *AH* I.23.1–5.

36. *AH* I.23.2.

37. J. Frickel, *Die 'Apophasis Megale' in Hippolyts Refutatio* (Rome, 1968), and J. M. Salles-Dabadie, *Recherches sur Simon le Mage* (Paris, 1969).

38. *Refutatio* VI.18.2.

39. Arai, 'Simonianische Gnosis', pp. 188–9. Even though the hypothesis of Frickel and Salles-Dabadie that the *Apophasis* is an early writing of Simonian Gnosis datable to the first century AD may seem unfounded, it is difficult to agree with Beyschlag and Aland in rejecting its Gnostic character.

40. C. Schmidt, *Studien zu den Pseudo-Clementinen* (Berlin, 1929), pp. 47ff.

41. *Acta Petri* 7–29.

42. *Homilies* II.22.1–4 and 23.

43. Beyschlag, *Simon Magus*, pp. 58ff.

CHAPTER 10   VISIONARIES, PROPHETS AND DIVINES

1. *AH* I.23.4 = *Refutatio* VI.20.1 (see also Tertullian, *Apol.* 23.1). The same accusation is made about Basilides (*AH* I.24.5) and the Carpocratians (*AH* I.25.3 and Eusebius, *HE* IV.9.7). Tertullian also makes the connection between magic and libertinism in *De praescriptione* 43.1. On the one hand, there are various indications that we are dealing here with a typical heresiological *topos* that is, in fact, without any foundation. Thus, the epithet *magos* (magician, magical) is also attributed to Menander because he is considered to be a disciple of Simon (*AH* I.23.5 and *HE* III.26.3).

Hippolytus (*Refutatio* IX.14.2) accuses the Elcasaites of practising magic, though this turns out (*Ref.* X.29.3) to be no more than simple divination. This raises the more general problem (see below, n. 3) of what is to be understood as 'magic' in these religio-historical contexts. On the other hand, there are various clear indications within the texts of a resort to magical practices; in addition to the texts assembled by W. Anz, *Zur Frage nach dem Ursprung des Gnostizismus* (Leipzig, 1897), pp. 5–8, there are also the *voces mysticae*, or mystical voices, and arithmetical speculations of NHC X (the whole of the second part; see Pearson, *Marsanes*, p. 380); NHC XIII.1.38.25ff.; XI.3.53.32; VI.6.56.17ff. and 61.10ff.

2. Even if it is true that certain Gnostic texts (*Pistis Sophia* 18; NHC II.5.123.8ff.) polemicize against magical practices and that Gnosis is soteric knowledge, these do not seem to us (as they do to others, e.g. W. Forster, 'Das Wesen der Gnosis', *Die Welt als Geschichte* (1955)2.113) adequate reasons for maintaining that magic is unknown in Gnosis. As W. Ullmann, 'Bild- und Menschenbild-Terminologie in koptisch-gnostischen Texten' in Nagel (ed.), *Studien*, p. 54, points out, 'thus magical tendencies in Gnosis deserve to be taken more seriously than hitherto.'

3. J. Beattie, *Other Cultures* (London, 1964), p. 212: 'In fact, however we formulate the distinctions, beliefs and practices which are usually called religious often contain a magical element, even in Western cultures.' See also A. Brelich, 'Tre note' in *Magia. Studi in memoria di Raffaela Galosi* (Rome, 1976), pp. 103ff., and A. A. Barb, 'The survival of the magical arts' in A. Momigliano (ed.), *Paganism and Christianity in the Fourth Century* (Oxford, 1963), p. 101.

4. Origen, *Contra Celsum* I.6; II.50–1, and G. Bardy, 'Origène et la magie', *RSR* 18 (1928), 126–42.

5. M. Mazza, 'L'intellectuale come ideologo: Flavio Filostrato ed uno *speculum principis* del terzo secolo' in *Il comportamento dell'intellettuale nella società antica* (Genoa, 1980), pp. 33–66.

6. *Vita Apollonii* V.12 and esp. VII.39, where Philostratus intervened personally to defend his hero from this infamous accusation.

7. H. Frankfort, *Kingship and the Gods* (Chicago, 1948); *The Sacral Kingship* (*La regalità sacra*) (8th International Congress for the History of Religions, Rome, 1955) (Leiden, 1959); E. O. James, *The Ancient Gods* (London, 1960), pp. 107–34.

8. W. Fagg, *Divine Kingship in Africa* (London, 1971); *Uomini e re* (Rome–Bari, 1971).

9. G. Fohrer, 'Neuere Literatur zur alttestamentlichen Prophetie', *ThRu* 19 (1951), 277–346; 20 (1952), 193–271.

10. This is, though true of classical prophecy in Israel, no longer the case for the figure of the *nabi*, or prophet, who does undergo possession and experiences loss of personality; see G. Fohrer, 'Prophetie und Magie' in *Studien zur alttestamentlichen Prophetie* (Berlin, 1967), pp. 242–64.

11. Dodds, *The Greeks and the Irrational*, pp. 70–5.

12. E. Fascher, *Der erste Brief des Paulus an die Korinther. Erster Teil* (Berlin, 1975), pp. 40ff.

13. 1 Cor. 8:1–3.

14. 1 Cor. 10:23.

15. 1 Cor. 15:29–32.

16. 1 Cor. 14:2–19.

17. W. Schmithals, *Die Gnosis in Korinth* (Göttingen, 1956).

18. *AH* I.14.1 = *Refutatio* VI.42.2.

19. Benz, 'Vision'; V. Macdermot, *The Cult of the Seer in the Ancient Middle East* (Berkeley, 1971).

20. On visions in dreams or in a state of waking, see Dodds, *The Greeks and the Irrational*, p. 119; A. Wilkenhauser, 'Die Traumgeschichte des Neuen Testaments in religionsgeschichtlicher Sicht' in *Pisciculi. F. J. Doelger dargeboten* (Münster, 1939), pp. 320–33; S. Zeuitlin, 'Dreams and their interpretations from the Biblical period to Tannaitic times', *Jewish Quarterly Review* 66 (1975), 1–18.

21. See above, ch. 2, n. 73.

22. In other words, these two visions present certain significant features: they are not allegorical, but direct; the auditory element is important; the nature of the soteric message is fundamental. These place them among the type known as *Lehrvisionen* or teaching visions, whose chief characteristic is their ability to bring about a profound change in the life of the individual. On the authenticity of these visions see Pfister, 'Ekstasis', p. 937, and G. Quispel, 'La conception de l'homme dans la gnose valentinienne', *ErJ* 15 (1947), 250.

23. BG 10.10ff.

24. BG 91.10ff.

25. BG 21.3–13.

26. In fact John sees a child first, then an old man. But we learn from the later declaration of the revealer that he also saw a woman or mother figure. By means of the polymorphy of Christ (see the texts collected by H. C. Puech in *Annuaire. École Pratique des Hautes Études* 74 (1966–7), 128–30, and Quispel, 'Demiurge in Apocryphon of John', pp. 1–5) the Divine Triad is thus made manifest in its Father–Mother–Son form.

27. We have already seen in ch. 4 that the spirit is the inspiring breath of the Pleroma. Thanks to the spirit (*en pneumati*) the Gnostic has his pneumatic vision, which is merely the predecessor of the beatific vision of the celestial world; see NHC XIII.1.38.27; VII.5, *passim*; VI.3.22.21; VI.6.57.6; VII.2.51.17ff.

28. W. Förster, 'Die ersten Gnostiker Simon und Menander' in Bianchi (ed.), *Origini*, pp. 190ff.

29. R. M. Grant, 'Jewish Christianity at Antioch', *RSR* 60 (1972), 98–9.

30. *AH* I.24.1.

31. *AH* I.24.1: see S. Pétrement, 'Le mythe des sept archontes créateurs' in Bianchi (ed.), *Origini*, pp. 460ff.

32. For parallels see above ch. 6, n. 25.

33. *AH* I.24.1. On Saturninus (or Satornilus) see Hilgenfeld, *Ketzergeschichte*, pp. 194–5; Grant, *Gnosticism*, pp. 108ff.; Wilson, *Gnostic Problem*, pp. 103ff.

34. F. Bolgiani, 'La tradizione eresiologica sull' encratismo I: Le notizie di Ireneo', *Atti dell' Accademia Scientifica di Torino* 96 (1956), 343–419.

35. Apart from the works cited above, ch. 5, n. 73, see Hilgenfeld, *Ketzergeschichte*, pp. 195ff.; Leisegang, *Gnosis*, pp. 195ff.; Grant, *Gnosticism*, pp. 142ff.

36. Hegemonius, *Acta Archelai* 67.4–12.

37. Eusebius, *HE* IV.7.

38. *Refutatio* VII.20.

39. Clem. Alex. *Stromateis* VI.6.53.

40. A. Orbe, 'Ideas sobre la tradición en la lucha antignostica', *Aug* 12 (1972), 19–32.

41. T. Klauser, 'Auswendiglernen', *RAC* I.1031ff.; H. Karpp, 'Viva Vox' in Stuiber and Hermann (eds), *Mullus*, pp. 190ff.

42. Some scholars believe that Gnostic thinkers were the first to work out the theological concept of *paradosis* (tradition); see M. Hornschuh. 'Die Apostel als Träger der Überlieferung' in Hennecke-Schneemelcher, *Neutestamentliche Apokryphen* II.43; Brox, *Offenbarung*, p. 132; for a contrary view see J. Daniélou, 'Traditions secrètes des Apôtres', *ErJ* 31 (1962), 204.

43. *Panarion* 24.6; U. Bianchi, 'Basilide o del tragico' in his *Prometeo*, pp. 163–71.

44. Clem. Alex. *Stromateis* IV.82.1–2.

45. Ibid. II.113.4.

46. Ibid. IV.86.1.

47. Bianchi, *Prometeo*, pp. 166–7.

48. Wilson, *Gnostic Problem*, pp. 126–7.

49. *AH* I.24.3–7.

50. *AH* I.24.5.

51. *AH* 24.4.

52. Hilgenfeld, *Ketzergeschichte*, pp. 397ff., and Leisegang, *Gnosis*, p. 200.

53. H. Kraft, 'Gab es einen Gnostiker Karpokrates?', *TZ* 8 (1952), 434–43.

54. *Stromateis* III.5.2–3.

55. Ibid. 6.1–8.

56. Ibid. 7.4–8. On the importance of the model of Platonic communism see J. Bidez, *La Cité du monde et la cité du soleil chez les Stoïciens* (Paris, 1932); Andresen, *Logos und Nomos*, pp. 248ff.; Schneider, *Geistesgeschichte* 1.680.

57. *Stromateis* III.9.2.

58. F. Bolgiani, 'La polemica di Clemente di Alessandria control gli gnostici libertini nel terzo libro degli "Stromati"' in *Studi in onore di A. Pincherle* (Rome, 1967), p. 95, n. 13.

59. *AH* I.25 = *Refutatio* VII.32.

60. Daniélou, *Théologie*, p. 81.
61. On Marcion see A. von Harnack, *Marcion. Das Evangelium vom fremden Gott*[2] (Leipzig, 1924); E. C. Blackman, *Marcion and his Influence* (London, 1948); Jonas, *Gnostic Religion*, pp. 137ff.; B. Aland, 'Marcion', *ZThK* 70 (1973), 420–7.
62. Harnack, *Marcion*, pp. 3–30.
63. Ibid., p. 23.
64. Ibid., p. 24.
65. *AH* III.3.4.
66. Harnack, *Marcion*, pp. 25–6.
67. *AH* I.27.1.
68. Harnack, *Marcion*, pp. 30–9; Grant, *Gnosticism*, pp. 124–5.
69. *AH* I.27.2.
70. On this date see A. von Harnack, *Die Chronologie der altchristlichen Literatur* 1 (Leipzig, 1897), 296ff. and 306ff.
71. *Panarion* 42.3–4.
72. 1 *Apol.* 26.58.
73. Tertullian, *Adversus Marcionem* V.19; Harnack, *Marcion*, pp. 153ff. and 314ff.
74. Harnack, *Marcion*, pp. 156ff. and 356ff.
75. Ibid., pp. 35ff. and 149ff.
76. *Adv. Marcionem* I.13.
77. Harnack, *Marcion*, pp. 74ff. and 256ff.
78. *Adv. Marcionem* I.17.
79. Jonas, *Gnostic Religion*, pp. 150ff.
80. Aland, 'Marcion', pp. 438–9.
81. Harnack, *Marcion*, pp. 131ff.
82. Ibid., pp. 196–7, n. 1.
83. *Gnostic Religion*.
84. *Stromateis* III.4.25.
85. Aland, 'Marcion', pp. 445–6. She reinterprets Harnack's thesis critically. For a contrary interpretation see Pétrement, *Dualisme*, p. 142, n. 18. See also U. Bianchi, 'Marcion: théologien biblique ou docteur gnostique?', *VigChr* 21 (1967), 141–9.
86. Harnack, *Marcion*, pp. 177ff. and 404ff.
87. Ibid., p. 188.
88. Ibid., pp. 178–9.
89. Eusebius, *HE* V.13.2–4; Harnack, *Marcion*, pp. 177f., 408f.
90. Tertullian, *De anima* 23.
91. *AH* III.4.3. For patristic sources see Hilgenfeld, *Ketzergeschichte*, pp. 283ff.
92. Tertullian, *Adv. Valentinum* 4.
93. *AH* III.4.3.
94. *Adv. Valentinum* 4, and Jerome, *In Hoseam* II.10.
95. *Stromateis* IV.89.1–3.
96. G. C. Stead, 'In search of Valentinus' in Layton (ed.), *Rediscovery* 2.

75–95. Tertullian (*Adv. Val.* 4) tells us that Valentinus did not create his system from nothing. On its relationship to that of the Revelation of John, see G. Quispel, 'Valentinian Gnosis and the Apokryphon Johannis' in Layton (ed.), *Rediscovery* 1.118ff.

97. This is true of *EvVer* and *Rheg*.

98. *Refutatio* VI.35.3–7.

99. W. Förster, 'Grundzüge der ptolemaischen Gnosis', *NTS* 6 (1959), 18.

100. On Heracleon see A. E. Brooke, *The Fragments of Heracleon* (Cambridge, 1891); Y. Janssens, 'Héracléon', *Muséon* 72 (1959), 100ff. and 277ff.; M. Simonetti, 'Eracleone e Origene' *VetChr* 3 (1966), 111ff. and 4 (1967), 23ff.; E. Mühlenberg, 'Wieviel Erlösungen kennt der Gnostiker Herakleon?', *ZNW* 66 (1975), 170ff.; B. Aland, 'Erwählungstheologie und Menschenklassenlehre' in Krause (ed.), *Gnosis* (1977), pp. 148–81; D. Devoti, 'Antropologia e storia della salvezza in Eracleone', *Atti dell'Accademia Scientifica di Torino* 2 (1978).

101. *Stromateis* IV.71.1.

102. F. M. Sagnard, *Clément d'Alexandrie. Extraits de Théodote* (Paris, 1948).

103. Leisegang, *Gnosis*, pp. 326–49.

104. *AH* I.13.3.

105. Filoramo, *Luce*, pp. 102ff.

106. Sagnard, *Gnose valentinienne*: 358ff. We know nothing of the other disciples mentioned in the heresiological sources (Secundus, Theotimus, Assionicus). As to (B)Ardesianus (*Ref.* VI.35.7), he does not have to be identified, as some think, with Bardesanes (d. 222), who lived at the court of Abgar the King of Edessa (179–216); see H. J. Drijvers, *Bardaisan of Edessa* (Assen, 1966).

107. E. Hänchen, 'Das Buch Baruch', *ZThK* 50 (1953), 123ff., and M. Simonetti, 'Note sul libro di Baruch dello gnostico Giustino', *VetChr* 6 (1969), 71ff.

108. Grant, *Gnosticism*, pp. 19ff.

109. *Refutatio* VIII.12–15.

110. Bolgiani, 'Polemica di Clemente', pp. 117–21.

111. Klijn, *Seth*, p. 112, and F. Wisse, 'Stalking those elusive Sethians' in Layton (ed.), *Rediscovery*, 2.575. But see also Schenke, 'Gnostic Sethianism', pp. 607ff. and Pearson, 'Figure of Seth', p. 504, n. 113.

112. See ch. 11.

113. For the following account see K. Koschorke, 'Patristische Materialien zur Spätgeschichte der valentinianischen Gnosis' in Krause (ed.), *Gnosis* (1981), pp. 120–39.

114. W. Bousset, *Jüdisch-christlicher Schulbetrieb in Alexandrien und Rom* (Göttingen, 1915); Donini, 'Filosofia antica', pp. 31ff. and 58ff.

115. Assuming, of course, that the Gnostics attacked by Plotinus were Valentinians; see Elsas, *Weltablehnung*, pp. 27ff.

116. A. le Bolluec, 'La place de la polémique antignostique dans le *Peri Archon*', *Origeniana* (1975), pp. 47–61.

117. *Panarion* 31.7.
118. Didymus, *Comm. in Psalmos* 20.1.
119. John Chrysostom, *Sermo I.3 in Genesim; De sac.* IV 4; *De verg.*3.
120. Julian, *Epistula* 3.
121. Ambrose, *Epistula* 41.1.
122. Eusebius, *Vita Constantinii* III.4.
123. Codex Theodosianus XVI.5.65.
124. Koschorke, 'Patristische Materialien', p. 125.
125. E. de Faye, *Gnostiques et Gnosticisme*² (Paris, 1925), pp. 476ff.; F. C. Burkitt, *Church and Gnosis* (Cambridge, 1932 repr. NY, 1978), pp. 40ff.
126. In texts such as the *Pistis Sophia*, *OrigMund*, *Mars*; see also Schenke, 'Phenomenon', pp. 614–15.
127. H. C. Puech, 'Archontiker', *RAC* I.633–43.

CHAPTER 11   ASCETICS AND LIBERTINES

1. Tertullian, *De praescriptione* 41.2–6.
2. E. Mendelsson, 'Some notes on a sociological approach to Gnosticism' in Bianchi (ed.), *Origini*, pp. 668–75; H. Kippenberg, 'Versuch einer soziologischen Verortung des antiken Gnostizismus', *Numen* 17 (1970), 211–31; P. Munz, 'The problem of "Die soziologische Verortung des Gnostizismus"', *Numen* 19 (1972), 4–15 (a critique of Kippenberg); H. A. Green, 'Suggested sociological themes in the study of Gnosticism' *VigChr* 31 (1977), 169–80, and *The Economic and Social Origins of Gnosticism* (Missouri, 1985); K. Rudolph, 'Das Problem einer Soziologie, soziologischen Verortung und Rolle der Gnosis in der Spätantike' in Nagel (ed.), *Studien*, pp. 19–29; K. Koschorke, 'Gnostic instructions on the organization of the community: the tractate "Interpretation of Knowledge"' in Layton (ed.), *Rediscovery* 2.762–3.
3. See the criticisms of Plotinus, *Ennead* II.9.18, and the observations of Jonas on the ethics of brotherhood in *Mythologische Gnosis*, pp. 170ff.
4. Rudolph, *Gnosis*, pp. 220–1.
5. NHC I.3.25.19ff.
6. See above, ch. 4, n. 30.
7. *AH* I, praef. 1.
8. *AH* I.24.6.
9. For this model of the 'sect' see B. Wilson, 'An analysis of sect development' *American Sociological Review* 24 (1959), 3–15, and *Magic and the Millennium* (St Albans, 1973), pp. 9–30. On the present limits of the use of the category 'sect' with regard to this historical period see the justifiable reservations of E. Tröltsch, *Die Soziallehre der christlichen Kirche und Gruppen* (Tübingen, 1912), pp. 353ff. See also L. Berger, 'The sociological study of sectarianism', *Social Research* 21 (1954), 467ff.
10. P. Pokornyi, 'Der soziale Hintergrund der Gnosis' in Tröger (ed.), *Gnosis*, pp. 77ff.

11. M. J. Vermaseren, *Mithras the Secret God* (London, 1963), pp. 37ff.; 129ff.; 138ff.

12. On the Hypogeum of the Aurelii and related inscriptions see J. Carcopino, *De Pythagore aux Apôtres* (Paris, 1956), pp. 85ff.

13. Böhlig, 'Zum Hellenismus', pp. 16ff.

14. Ibid., pp. 30–1.

15. Eusebius, *HE* VI.23.1ff.

16. M. Hengel, *Eigentum und Reichtum in der frühen Kirche* (Stuttgart, 1973), pp. 44. and 65ff.

17. Rudolph, *Gnosis*, pp. 288–90.

18. G. Quispel, 'L'inscription de Flavia Sophē' in his *Gnostic Studies* 1.58ff.

19. C. Schmidt, *Gnostische Schriften in koptischer Sprache aus dem Codex Brucianus* (Leipzig, 1892), pp. 452ff.; Perkins, *Gnostic Dialogue*, pp. 132ff.

20. *Acta Philippi* 94, where she is referred to as *eklelegmenē gynaikōn* (chosen of women); Bornkamm, *Mythos und Legende*, pp. 97ff. In the Manichaean Psalm Book (192.21 and 194.19) she appears described as *pneuma tēs Sophias* (spirit of Sophia). She is also important for the Cathars; see A. Borst, *Die Katharer* (Stuttgart, 1953), p. 164.

21. *EvMar*; see Perkins, *Gnostic Dialogue*, pp. 133–7.

22. Ménard, *Évangile selon Philippe*, pp. 150–1; on the relationship with the myth of Sophia see W. Henss, *Das Verhältnis zwischen Diatessaron, christlicher Gnosis und 'Western Text'* (Berlin, 1967), pp. 46–7.

23. NHC II.2.51 log. 114; see also ibid., log. 22, 61, 76, 105, 106.

24. *Refutatio* V.8.44 (Naassenes); *Excerpta ex Theodoto* 79; BG 9.20.

25. NHC II.7.144.8–10; III.5.144.15; VII.2.65.24; VIII.1.131.5ff. See also VII.1.27.2–6; VIII.1.1.10ff.

26. *Moralia* 1125 D-E.

27. *AH* I.21.4.

28. Rudolph, *Gnosis*, pp. 233ff.; J. Sevrin, 'Les rites et la gnose d'après quelques textes gnostiques coptes' in Ries (ed.), *Gnosticisme*, pp. 440–50. A wide-ranging survey of interpretations is given by Gaffron, *Studien*, pp. 76–99.

29. *CH* IV.4.

30. Ibid.

31. K. W. Tröger, *Mysterienglaube und Gnosis in Corpus Hermeticum XIII* (Berlin, 1971), pp. 56–57.

32. S. Angus, *The Religious Quest of the Graeco-Roman World* (London, 1929), p. 340.

33. G. van Moorsel, *The Mysteries of Hermes Trismegistus* (Leiden, 1955), p. 71.

34. NHC V.5.85.25; II.6.131.34.

35. NHC II.4.144.33ff.

36. This does not include the discourse on eschatological baptism, which will take place in the pure waters of light and is contrasted, in various Sethian texts (see F. Morand, 'L'Apocalypse d'Adam de Nag Hammadi' in Krause

(ed.), *Gnosis* (1977), pp. 38–41, and Schenke, 'Phenomenon', pp. 602–6 and non-Sethian texts (Jervell, *Imago Dei*, p. 160, n. 41, and Arai, 'Simonianische Gnosis', p. 197, n. 54), with terrestrial baptism, against which there is fierce polemic e.g. *ApcAd*; see Böhlig, *Mysterion und Wahrheit*, p. 152.

37. *AH* I.21.2.
38. Orbe, *Teología bautismal*, pp. 423–4.
39. *AH* I.21.3.
40. Bousset, *Hauptprobleme*, pp. 297ff.; Krause, 'Christlich-gnostiche Schriften', pp. 6–65; Rudolph, *Gnosis*, pp. 244–8.
41. NHC VI.8.65.15ff. See J. P. Mahé, 'Le sens des symboles sexuels dans quelques textes hermétiques et gnostiques' in Ménard (ed.), *Textes*, pp. 123–45.
42. M. Eliade, *Traité d'histoire des religions* (Paris, 1949), pp. 211ff., and Heiler, 'Erscheinungsformen', pp. 243–8.
43. J. Schmid, '(Heilige) Brautschaft', *RAC* II.528–64, and James, *Ancient Gods*, pp. 77–106.
44. Schmid, 'Brautschaft', pp. 543–4.
45. A. Dieterich, *Eine Mithrasliturgie*³ (Leipzig–Berlin, 1923), pp. 122–34; Reitzenstein, *Mysterienreligionen*, pp. 34–7, 100–1, 242–52; Nilsson, *Gechichte*, p. 691. The mystical union preached by the followers of Attis remains the subject of controversy: Clem. Alex. *Protrepticus* II.15. See D. Cosi, 'Salvatore e salvezza nei misteri di Attis', *Aevum* 50 (1976), 58–9.
46. R. A. Batey, *The New Testament Nuptial Imagery* (Leiden, 1971).
47. J. Bugge, *Virginitas* (The Hague, 1975).
48. P. F. Beatrice, 'Continenza e matrimonio nel cristianesimo primitivo (secc. I–III)' in R. Cantalamessa (ed.), *Etica sessuale e matrimonio nel cristianesimo delle origini* (Milan, 1976), pp. 3–68.
49. G. Kretschmar, 'Ein Beitrag zur Frage nach dem Ursprung der frühchristlicher Askese' *ZThK* 61 (1964), 27ff.
50. J. Fontaine, 'Valeurs antiques et valeurs chrétiennes dans la spiritualité des grands propriétaires terriers à la fin du IVe siècle occidental' in J. Fontaine and C. Kannengiesser (eds), *Epiktesis. Mélanges patristiques offerts au Cardinal Jean Daniélou* (Paris, 1972), pp. 571ff.
51. T. O'Dea, *The Mormons* (Chicago, 1957), p. 35.
52. H. Desroche, *Gli Shakers americani* (Milan, 1960), p. 196.
53. G. Welter, *Histoire des sectes chrétiennes* (Paris, 1950), p. 233.
54. V. Turner, *The Forest of Symbols* (Ithaca, NY, 1967), p. 58, and *The Ritual Process* (Boston, 1970), p. 94.
55. It is no accident that the interpretation of the ritual kiss in the sacrament of matrimony is disputed. Some (see Gaffron, *Studien*, pp. 214ff.) tend to diminish its importance. Others rightly emphasize its conspicuous symbolism, some tending to identify the ritual kiss with matrimony itself (H. M. Schenke, 'Das Evangelium nach Philippos', *ThLZ* 84 (1959), 5, and E. Segelberg, 'The Coptic-Gnostic Gospel according to Philip', *Numen* 7

(1960), 188), while others separate the two moments of the kiss and spiritual union; see J. Sevrin, 'Les noces spirituelles dans l'Évangile de Philippe', *Muséon* 87 (1974), 181ff. Against the latter interpretation should be remembered the rich symbolism of the kiss; see C. Trautmann, 'La parenté dans l'Évangile de Philippe' in Barc (ed.), *Colloque*, pp. 272–3.

56. *AH* I.21.3.
57. NHC II.3.69.1ff.; see R. M. Grant, 'The mystery of marriage in the Gospel of Philip', *VigChr* 15 (1961), 129–40; A. Orbe, 'Los valentinianos y el matrimonio espiritual', *Greg* 58 (1977), 5–53.
58. NHC II.3.63.1ff.
59. NHC II.3.78.12ff.
60. NHC II.3.82.8.
61. *Excerpta ex Theodoto* 63.2.
62. Ibid. 64. For other Gnostic parallels see Krause, 'Dialog des Soter', pp. 33–4.
63. J. E. Ménard, 'L'Évangile selon Philippe et l'Exégèse de l'Âme' in Ménard (ed.), *Textes*, p. 57.
64. Gaffron, *Studien*, p. 198.
65. *Panarion* 26.17.4.
66. Ibid. 26.4–5.
67. L. Fendt, *Gnostische Mysterien* (Munich, 1922), pp. 4ff.; J. Dümmer 'Die Angaben über die gnostische Literatur bei Epiphanius, Panarion 26' in P. Nagel (ed.), *Koptologische Studien in der DDR* (Halle–Wittenberg, 1965), pp. 191–219; S. Benko, 'The libertine Gnostic sect of the Phibionites according to Epiphanius', *VigChr* 21 (1967), 103–19.
68. *Panarion* 26.1 and 9.
69. M. Wellmann, 'Die pneumatische Schule', *Philosophische Untersuchungen* 14 (1895), 148ff.
70. H. C. Puech, 'Gnostische Evangelien' in Hennecke–Schneemelcher (eds), *Neutestamentliche Apokryphen* I.166–8.
71. Leisegang, *Gnosis*, p. 187.
72. H. Chadwick, 'The Domestication of Gnosis' in Layton (ed.), *Rediscovery* 1.5ff.
73. R. Griffiths, *The Reactionary Revolution: The Catholic Revival in French Literature 1870–1914* (London, 1966), ch. 7.
74. B 63.
75. *AH* I.6.2.
76. *Ennead* II.9.5.
77. F. Wisse, 'Die Sextus-Sprüche und das Problem der gnostischen Ethik' in Böhlig–Wisse, *Hellenismus*, pp. 62ff.
78. K. W. Tröger, 'Moral in der Gnosis' in Nagel (ed.), *Studien*, pp. 95–106.
79. *PS* 147 and 2 *LJ* 43.
80. A partial Coptic translation of a text whose entire Greek original has survived; see H. Chadwick (ed.), *The Sentences of Sextus* (Cambridge, 1959).

81. Wisse, 'Sextus-Sprüche', p. 75.
82. See above, ch. 1, n. 75.
83. J. Zandee, 'Les "Enseignements de Silvain" et le platonisme' in Ménard (ed.), *Textes*, pp. 158–79.
84. NHC VI.3.29.10ff.
85. Ibid. 30.28ff.
86. Ibid. 31.31ff.
87. Wisse, 'Sextus-Sprüche', pp. 81ff.
88. Pétrement, *Dualisme chez Platon*, pp. 244ff.
89. *Mythologische Gnosis*, pp. 234ff.
90. NHC VII.4.90.29ff.
91. Ibid. 93.3ff.
92. Ibid. 108.14.

Select Bibliography and Further Reading

Full bibliography in D. M. Scholer, *Nag Hammadi Bibliography*, published in *NT* 13–29 (1971–87); see also bibliography in the *Oxford Dictionary of the Christian Church*² (ed. and rev. F. L. Cross and E. A. Livingstone (Oxford, 1974), s.v. *Gnosticism*. The author's own revised bibliography appears in *Il risveglio della gnosi ovvero diventar dio* (Laterza, Rome–Bari 1990).

Facsimile Edition of the Nag Hammadi Codices, 13 vols (Leiden, 1978). Critical edition in progress: *The Coptic Gnostic Library*, 11 vols (Leiden, 1975ff.)

Translations: J. M. Robinson (ed.), *The Nag Hammadi Library in English*³ (Leiden–New York–Copenhagen–Cologne, 1988), from which many of the passages in this book are taken. A selection of Gnostic texts from secondary sources in R. McL. Wilson's English translation of W. Förster's *Gnosis* (Zurich, 1969; Oxford, 1972); some of these translations are also used in this book. Editions and translations of individual texts are given in the *Oxford Dictionary of the Christian Church*². See also Bentley Layton, *The Gnostic Scriptures* (London, 1987); and translations in *The Coptic Gnostic Library* (above).

Aland, B., 'Marcion', *ZThK* 70 (1973), 420–7.
—— (ed.), *Gnosis, Festschrift für Hans Jonas* (Göttingen, 1978).
Andresen, C., 'Erlösung', *RAC* VI.54ff.
—— *Logos und Nomos. Die Polemik des Celsus wider das Christentum* (Berlin, 1955).
Angus, S., *The Religious Quest of the Graeco-Roman World* (London, 1929).
Anz, W., *Zur Frage nach dem Ursprung des Gnostizismus* (Leipzig, 1897).
Arai, S., *Die Christologie des Evangelium Veritatis* (Leiden, 1964).
Arnaldez, R., *Philon d'Alexandrie. De Opificio Mundi* (Paris, 1951).

Baer, R. A., *Philo's Use of the Categories 'Male' and 'Female'* (Leiden, 1970).

Barc, B. (ed.), *Colloque International sur les Textes de Nag Hammadi* (Quebec–Louvain, 1981).

—— and Roberge, M., *Hypostase des Archontes et Noréa* (Quebec–Louvain, 1980).

Barns, J. W. B., Browne, G. M., and Shelton, J. C., *Nag Hammadi Codices. Greek and Coptic Papyri from the Cartonnage of the Covers* (Leiden, 1981).

Bauer, W., *Rechtgläubigkeit und Ketzerei im ältesten Christentum* (Tübingen, 1934), with addition by G. Strecker (1964); Eng.: *Orthodoxy and Heresy in the Earliest Church* (Philadelphia, 1971).

Baumann, H., *Das doppelte Geschlecht* (Berlin, 1955).

Baur, F. C., *Die christliche Gnosis* (Tübingen, 1835).

Baynes, C. A., *A Coptic Gnostic Treatise in the Codex Brucianus* (Cambridge, 1933).

Bazan, F. G., *Plotino y la gnosis* (Buenos Aires, 1981).

Benko, S., 'The libertine Gnostic sect of the Phibionites according to Epiphanius', *VigChr* 21 (1967), 103–19.

Benz, E., *Adam. Der Mythus vom Urmensch* (Munich, 1955).

—— *Die Vision. Erfahrungsformen und Bildwelt* (Stuttgart, 1969).

—— *Urbild und Abbild* (Leiden, 1974).

Betz, H. D., 'The Delphic maxim *gnōthi seauton* in Hermetic interpretations' *HThr* 63 (1970), 465–84.

—— (ed.), *Greek Magical Papyri in Translation, including Demotic Spells* (Chicago, 1986).

Beyschlag, K., *Simon Magus und die christliche Gnosis* (Tübingen, 1974).

Bianchi, U., 'Marcion: théologien biblique ou docteur gnostique?', *VigChr* 21 (1967), 141–9.

—— *Prometeo, Orfeo, Adamo* (Rome, 1976).

—— *Le origini dello gnosticismo* (Leiden, 1967).

—— and Vermaseren, M. J. (eds), *La soteriologia dei culti orientali* (Leiden, 1982).

Bidez, J., and Cumont, F., *Les Mages hellénisés*, 2 vols (Paris, 1938).

Bieler, L., *Theios Anēr. Das Bild des göttlichen Menschen im Spätantike und Frühchristentum* (Vienna, 1935–6).

Blackman, E. C., *Marcion and his Influence* (London, 1948).

Bleecker, C. J., and Vermaseren, M. J. (eds), *Historia Religionum* (Leiden, 1969).

Bloom, H., *The Journey to Lucifer* (New York, 1979).

Böhlig, A., *Mysterion und Wahrheit* (Leiden, 1968).

—— and Wisse, F.,*Nag Hammadi Codices III,2 and IV, 2. The Gospel of the Egyptians* (Leiden, 1975).

—— —— *Zum Hellenismus in den Schriften von Nag Hammadi* (Wiesbaden, 1975).

Bolgiani, F., 'La tradizione eresiologica I: Le notizie di Ireneo', *Atti dell' Accademia Scientifica di Torino* 91 (1956), 77ff.

248   *Select Bibliography and Further Reading*

—— 'La tradizione eresiologica II: La confutazione di Clemente Alessandrino', ibid. 96 (1961), 1–128.

—— 'La polemica di Clemente Alessandrino contro gli gnostici libertini nel III libro degli Stromati', in *Studi in onore di A. Pincherle* (Rome, 1967), pp. 86–136.

Borchert, G. L., 'Is Bultmann's theology a new Gnosticism?' *Evangelical Quarterly* 36 (1964), 222–8.

Bornkamm, G., *Mythos und Legende in den Apokryphen Thomasakten* (Göttingen, 1933).

—— 'Ophiten', PW XVIII.654–8.

Borsch, F., *The Christian and Gnostic Son of Man* (London, 1970).

Bousset, W., 'Gnosis–Gnostiker', PW VII.1503–47.

—— *Hauptprobleme der Gnosis* (Göttingen, 1907).

—— *Religionsgeschichtliche Studien* (Leiden, 1979).

Boyce, M., *Zoroastrians. Their Beliefs and Religious Practices* (London, 1975).

Bréhier, E., *Les Idées philosophiques et religieuses de Philon d'Alexandrie* (Paris, 1925).

Broeck, R. van, 'The Authentikos Logos: a new document of Christian Platonism', *VigChr* 33 (1979), 260ff.

Brown, P. R. L., *The World of Late Antiquity* (London, 1971).

—— *The Making of Late Antiquity* (Cambridge, Mass., 1978).

Brox, N., *Offenbarung. Gnosis und gnostischer Mythos bei Irenäus* (Salzburg–Munich, 1966).

Bullard, R. A., *The Hypostasis of the Archons* (Berlin, 1970).

Bultmann, R., γιγνώσκω, TW I.68ff.

—— *Exegetica*, ed. E. Dinkler (Tübingen, 1967).

Burckhart, J. E., 'Gnosis and contemporary theology', *McCormick Quarterly* 18 (1965), 43–9.

Burkitt, F. C., *Church and Gnosis* (Cambridge, 1932).

Butler, E. M., *The Myth of the Magus* (Cambridge, 1979).

Carmignac, J., *Le Mirage de l'eschatologie* (Paris, 1979).

Caster, M., *Lucien et la pensée religieuse de son temps* (Paris, 1937).

Cerfaux, L., 'Gnose', *DB* Sup. III.659.

Charlesworth, J. (ed.), *The Odes of Solomon* (Oxford, 1973).

Cilento, V., *Paideia Antignostica* (Florence, 1971).

Colpe, C., 'Gnosis', *RGG*³ II. 1649ff.

—— 'Gnosis II (Gnostizismus)', *RAC* XI.537–659.

—— 'Heidnische, jüdische und christliche Überlieferung in den Schriften aus Nag Hammadi', *JAC* 15 (1972)–23 (1980), nine articles, one in each issue.

—— *Die religionsgeschichtliche Schule* (Göttingen, 1961).

Cornelis, H., and Léonard, A., *La Gnose éternelle* (Paris, 1959).

Culianu, I. P., *Iter in Silvis* (Messina, 1981).

—— 'Recherches sur les dualismes d'Occident' (microfiche Lille-Thèses, Doct. d'État, 1986); Italian trans. Milan, 1989; French: *Les Gnoses dualistes d'Occident*, Paris, 1989.

Cullman, O., *The Christology of the New Testament* (London, 1963).

Cumont, F., *Afterlife in Roman Paganism* (New Haven, Conn., 1922).

—— *L'Égypte des astrologues* (Paris, 1937).

—— *Oriental Religions in Roman Paganism* (London, 1911).

—— *Recherches sur Manichéisme*, I *La Cosmogonie manichéenne* (Brussels, 1908).

—— *Recherches sur le symbolisme funéraire des romains* (Paris, 1942).

Daniélou, J., *Message évangélique et culture hellénistique* (Tournai, 1961).

—— *Théologie du judéo-christianisme* (Paris, 1961).

Delcourt, M., *Hermaphrodite. Mythes et rites de la bisexualité dans l'antiquité classique* (Paris, 1958).

Des Places, É., *Oracles chaldaïques* (Paris, 1971).

Detienne, M., *Dionysos mis à mort* (Paris, 1977).

—— *Les Maîtres de vérité dans la Grèce archaïque* (Paris, 1967).

Devoti, D., 'Antropologia e storia della salvezza in Eracleone', *Memorie dell'Accademia Scientifica di Torino* 2 (1978).

—— 'Temi escatologici nello gnosticismo valentiniano', *Aug* 18 (1978), 47–61.

Dey, J., *Palingenesia* (Münster, 1937).

Dillon, J., *The Middle Platonists* (London, 1977).

Dodds, E. R., *The Greeks and the Irrational* (Berkeley, 1951).

—— *Pagan and Christian in an Age of Anxiety* (Cambridge, 1965).

Dörrie, H., 'Kontroversen um die Seelenwanderung im kaiserzeitlichen Platonismus', *Hermes* 85 (1957), 414–35.

—— *Platonica Minora*, ed. V. Buchheit (Munich, 1976).

Donini, P. L., *Le scuole, l'anima, l'impero: la filosofia antica da Antioco a Plotino* (Turin, 1982).

Doresse, J., *L'Évangile de Thomas* (Paris, 1959).

—— *The Secret Books of the Egyptian Gnostics* (London, 1960).

Drijvers, H. W. J., *Bardaisan of Edessa* (Assen, 1966).

Dubois, J., 'Le contexte judaïque du "nom" dans l'Évangile de Vérité', *RThPh* 24 (1974), 188–216.

Duchesne-Guillemin, J., 'Dualismus', *RAC* VI.344–50.

Dümmer, J., *Die griechischen christlichen Schriftsteller. Geschichte, Gegenwart und Zukunft* (Berlin, 1977).

Dupont, L., *Gnosis. La connaissance religieuse dans les Épîtres de Paul* (Paris, 1949).

Elsas, C., *Neuplatonische und gnostische Weltablehnung in der Schule Plotins* (Berlin–New York, 1975).

Eltester, W. (ed.), *Christentum und Gnosis* (Berlin, 1969).

Fallon, F. T., *The Enthronement of Sabaoth* (Leiden, 1978).

—— 'The Gnostic apocalypses', *Semeia* 14 (1979), 123ff.

—— 'The Gnostics: the undominated race', *NT* 21 (1979), 271–8.

Fauth, W., 'Seth-Typhon, Oroel und eselköpfige Sabaoth. Zur Theriomorphie der ophitisch-barbelo-gnostischen Archonten', *Oriens Christianus* 57 (1973), 79–120.

Faye, E. de *Gnostiques et gnosticisme*[2] (Paris, 1925).

Fendt, L., *Gnostischen Mysterien* (Munich, 1922).

Festugière, A.-J., *L'Astrologie et les sciences occultes* (Paris, 1944): *Le Dieu cosmique* (Paris, 1949); *Les Doctrines de l'âme* (Paris, 1953); *Dieu inconnu* (Paris, 1954).

—— *L'Idéal religieux des grecs et l'Évangile* (Paris, 1932).

—— *La Révélation de hermès Trismegiste*, 4 vols (Paris, 1944–54)

—— *Personal Religion among the Greeks* (Berkeley, 1954).

—— Hermétisme et mystique païenne (Paris, 1967).

Filoramo, G., 'Aspetti del dualismo gnostico', *Memorie dell'Accademia Scientifica di Torino* 2 (1978), 239–307.

—— 'Rivelazione ed escatologia nello gnosticismo cristiano', *Aug* 18 (1978), 70–95.

—— 'Nuove religioni: problemi e prospettive', *RSLR* 15 (1979), 445–72.

—— *Luce e Gnosi* (Rome, 1980).

—— 'Gli apocrifi gnostici: il genere letterario delle apocalissi', *Aug* 23 (1983), 124ff.

—— and Gianotto, C., 'L'interpretazione gnostica dell'Antico Testamento', *Aug* 22 (1982), 69ff.

Flamant, J., *Macrobe et le Néo-Platonisme latin à la fin du IVe siècle* (Leiden, 1977).

Förster, W., *Von Valentin zu Herakleon* (Giessen, 1928).

—— 'Das Wesen der Gnosis', *Die Welt als Geschichte*, (1955–2), pp. 100ff.

—— 'Grundzüge der ptolemäischen Gnosis', *NTS* 6 (1959), 18ff.

—— 'Das System des Basilides', *NTS* 9 (1969), 233–55.

—— (ed.), *Die Gnosis*, 2 vols (Zurich, 1969–71); Eng. version, ed. R. McL. Wilson, *Gnosis* (Oxford, 1972).

Fossum, J. E. *The Name of God and the Angel of the Lord* (Tübingen, 1985).

Frickel, J., *Die Apophasis Megale in Hippolyts Refutatio* (Rome, 1968).

Funk, W. P., *Die zweite Apokalypse des Jakobus aus Nag Hammadi Codex V* (Berlin, 1976).

Gaffron, H., 'Studien zum koptischen Philippusevangelium unter besonderen Berücksichtigung der Sakramente', Bonn Ph.D. thesis, 1969.

Giversen, S., *Apokryphon Johannis* (Copenhagen, 1963).

Gladigow, B., 'Jenseitsvorstellungen und Kulturkritik' *ZRGG* 26 (1974), 301ff.

Grant, R. M., 'The mystery of marriage in the Gospel of Philip', *VigChr* 15 (1961), 129–40.

—— *Gnosticism and Early Christianity*[2] (New York, 1966).

—— 'Jewish Christianity at Antioch', *RSR* 60 (1972), 98ff.

Green, H. A., *The Economic and Social Origins of Gnosticism* (Missoula, 1985).

Grese, W. C., *Corpus Hermeticum XIII and Early Christian Literature* (Leiden, 1979).

Grünewald, I., 'Knowledge and vision', *Israel Oriental Studies* 3 (1979), 63ff.

Haack, F. W., *Geheimreligion der Wissenschaft. Neugnostische Bewegungen* (Stuttgart, 1966).

Hallowel, J. (ed.), *From Enlightenment to Revolution* (Chapel Hill, NC, 1975).

Haman, E., 'Hippolyte', *DTC* VI.2487–511.

Hänchen, E., 'Gab es eine vorchristliche Gnosis?', *ZThK* 49 (1952), 316ff.

—— 'Das Buch Baruch', *ZThK* 50 (1953), 123ff.

—— 'Aufbau und Theologie', *ZThK* 53 (1956), 141–91.

Hanratty, G., 'Gnosticism and modern thought', *Irish Theological Quarterly* 47 (1980), 3–23 and 119–32; 48 (1981), 80–92.

Happ, H., *Hyle* (Berlin, 1971).

Harnack, A. von, 'Zur Quellenkritik der Geschichte des Gnostizismus', *Zeitschrift für historische Theologie* (1874), 143–226.

—— *Lehrbuch der Dogmengeschichte*³, I (Freiburg–Leipzig, 1894³).

—— *Marcion. Das Evangelium vom fremden Gott*² (Leipzig, 1924²).

Hauschild, W. D., *Gottes Geist und der Mensch* (Munich, 1972).

Heiler, F., *Erscheinungsformen und Wesen der Religion* (Stuttgart, 1961).

Hennecke, E., and Schneemelcher, W., *Neutestamentliche Apokryphen*⁴, 2 vols (Tübingen, 1971); Eng. version *New Testament Apocrypha* (London, 1963–5).

Herzhoff, B., *Zwei gnostische Hymnen* (Bonn, 1973).

Hilgenfeld, A., *Die Ketzergeschichte des Urchristentums* (Leipzig, 1884).

Hodgson, P. C., *The Foundation of Historical Theology: A Study of F. C. Baur* (New York, 1966).

Hutin, S., *Les Gnostiques* (Paris, 1963).

Hyldahl, N., *Philosophie und Christentum* (Copenhagen, 1966).

Institutum Historicum Augustinium, *Ricerche su Ippolito* (Rome, 1976ff.).

Janssens, Y., 'Heracléon', *Muséon* 72 (1959), 10ff. and 277ff.

—— *La Prōtennoia trimorphe* (Quebec, 1978).

Jaspert, B. (ed.), *Tradition-Krisis-Renovatio* (Marburg, 1976).

Jensen, S. S., *Dualism and Demonology: The Function of Demonology in Pythagorean Thought* (Copenhagen, 1960).

Jervell, J., *Imago Dei* (Göttingen, 1960).

Jessen, O., 'Hermaphroditos', *PW* VIII.714–21.

Jonas, H., *Gnosis und spätantiker Geist*, I *Die mythologische Geist* (Göttingen, 1939, 1954², 1964³) II.I: *Von der Mythologie zur mystischen Philosophie* (Göttingen, 1954, 1966²).

—— 'Gnosticism and modern nihilism', *Social Research* 19 (1952), 430–52.

—— *The Gnostic Religion*² (Boston, 1963).

Jung, C. G., *Collected Works in English* (trans. R. F. Hull), 20 vols (London, 1902ff.)

Kirk, G. S., *Myth. Its Meaning and Function in Ancient and Other Cultures* (Cambridge, 1970, repr. Cambridge–Berkeley, 1971–4).

Klijn, A. F.J., *Seth in Jewish, Christian and Gnostic Literature* (Leiden, 1977).

Klimheit, H. J. (ed.), *Tod und Jenseits im Glauben der Völker* (Wiesbaden, 1978).

Koep, L., *Das himmliche Buch in Antike und Christentum* (Bonn, 1952).

Koschorke, K., '"Suchen und finden" in der Auseinandersetzung zwischen gnostischen und christlichen Christentum', *Wort und Dienst* 14 (1972), 51ff.

—— *Hippolyts Ketzerbekämpfung und Polemik gegen die Gnostiker* (Wiesbaden, 1975).

—— *Die Polemik der Gnostiker gegen das kirchliche Christentum* (Leiden, 1978).

Kraft, H., 'Gab es einen Gnostiker Karpokrates?' *TZ* 8 (1952), 434–43.

Krämer, H. J., *Der Ursprung der Geistesmetaphysik²* (Amsterdam, 1967).

Krause, H., *Gnosis and Gnosticism* (Leiden, 1977, 1981).

—— (ed.), *Essays on the Nag Hammadi Texts* (Leiden, 1972, 1975).

—— and Labib, P. *Die drei Versionen des Apokryphon Johannis im Koptischen Museum zu Alt-Kairo* (Wiesbaden, 1962).

Kroll, J., *Die Lehren des Hermes Trismegistos* (Münster, 1914).

Langerbeck, H., *Aufsätze zur Gnosis* (Göttingen, 1967).

Layton, B. (ed.), *The Rediscovery of Gnosticism*, 2 vols (Leiden, 1980–1).

Leipoldt, J., *Die Frau in der antiken Welt und im Urchristentum* (Leipzig, 1953).

Leisegang, H., *Die Gnosis* (Leipzig, 1924).

—— 'Pistis Sophia', PW XX. 1813–21.

Lenz, C., 'Apokatastase', *RAC* I. 510–16.

Lesky, E., *Die Zeugungs- und Vererbungslehren der Antike und ihre Nachwirken* (Wiesbaden, 1951).

Lipsius, R. A., *Die Quellen der ältesten Ketzergeschichte* (Leipzig, 1875).

Lewy, H., *Sobria Ebrietas* (Giessen, 1929).

Loos, M., *Dualist Heresy in the Middle Ages* (Prague–The Hague, 1974).

Lüdemann, G., *Untersuchungen zur simonianischen Gnosis* (Göttingen, 1975).

Macdermot, V., *The Cult of the Seer in the Ancient Middle East* (Berkeley, 1971).

—— *Pistis Sophia* (Leiden, 1978).

—— *The Books of Jeu and the Untitled Treatise in the Bruce Codex* (Leiden, 1978).

Mack, B. L., *Logos und Sophia. Untersuchung zur Weisheitstheologie im hellenistischen Judentum* (Göttingen, 1973).

Macrae, G. W., 'The Jewish background of the Gnostic Sophia Myth', *NT* 12 (1970), 86–101.

Mahé, J.-P., *Hermès en Haute Égypte. Les textes hermétiques de Nag Hammadi et leurs parallèles grecs et latins* (Quebec, 1978).

Martin, H., 'The anti-philosophical polemic and Gnostic soteriology of the Treatise on the Resurrection', *Numen* 20 (1973), 20–37.

Mead, G. R. S., *Pistis Sophia* (London, 1896).

Meeks, W. A., 'The image of the androgyne: some uses of a symbol in earliest Christianity', *HR* 13 (1970), 165–208.

—— 'Simon Magus in recent research', *RSR* 3 (1977), 137–42.

Ménard, J.-É., *L'Évangile selon Philippe* (Paris, 1967).

—— *L'Évangile de Vérité* (Leiden, 1972).

—— *L'Évangile selon Thomas* (Leiden, 1975).

—— *La Lettre de Pierre à Philippe* (Quebec, 1977).

—— 'Repos et salut gnostique', *RevSR* 51 (1977), 71–88.

—— (ed.), *Les Textes de Nag Hammadi* (Leiden, 1975).

Mensching, G., *Das heilige Schweigen* (Giessen, 1926).

Moorsel, G. van, *The Mysteries of Hermes Trismegistos* (Leiden, 1955).

Moreau, P., *L'Âme du monde de Platon aux stoïciens* (Paris, 1939).

Mortley, R., 'Gnosis', *RAC* X.485ff.

Mühlenberg, E., 'Wieviel Erlösungen kennt der Gnostiker Herakleon', *ZNW* 66 (1975), 170ff.

Müller, K., *Beiträge zum Verständnis der valentinianischen Gnosis* (Göttingen, 1920).

Munck, J., 'Bemerkungen zum koptischen Thomasevangelium', *Studia Theologica* 14 (1960), 140ff.

Murdock, W. R., and Macrae, G. W., *Nag Hammadi Codices V,2–5 and VI* (Leiden, 1979).

Nagel, P., *Studia Coptica* (Berlin, 1974).

—— *Studien zum Menschenbild in Gnosis und Manichäismus* (Halle–Saale, 1979).

Nag Hammadi Codices Facsimile edn, 13 vols (Leiden, 1972–7).

Nautin, P., *Hippolyte et Josipe* (Paris, 1947).

—— 'La controverse sur l'auteur de l'Élenchos', *RHE* 47 (1952), 5–43.

Nilsson, M., 'Sophia-Prunikos', *Eranos* 45 (1947), 169–72.

—— *Geschichte der griechischen Religion*² (Munich, 1961).

Nock, A. D., *Conversion* (Oxford, 1961).

—— *Essays on Religion and the Ancient World*, ed. Z. Stewart, 2 vols (Oxford, 1972).

—— and Festugière, A.-J., *Hermès Trismégiste*, I–IV (Paris, 1980).

Norris, R. A., *God and World in Early Christian Theology* (London, 1966).

Nygren, A., *Agape and Eros* (London, 1938).

Opitz, P. J., and Sebba, G., *The Philosophy of Order* (Stuttgart, 1981).

Orbe, A., *En los albores de la Exegesis Iohannea* (Rome, 1955).

—— *Los primeros herejes ante la persecución* (Rome, 1956).

—— *Hacia la primera teología de la procesión del Verbo* (Rome, 1958).

—— *La unción del Verbo* (Rome, 1961).

—— 'Spiritus Dei ferebatur super aquas', *Greg* 44 (1963), 712ff.

—— *La teología del Espiritu Santo* (Rome, 1966).

—— *Antropología de S. Ireneo* (Madrid, 1969).

—— 'Ideas sobre la tradición en la lucha antignostica', *Aug* 12 (1972), 19–32.

—— *Cristología gnostica*, 2 vols (Madrid, 1976).

—— 'Los valentinianos y el matrimonio espiritual', *Greg* 58 (1977), 5–53.

Pagels, E., *The Gnostic Gospels* (London, 1980).

—— *Adam, Eve and the Serpent* (New York, 1988).

Painchaud, P., *Le Deuxième Traité du Grand Seth* (Quebec, 1982).

Pax, E., *Epiphaneia* (Munich, 1955).

Pellicani, L., *I rivoluzionari di professione. Teoria e prassi dello gnosticismo moderno* (Florence, 1975).

Pépin, J.-P., *Mythe et allégorie* (Paris, 1958).

—— *Idées grecques sur l'homme et sur Dieu* (Paris, 1971).

Peel, M. L., *The Epistle to Rheginus* (Philadelphia, 1969).

—— 'Gnostic eschatology and the New Testament', *NT* 12 (1970), 14ff.

Perkins, P., 'Irenaeus and the Gnostics', *VigChr* 30 (1976), 193–200.

—— *The Gnostic Dialogue* (New York, 1980).

Peterson, E., *Frühkirche, Judentum und Gnosis* (Rome, 1959).

Pétrement, S., *Le Dualisme chez Platon, les gnostiques et le manichéens* (Paris, 1947).

—— *Le Dieu séparé. Les origines du Gnosticisme* (Paris, 1984).

Pohlenz, M., *Stoa*[4] (Göttingen, 1970).

Poirier, P. H., *L'Hymne de la Perle des Actes de Thomas* (Louvain, 1980).

Preisendanz, K. (ed.), *Papyri Graecae Magicae* (Leipzig, 1928).

Prigent, P., *Justin et l'Ancien Testament* (Paris, 1964).

Prümm, K., *Gnosis an der Wurzel des Christentums* (Salzburg, 1972).

Puech, H. C., 'Archontiker', *RAC* I. 633–43.

—— *Le Manichéisme* (Paris, 1949).

—— *Plotin et les gnostiques* (Paris, 1958).

—— 'Doctrine ésotériques et thèmes gnostiques dans l'Évangile selon Thomas', *Annuaire. Collège de France* 63 (1963), 199ff.; 66 (1966), 259ff.; 68 (1968), 292ff.

—— (ed.), *Histoire des religions* (Paris, 1970–2).

—— and Vaillant, A., *Le Traité contre les Bogomiles de Cosmos le Prêtre* (Paris, 1945).

Quispel, G., 'La conception de l'Homme dans la Gnose Valentinienne', *ErJ* 15 (1947), 250ff.

—— L'homme gnostique (la doctrine de Basilide)', *ErJ* 16 (1948), 89–139.

—— *Ptolémée. Lettre à Flora* (Paris, 1949).

—— *Gnosis als Weltreligion* (Zurich, 1951).

—— 'Faust: symbol of western man', *ErJ* 33 (1966), 241–65.

—— *Makarius, das Thomasevangelium und das Lied von der Perle* (Leiden, 1967).

—— 'Jung und die Gnosis', *ErJ* 37 (1968), 277–·98.

—— 'From mythos to logos', *ErJ* 39 (1970), 161ff.

—— *Gnostic Studies*, 2 vols (Istanbul, 1974).

—— 'Origen and Valentinian Gnosis', *VigChr* 28 (1974), 29–42.

Reitzenstein, R., *Die hellenistischen Mysterienreligionen*[3] (Leipzig, 1927).

—— *Poimandres* (Leipzig, 1904).

Ricerche su Ippolito: *see* Institutum Historicum Augustinianum.

Ries, J. (ed.), *Gnosticisme et monde hellénistique* (Louvain, 1982).

Robinson, W. C., 'The Exegesis of the soul', *NT* 12 (1970), 102–17.

Roloff, D., *Plotin. Die Gross-Schrift III,8; V,8; V,5; II,9* (Berlin, 1970).

Rousseau, A., and Doutreleau, L., *Irénée de Lyon. Contre les Hérésies* (Paris, 1952–79).

Rudolph, K., *Die Mandäer*, I *Prolegomena: Das Mandäerproblem* (Göttingen, 1961).

—— 'Gnosis und Gnostizismus: ein Forschungsbericht', *ThRu* 34 (1969), 121–75, 181–231, 358–61; 36 (1971), 1–61, 89–124; 37 (1972); 289–360; 38 (1973), 1–25.

—— *Die Gnosis* (Göttingen, 1978); Eng. *Gnosis*, ed. R. McL. Wilson (Edinburgh, 1983).

—— (ed.), *Gnosis und Gnostizismus* (Darmstadt, 1975).

Ruether, R., and McLaughlin, E. (eds), *Women of Spirit* (New York, 1979).

Russell, D. S., *The Method and Message of Jewish Apocalyptic* (Philadelphia, 1974).

Ruyer, R., *La Gnose de Princeton. Des savants à la recherche d'une religion* (Paris, 1974).

Saake, H., 'Pneuma', PW Suppl. XIV. 399ff.

Sagnard, F. M., *La Gnose valentinienne et le temoignage de S. Irénée* (Paris, 1947).

—— *Clément d'Alexandrie. Extraits de Théodote* (Paris, 1948).

Salles-Dabadie, J. M. A., *Recherches sur Simon le Mage* (Paris, 1969).

Samek Lodovici, E., *Metamorfosi della gnosi* (Milan, 1979).

Schenke, H. M., 'Das literarische Problem des Apokryphon Johannis', *ZRGG* 16 (1962), 56–63.

—— *Der Gott 'Mensch' in der Gnosis* (Göttingen, 1962).

Schlier, H., *Religionsgeschichtliche Untersuchungen zu den Ignatiusbriefen* (Giessen, 1929).

—— 'Das Denken der frühchristlichen Gnosis' in W. Eltester (ed.), *Neutestamentliche Studien für R. Bultmann*[3] (Berlin, 1957).

—— αιρεσιϛ, TW I.180–2.

Schmidt, C., *Gespräche Jesu mit seinen Jüngern nach der Auferstehung* (Leipzig, 1919).

—— *Pistis Sophia* (Copenhagen, 1925).

—— *Koptisch-gnostische Schriften*, I *Die Pistis Sophia. Die beiden Bücher des Jeu. Unbekanntes altgnostisches Werk*, ed. W. Till (Berlin, 1962).

Schmithals, W., *Die Gnosis in Korinth* (Göttingen, 1956).

—— *Die Apokalyptik* (Göttingen, 1973).

—— 'Gnosis und Neues Testament', *Verkündigung und Forschung* 21 (1976), 22–46.

Schmitt, E. H., *Die Gnosis*, II *Die Gnosis des Mittelalters und der Neuzeit* (Leipzig, 1907).

Schneemelcher, W., 'Epiphanius von Salamis', *RAC* V.909–27.

Scholem, G., *Major Trends in Jewish Mysticism* (Jerusalem, 1941).

—— 'Die Vorstellung von Golem', *ErJ* 22 (1953), 240ff.

Scholten, C., *Martyrium und Sophiamythos im Gnostizismus nach den Texten von Nag Hammadi* (Münster, 1987).

Schotroff, L., *Der Glaubende und die feindliche Welt* (Neukirchen, 1970).

256 *Select Bibliography and Further Reading*

Schürer, E., *The History of the Jewish People in the Age of Jesus Christ* (trans. G. Vermes, F. Millar and M. Black, 2 vols (Edinburgh, 1973–9).

Schwabl, H., 'Weltschöpfung', PW Suppl. IX.1540.

Schwanz, P., *Imago Dei* (Halle, 1970).

Scopello, M., 'Le mythe de la chute des anges dans l'Apocryphe de Jean', *RevSR* 54 (1980), 220–30.

Secret, F., *Les Kabbalistes chrétiens de la Renaissance* (Paris, 1964).

Segal, A. F., *Two Powers in Heaven* (Leiden, 1977).

Sevrin, J. M., 'Les noces spirituelles dans l'Évangile de Philippe', *Muséon* 87 (1974), 181ff.

—— 'A propos de la Paraphrase de Shem', *Muséon* 88 (1975), 66–96.

Sieber, J., 'An introduction to the tractate Zostrianos', *NT* 15 (1973), 237ff.

Siegert, F., 'Selbstbezeichnung der Gnostiker in den Nag Hammadi Texten', *ZNW* 71 (1980), 129–32.

Simonetti, M., '*Psyche* e *psychikos* nella gnosi valentiniana', *RSLR* 1 (1961), 1ff.

—— 'Note di cristologia gnostica', *RSLR* 5 (1969), 529–53.

—— 'Note sul libro di Baruch dello gnostico Giustino', *VetChr* 6 (1969), 71ff.

—— *Testi gnostici cristiani* (Bari, 1970).

—— 'Note sull' interpretazione gnostica dell' Antico Testamento', *VetChr* 9 (1972), 358ff.

Spanneut, M., *Les Pères de l'Église* (Paris, 1951).

Spark, H. D. F., *The Apocryphal Old Testament* (Oxford, 1985).

Stead, G. C., 'The Valentinian myth of Sophia', *JTS* 20 (1969), 75–104.

Stroumsa, G. A. G., *Another Seed: Studies in Gnostic Mythology* (Leiden, 1984).

Talbert, C. H., 'The myth of the descending–ascending redeemer in Mediterranean antiquity', *NTS* 22 (1975), 418–40.

Tardieu, M., 'Les Trois Stèles de Seth: un écrit gnostique retrouvé à Nag Hammadi', *RSPhTh* 57 (1973), 545–73.

—— *Trois mythes gnostiques* (Paris, 1974).

—— 'Le titre du deuxième écrit du Codex VI', *Muséon* 87 (1974), 523–30; 88 (1975), 365–9.

—— *Écrits gnostiques. Codex de Berlin* (Paris, 1984).

—— and Dubois, J.-D., *Introduction à la littérature gnostique* I (Paris, 1986).

Taubes, S. A., 'The Gnostic foundations of Heideggerian nihilism' *Journal of Religion* 34 (1954), 155f.

—— (ed.), *Gnosis und Politik* (Munich, 1984).

Taylor, A. E., *Plato* (London, 1926).

Theiler, W., 'Demiurg' *RAC* III.694–711.

Thomas, L. V., *The Anthropology of Death* (London, 1970).

Topitsch, E., *Sozialphilosophie zwischen Ideologie und Wissenschaft*[2] (Luchterhand, 1966).

Tröger, K. W., *Mysterienglaube und Gnosis in Corpus Hermeticum XIII* (Berlin, 1971).

—— (ed.), *Gnosis und Neues Testament* (Berlin, 1973).

—— (ed.), *Altes Testament-Frühjudentum-Gnosis* (Berlin, 1980).

Turner, H. E. W., *The Pattern of Christian Thought* (London, 1954).

Turner, J. D., *The Book of Thomas the Contender* (Missoula, 1975).

Unger, R., 'Zur sprachlichen und formalen Struktur des gnostische Textes "Der Donner: vollkommener Nous"', *Oriens Christianus* 59 (1975), 78–107.

Verbeke, G., *L'Évolution de la doctrine du Pneuma des stoïciens à St Augustin* (Paris–Louvain, 1945).

Verheule, A. F., *Wilhelm Bousset: Leben und Werk* (Amsterdam, 1973).

Vermaseren, M. J., 'Hellenistic religions' in C. J. Bleecker and M. J. Vermaseren, *Historia Religionum* 1. 495–532.

—— *Mithras the Secret God* (London, 1963).

—— (ed.), *Studies in Hellenistic Religions* (Leiden, 1979).

Vernant, J.-P., *Les Origines de la pensée grecque* (Paris, 1962).

—— *Mythe et pensée chez les grecs* (Paris, 1965; London–Boston, 1983).

—— *Mythe et société en Grèce ancienne* (Paris, 1974).

—— and Detienne, M., *Les Ruses de l'intelligence. La Métis des grecs* (Paris, 1974).

Vernière, Y., *Symboles et mythes dans la pensée de Plutarche* (Paris, 1977).

Vincent, L. H., 'Le culte d'Hélène à Samarie', *RevBib* 45 (1936), 221ff.

Vögelin, E., *Order and History,* IV *The Ecumenic Age* (Baton Rouge, 1974).

Völker, W., *Der wahre Gnostiker nach Clemens Alexandrinus* (Leipzig, 1952).

Volz, P., *Eschatologie der jüdischen Gemeinde im Neutestamentlichen Zeitalter* (Tübingen, 1934).

Waitz, H., 'Simon Magus in der altchristlichen Literatur', *ZNW* 5 (1904), 121–43.

Waszink, J. H., *Tertulliani De Anima* (Amsterdam, 1947).

Wehr, G., *Alle Weisheit ist von Gott* (Gütersloh, 1980).

Welburn, A. J., 'The identity of the Archons in the "Apokryphon Johannis"', *VigChr* 32 (1978), 241–54.

Wetter, G. P., *Charis* (Leipzig, 1913).

—— *Phōs* (Uppsala, 1915).

Whittaker, J., 'Basilides on the ineffability of God', *HThR* 62 (1969), 367–71.

Widengren, G. (ed.), *Proceedings of the International Colloquium on Gnosticism Stockholm August 20–25 1973* (Stockholm–Leiden, 1977).

Williams, M., *The Immovable Race* (Leiden, 1985).

Wilson, R. McL., 'Simon, Dositheus and the Dead Sea Scrolls', *ZRGG* 9 (1957), 21–30.

—— *The Gnostic Problem²* (London, 1964).

—— 'Jewish "Gnosis" and Gnostic origins: a survey', *Hebrew Union College Annual* 45 (1974), 179–89.

—— (ed.), *Nag Hammadi and Gnosis* (Leiden, 1978).

Wisse, F., 'The redeemer figure in the Paraphrase of Shem', *NT* 12 (1970), 130–40.

Wolfson, H. A., 'Negative attributes in the Church Fathers and the Gnostic Basilides', *HThR* 50 (1951), 145–56.

—— *The Philosophy of the Church Fathers* (Harvard, 1956, 1970[3]).

Yamauchi, E., *Pre-Christian Gnosticism* (London, 31973).

—— 'Pre-Christian Gnosticism in the Nag Hammadi texts', *Church History* 48 (1979), 130–5.

Les Yeux de Chair et les Yeux de Feu. La Science et la Gnose. Colloque tenu à Paris (Cahiers, no. 5, Université St Jean: Jerusalem, 1979).

Zaehner, R. C., *The Teachings of the Magi* (London, 1975).

Zandee, J., 'Gnostic ideas on fall and salvation', *Numen* 11 (1964), 19–68.

—— 'L'exemplarisme du monde transcendant par rapport au monde visible dans le Tractatus Tripartitus du Codex Jung', *Revue d'Égyptologie* 24 (1972), 224–8.

Index

259